Working Through
Environmental Conflict

Working Through Environmental Conflict

The Collaborative Learning Approach

Steven E. Daniels and Gregg B. Walker

 PRAEGER

Westport, Connecticut
London

Library of Congress Cataloging-in-Publication Data

Daniels, Steven E.
  Working through environmental conflict : the collaborative learning approach / Steven
E. Daniels and Gregg B. Walker.
    p. cm.
  Includes bibliographical references and index.
  ISBN 0–275–96473–6 (alk. paper)
    1. Environmental policy—United States—Citizen participation.   2. Conflict
management—United States.   3. Team learning approach in education—United States.   I.
Walker, Gregg B.   II. Title.
GE180.D36   2001
363.7′0525′0973—dc21   00–025460

British Library Cataloguing in Publication Data is available.

Library of Congress Catalog Card Number: 00–025460
ISBN: 0–275–96473–6

First published in 2001

Praeger Publishers, 88 Post Road West, Westport, CT 06881
An imprint of Greenwood Publishing Group, Inc.
www.praeger.com

Printed in the United States of America

The paper used in this book complies with the
Permanent Paper Standard issued by the National
Information Standards Organization (Z39.48–1984).

10 9 8 7 6 5 4 3 2

Copyright Acknowledgments

The author and publisher gratefully acknowledge permission for use of the following material:

Figure 5.1, Kolb's Model of the Learning Cycle from EXPERIENTIAL LEARNING: EXPERI-
ENCE AS THE SOURCE OF LEARNING AND DEVELOPMENT by Kolb, D., © 1984. Reprinted
by permission of Prentice-Hall, Inc., Upper Saddle River, NJ.

Figure 6.2, Checkland's Model of Soft System Inquiry from P. Checkland, *Systems Thinking, Systems Practice*. Copyright © 1981 P. Checkland. Reproduced by permission of John Wiley & Sons
Limited.

Excerpts from Chapter 10 reprinted from *Environmental Impact Assessment Review*, vol. 16, S.E.
Daniels and G.B. Walker, Collaborative Learning: Improving Public Deliberation in Ecosystem-
Based Management, pp. 71–102, Copyright © 1996, with permission from Elsevier Science.

To our parents, for teaching us that hard work is more important than play.

To our children, for teaching us just the opposite.

And most importantly, *to our wives,* for their unwavering support and encouragement (and because they never changed the locks on the house during one of our trips, even though they had ample justification to do so).

Contents

Tables and Figures

TABLES

FIGURES

Preface

Many of the leading thinkers in social science and politics believe that there is something fundamentally wrong with how government currently functions. Prominent social commentators such as Peter Drucker, James Q. Wilson, and Robert Reich all contend that things are amiss, although they present widely differing views and solutions to the problem. Every successful American presidential candidate back to Jimmy Carter in 1976 has run on a platform of what has been wrong with government; it was too large, expensive, obtrusive, inefficient, and so on. These perspectives are a collective indication that we increasingly lack a clear sense of purpose in our public policy. As a result, it is easy to criticize any policy, because without a purpose against which to judge performance, all decisions can appear nonsensical.

Why do public policy processes appear to have become so rudderless? Certainly, the various laws and regulations that constitute public policy have not disappeared—just the opposite is true, because each year there are more of them. Rather than disappear, they seem to lack social legitimacy and a definable sense of purpose. The latter Twentieth century witnessed a growing public dissatisfaction, detachment, and disillusionment toward policy and policy making in this country. There are ample social science measurements of this chasm, this gap between what people feel they *should* get in terms of public policy decisions and what they feel they *are* getting. There are likewise numerous social manifestations of the dissatisfaction: the wise use and home rule movements ("if government can't manage public land well, we'll just give it back to the counties"), property tax rollbacks ("if government can't spend my money well, I'll just take it back"), and the rise of broad-based conservatism ("if government can't do anything well, let's just shrink it").

Clearly, the attitudes toward public policy in the latter Twentieth century differed markedly from those of the century's first decades. The Progressive Era (roughly 1890–1915) was perhaps the high water mark in the social legitimacy and discretion granted to policymakers in the United States. The prevailing notion was that the best public policy decisions were made through technocratic governance: professional managers, well trained in their technical specialties, working on behalf of the citizenry at large. The era was a response to a set of principles that had emerged many decades earlier during the presidency of Andrew Jackson. These Jacksonian notions—that any person of average intelligence should presumably be able to hold government office and successfully discharge the responsibilities of the office—led to the most blatant forms of political patronage and misanthropic regulatory decisions and provided an impetus for a movement toward professionalism in government service.

Why has the Progressive era evolved, albeit with some intermediate steps, into our current postmodern malaise? The premise underlying this book is that the nature of the problems facing public policy makers has changed. The "easy" problems—those that lie neatly within the intellectual bounds of a particular discipline, those that are within the purview of a single agency, and those for which there is a widely preferred outcome—have largely been addressed.

Consider, for example, the problem of designing earthquake-resistant buildings and public works in high risk areas such as parts of California. A well-defined field of seismic engineering has emerged (an overlap between civil and geotechnical engineering), and there is a strong public preference for safer structures. As a result, considerable progress has been made in terms of construction safety. That is not to say that building new structures or retrofitting old ones is cheap, nor does this priority ignore those critics who say that we have not gone far enough in our efforts. But we certainly share the motivation and technical means needed to make progress.

This perspective does not imply that our generation faces tough problems and that all others had it easy. That would be the worst type of hindsight bias and hubris. Every generation engages problems that take its brightest thinkers to the edge of their technology and creativity. But the nature of the vexing problems appears to be changing, not merely because of complexity but also because they cut across disciplines and types of values. How can policy processes reconcile incommensurate values such as species conservation and individual liberty? Webber and Rittel (1973) coined a term—"wicked problems"—for those problems that defy typical disciplinary analysis and confound conventional policy processes. Our generation of public policy makers must wrestle with these wicked problems that confound conventional policy processes. The obvious building code improvements, the easy siting decisions for oil fields, wildernesses, prisons and parks, and the "no-brainer" immunization programs have all been completed. What we face are situations for which there is no single obviously right answer or where the results of individual decisions, each undertaken for arguably sound reasons, interact in unexpected and perplexing ways.

Perhaps just as frequently, public policy processes face significant value differences within the citizenry. Public decisions often face a wide set of opinions about what changes to the current situation would constitute an improvement. These differences in preferences run the gamut from self interest-driven "not in my backyard" (NIMBY) politics, to fundamental differences in worldviews about the role for government or the appropriate relationship between society and natural environments.

So what are decision makers to do? One response that is becoming uncomfortably common is to seek *equilibrated dislike*. When you hear someone say, "Well, both sides dislike my decision, so it must be fair," she or he is engaging a frame of reference that, in the long run, will have a corrosive effect on our ability to govern our public affairs. Perhaps both sides dislike the outcome because the decision is a bad idea, regardless of anyone's perspective. The long-run effect of an equilibrated dislike approach is that it does not build a constituency for either specific policies or government in general.

Public policy must move beyond simplistic attempts to balance competing interests, efforts that often yield compromise solutions that none of the participants desire. We must craft policy processes whose outcomes achieve a high level of both technical competence and social discourse. This book presents a particular framework, Collaborative Learning, which we feel is a useful tool in addressing today's confounding policy problems. But it can neither make them disappear nor make them become simple; they will always be challenging to scientists, elected officials, and citizens alike. Collaborative Learning is motivated out of the need to make progress in the face of potentially paralyzing social and technical complexity.

The design of Collaborative Learning is predicated on a set of premises. If you accept these premises as valid in a particular situation, then Collaborative Learning emerges as a quite logical response. But to the extent that the premises are not valid, Collaborative Learning is not such an obvious or helpful choice. Consequently, it is not a "silver bullet" that can apply to every situation. But given the variation and complexity of public policy situations, no method or technique can be universally applicable.

COLLABORATIVE LEARNING PREMISES

Collaborative Learning draws upon five fundamental premises about public policy decision making:

1. Public policy must make progress on the Fundamental Paradox, which is to craft technically competent decisions through processes that create and involve an informed citizenry.
2. Good decisions are characterized by the amount and nature of learning that both precedes and follows them.
3. Social learning is fundamental to good public policy decisions. In many settings, social learning occurs most appropriately in learning teams. Sometimes these learning teams are agency-led, with the public as adjunct members, and sometimes the reverse is the case.
4. The complex, transdisciplinary nature of many public policy problems requires a systems learning approach.
5. The learning process must be able to accommodate value differences and the potential for contentious behavior by the participants.

Collaborative Learning responds to these challenges by synthesizing the work of several fields. At its core, Collaborative Learning integrates systems thinking and conflict management; this allows the framework to address the fundamental complexity and controversy that define public policy decisions. It supplements these ideas with concepts from adult and experiential learning theory as well as organizational communication/team learning. As such, it applies to both decision teams that arise entirely within organizations and various public involvement activities that transcend organizational boundaries.

All the situations to which we have applied Collaborative Learning are public lands decisions in the United States, where our particular interests and expertise lie. Our readers must determine if Collaborative Learning principles can be tailored to meet the challenges posed by other fields and in other locales. Certainly, our experience is that public land management involves all of the complexity and controversy that a sane person would choose to confront. Because Collaborative Learning has produced some satisfying results in that milieu, it is reasonable to expect progress in other areas as well.

This book has two broad objectives. First, it should enable the reader to make informed decisions about whether to use Collaborative Learning in a particular situation. This objective flows out of our belief that no method or approach should be viewed as universally applicable. Choosing not to use any particular method requires as much knowledge as choosing to use it, and perhaps more courage.[1] The second objective is to provide enough practical detail about the framework—its techniques and applications—so that the reader can begin to use Collaborative Learning.

Our Collaborative Learning applications to date have been situationally responsive—they have been our best attempts to address the particular attributes of situations as they unfolded. The ways in which we have modified our approach have been based on a combination of theory and intuition, and in retrospect we can only partially articulate the thinking behind every choice. It is therefore overly prescriptive to say that one is using *the* Collaborative Learning method or format but probably more accurate to say that one is employing Collaborative Learning principles, processes, and techniques.

OVERVIEW TO THE CHAPTERS

Setting the Stage

Collaborative Learning is specifically designed to work in multiparty policy decision situations, which are typically complex and controversial. Before we can understand the details of Collaborative Learning, a shared understanding of policy decisions and their conflictual nature must be created. Chapter 1 introduces the Fundamental Paradox of modern policy formation and presents social learning as a response to the paradox. It stops short of saying exactly how to design a social learning process. Chapter 2 provides a brief introduction to the Collaborative Learning approach. It features an overview of the method that provides a context for understanding the three more detailed chapters that follow.

Foundation

The next four chapters elaborate on the premises discussed in the introductory chapters by presenting the theoretical basis for Collaborative Learning. Chapter 3 presents a perspective on conflict management in general and multiparty public policy conflicts in particular. Chapter 4 discusses collaboration as a particular set of behaviors that is a useful means for managing natural resource conflict. Chapter 5 provides the theoretical background on adult, experiential, and organizational learning. This is an essential foundation for the "how to" chapter (Chapter 8) because it establishes a framework for creating learning environments. Chapter 6 briefly describes a systems approach to understanding complex situations. It relies on the classic systems concepts (e.g., Churchman, 1971) but focuses more specifically on soft systems methods (e.g., Checkland, 1981; Wilson & Morren, 1990).

Techniques

But the benefits of Collaborative Learning emerge from *using* it, not *talking about* it. Specific techniques translate the theoretical ideas presented in Chapters 3–6 into action. Chapter 7 introduces specific concepts and skills of communication competence. The range of topics includes communication issues, communication competence skills, and cultural concerns. Chapter 8 presents techniques for designing and implementing Collaborative Learning projects. Activities pertain to analyzing conflict situations, conducting training programs, and facilitating Collaborative Learning processes. Within these areas, specific techniques for systems thinking are featured. Chapter 8 provides material such as situation mapping, using work sheets to elicit concerns and interests and using single-negotiating texts.

Applications

Chapters 9 and 10 describe some Collaborative Learning applications. Chapter 9 focuses on the Wenatchee National Forest Fire Recovery project. In 1994 some 180,000 acres burned in a series of wildfires in the Wenatchee National Forest of central Washington. The authors were retained to design and lead a collaborative public involvement process that could help craft a recovery strategy for the forest. A series of public meetings, held over some five months, helped Forest Service personnel identify values, issues, and key locations and refine proposals for various fire recovery projects. The Wenatchee National Forest subsequently received a national award from the U.S. Department of Agriculture for the effectiveness of this effort, and agency personnel have been kind enough to attribute some of that progress to the Collaborative Learning activities.

Chapter 10 presents three less comprehensive and more time-specific applications of the Collaborative Learning approach. The Wenatchee project was a large endeavor, perhaps larger than is necessary or feasible in many situations. These additional cases demonstrate a range of applications. Examples provided include the Oregon Dunes National Recreation Area (ODNRA), Chugach National Forest (Alaska) management plan revision, and Marys Peak (Oregon) recreation management planning. These cases illustrate different ways in which Collaborative Learning can be applied and a variety of techniques that may be employed. Of these three applications, the Chugach National Forest project is the most substantial, with agency personnel leading the Collaborative Learning (CL) after having gone through a training program and initial CL citizen workshops. As of this writing, the Chugach process is on-going.

CONCLUSION

The final chapter places Collaborative Learning in the context of emerging challenges in natural resource policy. It discusses some of the pitfalls and potentials to the approach. Despite whatever potential benefits Collaborative Learning might offer, there are inevitably some situations where the obstacles are too great for collaboration to succeed. Acknowledging that those situations exist and being vigilant to identify them may be, in some cases, the best one can do to deal with them. Once an intractable situation begins to unfold it is often too late to avoid the problem. There is little one can do at that point but damage control and allowing for a cooling-off period. But by the same token, a number of advances could be integrated into Collaborative Learning that seem worthwhile to us but have not yet been explored. One possibility would be to use simulation modeling to allow real-time "what if" exercises in latter stages of the learning process.

This chapter presents our vision for what Collaborative Learning might accomplish. In brief, we hope that the framework and its techniques become part of the "tool kits" of agency personnel and community members and that they can competently draw from Collaborative Learning, modify it, and move beyond it as situations unfold and their capacities evolve.

A LETTER TO OUR READERS

In many ways, the publication of this book is a joyous event culminating several years of effort. But it has one drawback. To this point, people have learned about Collaborative Learning by interacting directly with us through applications, training, or lectures. We have benefited greatly from these experiences. We have met many passionate, talented, thoughtful people, and their ideas and responses have influenced our thinking. By comparison, this book is an impersonal way to share our ideas. We hope this letter provides some degree of personalization.

There is certainly a huge interest in collaborative approaches to governance in general, and to natural resource management more specifically. Daniel Kemmis, a philosopher and practitioner of local politics, concluded several years ago that a politics of engagement was perhaps the only way that might preserve the values that had allowed his Montana home to remain the "last best place." He, in turn, had been influenced by a comment by the author Wallace Stegner that when the West "fully learns that cooperation, not rugged individualism, is the quality that most characterizes and preserves it, then it will have achieved itself and outlived its origins. Then it has a chance to create a society to match its scenery" (1969, pp. 37–38). Speaking in a much broader context, Robert Reich, a professor and practitioner of public administration at the national level, has regarded collaboration as part of the "next American frontier."

While the stylish writings of such sages can move people to action, just wanting to collaborate is unfortunately not the same as making it happen. No matter how committed you might be to bringing people together, no matter how strongly you might feel about the value of deliberative governance, at some point you are going to have to address the questions of *when* and *how*. It is to these questions that this book devotes much of its attention.

The *when* of collaboration acknowledges that not all situations are equally well suited to a collaborative approach at all times. An entire constellation of factors— for example, a lack of decision space, the probability of being "trumped" by decisions in other venues, parties that need to address internal issues before they can meaningfully engage others—limits the collaborative potential in particular situations. An advocate for collaboration must be both willing and able to size up a situation and conclude, "Not here, not now." The failure to make those tough judgments raises several risks for the participants, the issues, and the acceptance of collaborative approaches in general.

A second dimension of the *when* question relates to the skill level of the conveners and participants in a collaboration. A deep-seated optimism about what might be possible may be a defining trait of process designers of all stripes; we have to be looking for the opportunities embedded in a situation, or the manifold risks and uncertainties in their craft would paralyze us. But by the same token, we have a moral obligation to be equally realistic as we critique our skills relative to the challenges that a situation contains. All facilitators, mediators, or conveners bring with them their particular experiences, styles, and preferences. Each of them is unique, just as is every negotiation or collaboration. For any person, then, there are situations to which his or her style and experience are tremendously well suited and those for which they are not so well matched. In these latter cases, the facilitator arguably must be willing to conclude, "Perhaps here, now, but not for me."

A common pattern in life is when people dissatisfied with the status quo learn of an alternative approach that appears to have some advantages and become desperately impatient to apply that new-to-them technique. This pattern occurs to some people as they are introduced to the notions of collaboration and conflict management. People who are going through this conversion experience often want to initiate collaborative discussions on the most intractable, complex, and confounding problems that they are confronting. While we all want to make progress on difficult, contentious situations, we must also wonder if those are the best kinds of projects in which to gain experience as an apprentice collaborator. The risks of such unleavened enthusiasm are not unlike starting down an expert-level ski slope when your skills are better suited to more gentle terrain. We believe that the skills and confidence that people develop in easy situations prepare them to engage the tough ones, in public deliberation as in skiing. To short-circuit that process is risky in either arena, but in skiing an accident usually harms only yourself. In collaborative process, overconfidence means taking all of the participants on the same perilous ride.

The responsible choice, then, is to err on the side of thorough skill development through experience and not allow your enthusiasm to lead to cavalier choices. We must never forget that real acres, real people's lives, and real relationships and trust are at issue, and we must engage them with all of the effort, authenticity, and persistence that they deserve.

But once the various *when* questions have been addressed, the *how* questions remain. Fortunately for the apprentice convener, many similar efforts have preceded yours, and a great deal of rigorous thought by both practitioners and researchers is available. While your situation is certainly unique, there are principles that cut across both the field experiences and abstract theories. In addition, a number of specific frameworks attempt to organize the principles into structured approaches to deliberative processes. To some extent these frameworks are double-edged swords.

Recall our earlier comment that each convener brings a unique ensemble of skills and preferences, and that those attributes may or may not match the attributes of any given situation. The frameworks have a similar situational relevance: each is more or less suited to different situations because of the correspondence between the framework's strengths and the challenges posed by the situation. It doesn't make sense to use a visioning framework in a clearly defined "get closure on contract clause X" situation, nor does it make sense to use a hard-driving negotiation approach with a community that is not well organized and has not yet addressed the fundamental questions about its values and future. As a result, the choice of a framework must be grounded in a rich understanding of the situation at hand.

But after you have chosen your framework, you must be willing to modify it and make it suit the dynamic complexities of your situation. All negotiation or collaborative frameworks, including the Collaborative Learning approach presented in this book, can best be thought of as ways to ask questions about your situation, not as answers to be used in a regimented or formulaic manner. As we have used Collaborative Learning in various settings, we have never done exactly the same thing twice. We are forever modifying how we do things to adjust to new issues, limitations in room availability or scheduling, legal constraints, or whatever. The key point is that the Collaborative Learning ideas give us a point of departure, a way to think through the situation. Without them, we would be guessing about what might be best as the situation unfolds, and that guessing would make us very nervous, indeed.

The best way to think about Collaborative Learning is not as a method or technique, perhaps not even as a framework, but as an orientation or style. While this book goes into considerable detail about the ideas behind this approach, there are three concepts that we would like you to bear in mind as you read the book, and as you embark upon collaborations: authenticity, thoughtful effort, and persistence. Authenticity refers to the honesty, respect, and maturity with which you engage others. Thoughtful effort embodies the notions of design savvy and effective implementation. Persistence is just that: the willingness to see the process through to the end. If your efforts can embody these three values, then your choice of whether or not to use any particular framework is less important. In all likelihood, you are not going to make things worse and prospects are good that you can make things better than you might have expected beforehand. Given the rancorous nature of many environmental policy debates, that is certainly progress.

NOTE

1.   In our experience, employees of natural resource agencies are often very willing to try Collaborative Learning, often without much detailed knowledge of it. This enthusiasm makes us nervous because it implies that either they are not critical consumers, they have few alternative approaches, or both.

Acknowledgments

In a work of this size, a large number of people share in the credit. That is even more the case when the subject is collaboration. One person, or even the two people whose names are on the cover, could not have accomplished alone the work documented in this book.

First, we acknowledge the supportive work environment provided by Oregon State University, which employed both authors while the bulk of this work was undertaken. While it is true that our colleagues and supervisors did not always understand our work ("why is a forestry guy hanging out with a communication guy?"), we were given the latitude to try new things and take risks. In particular, Dean George Brown provided funding to the Sustainable Forestry Partnership that allowed us to bring Kathy Wilson to campus in 1991. Her introduction to soft systems methods, and her support over the years has been invaluable. Dean Kay Schaffer supported the second author's sabbatical fellowship at the Udall Center for Public Policy, where work on the book occurred. Our students at Oregon State University have been a particular joy over the years. They have tolerated inconvenient course schedules necessitated by off-campus travels, and endured long war stories about the "real world." A number of students (e.g., graduate students Tony, Rick, Corrine, Angela, and Janet) participated in some Collaborative Learning projects and read drafts of this book. International students (e.g., Liisa, Teppo, Magnus, Yoshi, and Nico) who took the personal and cultural risks to travel all the way to Oregon will always have a special place in our hearts.

The agency people we have worked with throughout the past decade have taught us a tremendous amount. Collaborative Learning has evolved over the years in part because we have watched agency and community leaders doing wonderful things on behalf of communities and ecosystems. We have merely tried to figure out what principles could explain their success so that we might be able to achieve similar results elsewhere. Some line officers in the Forest Service (e.g., Jim Furnish, Rebecca Heath, Abigail Kimball, Ed Becker) have shown true leadership on Collaborative Learning projects, which is vitally important because the buck stops with them if a project does not go well and because their employees watch them carefully for an earnest commitment to collaboration. Other Forest Service employees (e.g., Mark Hummel, Pat Reed, Bob Stehr, Margaret McHugh, Buddy Rose, Gary Lehnhausen, Doris Tai, Bernie Bornong, Rick Alexander, Mike Harvey) have also been great to work with because of their interest in learning new ideas and their strong commitment to work effectively with their communities.

Faculty colleagues have also been active partners in, and proponents of, our projects. In particular, Matt Carroll and Keith Blatner from Washington State University and Tarla Peterson from Texas A&M University have built Collaborative Learning principles into their own projects.

A number of people affiliated with non-profit organizations have given us opportunities to try out our ideas and have helped us learn. Wendy Sanders of the Great Lakes Forestry Alliance; Kate Clancy, Liz Higgins, and Lydia Oberholtzer of the Wallace Institute for Alternative Agriculture; Robert Ruffner of the Kenai Watershed Forum; Charlie Sperry of the Henry's Fork Foundation; and Kirk Emerson (now director of the U.S. Institute for Environmental Conflict Resolution), Ann Moote, and Robert Varady of the Udall Center for Studies in Public Policy stand out among the many who deserve our thanks.

This book would not have been completed without the editorial and publication assistance of a number of people. Professional editor Karen Skjei invested many hours editing the initial manuscript draft and preparing some the camera-ready copy. Loril Chandler helped with the camera-ready copy and the problems we encountered with Microsoft Word. Barbara Daniels prepared the final set of camera-ready copy and the index. Nina Duprey worked closely with the authors on final edits and camera-ready copy preparation. Catherine Lyons, Korene Lawton, Leanne Small, and Jim Sabin provided support from Greenwood Press.

And finally, we have worked with remarkable community members too numerous to name. Whether they are loggers from Washington, fishermen from Alaska, hikers from Oregon, or mayors from Wisconsin, the people who have come to our sessions have displayed admirable curiosity and native intelligence. Their desire to work with others—sometimes even people with whom they disagreed profoundly—in order to advance the broad civic interests of their community continually impresses us. That these people would entrust at least a part of their communities' discourse to a "couple of university guys" has always been a gesture of goodwill that never ceases to humble us.

Chapter 1

Crafting Effective Policy in a Contentious and Complex World

Complexity theory involves the study of many actors and their interactions.

Robert Axelrod
The Complexity of Cooperation

On 6 July 1995, President William Jefferson Clinton spoke to a Georgetown University audience on the subject of "citizenship and the American community." He told his listeners that "democracy requires a certain amount of common ground. I do not believe you can solve complex [policy] questions . . . at the grass-roots level or at the national level or anywhere in between if you have too much extremism of rhetoric and excessive partisanship."

Later that year, Dr. Jack Ward Thomas, then Chief of the Forest Service, voiced a similar theme in a speech at Syracuse University. "Despite serious decline," Thomas noted, "there is still a cooperative spirit alive in the land. It is the spirit of the earliest days of the republic." He concluded that "ordinary citizens can help solve problems that affect their lives [including] even relatively complex problems of natural resource management. However, they must be truly engaged in the process. They must learn from one another about the issues, and they must gain the skills necessary to fully participate in democratic governance."

Both President Clinton and Dr. Thomas spoke to a theme of this book: that citizens can and will participate meaningfully in policy development. People with diverse viewpoints can find common ground, can disagree respectfully, can learn from each other, can engage in civic discourse, and can make progress on the policy controversies that their society confronts. Collaborative Learning is a process that promotes this type of involvement

Understanding collaboration in general and Collaborative Learning specifically begins with learning about the policy arena in which collaboration can occur.   This chapter provides that starting point by addressing why collaborative processes might have a useful role in public policy formation.   It begins with a definition of policy effectiveness, because a major motivation of collaboration is to somehow increase policy effectiveness.   Fortunately, several authors have persuasively addressed the link between collaboration and policy effectiveness; our task is to synthesize their thinking and extend it into the natural resource arena.   It is also important to characterize public policy situations in a way that allows us to see how Collaborative Learning addresses them.

POLICY EFFECTIVENESS

Sorting through the volumes that have been written about policy, four basic concepts appear to capture the essence of policy effectiveness.   An effective policy:

- Is an adaptive process.
- Uses the most appropriate science and technology.
- Is implementable.
- Has low transaction costs.

Adaptive processes recognize that all management decisions are inevitably field experiments that apply the current stock of knowledge and assumptions as implicit operating hypotheses.   Using this observation as a guiding precept, the participants in adaptive processes strive to learn from those field experiments as quickly and reliably as possible, in order to test those fundamental assumptions and knowledge levels. If a policy does not yield the intended outcome, then it is not merely a failure but also an opportunity to examine which of its motivating assumptions might be faulty.   Much of the focus of adaptive management is on natural systems; Lee (1993) is an important recent attempt to integrate adaptive management into the policy arena.   Much of Senge's (1990) writing about companies as learning organizations resembles the concepts of adaptive management, although he does not use the term. Public policy addresses systems where the cost of failure is high: airline safety, nuclear power, species conservation, and so on.   The adaptive management scholars would have us conclude that some failures are inevitable because of the complexity of the situation.   Given that some failures will occur, policy systems must learn from those failures quickly so that the damage can be minimized and so that they do not recur.

Utilizing the most appropriate science and technology would seem to be an obvious criterion for policy formation, particularly when complex situations are involved.   However, "most appropriate" is a value statement, and for many technically trained specialists, it is synonymous with "most advanced" or "state-of-the-art."   But there are certainly cases where the most advanced technical solutions to policy problems are not the most appropriate, particularly when their costs are too high, or they result in policy recommendations that are not culturally or politically viable. The international development literature is full of examples of highly technology-oriented proposals for development projects that largely failed. They remind us that most advanced technology and most appropriate technology are not necessarily synonymous.

Implementability is another core component of policy effectiveness. It is difficult to imagine how a policy can be defined as effective if it never produces tangible results. Elegant models, intricate flowcharts, and bureaucratic plans may have their place in policy formation, but the benefits of policy are derived from accomplishments. (While much of recent political science and public choice theory argues that policies are primarily crafted to perpetuate bureaucracies, we are going to set that more cynical perspective aside for the time being.) Certainly the federal forest planning process that was conducted pursuant to the National Forest Management Act of 1976 exemplifies elegant policy that had limited implementation. The linear programming models that supported each forest's plan were immense, with thousands of rows and columns of data. Even so, the land allocations that many of the plans generated were subsequently appealed, and some have never been fully implemented. In regions such as the Pacific Northwest, the plans bear little resemblance to the ecosystem-based management efforts currently under way.

Finally, *low transaction cost* is a facet of policy effectiveness that is tied to implementability. Transaction costs are those expenses that society incurs to implement a policy, and, all other things being equal, lower transaction costs imply more effective policy formation. If one policy creates a given set of benefits while avoiding expensive administrative appeals or litigation, it is arguably more effective than one that incurs those costs. The ratio between the benefits of implementing a project and its transaction costs is a standard benefit-cost analysis of policy effectiveness. A policy that never can be implemented is mathematically equivalent to one with infinite transaction costs. In either case the benefit-cost ratio is driven toward zero.

Taken together, these concepts of policy effectiveness can be merged into a single notion: *social legitimacy*. If segments of society do view a policy process as lacking legitimacy, and the stakes are high enough, they are likely to coalesce into interest groups intent on impeding or preventing its implementation. The power of the government to act flows ultimately from the discretion granted to it by the governed. In addition, social psychological research from fields, such as procedural justice, show us that satisfaction with policy processes comes not only from the outcome that one receives but from the procedures that produced that outcome (e.g., Lind & Tyler, 1988).

SOCIAL LEGITIMACY

Recognizing that social legitimacy is a culturally located concept, that is, that its definition differs across societies and eras, we can use two criteria to define social legitimacy in contemporary American public policy:

- Decisions should be made in a rational manner; policy solutions must be recognized as technically sound.
- If people's lives may be affected by policy processes, then they should have a voice in those processes.

It is no coincidence that the first criterion broadly captures the more technical "adaptive" and "most appropriate science" criteria provided above and that the second corresponds to the more process-oriented "implementable" and "low transaction costs" criteria.

The Fundamental Paradox

This juxtaposition between technical competence and open process is a defining characteristic of American policy formation. But it is largely paradoxical as well, because achieving one value may compromise our ability to achieve the other. Citizens demand technically sound decisions, but as situations become more complex, fewer people have the technical background needed to either meaningfully contribute to, or critique, the decisions. By the same token, these complex situations often touch people's lives in fundamental ways. Our traditions of participatory democracy imply that those people should be at least consulted or even directly involved if they desire to be. These dual goals— technical competence and participatory process—create a compelling dynamic between a narrow politics of expertise and a broad politics of inclusion, a dynamic that cuts across public policy disputes such as nuclear waste disposal, health care, and land management. People feel that they should have a voice in public decisions that affect their lives, but how can that voice be meaningful if the terms, concepts, and technical trade-offs are all new to them? Finding ways to increase the quality of technical expertise, while simultaneously increasing the inclusivity of decision processes, is perhaps the fundamental challenge of effective policy formation. This paradox will continue to plague policy processes as long as complex issues are discussed in democratic deliberations, and it will likely grow in importance as society's technological sophistication increases.

This Fundamental Paradox has also captured the attention of scholars from several disciplines. From these different perspectives—public administration, public opinion polling, environmental science, and political science—emerges a composite perspective on the paradox of technical competence and inclusive process.

In a 1985 essay on public administration, Robert Reich examined what he viewed as the low level of success of public administration since World War II. His conclusion is that both the theory and practice of public administration have been dominated by two schools of thought—interest group intermediation and net welfare maximization—and that they are individually insufficient and jointly incompatible. Interest group intermediation is the process of weighing the competing claims of interest groups to craft policies that are a political settlement among their claims:

The public administrator's central responsibility came to be understood as ensuring that *all* those who might be affected by agency action were represented in decision making deliberations.   The job of the public administrator, according to this vision, was to accommodate—to the extent possible—the varying demands placed upon government by competing groups.   The public administrator was a referee, a skillful practitioner of negotiation and compromise. (pp. 1619–1620)

The limitations of this approach are threefold.   First, it requires that the agency operate with the wisdom of Solomon[1] as it attempts to craft the solution. The limitations of this strategy were articulated as the four-stage "Solomon-trap" by Carpenter and Kennedy (1988):   manager collects information, manager prescribes a solution, groups attack the solution, and manager defends the solution.   Second, the agency finds itself operating as an arbiter in an environment where each party faces incentives that encourage extreme behavior and the worst sort of positional rhetoric, but faces no incentive to learn from or accommodate one another.   Third, there are no structural guarantees that the process will result in an outcome that will be technically sound.   As such, Bryson's subsequent (1988) critique of negotiated outcomes is relevant:

The main weakness of negotiation approaches, as expounded, for example, by Fisher and Ury (1981) in *Getting to Yes*, is that although they show planners how to get politically acceptable results, they are not very helpful in assuring technical workability or democratic responsibility of results. (p. 40)

Net welfare maximization, on the other hand, is the term that Reich applies to a full suite of more technocratic approaches to policy formation that have economic methods at their core. Rather than engage in political negotiation to craft a mutually acceptable solution, net welfare maximization employs a rational-comprehensive process of formulating alternatives, identifying criteria, analyzing the alternatives relative to the criteria, and then selecting the optimal alternative. "In this vision of public administration, the administrator was primarily an analyst, rather than a referee. His first responsibility was to figure out the theory of market failure underlying a broad enabling statute, and then to apply that theory to the circumstances at hand by determining whether intervention would improve overall efficiency" (p. 1621).

But if the interested parties fail to recognize the optimality of the solution that the analyst generates, either their gamesmanship is revealed or the analyst learns that the decision process might have omitted a consideration and can conduct a more refined second iteration that the stakeholders will presumably accept.   But in any case, a net welfare maximization approach seeks an objectively "right" solution, with the expectation that its "rightness" will overwhelm any conflict. As with interest group intermediation, a number of criticisms can be leveled against a technocratic maximization approach to policy formation. First, one challenge in modeling large, complex situations is that the fundamental nature of the policy problem may change more rapidly than the modeler can adapt. As a result, the analyst may generate an elegant solution to last year's problem. Second, those groups with a stake in the outcome soon become savvy in the ways of the model and argue for different methods or assumptions because it makes their politically preferred outcome more analytically preferred as well. This dynamic can digress into a policy debate of warring experts, where every side has experts who generate support for their position. Third, policy situations often have distributive consequences or involve incommensurate values that confound analytical approaches. These situations go beyond merely complex; they are what Webber and Rittel (1973) referred to as "wicked problems" because of their analytical intractability.

Reich (1985) concludes that the current quagmire in public administration is caused by several factors: (1) that both interest group intermediation and net welfare maximization are insufficient, (2) that sometimes they may even be incompatible, and (3) that we sometimes try to use them interchangeably or switch back and forth between them (pp. 1623–1624). He contends that public administrators must fundamentally rethink their roles and go from being referees or analysts to emphasizing the deliberative aspects of governance.

Neither interest-group intermediation nor net-benefit maximization necessarily entails public deliberation about common values and the community's future. Yet public deliberation is a foundation of democracy. Such deliberation can lead individuals to revise opinions (about both facts and values), alter premises, and discover common interests. Disagreements and inconsistencies encourage individuals to balance and rank their wants. The discovery that solely personal concerns are shared empowers people to act upon them. Thus, public deliberation helps transform individual valuations into social values; it helps forge collective purposes, and, even more important, helps define and refine public morality. Through such deliberations, individuals become *citizens*. (pp. 1630–1631)

This more deliberative view of public administration requires that administrators conceive of themselves as leading *social learning*. "The job of the public administrator is not merely to make decisions on the public's behalf, but to help the public deliberate over the decisions that need to be made. Rather than view debate and controversy as managerial failure that make policymaking and implementation more difficult, the public administrator should see them as natural and desirable aspects of the formation of public values, contributing to society's self-understanding" (p. 1636). Reich did not go beyond providing some broad definitions of social learning in his 1985 essay, but as we shall see later, he provided additional insight in a 1988 book, *The Power of Public Ideas*. In both efforts he was largely silent about *how to do* social learning, however.

Daniel Yankelovich addresses the same conundrum—how to make policy on complex issues. In his 1991 book, *Coming to Public Judgment: Making Democracy Work in a Complex World*, Yankelovich contends that the complexity of modern societies requires citizens who are capable of making public judgments:

A particular form of public opinion that exhibits more thoughtfulness, more weighing of alternatives, more genuine engagement of the issue, more taking into account a wide variety of factors than ordinary public opinion as measured by opinion polls, and (2) more emphasis on the normative, valuing, ethical side of questions than on the factual informational side. (p. 5)

It is interesting to consider Yankelovich's belief that opinion-based governance is inadequate, given his career as a public opinion pollster. It would seem that someone who has made a career of measuring opinion would see them as an important foundation of policy decisions. His conclusion to the contrary is based on the recognition that anyone can have an opinion, and it is virtually impossible for policy processes to differentiate between an opinion that might be based on years of effort and involvement versus one that is little more than a guess. It is hard for Yankelovich to imagine, therefore, why opinion-based governance will yield outcomes that are sufficiently technically sophisticated to address the issues that are involved in managing our increasingly complex society.

The conclusion that Yankelovich reaches is that the kinds of policies that can meet today's challenges need to be based not on opinion, but on informed judgments. Those judgments are the result of a three-step process:

- Consciousness-raising
- Working through
- Resolution

The first stage, *consciousness-raising*, or heightened awareness, is largely informed opinion; it is being aware of an issue and concerned about it. The various news media do a credible job of generating awareness. *Working through* is an active process in which the person engaged in the issue recognizes the need for change. *Informed judgment*, on the other hand, differs from awareness in that the person has had to wrestle with the fundamental complexity of the situation. Whether the issue is driven by scientific uncertainty, budgetary constraints, differing conceptions of morality, or some combination of these and other factors, the pros and cons of various viewpoints and outcomes have been engaged. *Resolution* is the process of coming to judgment and involves coming to terms with the cognitive, emotional, and moral implications of one's position (pp. 63–65). When based on informed judgments, the vote that is cast, the donation granted, or the purchase made are qualitatively more sophisticated acts than if they had been grounded merely in opinion.

A significant limitation that Yankelovich sees in our collective ability to improve public opinion—and therefore the public policy decisions that attempt to incorporate or accommodate them—is that we lack opportunities for working through:

Unlike the consciousness raising stage, our society is not well equipped with the institutions or knowledge it needs to expedite working through. Our culture does not understand it very well and by and large does not do a good job with it. In brief then, there is a wrenching discontinuity between consciousness raising and working through that is a major source of difficulty in any effort to improve the quality of public opinion. (p. 65)

There are few opportunities for individuals with differing viewpoints on a matter of public policy to join together in a safe environment that nurtures inquiry and self-examination or where it is acceptable to raise doubts or explore alternatives. One avenue to improving public policy decisions may be to create opportunities for working through.

DOES THE FUNDAMENTAL PARADOX APPLY TO ENVIRONMENTAL POLICY?

In the United States, government agencies responsible for enforcing environmental laws and managing the nation's public lands prepare exhaustive environmental documents whenever significant management actions are considered. Under the requirements of the National Environmental Policy Act of 1969 (NEPA), federal agencies conduct environmental assessments and write environmental impact statements. Most state or federal agencies complete comprehensive plans pursuant to a wide range of procedural requirements. These assessments and plans typically address controversial management situations. In this context, government agencies have relied on two approaches for dealing with public lands conflicts. Each approach operationalizes one of the dimensions of the Fundamental Paradox: either interest group intermediation or technocratic net welfare maximization.

Formal Public Participation

Public participation is predecisional communication between an agency responsible for a decision and the public. The most basic format for the public participation activities conducted by natural resource management agencies in the United States involves three specific activities: *notification, issue surfacing,* and *comment on draft decisions. Notification* means communicating to the public through various media that an agency decision process is beginning and what the agency might know at that time about the basic structure of the decision process (issues, purpose, constraints, schedule etc.). Notification activities commonly include newsletters, direct mailings to interested individuals, and publication in the *Federal Register. Issue surfacing,* also referred to as scoping, is the canvassing of interested members of the public to determine what their interests, goals, and concerns might be. Typical issue surfacing involves workshops, field trips, soliciting letters, and one-on-one communication. *Comment on draft decisions* takes different forms, but the most common activities are public meetings/hearings and comment letters from the public.

The basic public participation model has been broadly criticized as ineffective. Although formal public participation processes provide easy access and predictability, the disadvantages concentrate on the impact of that access. It is immaterial that a process is convenient if being involved has no effect.

Research substantiates the sense that in many U. S. public lands conflicts most public participation efforts have few positive effects. Surveys indicate that substantial portions of participants feel that their input had little or no impact (Lyden et al., 1990; USDA-Forest Service, 1990), are dissatisfied or mistrustful (Dixon, 1993), value interactive participation methods that involve two-way communication and shared decision making over formal public hearings or letter writing (Force & Williams, 1989), feel that public meetings may become venting sessions motivated out of generalized resentment and mistrust of public officials (Twight, 1977), and believe that public meetings do little to dispel stereotyped perceptions of disagreement with agency positions (Twight & Paterson, 1979).

The relatively formal nature of communication during public involvement processes also affects the quality of the information that the agency receives. To comment at a hearing-type meeting, a participant must speak for the record, which often means making a short speech into a microphone before a relatively large assembly. Because many people feel anxious about public speaking, it is likely that the quality and quantity of the comments are reduced by such a formal protocol and that only the most motivated people will overcome their fears and address the group. As a result, the comments tend to be more extreme than they might be in a setting where dialogue is more natural.

Formal public participation methods used by government agencies seem to exhibit a "Three-'I' Model": "inform, invite, and ignore." A public land management agency can inform the public about a proposed action, invite the public to a meeting to provide comments on that action, and ignore what members of the public say. While this may be a somewhat cynical view, it is clear that there has been more measured dissatisfaction with public participation than satisfaction (Hendee et al., 1974; Blahna & Yonts-Shepard, 1989; Dixon, 1993; Twight, 1977; Twight & Paterson, 1979; Force & Williams, 1989). It seems that, on balance, the public participation activities of land management agencies are not contributing to any successes they may be enjoying; it is, in fact, more likely that they are part of the agencies' current difficulties.

Scientific and Technical Expertise

A second approach that public land management agencies have employed to make decisions relies on the insights from science and technology. This approach holds that if the task of analyzing a controversial situation is assigned to technical specialists, their scientific knowledge and solutions will be sufficiently convincing to mitigate or even eliminate conflict. In short, it assumes that complexity is creating the controversy, and if the complexity can be resolved, then perhaps the controversy will dissipate.

Using the most appropriate science and technology may seem like the obvious way to deal with environmental and natural resource policy conflicts. Indeed, expert panels are increasingly used to devise management strategies in situations where conventional means have run aground. Using the federal lands in the western United States as an example, at least three large teams of scientists have been convened in recent years to address bioregional species conservation issues: for the range of the northern spotted owl in the Pacific Northwest, for the interior Columbia River basin, and for the Sierra Nevada region in California. These scientific SWAT (Special Weapons and Tactics) teams are convened in the hopes that there is some unambiguous and objective "right answer" to questions of huge significance and complexity. Public acceptance of their "right answers" has been slow in coming: neither the plans for the northern spotted owl region nor those for the interior Columbia River basin have been heartily embraced by the communities in their respective regions (the Sierra Nevada process is too young to judge in this regard). The plan for the northern spotted owl region was ruled as violating the Federal Advisory Committee Act, and Congress has made several attempts (heretofore unsuccessful) to eliminate funding for the interior Columbia River basin planning process.

We might all wish that teams of experts could arrive—like the cavalry riding over the hill—and solve our fundamental questions about the interactions between ecological integrity, economic well-being, cultural values, and private property rights. An expert-driven approach would certainly relieve the rest of us from the huge burden of debating a large class of public policy issues. But such an approach may be destined to fail because it seeks technical solutions to policy conflicts that encompass differing values and worldviews. Those plural values probably mean that there may never be unambiguous or objective answers to these questions, no matter how many experts are convened or how sophisticated their models might become.

THE ROLE FOR COLLABORATIVE PROCESSES IN GOVERNANCE

The conclusions of scholars such as Reich or Yankelovich and the limited success of the agencies' public involvement activities argue for a new twist on public decision processes. To return to an earlier notion, public policy must strive to make progress on the Fundamental Paradox of technical competence and inclusive deliberation. We cannot accept wild swings from purely technocratic processes, to purely inclusive ones as progress. Our capacity to develop processes that can truly identify and advance the public interest hinges on our ability to enhance both. Collaborative processes that are inclusive, sincere, and thorough offer some important potential in achieving that balance. Collaboration involves interdependent parties identifying issues of mutual interest, pooling their energy and resources, addressing their differences, charting a course for the future, and allocating implementation responsibility among the group. As such, it is fundamentally a process for social learning (à la Reich) and working through (à la Yankelovich).

The challenge in any situation, of course, is to craft a collaborative process adequate to the task. Given the complex, almost wicked nature of many contemporary policy problems collaborative processes must be well grounded in learning theory. It will not suffice to convene a group and merely assume that they can address the technical issues with adequate competence. They must learn their way to the level of sophistication that their input must achieve if it is to be valuable. By the same token, these situations are often paralyzingly controversial. Natural resource debates are often so contentious that the best outcome some policymakers can envision is *equilibrated dislike:* "Everyone is equally mad, so I must have made a good decision." But such a standard of performance can have harmful, long-term effects on the trust between the public and agencies, as Reich pointed out:

The failure of conventional techniques of policy making to permit civic discovery may suggest that there are no shared values to be discovered in the first place. And this message—that the "public interest" is no more than accommodation or aggregation of individual interests—may have a corrosive effect on civic life. (1988, pp. 146–147)

Collaboration may allow the discovery of shared values, but only if the participants "walk the talk." If agency personnel or community leaders convene a process, it will not be adequate to merely decree that it is collaborative; rather, collaborative behaviors will have to be modeled by the conveners, encouraged by the process, and discouraged by group norms and behavior.

An enthusiasm for collaboration should not be grounded in a presumption that it is either quick or easy; in fact, experience shows that it is often neither. Under the best of circumstances it taxes our collective ability to communicate competently, to debate constructively, and to explore thoroughly. The integrative nature of collaboration requires that experts de-jargonize their work and acknowledge the fundamental value preferences that their views inevitably reflect. It also requires that citizens give generously of their time, that they openly engage worldviews and political preferences different from their own (and often in conflict with them), and that they be responsible and pragmatic in terms of the demands they place on agency personnel and the public purse. In short, it requires that all participants exhibit behaviors that embody the highest ideals of civic engagement, something that we all fall short of accomplishing. As such, collaborations never accomplish what a starry-eyed idealist might hope for. But by the same token, they can also accomplish more than the most tense-jawed pessimist might predict.

Collaborative Learning is the particular technique that we have designed to embody these values of social learning and working through. Its goal is to improve the quality of public decisions by improving social deliberation and by moving environmental decision making beyond positional advocacy and sound-bite media campaigns. This is not an easy task, but it is fundamental to moving forward, because as William Cronon, esteemed professor of environmental history, noted:

We must recognize that advocacy and critical understanding are often in tension with each other, and we must always be willing to stand back from advocacy—however briefly—to make sure that our reasons for acting as we intend to do are in fact sound.

One problem with advocacy politics is that it feeds the sound-bite political culture that has so corrupted our civil life in the past quarter century, in which extreme advocates caricature each others views in the interest in generating outrage to fuel and raise funds for their own cause while doing nothing to build genuine consensus within the culture and the political economy as a whole. Ironically, the extreme advocates at opposite poles actually need each other to sustain their own positions. Their extreme dualism sustains itself by denying the possibility of a common ground. Wise Use and Earth First! sustain each other in peculiar ways that produce an odd symbiosis at opposite ends of the political spectrum. (1998)

Collaborative Learning is certainly is not the only technique that can be used to achieve collaborative deliberation; indeed, it is possible to collaborate effectively without relying on a particular technique. Collaborative Learning offers a synthesis of ideas from dispute management theory and systems thinking that allows it to address controversy and complexity. It provides a framework through which the conveners of collaboration can make choices about the kinds of activities that are appropriate as the discussions unfold and allows them to anticipate some of the behaviors that may emerge at different points.

CONCLUSION

Collaboration is a useful means of crafting public policy because it offers a rich opportunity for deliberative political discourse. One of its major advantages is its flexibility; it is not as rule-bound as either legislative or litigative approaches to policy formation. But by the same token, that flexibility requires that both the *design* and *implementation* of the collaboration be sufficiently thoughtful as to capture that potential. The absence of a priori rules creates a certain vulnerability. A process is not collaborative just because someone labels it so, but the collaboration emerges from the interactions of the participants, which, in turn, is encouraged by the thoughtfulness of the design. As David Mathews, former secretary of Health, Education and Welfare and president of the Kettering Foundation noted (1994):

If the question of what turns a collection of people into a public could be answered in just one word, the word would be *deliberation*. People become a public through the connecting process of deliberation. To deliberate is not just to "talk about" problems. To deliberate means to weigh carefully both the consequences of various options for action and the views of others. Deliberation is what we require of juries. It is what makes twelve of our peers a group to whom we literally give life-and-death powers. We don't just trust twelve people with those powers under any condition. We only trust them under the condition that they deliberate long and carefully. The same is true of democratic politics. Without the discipline of serious deliberation, it is impossible for a body of people to articulate what they believe to be in the best interest of all—in the "public" interest. Deliberations are needed to find our broader and common concerns. (p. 111)

The goal of Collaborative Learning is to create opportunities for deliberation. There are three foundations upon which we build that deliberative potential: learning theory, systems theory, and conflict management. The learning theory is important because deliberation must be more than profound contemplation—it can be an active process of engaging facts and values in ways that correlate well with the learning styles of adults, many of whom bring a great deal of knowledge and experience to the process. Second, the systems theory is important because it can provide some clever ways to deal with the interrelationships and complexity that are often involved in contemporary policy situations. Finally, the conflict management is important because this deliberation is fundamentally political, because many situations have a long history of controversy, and because adversarial politics is part of the human condition. Initiating a collaboration hoping that everyone will be pleasant and without hidden agendas invites disaster. This book now devotes a chapter each to theories of conflict management, collaboration as a conflict management philosophy, learning theory, and systems theory.

NOTE

1. King Solomon was asked to settle a dispute between two women, each of whom claimed to be the mother of a particular infant. He proposed that the child be split in two, so that each mother could have half. At that point, one mother agreed to drop her claim. Solomon declared her the mother, on the logic that only a mother would give the child away to save its life (1st Kings 3:16–27).

Chapter 2

The Essence of
Collaborative Learning

> Common ground is the shared basis from which we must think and then act to resolve complex issues such as those in the environmental arena.
>
> —Carol Rosenblum Perry
> *The Environment of Words*

This chapter provides a compact, yet comprehensive, overview of Collaborative Learning. The depth of understanding that is required to apply Collaborative Learning comes from the other chapters, but no other chapter provides a complete description of the method.

WHAT IS COLLABORATIVE LEARNING?

Collaborative Learning is a framework and set of techniques intended for multiparty decision situations. It is a means of designing and implementing a series of events (meetings, field trips, etc.) to promote creative thought, constructive debate, and the effective implementation of proposals that the stakeholders generate. This approach can be used when there are multiple stakeholders who are *interdependent* because they are all affected by the same situation but are also *independent* because they may have distinctly different views and values regarding it. There may also be substantial differences between the improvements that different stakeholders prefer. Collaborative Learning is equally applicable to decision-making situations within a single organization (e.g., managing a project team) and to situations between organizations and in the public policy sphere.

Collaborative Learning begins with a series of assumptions about the world and the nature of the decisions to which the method is being applied:

1. Conflict is inevitable.
2. Conflict is irresolvable, but manageable.
3. Truly vexing situations are often rich in systems complexity.
4. Much of the value of collaborative processes comes from their value as learning opportunities.
5. The best way to improve decisions in highly complex situations is to understand the decision making as a learning process.

These assumptions begin to clarify the ways in which Collaborative Learning differs from other approaches. First, by accepting conflict as an inherent part of many decisions, it departs from the prevailing mind-set among many negotiation and mediation practitioners and researchers. The most common term in the field is conflict *resolution*, which implies that the root cause of the conflict can be identified and excised from society. The Collaborative Learning approach is more modest—perhaps more realistic—in admitting that there will always be complex and controversial decisions to be faced. Our task is to learn how to *manage* their conflict dimensions so that rancor does not begin to dominate the discussion and diminish the possibility of substantive improvements.

A second departure is that some facilitative approaches use an "Abundance Principle" (Krueger, 1992; Levine, 1998), that is, that there will be plenty of resources for everyone if we can just sit down and talk our way through the issues that constrain our true potential. In a situation characterized by untapped abundance, the facilitator's task is to generate a supportive and creative environment so that the heretofore-unrecognized opportunities can emerge. We do not embrace the presumption of abundance in the natural resource/environmental arena. It would be imprudent to apply a technique that implicitly assumes that in any locale there could be more acres, water, wildlife, or biological productivity than there is.   Such an approach could promote unrealistically optimistic efforts, contradict scientific information, and waste the participants' time and effort in developing desirable—yet infeasible—proposals.[1]   Collaborative Learning is a very pragmatic approach. It intends to help people make progress in difficult situations, where the difficulty emerges from a combination of complexity and controversy. It does not promise that everyone (or even anyone) will get everything that she or he might desire. It does not promise that the underlying value differences that often drive natural resource controversies will disappear. It does not even promise that everyone will necessarily like everyone else more when the process is over. The social contract, if you will, between Collaborative Learning facilitators and stakeholders is quite simple. If the stakeholders will strive to give the process a chance, the facilitators will strive to conduct a process that is efficient, promotes civility, respects the knowledge and time that the participants contribute, and fosters learning. The expected outcome is an action plan to improve the situation.

MANAGING CONTEXT AND CONTENT

One of the key lessons that we have learned is that the success of Collaborative Learning projects often depends on factors far different from the specific set of issues about which we have ostensibly been asked to help. Often additional factors that lie outside the narrow bounds of the problem at hand have a great deal to do with the ultimate success of our efforts. We have come to distinguish between content and context as a way of clarifying these different realms. Content refers to the specific issues the collaboration is intended to address: the grazing allotment, the landscape level plan, the site for a landfill, and so on. Content may also include various legal or procedural requirements affecting how the collaboration can proceed. Context pertains to the organizational setting in which the collaboration is intended to operate. Often we are invited to lead a Collaborative Learning project by a lead stakeholder, such as the United States Department of Agriculture (USDA) Forest Service (the most frequent convener of the projects we have undertaken). By considering context, issues like the skill and morale of key employees, the commitment of decision makers to collaboration, and the relationship between the organization and key external stakeholders all become important considerations in deciding if, how, and when to initiate a Collaborative Learning project.

Five distinct phases characterize an overall Collaborative Learning project that address issues of content and context (Figure 2.1, outer circle):

- Assessment
- Training
- Design
- Implementation/Facilitation
- Evaluation

Taken together, these five phases constitute a comprehensive Collaboration Learning *project*, while the specific techniques featured in the design and implementation/facilitation phases define the Collaborative Learning *process* core. Assessment is essentially a thoughtful evaluation of the situation's potential for collaboration. Training emphasizes the development of an appreciation for collaboration among key organization employees and stakeholders as well as some grounding in the specific techniques of Collaborative Learning. Design centers on the development of a situation responsive strategy for involving participants in a meaningful process. Implementation/facilitation involves the direct conduct of meetings, field trips, workshops, designed to promote mutual learning, innovative, constructive debate, and decision-making. Finally, evaluation includes data gathering and reflection to learn from participants what choices were most and least effective, and what lessons can inform future projects.

Figure 2.1
Collaborative Learning Project Phases and Process Stages

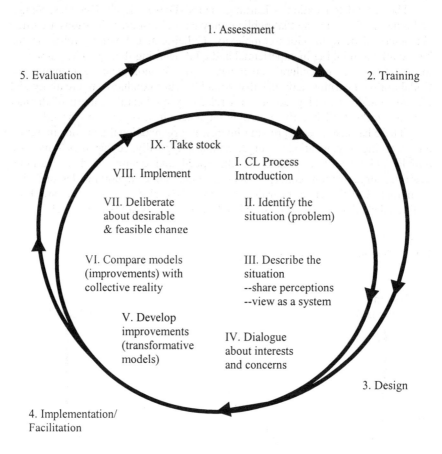

1. Assessment

5. Evaluation

2. Training

IX. Take stock

VIII. Implement

I. CL Process
Introduction

VII. Deliberate
about desirable
& feasible change

II. Identify the
situation (problem)

VI. Compare models
(improvements) with
collective reality

III. Describe the
situation
--share perceptions
--view as a system

V. Develop
improvements
(transformative
models)

IV. Dialogue
about interests
and concerns

3. Design

4. Implementation/
Facilitation

COLLABORATIVE LEARNING IS A HYBRID OF SEVERAL FIELDS

Figure 2.2 shows the different lines of research that have been synthesized to create Collaborative Learning. This diagram may be thought of as an academic pedigree, a map of the conceptual parents that have been combined to yield this approach. Each of these different bodies of thought provides principles that inform the choices that Collaborative Learning project developers and facilitators make.

Collaborative Learning has three conceptual foundations, and each is equally important. The first is conflict management (Deutsch, Fisher, Pruitt, Carnevale, Susskind, and others). There is a huge field of practice and research into the causes, characteristics of, and responses to, conflict. Disputes of all kinds—family, labor management, international diplomacy, public policy—have been extensively studied, and the results of these efforts provide a crucial springboard for Collaborative Learning.

The second foundation is learning theory (Dewey, Kolb, Knowles, Senge, and others). Recognizing that public policy/natural resource situations are often characterized by tremendous complexity, Collaborative Learning relies on the best available thinking in experiential and adult learning theory. The purpose is to identify the procedural attributes and chronological sequencing of Collaborative Learning activities that would be most conducive to creativity and critical thought. Learning occurs in a relatively predictable pattern of distinct cognitive tasks; Collaborative Learning sequences its tasks in a similar order.

There has also been a growing interest in organizational behavior literature on "learning organizations": organizations—typically, companies—that are nimble and responsive because of the speed and quality of their learning. Learning organization concepts also provide some important lessons that strengthen Collaborative Learning because they clarify that there are both additional challenges and benefits when learning occurs at the team level.

Figure 2.2
Foundations of Collaborative Learning

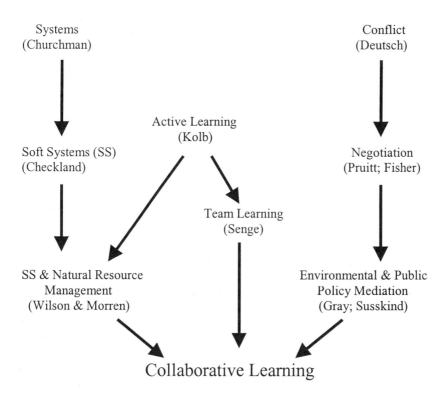

The third foundation to Collaborative Learning is systems thinking (Churchman, Checkland, Wilson & Morren, and others). This discipline assumes that many situations are characterized by a complex set of relationships. Thinking about those situations at any less than the systems level (such as linear thinking) is therefore an incomplete and potentially limiting understanding. In particular, such thinking fails to recognize certain properties that emerge only at the systems level, and may ignore the possibility that any act may generate unintended consequences as its effects ripple through the system. The proposed "solutions" that emerge from an incomplete understanding are therefore likely to either solve the wrong problem, solve a symptom rather than the cause, or create additional problems that were not foreseen.

Collaborative Learning is a rare approach in some ways. First, it is an academically eclectic approach, since it draws on three different theoretical fields that to our knowledge have never been purposively integrated. This integration makes Collaborative Learning distinctive because theoreticians tend to stay in their own "pastures", and very rarely cross the disciplinary fences that divide them.[2] Its second unique feature is its use of theory to directly inform practice. Our interaction with conflict resolution professionals leads us to conclude that the field has a substantial chasm between practitioners and academics. The former have a wealth of experience but rarely have the luxury to reflect on why things worked out as they did or how things might have been done differently. The latter have a wealth of explanations and principles but rarely face the reality of having to conduct meetings in unpredictable and volatile environments.

Collaborative Learning is one effort to bridge that chasm; it has robust theoretical roots that shape and instruct the practice. While Collaborative Learning is intentionally designed as a means to help agency managers, elected officials, and citizens make progress in vexing situations, its value comes from its strong foundation in the best contemporary thinking about how people process information, how they deal with different viewpoints and goals, and how to best organize their thinking about complex situations.

THE STAGES OF THE COLLABORATIVE LEARNING PROCESS

The inside circle of Figure 2.1 presents the Collaborative Learning process as a series of distinct activities. Stage 1, Assessment, begins at a point analogous to roughly 1:00 on a clock face. Both the general circular flow, as well as the particular starting point, comes from David Kolb's models of experiential learning (see Chapter 5). The specific kinds of activities that occur in Stage 1 comes from conflict theory literature, which emphasizes understanding the nature of the situation and the stakeholders before beginning any process. The remaining steps in the process come from the soft systems approach of Peter Checkland, as modified by Kathy Wilson and George Morren (1990). The conflict management techniques are important throughout these steps because behaviors can escalate at any time in the process. Still, the point where managing the potential for conflict is most important is Stage 7, which involves collaborative argument (deliberation) about desirable and feasible change. Here the stakeholders commit to a course of action by selecting a set of changes to implement. This is the decision-making moment in a process that has built gradually to this point. Applying concepts from mediation and negotiation is crucially important at this point because if this stage is not competently facilitated, much of the progress to this point can be lost.

WHAT IS THE GOAL OF COLLABORATIVE LEARNING?

Collaborative Learning seeks to help stakeholders generate a set of improvements in a situation of mutual concern. These changes are undertaken because the stakeholders recognize them as meeting the dual test of desirability and feasibility. In a nutshell, Collaborative Learning seeks improvement through creativity, and creativity derives from a rich understanding of the complexity of the situation at hand.

Unlike some other decision-making methodologies, stakeholder participation in Collaborative Learning is not optional or peripheral; it is essential. The stakeholders—not the facilitators—must understand the situation. The stakeholders—not the facilitators—generate potential improvements to the situation. The stakeholders—not the facilitators—ultimately judge the desirability and feasibility of potential improvements. As Brown noted, when reviewing the role of stakeholder participation in soft systems, "Participation is evidently central to Checkland's thesis of problem solving . . . the logic-based inquiry begins with pragmatic real-world thinking, via a discussion of the problem with those chosen to be involved in the methodology. This ideally incorporates the people involved in the situation, or at least representatives of all of the interest groups" (1996, p. 204).

Although the word "empowered" has become somewhat clichéd, it nevertheless applies nicely to Collaborative Learning. The empowering comes neither from somehow transforming the individuals (which techniques such as Bush and Folger's [1994] Transformative Mediation attempt to do) nor from somehow transforming the situation (which techniques such as those of Maser [1996] or Levine [1998] attempt to do). Rather, the empowerment comes from creating a constructive environment that allows the knowledge and values held by individuals to be combined into a larger understanding of the situation. When that understanding emerges at the group level, it creates a learning team that can deliberate more powerfully than any of the individuals could have alone. Collaborative Learning does not empower people with the promise that complex and controversial decisions will now become easy to solve; rather, people are empowered to work very hard for ongoing improvement.

The primary focus of Collaborative Learning is outcome-oriented, that is, CL produces implementable improvements to the situation. It does not seek to change stakeholders' values or the relationships among stakeholders, although these may emerge from a CL project. Collaborative Learning processes do not include explicit team building or "group encounter" activities. A suite of therapeutic/group counseling techniques has been developed and there are consultants/counselors who use them effectively. But this is not the orientation that Collaborative Learning adopts.

Nevertheless, Collaborative Learning has some secondary benefits that emerge largely as by-products of making progress on the primary goal. Notable among these are an enhanced sense of accomplishment among the participants, a deeper sense of community, and an increased acceptance of the legitimacy of the values of other groups. This relational change stops well short of any sort of spontaneous "group hug," and certainly the stakeholders hold strongly to their values and will advocate forcefully for them. But when people make more progress than they expected to achieve and do so while working in a multiparty setting with groups that they may dislike or distrust, they can begin to re-think the negative assumptions and stereotypes they hold about the other stakeholders. As we have repeatedly seen, making progress on some issues creates a window of opportunity for addressing a second set of issues that perhaps would have been too controversial to be addressed at the outset.

WHAT ARE *NOT* GOALS OF COLLABORATIVE LEARNING?[3]

Collaborative Learning has not been designed to somehow "market" decisions that have already been made. CL objectives do not include enhancing the public acceptability of a plan through a public relations campaign that can generate support while requiring few, if any, substantive changes to the plan. In all fairness, Collaborative Learning (or any other collaborative process) probably could be used to sell an agenda to an unsuspecting public because of the way it uses compelling words like "respect," "learning," "progress," and "improvement." But the central role that stakeholder participation plays in Collaborative Learning means that it would be difficult to use Collaborative Learning to sugarcoat a fait accompli decision. If someone were looking for a means to legitimate a pre-established decision, Collaborative Learning would not the best choice because its rich involvement of diverse stakeholders makes any particular outcome unpredictable.

A second objective that Collaborative Learning does not pursue is the manipulation of the process to favor one group over another. Collaborative Learning values inclusiveness, and that may mean that the facilitators go to extraordinary lengths to provide access to the sorts of participants who normally do not have much power in conventional decision processes (e.g., finding ways to accommodate and reassure people whose literacy skills may be marginal). But providing equality of opportunity is not the same as trying to steer the outcome toward the preferences of any particular group. Although advocacy groups that feel threatened by collaborative processes contend that their constituents are uniquely unqualified to participate in collaborations (and therefore should not participate because of this competitive disadvantage), processes such as Collaborative Learning are quite egalitarian in creating opportunity for mutual persuasion.

By the same token, Collaborative Learning is not undertaken as a means to pursue the facilitators' (or trainers, designers, assessors) values regarding the outcome. Certainly facilitators have their own personal values, but facilitators have an ethical obligation to recognize that for this situation, at this time, and in this locale, the facilitators' *values regarding the outcome* are subordinated to the values of the stakeholders. Instead, the facilitator should strive to lead the group's discussion of their *values about the process*, and be a champion, coach, and role model in that arena.[4]

WHAT DO COLLABORATIVE LEARNING PROCESSES LOOK LIKE?

Because Collaborative Learning is a set of design principles, there is no single Collaborative Learning approach or format. That being said, there would be a number of identifiable attributes to a Collaborative Learning project:

1. The facilitators are grounded/they understand the situation from the stakeholders' perspectives. They are particularly aware that there are multiple worldviews about the situation, and therefore multiple ways to think about improving it. This knowledge of the situation may arise because the facilitators live in the area, or have made a systematic effort to become familiar with the various stakeholders.
2. A series of public events (meetings, field trips, etc.) involving as many different kinds of stakeholders as possible, in order to create a shared understanding of the situation, as well as the different concerns that people have toward it. These can be relatively small meetings; the emphasis on large meetings is much higher in public hearing processes such as NEPA. The key attribute of Collaborative Learning meetings is not so much the *number* of participants at any given meeting, but the *range* of viewpoints that those participants represent and the quality of the deliberation that results.
3. An analytic phase when the concerns are converted into alternatives or models of the transformed system. This phase is typically conducted by specialists or working teams, and it involves less public/large group interaction that do other phases.
4. An evaluative process that allows the stakeholders to debate the desirability and feasibility of different strategies for change. This debate, particularly in terms of feasibility, is informed by the results of the analytic phase.
5. A decision point. This may consist of people making individual decisions over issues where they have the sole authority for doing so (such as an agency official making the formal regulatory decision or a private landowner committing to a course of action on her own land), or it may be a group decision to move forward on a project together.
6. Implementation and evaluation.

CONCLUSION

In sum, Collaborative Learning:

- Stresses *improvement* rather than solution.
- Emphasizes *situation* rather than problem or conflict.
- Focuses on *concerns and interests* rather than positions.
- Targets *progress* rather than solution.
- Encourages *systems thinking* rather than linear thinking.

- Recognizes that *considerable learning*—about science, issues, and value differences—will have to occur before implementable improvements are possible.
- Emphasizes that learning and progress occur *through communication and negotiation interaction.*

These features have the combined potential to reconfigure decision making into an active learning process that provides stakeholders—employees, citizens, and neighbors—with a meaningful voice and provides decision makers—managers, elected officials, and agency planners—with relevant, timely, and useful input.

NOTES

1. In partial defense of the Abundance Principle, a compelling body of experimental negotiation research shows that people typically underestimate the opportunity for mutual gain outcomes when they negotiate (Bazerman, 1998).   This finding, known as the "fixed pie bias," implies that facilitators should actively push stakeholders to move beyond their fixed pie assumptions and look for mutual gain opportunities. If facilitators invoke the Abundance Principle they are clearly doing just that. Our discomfort with the Abundance Principle is that it optimistic in the extreme, essentially substituting an infinite or unlimited pie for a fixed one.

2. Our efforts at interdisciplinary integration are in the spirit of the explorer Thor Heyerdahl, who said "In order to penetrate even farther into their subject, the host of specialists narrow their field and dig down deeper and deeper till they can't see each other. But the treasures their toil brings to light they place on the ground above. A different kind of specialist should be sitting there, the one still missing. He would not go down any hole, but would stay on top and piece all of the different facts together" (1960).

3. A disclaimer is warranted at this point, because we are making statements that in investment law would be referred to as "forward looking statements": true to the best of our current knowledge, but changing conditions that cannot be foreseen may cause the future to be somewhat different. In particular, we are making statements about how other people might use Collaborative Learning when we can neither control nor foresee what other people will do.

4. This discussion foreshadows an in-depth treatment of different roles and the need for role clarity that appears in Chapter 3.

Chapter 3

Understanding Conflict Situations

> Instead of suppressing conflicts, specific channels could be created to make this conflict explicit, and specific methods could be set up by which the conflict is resolved.

> —Albert Low
> *Zen and Creative Management*

As presented in the previous chapter, Collaborative Learning provides a method for mutual learning about environmental conflicts and generating improvements in the management of those situations. With its emphasis on dialogue and deliberation, Collaborative Learning offers a setting for asking the appropriate questions and "solving the right problem" (Mitroff, 1998). As a framework for public participation and decision-making, Collaborative Learning is particularly relevant to situations in which conflict plays a significant role. Its development has been motivated by the numerous environmental and natural resource policy conflicts that people and organizations escalate and often litigate. Consequently, this chapter presents our view of environmental and natural resource policy conflicts.

Methods for effectively managing environmental and natural resource conflicts, such as Collaborative Learning, must be responsive to their complexity. Understanding this complexity begins with a basic review of the nature of conflict situations, which this chapter provides. First, we offer a primer on the fundamentals of conflict and its management as a component of Collaborative Learning. After the primer, we focus specifically on the nature of environmental conflict and some of the complexities that define it.

On Terminology

This book uses the terms "environmental" and "natural resource" interchangeably. We do so in a manner similar to that of Crowfoot and Wondolleck in *Environmental Disputes* (1990), who use the term "environmental dispute" to include both environmental and natural resource situations. Environmental policy, broadly construed, includes all actions by any policy-making agent that may potentially affect the quality of the natural world. Natural resource policy refers often to actions related to the proactive management of elements in nature that people intend to actively manipulate. For example, timber harvest management falls into the category of natural resource policy, while the remediation of a toxic waste site exemplifies environmental policy. But in other cases, any distinction between environmental and natural resource is blurry, at best. When we use the terms "environmental policy," "environmental conflict," and "environmental decision making," we are including "natural resource" as well, and vice versa.

As an interesting twist to this semantic distinction, in our Collaborative Learning work around the country we have noticed regional predispositions regarding these terms. In the western United States, more people frame decisions as "natural resource" than as "environmental." In the midwestern, eastern, and southern United States, citizens seem to invoke "environment" more often than "natural resource" when discussing the same sorts of policy issues. This serves as a reminder that conveners and facilitators need to be sensitive to regional variations in terminology.

THE NATURE OF CONFLICT

For as long as humans have encountered one another, there has been conflict. Conflict is an inevitable part of human interaction, regardless of the arena in which it occurs. "Conflict occurs in almost all social settings," write Folger et al. in *Working Through Conflict.* "As we enter more complex relationships and become involved in more diverse and public settings," they explain, "we often find that conflicts remain remarkably similar to those in our early lives" (1997, p. 6). In its simplest form, conflict consists of incompatibility involving issues, parties, processes (how, when, and by whom) and outcomes. But conflict is rarely considered simple. As Folger et al. remark, "conflict is one of the most dramatic—and sometimes traumatic—events in life" (1997, p. 12).

We have asked college students in conflict management and dispute resolution classes to provide examples of conflict. Students report varied personal experiences such as "fight with my boyfriend," "argument with my boss," "my parents' divorce," "not getting classes I need," and "financial aid hassles." They also recognize that conflicts occur at larger organizational and social scales as well, because they also mention "budget cuts," "the spotted owl mess," "the Arab-Israeli conflict," and "Northern Ireland" as illustrations of conflict.

These responses reveal common perceptions of conflict; we typically associate conflict with fights, games, debates, squabbles, arguments, shouting, violence, tension, and anger. Wilmot and Hocker (1998) present prevalent images of conflict as metaphors (see Table 3.1). They note that people often characterize conflict as war, disease, struggle, a trial, explosive, and as a mess; such images suggest that "many people view conflict as an activity that is almost totally negative and has no redeeming qualities" (p. 9). A recent study of conflict metaphors further illustrates this point. McCorkle and Mills (1992) surveyed 349 undergraduate social science students at a United States university about their past interpersonal conflicts. The researchers' questionnaire asked respondents to identify conflicts they had experienced, indicate whom they were with and what the conflicts were about, and write a paragraph describing each conflict. The researchers analyzed these paragraphs to determine what metaphors were employed to describe the conflicts. They found a variety of metaphor types (conflicts represented as animals, natural processes, one-way communication, confinement, etc.) and concluded the metaphors were consistently negative. "None of the metaphors were positive," McCorkle and Mills remark, and "this appears to confirm the Euro-American cultural assumption that conflict is by definition negative" (1992, p. 63).

Table 3.1
Common Conflict Metaphors

Negative Conflict Metaphors	Conflict is Warlike and Violent Conflict is Explosive Conflict is a Trial Conflict is a Struggle Conflict is an Act of Nature Conflict is Animal Behavior Conflict is a Mess Conflict is a Communication Breakdown
Neutral Conflict Metaphors	Conflict is a Game Conflict is a Heroic Adventure Conflict is a Balancing Act Conflict is a Challenge
Positive Conflict Metaphors	Conflict is a Bargaining Table Conflict is a Tide Conflict is a Dance Conflict is a Garden

While some people may assume that conflict is overwhelmingly negative, conflict scholars do not hold this view. A brief review of how leading scholars define conflict reveals that conflict is neither inherently positive nor negative. Rather, it has the potential to be either. Table 3.2 offers a compendium of scholars' definitions of conflict and their key terms. These definitions have much in common. First, they indicate the inevitability of conflict in human affairs. Second, they reveal key features of conflict situations. For example, many of the definitions stress that conflicts involve interdependent parties that perceive some kind of incompatibility.

Central Elements of Conflict Situations

From the definitions presented in Table 3.2, we conclude that conflicts generally involve:

- Perceived incompatibility
- Interests, goals, aspirations
- Two or more interdependent parties
- Incentives to cooperate and compete
- Interaction; communication
- Bargaining/negotiation
- Strategy/strategic behavior
- Judgments and decisions

From these definitions and this list, we have identified a set of elements we think are essential to understanding conflict situations. Incompatibility, goals and aspirations, parties and roles, interdependence, and judgments are addressed here.

Incompatibility. A central, defining feature pervades the conflict definitions in Table 3.2: incompatibility. Deutsch writes that "a conflict exists whenever incompatible activities occur . . . an action that is incompatible with another action prevents, obstructs, interferes, injures, or in some way makes the latter less likely or less effective" (1973, p. 10). Incompatibility may appear simply as different interests. "Conflict," Pruitt and Rubin propose, "means perceived divergence of interest, or a belief that the parties' current aspirations cannot be achieved simultaneously" (1986, p. 4). But it can also be reflected as different preferences regarding procedures.

Goals and Aspirations. Situations become conflictual when incompatibility arises about a goal, objective, or aspiration. Substantive matters include tangible (observable, definable, measurable) content issues parties perceive: "what to do, what decisions to make, where to go, how to allocate resources, or other externally objectifiable issues" (Wilmot & Hocker, 1998, p. 56). Parties may also experience conflict about the rules that guide their interaction, including how decisions are made. So discussion of procedural issues must sometimes precede discussion of substantive issues. Procedural issues are generally tangible. Relationship

Table 3.2
Definitions of Conflict

Author(s)	Definition	Key Terms
Coser (1956)	Social conflict is a struggle between opponents over values and claims to scarce status, power and resources.	struggle opposition scarcity
Schelling (1960)	Conflicts that are strategic are essentially bargaining situations in which the ability of one participant to gain his ends is dependent on the choices or decisions that the other participant will make.	strategy bargaining dependence decisions
Deutsch (1973)	A conflict exists whenever incompatible activities occur . . . one party is interfering, disrupting, obstructing, or in some other way making another party's actions less effective.	incompatibility interference effectiveness
Wall (1985)	Conflict is a process in which two or more parties attempt to frustrate the other's goal attainment . . . the factors underlying conflict are threefold: interdependence, differences in goals, and differences in perceptions.	goals interdependence perceptions
Pruitt & Rubin (1986)	Conflict means perceived divergence of interest, or a belief that the parties' current aspirations cannot be achieved simultaneously.	perception interests aspirations beliefs
Conrad (1990)	Conflicts are communicative interactions among people who are interdependent and who perceive that their interests are incompatible, inconsistent, or in tension.	perception communication interdependence tension
Tjosvold & van de Vliert (1994)	Conflict—incompatible activities—occurs within cooperative as well as competitive contexts . . . conflict parties can hold cooperative or competitive goals.	goals incompatibility cooperation competition
Folger et al. (1997)	Conflict is the interaction of interdependent people who perceive incompatible goals and interference from each other in achieving those goals.	perception interaction interdependence incompatibility
Wilmot & Hocker (2001)	Conflict is an expressed struggle between at least two interdependent parties who perceive incompatible goals, scarce resources, and interference from others in achieving their goals.	struggle interdependence perception scarcity

issues embrace intangible, subjective material such as each party's importance to the other, the emotional distance that they wish to maintain, the influence that each is willing to grant the other, the degree to which the parties are seen as a unit, or the rights that the parties accede to one another (Wilmot & Hocker, 1998). Power, authority, responsibility, control, and leadership may appear as overt relational issues. A less obvious type of relationship issue involves identity concerns, which relate to an individual's identification with a group that shares symbols, meanings, and norms/rules for conduct (Collier & Thomas, 1988). Within interpersonal relationships, people negotiate social roles and personal identities (Ting-Toomey, 1985). Identities provide individuals with purpose, meaning, and a sense of worth. They can be broad in scope, like nationalism, or narrow in scope, such as identification with an individual or even personality type. Typically intangible, identity issues feature concerns about self-esteem (Wilmot & Hocker, 1998), acknowledgment, achievement, reputation, and image or 'face' (Folger et al., 1997).

Conflict issues are characterized not only by type but by the nature of the incompatibility as well (Wehr, 1979). Based on Wehr's work, we note that incompatibility may be:

- *Fact-based*: disagreement over what the "facts" of the issue are; what is true or accurate; what is "reality."
- *Values-based*: disagreement over what should be the determinants (criteria, bases, priorities) of a policy decision, a relationship, or some other issue in conflict.
- *Interests-based*: disagreement over who will get what in the distribution of scarce resources, whether tangible or intangible (e.g., land, economic benefits, rights, privileges, control, respect).
- *Jurisdiction-based*: disagreement over who has authority or jurisdiction over the problems and issues of the conflict.
- *Person-based*: disagreement pertaining to personal factors, such as interaction styles, idiosyncratic actions, personality-related behaviors, effects of the physical setting, etc.
- *History-based*: disagreement related to the history of the issue(s), the conflict, and the conflict relationship, as perceived by the parties in conflict.
- *Culture-based*: disagreements emerge that pertain to cultural orientations, worldviews, and identities. Parties' different cultural foundations, when not addressed, may contribute to misunderstanding.

Parties in conflict have goals, preferences, aspirations, and interests about the issues that they have identified. These objectives mirror the 'parties' understanding of the ways in which those issues are incompatible. In any given situation, issues may involve several kinds of incompatibility. Public policy conflict issues, for example, often include all of the incompatibilities just listed above in varying degrees.

Parties and Roles. Parties are entities (individuals, groups, organizations, governments) capable of making decisions directly or indirectly related to the conflict. They have a stake in the outcome. Three kinds of parties may appear in any conflict situation: primary, secondary, and peripheral. *Primary* parties are major players in the conflict; they perceive that their goals or aspirations are incompatible with one another and interact directly with each other in pursuit of their objectives. *Secondary* parties have a vested interest in, or may be affected directly by, the conflict and its outcome but for some reason (such as inadequate resources, lack of access, perception of inappropriateness) are not directly involved. Secondary parties are potential coalition members and may become primary parties at some point. Secondary parties merely want to be kept informed of the progress in a negotiation but may stop short of being directly involved. *Peripheral* parties have an awareness of the conflict but are not as likely to be directly affected by the outcome. The media and general public may be peripheral parties in a conflict. Groups that are initially peripheral parties may evolve into either secondary or even primary parties.

A party may enact a variety of roles in a conflict, which affect their choice of strategies and tactics. Possible roles include:

- *Direct conflict party*: the party interacts and negotiates for herself or himself.
- *Conflict party as agent*: the individual interacts or negotiates on behalf of someone else (e.g., an attorney).
- *Secondary or indirect conflict party*: the individual uses a conflict agent; the conflict party advises the agent and may give the agent responsibility, while maintaining decision-making authority.

Related to a conflict party's roles is her or his responsiveness in those roles (Druckman, 1977). In any given negotiable conflict, a disputant must balance responsiveness and accountability to a number of parties. These include the conflict party's responsiveness to herself or himself, to the other direct conflict parties, to her or his own primary constituency, to secondary parties (those that influence self or other), to the public and community, to the media, and to precedent and principle.

Interdependence. As implied in scholars' definitions, a portion of the potential for significant communication and constructive conflict management is based on the parties' perceived interdependence. Without interdependence, there is little need or opportunity for meaningful interaction. "Conflict parties engage in an expressed struggle and interfere with one another," Wilmot and Hocker write, "because they are interdependent" (1998, p. 35). As interdependent parties engage conflict strategically, they interact within what Schelling (1960) calls a "precarious partnership." In a similar vein, Wall proposes that "conflict is a process in which two or more parties attempt to frustrate the other's goal attainment . . . the factors that underlie conflict are threefold . . . interdependence, differences in goals, and differences in perceptions" (1985, p. 155). Goal interdependence is an indicator of collaborative potential. The greater the goal interdependence, the greater the incentive for parties to manage their conflict collaboratively. Consequently, the extent to which goals are interdependent may directly affect communication patterns in conflict (Tjosvold, 1990).

A person who does not perceive his or her dependence on another person, "that is, who has no special interest in what the other does—has no conflict with that other person" (Braiker & Kelley, 1979, p. 137). An individual who perceives incompatibility but not interdependence might not consider engaging in conflict interaction, such as negotiation. A high-powered person may decide unilaterally to resolve the conflict by presenting a promise or threat or some other way of gaining compliance. A low-powered individual may decide unilaterally to accommodate, withdraw from, or avoid the conflict. When the disputants perceive interdependence, the prospect for direct, constructive communication to deal with the conflict begins to improve. Interdependence implies that each party has enough power, not necessarily equal, to warrant joint decision making (Bacharach & Lawler, 1981a).

Judgments, Cognitive Frames, and Biases. In conflicts, parties perceive the extent to which they are interdependent and their goals and interests are incompatible. These perceptions lead to judgments about the appropriate way to deal with the conflict. Parties in the conflict are susceptible to judgment biases that emanate from the individual's cognitive framing of the situation. One of the important findings from the decision-making research of recent years is that the cognitive frame that people employ affects their decision making at the most fundamental level. The concept of cognitive frame refers to how people structure their understanding of a situation, in terms of both the nature of the situation as well as the decision choices available to them. A situation can be framed in the realm of losses (i.e., "is this agreement a loss compared to what I might have ideally achieved") or gains (i.e., "is this agreement a gain compared to what I might have achieved acting alone"), depending on what base is chosen as the point of comparison.

This cognitive model of decision making has been extended successfully into the conflict and negotiation field by a number of researchers, including Bazerman, Neale, Northcraft, Thompson, and Hastie. An important finding from their work is that the ways in which disputants think about their negotiation task has a profound effect on how they interact with other parties, what kinds of offers they make, how they perceive the offers of other parties, and so on. Indeed, just invoking the terms "conflict" or "negotiation" gets most people in a cognitive frame of winning versus losing, as opposed to a joint problem-solving frame. As a result, the default behavior that emerges from that frame tends to be quite competitive, at least more competitive than the structure of the situation dictates. The kinds of behavior that result from an overly competitive stance include low levels of disclosure, inability to communicate so that any opportunities for mutual gain can be identified, suspicion regarding the motives of other parties, and referring to the other parties as "opponents" rather than "colleagues," "stakeholders," "partners," or "other citizens."

Summarizing the entire literature on decision maker and/or negotiator cognition exceeds the purpose and scope of this chapter. However, three biases illustrate the importance of cognition on behavior in conflict and negotiation situations: fixed-pie bias, reactive devaluation, and overconfidence.

Fixed-pie bias relates to negotiators' ability to recognize the integrative (mutual benefit) potential in a mixed-motive (i.e., involves both integrative and distributive incentives) bargaining situation (Bazerman, 1998). The fixed-pie bias has been identified by many researchers, most often in precisely constructed and controlled experimental settings (e.g., Thompson & Hastie, 1990). Because this bias involves underestimating the potential benefit from cooperative strategy, it produces behaviors that are more competitive than the situation would seemingly require. For most, merely invoking the cognitive frames of "conflict" and "negotiation" prompts them to assume that the other parties' preferences are diametrically opposed to their own and that the collective task is to divide a finite set of resources among competing parties. This dividing-the-spoils orientation gives rise to the fixed-pie terminology. The fixed-pie bias is so pronounced that in a well-known multitask negotiation simulation, negotiators are unable to capture much of the mutual gain that has been designed into the simulation. They are so concerned about not losing what they have or perhaps so suspicious of the other party's motives and statements that they fail to recognize that there are some tasks in which everyone prefers the same outcome (Bazerman, 1998).

The second bias, *reactive devaluation*, relates to a negotiator's interpretation of her or his own preferences based on the other party's reaction to the negotiator's offers. The typical scenario is that Party A makes an offer, Party B responds favorably, and Party A reacts (nonverbally) by lowering his or her internal valuation of the issue in question. This devaluation occurs because A is basing her or his valuation on how much B values it, at least in part. Stated another way, the sentiment "I sold my house the first week and got my asking price—I should have asked more for it" is a stereotypical manifestation of reactive devaluation.

Reactive devaluation occurs completely independently of more objective measures of the value of an issue and is largely paradoxical. We tend to regard our opponent's acceptance of our offers not as evidence of careful strategy or research on our part, but on our inappropriate valuation. Perhaps the house sold the first week because you enacted an exemplary strategy: you hired the best agent in town, carefully prepared the house for sale, put it on the market in the part of the year when many people move, and so on. Rather than focus on those possible explanations, it may be our human nature to look at the buyer's enthusiasm and wish that we had driven a harder bargain.

The third cognitive bias, *overconfidence*, is the tendency to presume that one is going to have a higher level of success in a negotiation or litigation than a priori probabilities would indicate. Overconfidence may result in various counter-productive behaviors, such as choosing a venue where you have a low probability of prevailing, insufficient concession making, strident rhetoric, and so on.

Taken together, these and other examples of the effects of cognition of negotiator performance are profound. They show that the way in which one cognitively frames the conflict situation at hand affects not only behavior but outcomes and satisfaction as well. As we think about conflicts in general and environmental conflicts specifically, we can look for useful frames from which to engage complex multiparty public policy conflicts. Part of the Collaborative Learning approach is to carefully manage the participants' cognitive frames regarding the task at hand, in an attempt to counteract, at least in part, the effect of biases such as the fixed-pie bias, reactive devaluation, and overconfidence.

Conflicts are Situational

Obviously conflicts do not occur in a vacuum. Deutsch (1973) notes that conflict, as social interaction, occurs in an authentic setting.

Social interaction takes place in a social environment—in a family, a group, a community, a nation, a civilization—that has developed techniques, symbols, categories, rules, and values that are relevant to human interactions. Hence, to understand the events that occur in social interaction one must comprehend the interplay of these events with the broader social context in which they occur. (p. 8)

The conflict situation, like conflict itself, is multi-faceted. First, *conflicts occur on many levels*, such as interpersonal, intercultural, group, or organizational. Putnam and Poole (1987) refer to levels as "arenas." They note, for example, that "relationships between disputants, issues, contextual features, and treatment of communication differ somewhat across the four arenas" (p. 551) of organizational conflict: interpersonal, bargaining and negotiation, intergroup, and inter-organizational. "For instance," they explain, "since interpersonal conflicts center on individuals and inter-organizational disputes generally involve collectivities, the message form, substance, and patterns of communication would typically reflect these diverse parties and their unique features" (1987, p. 551).

Second, *conflict varies according to scale*. Some conflicts are a relatively simple combination of limited issues, a small number of parties (e.g., two), and little conflict history. Other conflicts are quite complex and involved, including many issues, parties, and history. Conflicts range from relatively simple to extremely complex on a variety of scales: in and among families, neighborhoods, communities, states, and nations. More than one scale may be relevant to a particular conflict situation. A facility siting conflict, for example, may involve neighborhood, community, and regional interests. Conflicts over biodiversity and sustainability may occupy an international stage, while simultaneously being played out in national capitals as well as in local communities.

Third, *conflicts take place in varied settings*. This book focuses on environmental and natural resource conflict, but the public policy realm includes many other settings ripe for conflict, such as health care, immigration, transportation, welfare, and foreign relations. Conflicts in such settings may include impersonal conflict in which individuals encounter a seemingly faceless organization. People often feel powerless when dealing with bureaucratic organiza-tions. They perceive incompatibility but are frustrated by an organization that appears to be unresponsive, maintains decision-making ambiguity, and seems insulated against criticism and change. The citizen who encounters illegal dumping into a community's sewer system may experience conflict with a community administrator over monitoring and enforcement. The college student who gets the runaround in trying to obtain financial aid or schedule classes experiences conflict with the impersonal university. The taxpayer who receives an audit notice experiences conflict with the impersonal national revenue service. If the organization, in this case the revenue agency, does not perceive interdependence, that organization will likely not acknowledge a conflict. The individual has a problem with the organization, but the organization does not necessarily have a problem with the individual; any conflict remains impersonal. In order to resolve this conflict through a joint communication effort, the conflict must be transformed to one in which the parties perceive interdependence.

Finally, *conflicts play out in particular venues*. The notion of venue refers to a combination of setting and scale; it is where the conflict plays out. Some conflicts arise over the kitchen table, progress into the marriage counselor's office, and ultimately end up in divorce court. Each of these is a different venue, and the notion of appropriate procedure and acceptable behavior differs between them.

Different parties have more or less power in each venue and will work to assure that the conflict is settled in the venue in which they have the competitive advantage. That may mean that the parties negotiate over setting and scale, as they try to move the discussion into the venue that they prefer. Particularly in public policy conflicts, this notion of "venue shopping" may mean that each of several parties may be pursuing its agenda through their preferred means, and a face-to-face negotiation may not occur. One party may go to a sympathetic member of Congress, another might pursue a litigation strategy, and yet another might attempt to mobilize local groups or public opinion. Moreover, the dominance of a particular level, setting, or scale does not preclude linkages to other levels. For instance, it can be risky to attempt to resolve local disputes while there is a great deal of policy uncertainty at the national level, because there is a very real possibility that the local effort can be overridden by national-level decisions (Daniels & Walker, 1995a).

THE NATURE OF CONFLICT MANAGEMENT

Whatever the conflict situation and however it is characterized, conflict management strategies must be responsive to the particular situation in which a conflict occurs. It is one thing to recognize and define a conflict; it is quite another to attempt to manage it. In this next section, we highlight some fundamental elements of managing conflicts.

Conflict: Management versus Resolution

Many discussions of conflict turn to the term *resolution* to denote the settlement of either a conflict or dispute. We agree that specific disputes can be resolved but believe that many policy conflicts are both complex and enduring (often with social, political, cultural, economic, and scientific aspects). Complex conflict situations may never be resolved, in the sense that the parties reach an agreement that ends the core incompatibilities that gave rise to the conflict. Rather, many complex conflicts can be *managed* well, so that they do not become destructive. Consequently, we employ the term "management" as a broad notion that includes, but does not presume, resolution. Furthermore, managing conflict accommodates the view of "situation improvement;" that is, those desirable and feasible changes that will improve a problematic situation. This view is a central tenet of Collaborative Learning (Daniels & Walker, 1996; Daniels et al., 1996).

Conflict Management as Progress

We define management as the generation and implementation of tangible improvements in a conflict situation. Improvements in the ways that we manage a conflict situation constitute progress. Therefore, conflict management can be thought of as *making progress* (Walker & Daniels, 1997; Daniels & Walker, 1999). Drawing upon our earlier discussion of conflict issues, conflict management involves making progress on the three fundamental dimensions of a conflict situation: substantive, procedural, and relationship.   These dimensions can be viewed as part of a conflict management Progress Triangle, as presented in Figure 3.1.

Figure 3.1
The Progress Triangle

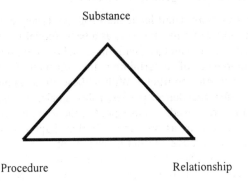

Portraying conflict management as a triangle of three interrelated dimensions—substance, procedure, and relationship—illustrates several points about managing conflicts. First, any conflict situation includes substantive, procedural, and relationship dimensions. Second, one addresses the conflict situation initially through any of the three dimensions. For example, a health care policy conflict situation might feature substantive concerns related to health care costs and service delivery. A natural resource conflict situation such as salmon recovery might emphasize procedural and relationship factors related to the sovereign status of native peoples.

Furthermore, the Progress Triangle can serve as a transformative cognitive frame. Recalling our discussion of cognitive frames earlier in this chapter, the Progress Triangle provides disputants with a nontraditional way to think about conflict situations.   It suggests that the appropriate goal for complex, multiparty conflict situations, like those related to environmental policy, is *progress*, rather than *success*. For example, thinking that a particular environmental policy conflict can be successfully resolved permanently reinforces the misperception that conflict is a transient, episodic, or aberrant feature of civic life.

This emphasis on *progress*, rather than *success*, as the appropriate metric of satisfaction in complex multiparty public policy disputes is part of the cognitive reframing that Collaborative Learning undertakes. It is not merely semantic nit-picking, because the words you choose create and reinforce your cognitive frame. We contend that public decision making, and the discourse that it engenders are inherently and inevitably conflictual, and that is doubly true in the environmental arena. The expectation that conflict can be resolved therefore creates false hopes and an all-or-nothing metric of satisfaction. *Success* as the measure of effectiveness assumes that consensus can be reached among the numerous parties on what constitutes success. *Progress*, on the other hand, implies that conflicts and their management are ongoing. The Progress Triangle is a cognitive frame that provides disputants with a more attainable goal—meaningful progress—against which to assess their efforts. Making "meaningful progress" on a challenging environmental policy situation is a more reasonable burden that invites collaboration rather than adversarial competition.

A Simple Conflict Management Framework

As we discuss in more detail later, the Progress Triangle has value beyond providing a new cognitive frame. It serves as a basic model for understanding the nature of a conflict situation and assessing its collaborative potential. Its design suggests the importance of determining the substantive, procedural, and relationship factors in any conflict. Within these dimensions, more specific elements such as interdependence, parties, roles, goals, issues, and sources of incompatibility can be reviewed. Consequently, the triangle may be useful as an assessment tool. Assessment, as we address in this chapter, is an important first step in a process of constructive conflict management.

Figure 3.2 offers a basic conflict management framework. Competent conflict management begins with a thorough appraisal of the conflict situation. Conflict parties can develop their own assessment approach or may draw upon assessment criteria that scholars offer. Examples include the Conflict Mapping Guide (Wehr, 1979); the Struggle Spectrum (Keltner, 1994); the Conflict Assessment Guide (Wilmot & Hocker, 1998); and the Conflict Analysis Framework (Carpenter & Kennedy, 1988). These approaches generally feature questions about such elements as the involved parties' perceptions, expectations, values, and goals; the issues; the conflict history and precipitating events; and past management strategies (Walker, 1996).

Figure 3.2
A Conflict Management Framework

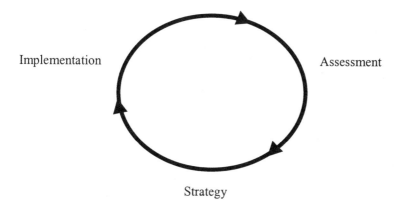

Implementation   Assessment

Strategy

Conflict Management as Strategic Choice

Based on your assessment of a particular conflict situation, the next step in constructive conflict management is to identify alternative management strategies. Conflict interaction means that the disputants are making strategic choices as they strive to manage or resolve their differences (Pruitt & Rubin, 1986; Lewicki et al., 1994). Whether your role is as a direct participant or as a mediator/facilitator, the likelihood of achieving a satisfactory outcome depends, at least in part, on how well you craft and implement an appropriate strategy. As Carpenter and Kennedy note, "In the complexity and uncertainly of public disputes, the more attention given at the beginning to preparing a conflict management program, the better the chances of a successful outcome" (1988, p. 68).

Strategic Choices and Dual Concerns. People respond to conflicts both spontaneously and intentionally. Spontaneous conflict responses often result in escalation. The alternative is developing an intentional response—a conflict management strategy. The ways in which people intentionally respond to conflict situations and the strategic choices they make reflect concerns for both themselves and other parties. These dual concerns can be represented as perpendicular axes (see Figure 3.3). Developed by Pruitt and Rubin (1986; also Rubin et al. 1994), the model indicates that when Party A's concerns for its own welfare increases, the likelihood of active engagement in a conflict situation increases. That active engagement may be competitive or collaborative, depending on the degree of Party A's concern for Party B's outcomes. Correspondingly, if Party A places much higher value on Party B's welfare than its own, Party A will likely accommodate as a passive response.

Figure 3.3
The Dual Concern Model

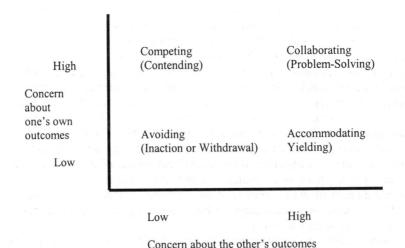

Strategic Alternatives. People consciously address conflict by choosing from among various strategies (group of tactics): contending (competitive, distributive); collaborating (problem solving, integrative); accommodating (yielding); and avoidance (withdrawal or inaction). Contending and collaborating are strategies of active engagement; the parties acknowledge the conflict and deal with it assertively. Both strategies presume joint decision making and social influence in the conflict management process (Pruitt & Rubin 1986; Rubin et al., 1994). The choice to pursue a contending or collaborating strategy acknowledges the mixed-motive character of the conflict and the parties' interdependence. In contrast, accommodation and avoidance are both unilateral decisions; a party can use one of these regardless of what the other conflicting parties might do. These strategies exhibit a passive, rather than active, response: accommodation by "giving in" is passive engagement, while the avoidance through withdrawal and inaction indicates passive non-engagement.

Competitive versus Collaborative Strategies. As active engagement conflict management strategies, competition and collaboration are clearly distinguishable. In the extreme, they occupy opposite ends of a strategy continuum, as Figure 3.4 displays. Collaboration corresponds to integrative negotiation while competition related to distributive negotiation (Lewicki et al. 1994; Wilmot & Hocker, 2001).

Figure 3.4
The Collaboration-Competition Strategy Continuum

Collaboration   Competition

Integrative Negotiation   Distributive Negotiation

Conflicts are inherently mixed-motive situations; in any conflict there are some incentives to compete and some incentives to cooperate. If a party perceives only purely competitive incentives, then the conflict situation is fundamentally a game in which the party acts unilaterally whenever possible to pursue its self interest. If a party's motivation is completely cooperative, on the other hand, then there probably is no meaningful incompatibility in the situation. Because conflict situations are rarely purely competitive or cooperative, the strategies that the parties frequently employ tend to be mixed as well. Both competitive and cooperative tactics may be interwoven into a single, overall approach. Still, one strategic orientation will likely be dominant in that approach or in the conflict "style" of the party. For example, an environmental organization may adopt an overall competitive strategy of litigation while maintaining signals of its willingness to collaboratively negotiate some issues. In contrast, a different environmental organization might advance a strategy of collaboration, including participation in public forums, negotiation, and dialogue, while maintaining the competitive options of litigation and political lobbying.

Firm Flexibility. In the next chapter we discuss collaboration extensively. As that discussion illustrates, collaboration is not synonymous with cooperation. Cooperation can appear as part of either an accommodative, a compromise, or a collaborative strategy. What distinguishes collaboration from mere cooperation is the assertiveness of a collaborative strategy. It features a willingness to cooperate and collaborate while remaining principled about your goals and values. Pruitt (1983) calls this "firm flexibility"; an orientation in which one is firm about goals and objectives but flexible about how one achieves them.

DEFINING ENVIRONMENTAL CONFLICT

In the introduction to their recent work, *Mediating Environmental Conflicts*, Blackburn and Bruce assert that "environmental conflict arises when one or more parties involved in a decision-making process disagree about an action that has potential to have an impact upon the environment" (1995, pp. 1–2). In an essay from that same work, Burgess and Burgess propose that "environmental conflict refers to long-term divisions between groups with different beliefs about the proper relationship between human society and the natural environment" (1995, p. 102).

These definitions reveal that environmental conflict involves some degree of incompatibility arising from issues related to the environment, rather than some other form of interpersonal or organizational conflict that merely happens to have arisen in the context of environmental decision making. As such, the definitions may offer more insight into the difficulty of devising a single-sentence definition of environmental values or policy than of characterizing environmental conflict itself. Understanding environmental and natural resource conflict requires much more than a minimalist definition. As Crowfoot and Wondolleck (1990) note, environmental conflicts have various sources: they are "rooted in different values of natural resources and environmental quality"; they are "incited by different stakes in the outcome of environmental and natural resource management decisions"; and they can be caused by "the uncertainly surrounding various environmental actions, and the different assessments of the risks associated with these actions" (1990, pp. 6, 7).

The sources of conflict in natural resource decisions that Crowfoot and Wondolleck identify reveal the difficulty of finding a simple definition. We can accomplish more by describing fundamental assumptions about environmental conflict.

Environmental Controversies Involve both Conflicts and Disputes

As environmental mediator Gerald Cormick notes, an environmental conflict occurs "when there is a disagreement over values or scarce resources" (1982, p. 3). Specific disputes arise as episodes in the longer-running social discourse over natural resource policy. Disputes are encounters "involving a specific issue over which the conflict in values is joined." Cormick explains that "the settlement of a dispute is achieved when the parties find a mutually acceptable basis for disposing of the issues in which they are in disagreement, despite their continuing differences over basic values" (1982, p. 3). Environmental conflicts are ongoing, and reflect the persistent value differences that Cormick features. These different values, interests, and fundamental views of the relationship between people and the natural environment are embedded in the body politic (Henning & Mangun, 1989; Hunter, 1989). These conflict factors may contribute to views of a conflict as intractable (Kriesberg, 1989). Disputes, on the other hand, are identifiable, issue-specific interactions that arise at particular points in time, often as episodes within longer-running conflicts (Crowfoot & Wondolleck, 1990). Consequently, enduring conflicts need to be managed, while the disputes that arise within them offer opportunities for settlement. Natural resource managers and organizational representatives must be able to distinguish between the disputes and the conflicts that are relevant to their roles. For example, conflicting views and philosophies over the importance of preserving old growth forests will continue over the long term, while specific timber harvest, stream buffer, and salvage disputes require decisions in the short term.

Environmental Conflicts are Complex

There may be no conflict setting more complex than environmental policy. Faure and Rubin (1993) have identified a number of "distinctive attributes" of environmental negotiations: multiple parties and multiple roles, multiple issues, meaningless boundaries, scientific and technical uncertainty, power asymmetry, joint interest, negative perceptions of immediate outcomes, history, long time frame, changing actors, public opinion, institutionalization of solutions, and new regimes and rules (pp. 20–26). Lang (1991) has featured five ways in which environmental negotiations are different from other conflict situations. First, lobbies (either for ecological or business interests), try to influence policy on both the national and intergovernmental levels. Second, media interest and scrutiny are greater on environmental issues than other matters, such as trade or arms control. Third, scientific evidence often competes with economic interests. Fourth, negotiated agreements on environmental issues are rarely final and are likely to be reopened as new evidence emerges and situations change. Fifth, agreements generally emerge from an incremental negotiation process that generates a series of decisions over a period of years (p. 355).

Consistent with Faure and Rubin's and Lang's ideas, we see seven salient sources of environmental conflict complexity:

- Multiple parties.
- Multiple issues.
- Cultural differences.
- Deeply held values and worldviews.
- Scientific and traditional knowledge.
- Legal requirements.
- "Conflict industry."

Multiple Parties. In our classes (natural resource decision making, forest policy, conflict management) and in our training programs on Collaborative Learning, we ask participants to identify an environmental or natural resource conflict that has only two parties. Over the years, no one has ever identified one. A given environmental conflict or dispute will include multiple parties, such as native peoples (Indian tribal members and tribal governments); interest groups (such as environmental or commodity-oriented activist groups); local communities (e.g., resource-dependent or tourism-oriented towns); commercial or business interests (agricultural and nonagricultural); nonaffiliated citizens (not identified with a specific interest group); government agencies; scientists (agency and nonagency), and nonresidents. Furthermore, some parties may be hard to identify or may emerge during an environmental conflict management process.

Although there are different parties in any environmental conflict, they are not likely to have equal standing in it. Furthermore, some parties may be regarded as primary, or having a direct stake in the outcome. Other parties may be secondary; that is, they are interested in the outcome but will not be involved as directly as stakeholders.

Multiple Issues. Environmental conflicts and disputes usually involve many issues rather than simply one or two. A conflict over a proposed timber sale, for example, is not just about harvesting a particular board-foot quantity. It includes issues of forest health, fire management, worker safety, vegetation, habitat, soils, recreation, visual quality, and economic viability. Each party may have its own set of salient issues and will likely place different emphases on those issues that it shares with other parties.

Issues can relate to any of the three conflict dimensions presented earlier: substance, relationship, and procedure. These issues can be tangible or symbolic. Examples of tangible issues in a landfill siting conflict could relate to the water table, proximity to residential areas, wetlands, roads, soil composition, decision authority, and citizen participation procedures. Symbolic issues could include the standing that a particular citizen group holds to have voice in the siting process, trust between citizens and siting authorities, the power of the various parties to implement or block the decision, and the credibility of the decision makers. But do not be lulled into thinking that symbolic issues are somehow less real or important than tangible issues; just the opposite may be true.

Cultural Differences. Differences between parties related to their perceived membership in cultural communities permeate environmental conflicts. Dean Barnlund, one of the first cross-cultural communication scholars, forecast that "we can expect to spend most of our lives in the company of neighbors who will speak in a different tongue, seek different values, move at a different pace, and interact according to a different script" (1991, p. 22). He predicted that "when people communicate between cultures, where communicative rules as well as the substance of experience differ, the problems multiply" (p. 31).

Barnlund's ideas refer to communication between two cultural communities; imagine the increased complexity when an environmental conflict includes people and groups identifying with many different cultures. Culture is a far more inclusive concept than race and refers to a historically transmitted system of symbols, meanings, and norms. Culture relates to ethnicity, gender, regional identity, profession, community, or "any other symbol system that is bounded and salient to individuals" (Collier & Thomas, 1988, pp. 102–103). Cultural communities pertinent to numerous environmental conflicts include rural and urban residents, newcomers to an area as well as old-timers, ethnic groups, and occupational groups.

Deeply Held Values and Worldviews. Natural resource conflicts are frequently ongoing, reflecting different values, interests, and fundamental views of the relationship between people and the natural environment (Henning & Mangun, 1989). Some conflicts exist at the profoundly fundamental level, featuring stakeholders with diametrically opposed value systems relative to the issues at hand (Hunter, 1989). The complexity of a conflict certainly increases when it is driven by people's fundamental values—about right and wrong, about entitlements, about humans' role in nature, and so on. Parties will not agree to outcomes that contradict their worldviews and may make little progress until they understand one another's value orientations and regard them as legitimate. There is no one right way to understand nature; there are many different value-based views of the natural environment and of humanity's relationship to it. Rolston (1988), for example, delineates various seminal values, including life-support, economic, recreational, scientific, aesthetic, historic, cultural-symbolic, character-building, diversity-unity, and religious. Many of these, while fundamental to value systems about natural resources, also seem incompatible. Economic values of a specific western rangeland, for example, may seem to deny some aesthetic or religious values related to that same land.

Scientific and Traditional Knowledge. Understanding of environmental policy situations is enhanced by integrating ideas from a variety of sources: physical/biological science, political/social science, and the local community. Policy decision making should respect traditional knowledge (both indigenous and local) just as it respects scientific knowledge; voices from nonscientific communities deserve to be heard alongside those of the scientists. An ecosystem-based management approach should include agencies, organizations, and community representatives learning about, and analyzing, conflict and dispute situations systemically and should enact appropriate strategies to deal with those disputes constructively. Learning and analysis demand forethought, time, and coordinated effort, although these are often scarce when crises erupt. Crises encourage "knee-jerk" reactions, rather than evaluating options systemically and making constructive, planned strategic choices. In crises, parties often rely on "trained incapacities," habitual methods of responding, even when aware that these methods may not work (Folger et al., 1997). Such habitual responses may thwart innovation, systems thinking, and good decisions.

Legal Requirements. A considerable body of laws, executive orders, regulations, and legal precedents defines what is acceptable procedure in terms of agency decision making and public involvement.[1] Certainly, the Administrative Procedures Act (APA) of 1946 establishes a fundamental benchmark for agency decision making with its prohibition of arbitrary and capricious decisions, which the courts have evolved into the "hard look" doctrine. (Agency decisions are assumed to not be arbitrary and capricious if the agency can show that it took a hard look at the issues. In this regard, it is similar to the concept of "due diligence" found in commercial law.) Much better known than APA is the National Environmental Policy Act (NEPA) of 1969, which requires interdisciplinary planning of major federal actions that could potentially affect the human environment. Even though NEPA now provides the core of the requirements for public involvement in agency decision making in the natural resource arena, most of its public involvement features come not from the law itself but from either executive orders issued shortly after the passage of NEPA, regulations promulgated by the Council of Environmental Quality, the rule-making body established by NEPA, or case law from the large number of NEPA-related lawsuits that have been contested over the past three decades. In addition, there are some "open government" laws that were passed during the Vietnam War era and its distrust of government, notably the Freedom of Information Act (FOIA) of 1966 and the Federal Advisory Committee Act (FACA) of 1972. FOIA makes the great preponderance of agency files open to public scrutiny. FACA requires that advisory committees function in an accessible and well-publicized manner. Both of these laws are philosophically motivated by a desire for transparent governance.

This large body of procedural requirements related to public involvement has arguably had a chilling effect on innovation in public involvement practice, which may be the exact opposite of what the laws' authors intended. The requirements for public notice have become quite specific; for example, legal notices must appear in a specified number of newspapers for a specified number of days. Because failure to meet these various mandates is grounds for having a project overturned, the prudent course of action is to do the legal requirement—no more, no less. This means that there is certainly no structural incentive for any innovation in public involvement; any creativity emerges in spite of the law, not because of it. This legal environment certainly adds a level of complexity to the planning of collaborative efforts. The case law is clear that efforts at collaboration do not substitute for other procedural requirements. That means that the collaborative process must include activities that are NEPA-compliant or that traditional NEPA activities (publish environmental documents, allow public comment periods, and so on) must occur at the same time as the collaborative process.

"Conflict Industry." A final overlay of complexity emerges from our largely contentious and litigious political tradition. The political and legal landscape around natural resource management is populated by a number of advocacy organizations whose roles are to fight for the preferred outcome of some constituency. These groups are on all sides of the political and ideological spectrum: they fight for the interests of particular industries, for geographic areas, for landowning people, for landless people, for elderly people, for unborn people, and for wildlife, wilderness, and water. Yet all of these groups face a similar incentive—they must convince their members and funders that they are fighting the good fight. One can realistically imagine situations where the interests of formal interest groups, including their staffs, may not be entirely compatible with the underlying goals and values of the constituency that they presumably serve. It is conceivable that their organizational niche and their job security as individuals depend more on the perpetuation of the conflict than on some calm, quiet settlement. We call these people the "conflict industry." It is not merely lobbyists or national-level organizers that we include in this category—anyone whose personal interests are better served by the perpetuation of a competitive and conflictual approach to environmental policy falls into this group. This can encompass anyone from the slickest environmental attorney in San Francisco or

Washington, D.C., to a rancher in Evanston, Wyoming, whose status among her peers comes from her willingness and ability to challenge local Bureau of Land Management employees over grazing policies and practices.

The important things for Collaborative Learning conveners and designers to recognize are (1) that the conflict industry exists, (2) that it evolved as a legitimate part of the system of government created by the framers of the Constitution, (3) that members of the conflict industry can feel that successful collaborations may undermine their importance and agenda, and (4) that members of the conflict industry may not want to participate in collaborative processes and may have good reasons to attempt to circumvent and "blindside" them (Daniels & Walker, 1999).

As an illustration of the threat that some national organizations may feel from a movement toward collaboration (particularly a movement that would devolve policy making to a large number of localized efforts), consider the opening paragraph of a speech that Michael McCloskey, executive director of the Sierra Club, gave to his board of directors in 1995:

A new dogma is emerging as a challenge to us. It embodies the proposition that the best way for the public to determine how to manage its interest in the environment is through collaboration among stakeholders, not through normal governmental processes.

There are three notable word choices in this sentence: dogma, challenge, and normal governmental process. *Dogma* often connotes a view or position that is overly rigid, or lacks adequate foundation. It is also instructive that McCloskey framed collaboration as a *challenge to us*, rather than as either a challenge to others or as an opportunity for the enhanced direct involvement of Sierra Club members. Finally, he draws a clear distinction between collaboration and *normal governmental processes*, implying that collaborations are abnormal, or in some way inconsistent with American traditions of governance and policy making. In short, this one sentence sets the stage for the message that ran throughout the speech; notably, that McCloskey feels the Sierra Club is profoundly threatened by any consideration of collaborative approaches. And it is not solely environmental groups who might feel that local collaborations are not in their best interest; commodity-production groups (who presumably are the "other side" to the Sierra Club) face exactly the same dynamic. Collaborative processes do not, by definition favor any one "side" over any other. Federal agencies may resist proposals with the potential to diminish their traditional discretion, and relocate the policy discussion out of their organizational hierarchy and into discussions that occur at the agency/stakeholder interface. But the fact that some organizations and individuals feel that collaborations pose a threat to them certainly adds to the complexity of convening and designing them. If these various players resist efforts at collaboration, their behavior does not arise because they are somehow evil or because collaboration is somehow flawed. Rather it is because these players occupy niches in the political landscape, and these niches derive their power and status from a competitive approach to addressing environmental problems, and because at a fundamental level these players' roles have shaped their strategic views of how decisions ought to be made.

Complexity and Columbia River Salmon

One of the most complex environmental policy conflicts of the last twenty years concerns restoring salmon in the Columbia River system of the Pacific Northwestern region of the United States. This conflict has a long, complicated history (Robbins, 1996). As William Lang writes, "The salmon crisis in the Pacific Northwest has generated an image of the unthinkable—a Columbia River without salmon" (1996, p. 348). Restoring salmon in the Columbia River system (the Columbia and Snake Rivers and their tributaries) seems to defy solutions. No one group has the answer and there is no simple remedy. If one group claimed the conflict resolution high ground, other parties would not likely agree. In late July 1999 Jonathan Brinkman of the *Oregonian* (one of the region's largest newspapers) described a "forum" of leaders formed to "solve" the Columbia River salmon "problem." "Facing a decision within months on whether to breach four dams [on the Snake River] to aid salmon, top federal, state, and tribal salmon recovery managers decided this week what the region's goal should be," Brinkman wrote. "They crafted a careful statement about healthy rivers and restoring salmon for tribal harvests. They agreed that the issues are complex. They agreed on the need for a regional consensus. But they disagreed about nearly everything else, and after a four-hour meeting in Spokane [Washington], members of the Columbia River Basin Forum appeared to be as far apart as ever about what can and should be done to save the Northwest's salmon and steelhead trout" (Brinkman, 1999b, pp. A1, A10).

The Columbia River salmon situation illustrates all the dimensions of environmental conflict complexity.

Parties. Identified stakeholders include seven federal agencies, thirteen sovereign Indian nations, four state governments, and numerous county governments, business and agricultural organizations, and interest groups, such as environmental and sport fishing organizations. A consultant retained by the Northwest Power Planning Council in the mid-1990s to facilitate a Columbia River salmon consensus process has identified 80 stakeholders (Orenstein, 1997).

Issues. Many issues endure, including the impact of dams, agricultural practices, timber harvest activities, river and stream conditions, commercial and sport fishing, Indian treaty rights, industry needs, and salmon as a cultural and spiritual symbol.

Cultural Differences. On the surface, the Columbia River may appear to involve two dominant cultural communities: native peoples (members of sovereign Indian nations) and Euro-Americans. A closer examination reveals that this situation includes a variety of ethnic, organizational, and community cultural groups: Native Americans, farm workers, government employees, rural community members, urban energy users, recreation interests, and more.

Deeply Held Values and Worldviews. Salmon are both substantive and symbolic to the quality of life in the Pacific Northwest. For some Pacific Northwest residents the value of salmon is cultural; for others spiritual; and for others still, economic (Cone, 1995). "As long as human memory," William Lang notes, "salmon have been the quintessential symbol of life and fecundity in the Columbia River basin, where thousands of miles of streams have provided anadromous salmon spawning beds for millions of years" (1996, p. 348). Michael Paulson of the *Seattle Post-Intelligencer* reported in March 1999 that "salmon, because of their revered status in the Northwest, seem to enjoy greater public sympathy than the rarely seen [spotted] owl." Paulson noted that "a poll taken last summer by Elway Research found that most residents are willing to spend money to save salmon, and most do not believe a listing of salmon under the Endangered Species Act will directly affect their lives." "Some argue that there is public sympathy for salmon because their plight, in some ways, echoes the plight of human residents of the area." Paulson also emphasized that salmon are an indicator of how the region responds to environmental problems (Paulson, 1999, p. B1).

Scientific and Traditional Knowledge. There may be no environmental controversy studied more than that of Columbia River salmon restoration. Over the past 15 years, millions upon millions of dollars have been spent on a multitude of studies, projects, and scientific meetings. Tribal scientists, agency scientists, university scientists, and interest group scientists have often been at odds with one another such that no scientific consensus has emerged. For example, a recent *Oregonian* article reported that

One-third of the 241 salmon recovery programs the Bonneville Power Administration finances fail to meet scientific standards and should no longer be funded, an independent review panel concludes in a new report. The report comes at a time of deep disagreement over the direction of the costly and largely ineffective effort to rebuild salmon populations in the Columbia River Basin . . . The panel's recommendations angered Northwest tribes that are proposing new types of hatcheries to restore salmon to tributaries where the fish have sharply declined, in some cases to the point of extinction. (Brinkman, 1999a, p. B1)

Legal Requirements. Just as there are many parties, there are numerous jurisdictions and laws pertinent to the Columbia River salmon restoration controversy. Pacific Northwest Indian tribes hold treaty rights to salmon. Environmental and conservation groups base lawsuits on the Endangered Species Act to protect salmon. The Columbia River system flows through four states. Numerous federal and state agencies hold regulatory or resource management missions germane to salmon restoration that may contradict one another.

Conflict Industry. Conflict over restoring salmon runs in the Columbia River basin has persisted for decades, becoming increasingly acute in the 1990s. It has spawned an "industry" that, according to some critics, has spent much while accomplishing little. As part of his 1997 "Year of the River" series in the *Tri-City Herald*, Don McManman writes:

Over the past 10 years, Northwesterners have paid no less than $3.5 billion to help bring back Columbia River salmon runs. That's $350 for every person— even children—in the Northwest. And very little of it has made a difference for the salmon. But it has created a powerful lobby of those who help spend it: biologists, bureaucrats, Indian commissions, lawyers. "I couldn't believe how they spent money here. A guy would write a four-page proposal and get $400,000," said Phil Mundy, a member of the power planning council's Independent Scientific Advisory Board. With that kind of money for ammo, it was easy to blast away at any target of opportunity, regardless of chances of strategic success. (McManman, 1997).

Additionally, numerous lawyers, consultants, mediators, and facilitators have received contracts to help with conflict management activities. National dispute resolution firms, such as Resolve, Inc. of Washington, D. C., have been brought in to help develop consensus processes, but to no avail.

MEDIATION AND ENVIRONMENTAL CONFLICT

There are many ways to respond to environmental and natural resource conflicts, approaches that run the gamut of struggle from mild disagreements resolved via civil discourse, to resolution through violence (Keltner, 1994). Environmental conflicts are frequently "settled" via litigation and legislation, both adversarial processes that seem to sustain conflict, creating as much new conflict as may be resolved. In the 1970s new approaches emerged under the umbrella term of "environmental alternative dispute resolution" (EADR). While the EADR movement includes a variety of activities (e.g., negotiated rule making, policy dialogues; see Gray, 1989; Dukes, 1996 for reviews), mediation seems the best known.

In *Resolving Environmental Disputes*, Gail Bingham tells the story of what many consider to be the "first [mediated] environmental dispute" (1986, p. 15):

In 1973, Daniel J. Evans, then governor of the state of Washington, invited mediators Gerald W. Cormick and Jane McCarthy to help settle a long-standing dispute over a proposed flood control dam on the Snoqualmie River (p. xvii.) . . . The controversy contained two elements essential to mediation attempts: the issues were seemingly intractable, and the parties were willing to try something new. There were few, if any, precedents to follow, either for the mediators or the parties. By December 1974, however, an agreement was signed . . . the mere fact of the agreement was enough to inspire individuals from across the United States with the idea that controversial environmental disputes could be settled through mediation. (pp. 14–15)

If environmental mediation was born in the early 1970s, it had perhaps its most significant coming out party in 1998. On 22 October 1998, 150 people gathered in Tucson, Arizona for the dedication of the U.S. Institute for Environmental Conflict Resolution (IECR). As the February 1999 *Udall Center Update* reported:

The Environmental Policy and Conflict Resolution Act of 1998 created the Institute, which will operate under the aegis of the Morris K. Udall Foundation, also located in Tucson. The Senate and the House unanimously passed the Act, which was signed into law by President Clinton in February 1998. Under the new law, federal agencies are authorized to use the Institute to assist in the resolution of disputes involving federal environmental, public lands, and natural resource issues. (Federal Institute, 1999).

The IECR Web site explains the purpose and focus of the Institute:

The 1998 Environmental Policy and Conflict Resolution Act (P.L. 105-156) created the U.S. Institute for Environmental Conflict Resolution to assist parties in resolving environmental conflicts around the country that involve federal agencies or interests. The Institute provides a neutral place inside the federal government but "outside the Beltway" where public and private interests can reach common ground. Its primary objectives are to:

- Resolve federal environmental, natural resources, and public lands disputes in a timely and constructive manner through assisted negotiation and mediation
- Increase the appropriate use of environmental conflict resolution (ECR) in general and improve the ability of federal agencies and other interested parties to engage in ECR effectively
- Engage in and promote collaborative problem-solving and consensus-building during the design and implementation of federal environmental policies to prevent and reduce the incidence of future environmental disputes

Congress authorized $1.25 million in Federal funds for annual operating expenses for each of five years, along with a $3 million capitalization fund. In October 1998, Congress appropriated the full authorization for the first year's operating expenses, as well as the full capitalization fund. In addition to the Congressional appropriation, the Institute receives support for its activities through interagency agreements and contracts for services. (U.S. Institute for Environmental Conflict Resolution, 2000).

The U.S. Institute for Environmental Conflict Resolution serves primarily as a facilitator and broker for public and private stakeholders. In his dedication ceremony speech, Senator John McCain of Arizona, chief sponsor of the legislation, noted the importance of the Institute:

The creation of this institute could not be more timely. We live in complicated times, and face a growing number of complex environmental challenges. As surely as the country's population grows and the edges of urbanization expand, pressure on the environment will increase.

  Too often solutions elude us because the issues are mired in governmental bureaucracy or consigned to the courts where common-sense outcomes are lost in a Byzantine legal system and the only certainty is that large sums of money will be squandered on lawyers . . . Mo Udall understood the importance of responsible stewardship, consensus building and problem solving. He knew that the path to progress is to give people an opportunity to be problem solvers rather than litigants. This Institute is charged with carrying on that treasured legacy. (McCain, 1998).

  The U.S. Institute for Environmental Conflict Resolution is significant for a number of reasons. First, it grants institutional legitimacy to environmental conflict management and dispute resolution practices, such as negotiated rule making, policy dialogues, mediation, and facilitation. Second, it increases the visibility of environmental alternative dispute resolution, hopefully to the extent that stakeholders see EADR practices as viable alternatives to adversarial strategies. Third, the institute features EADR beyond simply environmental mediation. Its work is multi-faceted. IECR activities correspond to a variety of program areas, such as: case management and contracting for professional ECR services; training and education on ECR for federal agency personnel and other stakeholder groups; and providing ECR services (including convening, assessment, facilitation, and mediation processes) by its staff or members of its roster of ECR professionals (U.S. Institute for Environmental Conflict Resolution, 2000).

  We have discussed the U.S. Institute for Environmental Conflict Resolution at some length because it is both substantively and symbolically important. The Institute symbolizes the compelling need to continue to develop and improve ways for people to meaningfully and constructively manage complex natural resource and environmental policy conflicts. What started in the early 1970s as environmental mediation has now evolved into methods that extend beyond the application of mediation to environmental conflict situations, while incorporating many mediation techniques. Collaborative Learning is one such method.

  Still, in order to understand conflict situations and collaboration, some discussion of environmental mediation seems useful. Mediation, regardless of context (e.g., environmental, labor management, community, commercial), "is third-party assistance to people who are trying to reach agreement in a controversy" (Pruitt & Kressel, 1989, p. 1). Mediation features disputant decision making; it "is a self-empowering process that emphasizes the participants' responsibility for making decisions that affect their lives" (Taylor, 1988, p. 61). Mediation proceeds through a series of stages with agreement as its goal (Moore, 1996; Lewicki et al., 1999). Negotiation characterizes mediation interaction. "Mediation is essentially negotiation," Moore explains, "that includes a third party who is knowledgeable in effective negotiation procedures, and can help people in conflict coordinate their activities and to be more effective in their bargaining" (1986, p. 14). The negotiation that a mediator promotes is essentially integrative or mutual gain; facilitated problem-solving negotiation that seeks a joint, mutually beneficial decision.

Environmental mediation, simply put, is mediation techniques applied to environmental conflict situations. As Blackburn and Bruce explain in the introduction to their edited work, *Mediating Environmental Conflicts: Theory and Practice*:

Mediation is a relatively new approach to managing conflict over environmental issues. It developed from attempts to apply labor and community mediation experience to environment-related conflicts, with the first documented instance of such mediation dating from 1974. Since then, a literature on the theory and practice of environmental mediation has evolved as practitioners reflect upon the techniques and approaches which have worked best and theoreticians attempt to pull together the key elements of successful mediation activities. (1995, p. 1).

One of the best reviews of mediation research appears in Blackburn and Bruce's book. Rosemary O'Leary's (1995) essay, "Environmental Mediation: What Do We Know and How Do We Know It?," examines a cross-section of empirical work on a number of different areas of environmental mediation. A more updated version of the paper appears on the Web site of the Indiana Conflict Resolution Institute, an organization O'Leary co-founded (O'Leary, 1997).

In this essay, O'Leary notes that environmental mediation research corresponds to a number of key dimensions of conflict management and mediation processes. She presents these dimensions as factors related to the success or failure of environmental mediation. These factors include structure and process, the parties, motivation, the role of government officials, goals, timing, issues, morals and values, the role of mediators and facilitators, power, implementation, and high-tech alternatives (1995, pp. 22–31). These factors suggest the challenges that environmental mediation or any other environmental conflict management process may face. Environmental conflict management efforts could be undermined by problems in any of these areas. For example, we conducted a case study of environmental mediation that dealt with forest management practices in a southern Oregon national forest. In it we discovered that a significant imbalance of power thwarted a mediated agreement (Daniels & Walker, 1995a).

Despite the growth of mediation as an environment conflict resolution approach, mediation techniques need to be adapted to the needs and complexities of environmental and natural resource conflict situations. Conventional mediation methods may be insufficient for addressing natural resource and environmental conflicts. Standard mediation theory and practice rely principally on a two-party conflict model, which is perfectly appropriate to the labor-management, divorce, and community dispute settings that dominate the field. Some mediation techniques that have a long and successful track record in two-party disputes may not be adequate for dealing with the multifaceted complexity of natural resource controversies. Richard Pacheco, a mediator and facilitator with Western Network of Santa Fe, New Mexico, questions the relevance of traditional mediation. He notes that conventional mediation techniques are often "culturally insensitive" and fail to balance culturally influenced power. He adds that the standard mediation model is too "problem oriented." Environmental conflict resolution models, he asserts, need to place more emphasis on "trust, credibility, and relationship building" (1997, p. 20).

The caucus technique provides another example of an area where conventional mediation needs adaptation when applied to environmental conflicts. Mediators in two-party disputes may employ caucuses (a series of one-on-one meetings with the parties, often shuttling offers between them) to advance the process toward settlement. A natural resource conflict may involve 10, 20, or more stakeholders, making caucuses impractical. Competent natural resource mediators must find other methods to achieve the benefits that a caucus might otherwise gain. Further, some argue that mediation is inappropriate in natural resource disputes no matter what its form, because natural resources (e.g., old-growth forests) cannot be compromised or negotiated away (Amy, 1987). As Amory Lovins has observed, "Our society has mechanisms only for resolving conflicts of interests, not conflicting views of reality" (1979, p. 12). Dealing with cutting-edge environmental issues will require cutting-edge innovation in our mediation/facilitation approaches.

Environmental mediation is an important aspect of the environmental and natural resource conflict arena. For it to be effective, it needs to be much more than simply carrying labor-management or community mediation techniques into environmental conflict situations (Dukes, 1996). Methods for managing environmental conflicts and resolving disputes need to address relationship and procedural aspects of conflict as well as substance. Mediation techniques can be useful within frameworks that emphasize all three of these areas of the Progress Triangle.

CONCLUSION

Conflict theory has historically emphasized human *behavior* and the *choices* that parties make under particular conditions. Many different behaviors are possible, both spontaneous and strategic. Recently, conflict and negotiation scholarship has increasingly considered *interaction, cognition,* and *situation* as well. The focus on interaction has drawn attention to communication factors and the meanings that parties create as interpretations of conflict behaviors. An explicit focus on cognition shows us that negotiators are by no means rational in their understanding of situations and their choice of tactics. Negotiation behavior is directly linked to their cognitive frame, and reframing may be an important facilitative technique. Closer examination of the situation has revealed three significant dimensions—substantive, procedural, and relationship—that conflict managers must assess in order to determine what strategies to use. The best strategy—a set of planned behaviors responsive to the unique characteristics of the situation at hand—is implemented through communication interaction in order to deal with the conflict constructively.

Natural resource and environmental public policy leaders should view conflict management as a core responsibility. In this arena, effective conflict management provides a key link of trust and communication between resource leaders and citizens. Natural resource and environmental management professionals should not be content with a strategy to convince citizens that "my organization is right, why don't they just let us decide?" Natural resource scientists should not be seduced by the hubris of "my science is right, can't they just see that?" Such strategies engender public cynicism and apathy and fail to recognize the need to manage the ongoing value differences that fuel many public controversies. Natural resource leaders need to be competent conflict managers, capable of assessing conflict situations, developing alternative strategies, and implementing the best action plans for constructive conflict management and public participation. In doing so, they will demonstrate the need for both the best available science as well as an involved citizenry.

Natural resource policy situations are both controversial and complex. Conflict consequently appears inevitable in these situations. Engaging the conflict directly is potentially beneficial, if good assessment takes place, and appropriate strategies are used. Writing about organizational conflict, psychology professor Dean Tjosvold (1991) notes that well-managed conflicts can lead to better decisions, improve social cohesion, stimulate innovation, and increase morale. The natural resource policy arena offers similar opportunities. Perhaps what matters most are conflict assessment and management strategies that make progress on the paradox of public deliberation: how to implement strategies that can generate technically sound decisions, while simultaneously allowing stakeholders a rich and meaningful voice in the process. The demands of natural resource management, combined with the range of interests in the mixed public/private lands, appear to require nothing less.

NOTE

1. This discussion focuses on federal legal requirements in the U.S. because it is the set of requirements most likely to be relevant to the largest portion of the readers of this book. Many of the state laws in the U.S. are patterned after the federal laws to some extent, and certainly the environmental impact reports required in a number of countries has been informed by the American experience. So even though there are important differences between federal laws in the U.S. and the various requirement in states and in other countries, this brief discussion of federal legal requirements can be extended by analogy into those other realms.

Chapter 4

Collaboration as a Deliberative Process

> Many environmental conflicts today pit advocates who are aware of their own place in the system, but not of relationships in the whole—pits them against each other. Environmentalists are as guilty of this as anyone, even though everyone is equally dependent upon the system . . . The rancher and the logger, for instance, know things about nature that the backpacker and kayaker do not, and vice versa as well. All are partial views that have much to learn from each other if only we are willing to open ourselves to the listening that is required for that mutual learning to occur.
>
> —William Cronon
> *Starker Lecture, Oregon State University, 20 November 1998*

As we noted earlier, the phrase "Collaborative Learning" appears most often as a concept in the fields of education and computer science. In education, merging "collaboration" with "learning" generally means "constructing knowledge collectively as people work, inquire, and learn together based on a shared purpose" (Collaborative Learning Project, 1998; Bosworth & Hamilton, 1994). In computer science, scholars distinguish between "computer-supported Collaborative Learning" and "computer-supported cooperative work." The computer science field views Collaborative Learning as an active system featuring "instructional methods that seek to promote learning through collaborative efforts among students working on a given learning task" (Kumar, 1998, p. 2).

This book is the first comprehensive effort to make Collaborative Learning a meaningful concept in the environmental and natural resource policy arena. Our integration of collaboration and learning is distinct from work in other disciplines. Understanding our Collaborative Learning approach requires an understanding of collaboration as a deliberative process.

In Chapter 1 we addressed the environmental and natural resource policy context in which conflicts occur, and Chapter 2 presented the fundamentals of Collaborative Learning. In Chapter 3 we discussed the nature of conflict, environmental conflict situations in particular. In this chapter, we continue to provide a foundation for Collaborative Learning by addressing collaboration in the policy context in which environmental conflicts occur. We first define collaboration and its relationship to important conflict management concepts such as collaboration and power. We then contrast collaboration with consultation and consensus.

THE NATURE OF COLLABORATION[1]

When Michael Dombeck became Chief of the USDA-Forest Service in January 1996, he told his fellow employees that "collaborative stewardship" would be among the key features of his resource management philosophy and tenure as chief. His message was consistent with collaboration and consensus themes coming from other federal agencies. Under the Clinton administration, the Environmental Protection Agency initiated a program in alternative dispute resolution that emphasizes using mediation and facilitation to promote collaborative problem solving among stakeholders. Similarly, the U.S. Department of the Interior Bureau of Land Management has launched a nationwide program that features collaboration and consensus as part of land management decision making.

Executive branch agencies and Chief Dombeck stress the importance of people's working together as part of the development of sound policy. This is certainly vital in the natural resource arena. For example, federal and state agencies that embrace ecosystem management as their natural resource management orientation must "recognize resource planning as a forum for public deliberation on the shape of a common future . . . planning needs to combine diverse viewpoints, ranging from perspectives of those who use public lands to views of those whose culture is shaped by the land" (Cortner & Shannon, 1993, p. 16). People can work together and deliberate through collaborative processes. Agency managers, such as foresters, "are realizing that collaborative approaches may be their best and only chance to influence the direction of natural resource policy" (Selin et al., 1997, p. 25).

Defining Collaboration

But just what is collaboration? Our use of the term collaboration is based on a standard, rather common-sense conception of it. Whenever we need to describe collaboration as it applies to public decisions, we turn to Barbara Gray's book *Collaborating* (1989):

Collaboration involves a process of joint decision making among key stakeholders of a problem domain about the future of that domain. Five features are critical to the process: (1) the stakeholders are interdependent, (2) solutions emerge by dealing constructively with differences, (3) joint ownership of decisions is involved,

(4) stakeholders assume collective responsibility for the future direction of the domain, and (5) collaboration is an emergent property. (p. 11)

There are perhaps two noteworthy comparisons between Gray's concept and our Collaborative Learning approach. First, Gray spends considerable time defining the *domain* of the problem, which refers to the context or milieu within which the problem has arisen. We likewise take a broad view of "problem," because the term can be symptomatic of other issues or be driven by forces that the immediate stakeholders cannot affect. The important difference is that we substitute the notion of *situation* for domain. In our experience, reducing the level of abstraction in public processes is always desirable, and we are more comfortable discussing the situation than the problem domain. The second noteworthy point is her use of the emergent property concept, which is drawn from systems theories on which we rely so heavily. Emergent properties appear as the result of synergy among the elements, functions, and environment of a system and are often invisible if one reduces the system down to any one of its components. (Morale in an organization is a good example of an emergent property; see Chapter 5 for a more detailed discussion of emergence.) As such, collaboration is an emerging and evolving process that is never fully predictable or manageable.

It is therefore important to regard collaborative processes more as improvisations than clearly orchestrated symphonies of coordinated effort. Of course, there are many skillful things that conveners and participants can do to enhance the collaborative potential. The point is that if you are going to embark on collaboration, then you must learn to tolerate a measure of unpredictability and ambiguity. At times that is both frustrating and disconcerting, but whether collaborative behaviors emerge depends first and foremost on the participants, and there is no practical way or ethical reason to force them to interact collaboratively. Collaboration cannot be forced, scheduled, or required; it must be nurtured, permitted, and promoted.

Collaboration is fundamentally a process in which interdependent parties work together to affect the future of an issue of shared interests (Gray, 1989). More specifically, Gray (1985) defines collaboration as "the pooling of appreciations and/or tangible concerns, e.g., information, money, labor, etc., by two or more stakeholders to solve a set of problems which neither can solve individually" (p. 912). Drawing upon Gray's ideas, Selin and Chavez (1995) assert that "collaboration implies a joint decision making approach to problem resolution where power is shared, and stakeholders take collective responsibility for their actions and subsequent outcomes from those actions" (p. 190). In collaborative conflict management and decision-making activities, people have meaningful opportunities for "voice," that is, to communicate as participants in significant ways. Their ideas and interactions matter in both the process and outcome of the situation.

Collaboration and Competition

Environmental conflicts and controversial decisions involve strategic choices as parties strive to settle differences (Rubin et al., 1991). Disputants' strategic orientations typically reflect their goals and appraisal of the conflict situation. As the Dual Concern Model presented in Chapter 3 (Figure 3.3), disputants may deal with a dispute directly through collaboration or competition, yield to, or accommodate, the other party, or avoid the dispute. Negotiation and decision making to settle disputes typically reflect a strategic choice between two dominant strategic orientations: collaborative/integrative and competitive/distributive (Walton & McKersie, 1965; Lewicki et al., 1999; Lewicki et al., 2001). Fisher and Ury's classic book on negotiation, *Getting to Yes* (1981), promotes collaborative, integrative negotiation as an alternative to competitive, adversarial, distributive negotiation. Understanding distributive and integrative negotiation strategy, therefore, provides a foundation for understanding the nature of collaborative processes. Collaboration is often associated with integrative bargaining or negotiation (Lewicki et al., 1999). Correspondingly, competition in conflict situations is generally associated with distributive negotiation. Table 4.1 presents a comparative view of competitive/distributive negotiation strategy and collaborative/integrative negotiation strategy.

Table 4.1
Comparing Competitive and Collaborative Strategic Orientations

Concept/Feature	Competitive/Distributive	Collaborative/Integrative
Party's goals	Maximize own share of benefits (individual gain)	Increase benefits for both both sides (mutual gain)
Theory base	Game theory, economic utility, collective bargaining	Human relations, systems, problem solving, communication
Utility orientation	Individual	Joint
Motivation	Self-interest	Mutual-interest
Relationship worth	Minimal, present focus	High, future-oriented
Relationship perception	Adversary, rival, competitor	Collaborator, partner
Trust	Limited, guarded	High
Communication	Controlled, selective, purposeful, tactical	Open

Table 4.1 continued

Concept/Feature	Competitive/Distributive	Collaborative/Integrative
Dissemination of information	Cautious, intentional	Full relevant disclosure
Position sought relative to the other party	Superiority; gain or maintain advantage	Respected equal
Power	Individual-centered; coveted, sought	Shared; in relationship, process
Norm of justice	Equity	Equality
Issue focus	Positions	Interests
Deception	Accepted as inherent, justified	Inappropriate, unnecessary
Intangible issues (e.g., face, respect)	Manipulated for advantage	Addressed openly
Rules, procedures	Dictated by conflict structure or imposed	Generated by the parties

Sources: Walton & McKersie (1965); Lewicki & Litterer (1985); Pruitt (1983); Fisher & Ury (1981); Tracy & Peterson (1986); Peterson & Tracy (1979), Lewicki et al, 1999).

A competitive/distributive strategy is likely when parties perceive resources as fixed or limited. Motivated by self-interest, each party wants to maximize its share. Consequently, the disputants employ competitive tactics designed to gain as much outcome as possible (Lewicki & Litterer, 1985). Each party takes a position (e.g., "timber harvest must be 20 million board feet per year" or "no timber harvest in roadless areas") and seeks power and control. A collaborative/integrative strategy is appropriate when parties perceive integrative potential, that the fundamental structure of the dispute offers the potential for both or all sides to achieve their objectives (Lewicki & Litterer, 1985). Whereas competitive/distributive negotiation involves positional bargaining, collaborative/integrative negotiation emphasizes the generation of alternative solutions to disputes through creative problem solving (Walton & McKersie, 1965; Fisher et al., 1991; Pruitt, 1983). When the parties adopt collaborative/integrative strategies it is easier to create an atmosphere of open communication and collaboration, where shared self-interest is the motivation, in a committed search for a mutually beneficial outcome through joint decision making. Consequently, collaborative/integrative negotiation is often called "mutual gains bargaining" (Susskind & Landry, 1991).

Environmental and natural resource conflicts provide opportunities for unilateral or joint decision making and for collaborative/integrative or competitive/distributive strategies. Given the complexities concerning issues, stakeholders, and interdependence, the likelihood that parties will be tempted to employ competitive/distributive strategies is high. With increasing complexity come increased uncertainty and a reluctance to trust or look beyond individual interest. As Table 4.1 illustrates, competitive/distributive strategies and tactics will be the dominant dispute settlement interaction when parties are motivated by self-interest, perceive resources as fixed, attempt to control communication, maintain little trust, seek power or advantage, stress positions, and regard other parties as adversaries or enemies. As environmental conflict situations become more complex and difficult, the parties may feel that competitive/distributive strategies and tactics are more secure and predictable. Yet this complexity also provides opportunities for collaborative, integrative dispute settlement approaches. Complex sets of issues can be divided into manageable concerns. Stakeholders can arrange concerns as priorities and "log roll" or trade off one party's low priority for another's high priority.

Often having a large number of stakeholders may appear to discourage collaborative, integrative dispute settlement. This is particularly true in situations where stakeholders come and go during the course of the dispute, changing the cast of characters at every meeting. But the numerous parties in a natural resource dispute also generate the potential for team efforts. Stakeholders can combine resources in problem-solving caucuses or committees that are organized by interests and concerns. Further, parties can recognize potential problems related to changing representation and stakeholder numbers and establish appropriate learning mechanisms, dispute settlement structures, and ground rules for negotiation.

Imbalances in interdependence could encourage mistrust and unilateral action. Consequently, stakeholders may try to maintain a strong, viable BATNA (best alternative to a negotiated agreement) as they operate from a controlled, distributive strategy (Fisher & Ury, 1981). Parties might attempt to use "facts," history, jurisdiction, and values as bases for power, control, and even separation. Some stakeholders may attempt to manipulate venues to their advantage and to strengthen their BATNA. Unless interdependence concerns are confronted, integrative negotiation strategies seem unlikely. Therefore, stakeholders must focus on structure and ground rules for negotiation and decision making before actual negotiations over substantive issues take place. Parties may employ pre-negotiation agreements or "protective contracts" that stipulate consequences if the participants do not adhere to the ground rules.

Since they have been entrusted to oversee natural resources and carry out legal mandates, government agencies such as the USDA-Forest Service often seem caught up in the complexities of disputes. Agencies may want to serve as impartial parties but are often viewed as stakeholders with their own specific agendas. As parties with legitimate power, agencies play a key role in settling natural resource disputes and in fostering a distributive/competitive or integrative/collaborative climate.

Collaboration or Competition: The Leslie Ranch Case

In 1990 a conflict arose over the management of public lands in the high desert region of central Oregon. The area affected covered 127,400 acres of USDI-Bureau of Land Management (BLM)-administered lands near a growing recreation and urban area of central Oregon. The catalyst for the conflict situation was a rancher who disagreed with a BLM change in management strategy on his grazing allotment. The rancher sought out a county extension agent and other ranchers to develop a Coordinated Resource Management Plan (CRMP) that would address his concerns and serve as the basis for a BLM Allotment Management Plan (AMP). The BLM was managing the area under the direction of a previous Environmental Impact Statement (EIS), in which a "no grazing" option had been considered but not adopted. Therefore, BLM managers believed their management options were limited to how, not whether, to graze the land. An apparent decline in sage grouse populations (a candidate for threatened or endangered species status) and concerns with available big game forage prompted wildlife habitat considerations.

The BLM had wanted a citizens' working group to address issues and make recommendations relevant to its management plan and endorsed the Land Issues Forum (LIF) group's work to organize and facilitate the process. Parties involved in this process included the Land Issues Forum (an ad hoc range management group, the initiator and sponsor), the Bureau of Land Management, Prineville District, Deschutes Resource Area (the decision authority), Oregon Department of Fish & Wildlife (ODF&W), Crook County Extension (Oregon State University), private citizens/landowners, ranchers, environmentalists, and university range and wildlife specialists.

Initially, a hired consultant facilitated the development of a CRMP on a pasture-by-pasture basis. The resulting plan incorporated grazing rates that were too high for the BLM, and the agency could not accept the recommendations. However, the objectives outlined by the group were carried forward to later discussions. Facilitation was subsequently done by three different individuals. Issue identification and decisions were often made by majority view rather than by consensus, with the majority often concerned primarily with livestock management issues. Often, dissenting interests were not present at meetings; therefore, those in attendance might have considered their unanimous agreement at the time to be consensus-based, while those not present might not have agreed with the decision. Meetings were usually held during weekdays, accommodating local, place-based parties better than regional parties based in urban areas. The process lasted about two years (1990–1992).

The process contributed to the BLM Environmental Assessment (EA) that was represented as receiving unanimous support of the working group. Some environmentalists, though, did not sign on, claiming that their issues and concerns were not expressed in the document. The ODF&W signed on to the AMP. Protests were filed on the plan by two of the environmental groups originally involved in the discussions.

Almost all parties expressed disappointment at the length of time involved in the discussions. Some environmentalists said they did not have enough time to go to all of the meetings. They claimed there was rarely a group consensus on common goals or process issues. These environmentalists did not perceive the facilitators to be totally impartial, and they felt that the nature and scope of the discussions focused on ranching concerns. Their dissatisfaction with the process and the scope of discussions led to one individual to withdraw from the process before completion. The environmentalists' doubts about the process' generating meaningful change may have contributed to their spotty attendance at meetings. These participants were dissatisfied that the extent of grazing set-asides (2,300 acres) did not come close to their desired amount ("at least 30–40% of the area left alone").

Others in the group were satisfied with the process. Some group members perceived a few environmentalists as just wanting to end cattle grazing on the public lands, without empirical support for such a policy action. They claimed that dissatisfied environmentalists were asked where and how much land should be set aside but were never specific about their prescription; also, certain environmentalists would not attend meetings and then would be upset at decisions reached at those meetings. In general, a number of group members (e.g., ranchers) felt they were going further than any previous range management effort had in recognizing non-grazing concerns.

The stakeholders in this dispute were so far apart in management philosophies that consensus on the main issues was problematic at best and evidently not resolvable in this case. With the BLM operating under a grazing mandate, certain agency employees and ranchers believed that the result was a large step forward in recognizing other resources. One environmentalist who was dissatisfied with the outcome said that the discussions had provided him an opportunity to meet others involved with the resource and that the result was at least a step in the right direction (Daniels et al., 1993).

Collaborative Potential

As Table 4.1 suggests, a collaborative orientation, such as mutual gain negotiation (Fisher et al., 1991) and transformative mediation (Bush & Folger, 1994), reflects the significant value that parties place on their relationships with one another, their willingness to trust and share power, their desire for open and constructive communication, and their respect for creative approaches to resource distribution. The elements of this table are the factors that influence the collaborative potential of a conflict situation. A party that chooses to adopt a collaborative/integrative strategy in an environmental conflict will likely perceive collaborative potential. This perception is based on two factors. First, the party believes that there is a possibility for meaningful, respectful communication interaction between the disputants. Second, the party believes that a mutual gain or integrative outcome is possible, that is, that the fundamental structure of the dispute offers the potential for both or all sides to achieve more of their objectives than would be likely in some other venue (Lewicki et al., 1999).

Key Features of Collaboration

Collaborative processes, as the previous discussion indicates, are fundamentally different from competitive conflict resolution processes such as litigation or highly structured, unilateral decision making. When a decision-making organization (e.g., a government agency) interacts with citizens and stakeholder groups (its publics), it has strategic options that emphasize either a competitive or collaborative approach. As an involvement strategy, collaboration differs considerably from the traditional public participation model of open houses, public hearings, and comment periods. Several key aspects of collaboration clarify these differences:

1. *It is less competitive* and more accepting of additional parties in the process because they are viewed more as potential contributors than as potential competitors.
2. *It is based on joint learning and fact-finding;* information is not used in a competitively strategic manner.
3. *It allows underlying value differences to be explored,* and there is the potential for joint values to emerge.
4. *It resembles principled negotiation,* since the focus is on interests rather than positions.
5. *It allocates the responsibility for implementation* across as many participants in the process as the situation warrants.
6. *Its conclusions are generated by participants* through an interactive, iterative, and reflexive process. Consequently, it is less deterministic and linear.
7. *It is an ongoing process;* the participants do not meet just once to discuss a difference and then disperse. However, collaborations may have a limited life span if the issues that brought the participants together are resolved.
8. *It has the potential to build individual and community capacity* in such areas as conflict management, leadership, decision making, and communication.

These distinctions between collaboration and traditional public participation can be encapsulated into two philosophical differences. First, an interest in collaboration grows out of the recognition that in some situations, any single natural resource or environmental management agency cannot adequately address the issues at hand by working independently. Collaborators bring to the process various additional resources that the agency may need: different perspectives on both the problem and potential improvements in it, understanding of rapidly changing social values, scientific data, traditional knowledge, political clout, agreement and coordination of other agencies and private landowners, finances, volunteer labor, and so on. For example, since the focus of land management is increasingly shifting away from specific resources (stands of trees, herds of big game, grazing acreage, etc.) toward landscapes and ecosystems, collaboration appears better suited to planning and implementation tasks than traditional public involvement. Collaboration arranges the relationships between the stakeholders in a manner that more closely matches the resources and responsibilities that each brings to the process. Just as ecosystem management emphasizes "system" relationships in the natural world, collaborative processes can illuminate "system" relationships in the social world.

Second, collaboration values cooperation, while traditional public involvement has evolved to emphasize competition. While there was no a priori reason that public involvement was destined to have a competitive orientation, it nonetheless has. Public involvement policy is firmly embedded in the adversarial comment/appeal/litigate/legislate mentality that characterizes much of environmental politics. A call for collaboration is not a starry-eyed proposal that ignores the current venom and rancor; rather it raises the possibility that energy currently devoted to competitive behaviors can, in some instances, be channeled into developing new approaches to natural resource management and environmental policy.

Theory suggests two keys to shifting the relationships in natural resource policy away from competition and toward collaboration: correctly select those situations where collaboration is an appropriate strategy and structure the process to encourage and reward cooperation rather than competition. Not all situations are amenable to collaboration. The complexity of natural resource conflict implies that it is often unrealistic to expect collaborative behaviors to emerge or persist. Some scholarship indicates that collaboration may be successful in the minority of cases (Amy, 1987; Buckle & Thomas-Buckle, 1986). It is also unrealistic to merely announce that a collaboration is beginning and expect the current relationships and patterns of behavior to change. Collaboration requires innovative decision-building structures designed with considerable attention to the incentives that they create. If they do not establish clear rewards for collaboration and disincentives for competition, there is no reason to expect much change in behavior (Daniels & Walker, 1999a; Vira et al., 1998).

Collaboration does not demand that participants set their self-interest aside, nor does the success of collaboration hinge on their doing so. Quite the contrary—participants are expected to voice their interests clearly and work energetically to achieve them. The key is that their efforts are not oriented strictly in opposition to those of their fellow participants, but more in concert. An environment needs to be created in which exploring differences is encouraged rather than hindered. When differences are not openly addressed, they may fester below the surface and eventually cause discontent with the process and dissatisfaction with the results. To counter this, collaboration strives to encourage integrative negotiation and dialogue among the stakeholders. This interaction is "dialectical" to the degree that it is motivated by the desire to examine issues critically by means of fair, just, and orderly procedures (Wenzel, 1990).

The President's Council on Sustainable Development (PCSD): Lessons Learned from Collaborative Approaches

In 1996 the U.S. President appointed the "New National Opportunities Task Force," with members drawn from industry and government. Among the task force's activities were the examination of cases in collaboration and reviewing the academic literature on collaboration. In April 1997 the task force presented a draft report, "Lessons Learned from Collaborative Approaches."

The task force explains its project mission as follows:

It is increasingly common for businesses, government, citizens and non-governmental organizations to find themselves participating in many collaborative efforts to solve environmental, social, and economic problems. They are doing so because collaborative approaches, it is commonly believed, lead to more comprehensive and acceptable outcomes at reduced cost than traditional regulatory and litigation-oriented approaches. Indeed, the PCSD, which is itself a collaborative process, recommended collaborative approaches to reform the environmental regulatory system, create an alternative regulatory path, and solve community- and ecosystem-based problems. The PCSD remains committed to collaborative strategies.

Yet, the majority of participants in formal collaborative processes know that with this great promise come great challenges. Success depends on many factors—some common sense, others less obvious, and many not always practiced or universally understood. For this reason, the New National Opportunities Task Force decided to examine some of the lessons that could be learned from a sampling of formal collaborative efforts now underway or recently completed. Specifically, the Task Force wanted to (1) document lessons learned from a diverse sample of collaborative processes; (2) identify when and under what circumstances collaborative approaches are useful and effective; (3) identify characteristics that are essential to successful collaborations and, conversely, the characteristics that cause collaborative processes to falter and fail; and (4) recommend next steps for evaluating collaborations. (President's Council, 1997).

The task force's summary findings are as follows:

1. Stakeholders often realize significant benefits through collaboration.
2. Collaboration is a process that is helping us learn how to solve society's complex problems, and evaluation is a key to learning.
3. Evaluations of collaborative efforts are rarely conducted either during or after a project.
4. Collaborations are becoming more complex, and evaluation processes must adjust accordingly.
5. Trust is essential, and ownership of the process and outcomes fosters trust.

The task force also identified the "key characteristics of collaborative processes" (President's Council, 1997):

1. Characteristics of the vision and objectives
   a. Shared vision and objectives
   b. Measurable outcomes
2. Characteristics of the process
   a. Process is equally managed by stakeholders
   b. Shared and defined decision-making process
   c. Up-front planning
   d. Conflict resolution
   e. Open communications among participants
3. Characteristics of the participants
   a. Balanced and inclusive stakeholder participation
   b. Strong leadership
   c. Create capacity for stakeholders to understand information
   d. Facilitators may help and should apply similar tools

COLLABORATION AND POWER

As noted earlier, Selin and Chavez (1995) emphasize that collaboration involves a joint decision-making approach in which power is shared, and "stakeholders take collective responsibility for their actions and subsequent outcomes from those actions" (p. 190). Balancing or sharing participatory power is an important feature of collaborative interaction, such as that which occurs as a part of Collaborative Learning. Collaboration locates control and power in the parties and their negotiation relationship. Disputants participate jointly in the decision-making process, maintaining ownership in agreements reached. In so doing, collaboration allocates the responsibility for implementation across as many participants in the process as the situation warrants. This effort is often an ongoing process, and power plays a somewhat different role that it does in situations where the participants might come together for a relatively short time to address a specific decision and then disperse.

A Relational View of Power

In conflict situations, power, "the ability to control or influence events," may be associated with individual parties rather than relationships (Folger et al., 1997). Power is often viewed as a resource, to be employed as part of a competitive strategy to achieve individual gain (Lewicki et al., 1999). Seeing power as part of an individual party's unilateral, competitive orientation disregards a critical feature of collaboration: the relationship. Collaboration relies on parties' perceiving themselves to be in an interdependent relationship. In a collaborative process, power is relational or social, stemming from relationships among the parties (Folger et al., 1997).

Folger et al. (1997) explain that individuals or parties can use a wide range of resources (e.g., skills, time, expertise, status, personal qualities, ability to reward or punish) to exert influence. They note that "any resource serving as a basis for power is only effective because others [parties, individuals] endorse this resource" (p. 100). They explain further that "because power is relational, the effectiveness of any resource is always negotiated in the interaction" between the parties (p. 111). This relational view of power is relevant to collaboration because of the importance that collaboration places on the relationship between the parties. Yet this discussion of power falls short of clarifying the extent to which power in environmental or natural resource collaboration becomes located as much in the relationship between the parties in conflict as in the parties themselves.

A Dependence Theory of Power

A view of power that seems particularly relevant to collaborative processes such as Collaborative Learning is Bacharach and Lawler's "dependence theory of power" (1981a). They see bargaining and negotiation as essential to resolving conflicts. For them, negotiation is a game of managing impressions and manipulating information. It is a competitive struggle for advantage, for with the advantage come beneficial outcomes. Bacharach and Lawler emphasize tactical action, that is, the manner in which negotiators bluff, argue for their positions, attempt to deceive and manipulate one another, draw upon potential power (objective sources of power) to shape impressions, and make power plays to gain and maintain advantage.

Bacharach and Lawler assert that negotiation power is *perceived power*. Meaningful power in a conflict relationship does not exist beyond the parties' perceptions of power. Power has an objective component (e.g., quantifiable control of a resource), but the subjective or cognitive dimension, which reflects disputants' judgments and perceptions, is more critical to understanding tactical action and potential power. "The objective dimension of power becomes important," Bacharach and Lawler explain, "only to the extent that bargainers translate it into tactical action" (1981a, p. 48).

As part of a conflict management strategy, whether competitive or collaborative, manipulating perceptions of power is critical to asserting influence. This manipulation is attempted through persuasive communication.

"Through tactics such as bluffing and argumentation," Bacharach and Lawler remark, "bargainers attempt to create a mutually accepted definition of the power relationship that is of some advantage to themselves" (1981a, pp. 49–50). In a later work, Bacharach and Lawler (1986) explain that "the central idea [of our theory] is that the bargaining power of a party—whether an individual, organization, or nation—is based on the dependence of others on that party." They add that "the dependence framework treats the ongoing [disputant] relationship as a power struggle in which each party tries to maneuver itself into a favorable power position" (pp. 167–168).

In Bacharach and Lawler's theory, dependence is the key power construct. Dependence generally refers to the degree that parties perceive themselves to have a stake in the conflict relationship. The dependence relationship is both variable and ambiguous. Like the issues in conflict, the nature of the disputants' dependence on one another is negotiable. Drawing upon the ideas of Blau (1964) and Emerson (1962, 1972a, 1972b), Bacharach and Lawler explain their dependency theory of power in a number of works (1976, 1980, 1981a, 1981b, 1986; Lawler & Bacharach, 1976, 1979). Fundamentally, one party's power reflects the extent to which another party is dependent on him or her for a particular outcome. Party A's power increases as Party B's dependence on Party A increases. Because interdependence permeates the conflict relationship, Party A's power within the relationship requires contrast with Party B's power. Party A's relative power consists of the ratio of Party B's dependence on Party A to Party A's dependence on Party B (see Figure 4.1).

Specifically, in Figure 4.1, A's power and B's power appear respectively as R and S, where X represents A's power over B (B's dependence upon A) and Y reflects B's power over A. According to this theory, disputants strive to minimize their dependence on their adversaries while maximizing their adversaries' dependence upon them. To the degree that they are successful, they control the conflict relationship, process, and outcome.

Figure 4.1
A Dependence View of Power

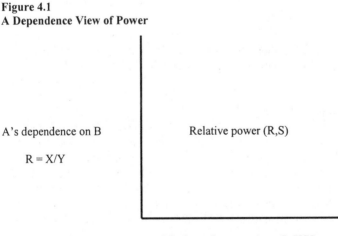

A's dependence on B

$R = X/Y$

Relative power (R,S)

B's dependence on A $S=Y/X$

Dependence emerges from the interaction of factors: alternatives and commitment. The former refers to the extent to which parties discern sources of alternative outcomes, and the latter relates to the degree of a bargainer's commitment to the outcomes at issue, that is, outcomes that the other party controls. Presented in terms of two-party bargaining, Bacharch and Lawler clarify that "four variables are essential to an analysis of bargaining power: A's alternatives, B's alternatives, A's commitment, and B's commitment" (1981a, p. 61). Cast in the earlier equation X, Party A's power over bargainer B encompasses B's alternatives to dealing with A and B's commitment to outcomes that A controls. The greater B's alternatives and the less B's commitment, the less A's power over B. A disputant's alternatives and commitment reflect that individual's awareness and understanding of these dimensions of dependence.

Collaboration and an Interdependence Theory of Power

Collaborative Learning and collaborative processes in general draw upon both relational and dependence theories of power to incorporate an "interdependence theory of power." Folger et al.'s (1997) explanation of the relational view of power locates that theory in the resources that people possess and how those resources affect the interpersonal interactions between disputants. In contrast, Bacharach and Lawler's dependence theory of power relies on the structure of the situation and its influence on disputants. They associate their theory of power with adversarial, competitive conflict and bargaining. The concept of power in Collaborative Learning integrates aspects of both relationship and dependence in a way that shifts the focus to interdependence. As parties perceive interdependence, shared power in the collaborative relationship is likely to increase.

Our interdependence theory of power draws heavily on Bacharach and Lawler's ideas about dependence resulting from alternatives and commitment. For Collaborative Learning and other collaborative processes to work, parties must believe the process is a viable alternative for them. They must be committed to giving the process a reasonable chance to succeed. The more attractive the collaborative alternative, the more likely that parties will make the necessary commitment. Collaborative processes like Collaborative Learning are dynamic and rely on constructive communication interaction. As parties interact, their perceptions concerning alternatives and commitment—their interdependence—may change.

Many conflict and dispute resolution scholars note the importance of interdependence. Conflict becomes significant communication interaction when it features perceived interdependence. "From a communication perspective," Wilmot and Hocker write, "conflict is an expressed struggle between at least two interdependent parties who perceive incompatible goals, scarce resources, and interference from the other party in achieving those goals" (1998, p. 21). Goal interdependence is an indicator of collaborative potential. Consequently, the extent to which goals are interdependent will most directly affect communication patterns in conflict (Tjosvold, 1991; 1993).

A party that perceives incompatibility but not interdependence may not consider conflict interaction, such as collaborative negotiation. A high-power/low-dependence party may decide unilaterally to resolve the conflict by presenting a promise or threat, or gain compliance in some other way. A low-power/high-dependence party may decide unilaterally to accommodate, withdraw from, or avoid the conflict (recall the Dual Concern Model, Figure 3.3). With the disputants perceiving interdependence comes the prospect for direct, constructive communication to deal with the conflict. Interdependence implies that each party has adequate power (not necessarily equal) to warrant joint decision making (Bacharach & Lawler, 1981a).

The focus that an interdependence theory of power puts on the collaborative relationship between the parties draws upon Bacharach and Lawler's work. Although they propose their theory as part of a competitive bargaining situation, their conceptualization of "total power" is relevant to collaboration. Returning to Figure 4.1, total power refers to the sum of Party A's and Party B's dependence on one another, "the absolute amount of dependence" in the disputant relationship (Bacharach & Lawler, 1981a, p. 99). Bacharach and Lawler propose that an increase in the total power in the disputant relationship, generated by a decrease in the total alternative outcome sources across disputants or an increase in the total commitment across disputants, "decreases the mutual toughness" of the parties (1981a, pp. 99–100). Applied to collaborative processes, their ideas suggest that as total power increases, competitive incentives decrease, and collaborative potential becomes greater. Cast within our interdependence theory of power, as the attractiveness of collaborative process increases, parties' commitment to that process also increases. The greater the commitment to, and viability of the process, the more power that parties will invest in the collaborative relationship, and the greater their perceptions of interdependence.

DISTINGUISHING COLLABORATION FROM OTHER POLICY CONFLICT PROCESSES

Environmental and natural resource policy decisions can involve one or more of a variety of processes, ranging from unilateral decision making (where one organization or entity is the sole decision maker, and no "public" is involved), to decisions based on pure consensus, durable agreement by all relevant parties or stakeholders. Unilateral decision making is beyond the scope of this discussion. We are interested in decision-making situations in which more than one party is involved, including potentially joint decision-making situations. In addition to collaboration, two general types of processes are common in multiparty environmental policy situations: consultation and consensus (see Table 4.2).

Table 4.2
Comparing Consultation, Consensus, and Collaboration

Factor	Consultation	Consensus	Collaboration
Goal	Information gathering and feedback	An outcome supported by all parties; agreement	Fair, inclusive process; full respectful inter-action; mutual gains outcome
Decision making	Little to no decision space; unilateral; retained by the decision authority	Shared decision space as dictated by the decision authority	Shared decision space; shared by jointly among the participants
Participation	Structured by the decision authority	Structured by the parties; controlled access	Accessible and inclusive
Negotiation	None	Likely, depending on procedural rules	Fostered; mutual gains; inter-action
Power and control	Sought and maintained decision authority	Shared, as dictated by the decision authority	Shared and negotiated
Philosophy	Inform and educate; command and control	Full support of the agreement	Active, learning-based participation

Consultation

Consultation refers to those activities that involve parties in the environmental policy decision process without sharing any aspect of the decision itself. It is a legitimate and viable decision-making strategy, but it is not collaborative. Its basic activities are information gathering and feedback. When a decision authority seeks input from other parties, it invites feedback on its terms. The decision authority might present a range of possible alternative decisions or propose a specific action and then seek the reactions of other parties, such as those likely affected by the decision. The decision authority may ask for ideas as it begins a planning process. In either case, the decision authority provides opportunities for participation in the decision situation without participating in the process of decision making itself.

In Chapter 1 we discussed formal public participation as part of the environmental policy governance framework. Formal public participation the consultation strategy. Traditional public participation activities, such as public hearings, letter writing, "comment" periods, open houses, and the like, stem from, and maintain, decision maker control. These techniques provide people and organizations with opportunities to communicate their concerns to a decision authority. The techniques seek to "inform and educate" and "invite feedback" while offering no guarantee of meaningful citizen input. In these settings, citizens do not know if and how their ideas will be used. Whether or not their comments influence the decision may depend on the benevolence of the decision authority. The consultative strategy and its traditional public participation techniques give rise to the various limitations that were discussed in Chapter 1: the uncertainty over how citizen comments are used, the limited impact that comments have on the outcome, the quasi-arbitration authority of the deciding official, the formality of the communication environment, and so on.

Consensus

As decision authorities and citizens have become disenchanted with the consultative strategy, "consensus" has emerged as an alternative approach for managing environmental conflicts. Consensus is typically defined as "either approval [of the agreement] or the absence of active opposition by each interest" (Dukes, 1996, p. 52). Consensus refers to an outcome in which an agreement, settlement, or solution is generated that all participating parties can support or at least will not oppose. Consequently, even though the public policy conflict literature freely uses the phrase "consensus process" (e.g., Susskind & Cruikshank, 1987; Ozawa, 1991), consensus refers to a type of *decision* rather than to a particular *process*.

Is there consensus on consensus? The Oregon Department of Land Conservation and Development (ODLCD) defines consensus as:

an agreement that is reached by identifying the interests of all concerned parties and then building a solution that maximizes satisfaction of as many of the interests as possible. The process does not involve voting, rather a synthesis and blending of proposed solutions. Consensus does not mean unanimity in that it may not satisfy each participant's interests equally or that each participant supports the agreement to the same degree. Consensus is considered to be the best decision for all participants because it addresses all interests to some extent. (Tarnow et al., 1996, p. 113)

Contrast this definition with the varied characterizations of consensus that appear in the small-group decision-making literature. In this area, consensus has been characterized in a variety of ways, including (1) the majority's will determined by democratic voting procedures, (2) unanimous agreement (consent or support), (3) the absence of any objection, (4) parties' commitment to implement a decision while not fully agreeing with the decision (partial consensus), (5) public support for a decision while maintaining opposition privately, and (6) group compliance (Fisher & Ellis, 1989).

The ODLCD in its 1993 booklet, *Collaborative Problem-Solving and Consensus Building in Resource Management and Planning*, explains that "consensus does not mean that all members are equally enthusiastic about a decision." Consensus may involve different levels of support. The ODLCD provides a six-item scale and notes that consensus can occur as long as no party is at level 6 (Lane Council of Governments, 1993, p. 9):

1. Wholeheartedly agree
2. Good idea
3. Supportive
4. Reservations—need to talk more about it
5. Serious concerns but will stand aside
6. Cannot participate in the decision and will work to block it

As this scale implies, consensus refers to the degree of support an agreement receives, not the process through which agreement is reached. Consensus decisions can result from highly collaborative processes, but they can also stem from very structured processes imposed by a decision authority. The latter can lead to false or *superficial consensus*. This type of consensus occurs when an agreement is made without all parties accepting the decision. It also may involve a particular party's submitting to internal group pressures to agree. Participants may also submit to consensus because an external authority pressures them to do so and threatens them with a negative consequence if they do not reach agreement.

Consensus and Diversity (Pluralism)

Consensus, whether viewed as unanimous agreement or group solidarity, can be a problematic notion in a decision-making situation where the participants value pluralism and diversity. First, consensus may not be possible, given plural values. Second, it may also not be a particularly desirable goal, given an emerging emphasis on creating institutions that can embrace and accommodate plural viewpoints. Third, it is not a prerequisite to making progress on vexing problems in natural resource management. Philosopher Nicholas Rescher (1993) critiques consensus from a pluralist perspective, with this premise:

The fact is that we live in an imperfect world. The resources at our disposal are limited, our own intellectual resources included. We have to be prepared for the fact that a consensus among people, be it global or local in scope, international or familial, is in general unattainable. In a world of pervasive disagreement we must take recourse to damage control. We must learn to live with dissensus with pluralism in matters of opinion. And we must *and can* bring to realization frameworks of social inclination that make collaboration possible despite diversity and that facilitate co-operation in the face of dissensus. In the setting of issues regarding social interaction, dissensus tolerance should prove positive and constructive. In the setting of issues regarding knowledge and inquiry it can, properly configured, lay the basis for a contextualistic rationalism intermediate between dogmatic absolutism on the one hand and relativistic nihilism on the other. (1993, p. 4)

In terms of the desirability of consensus outcomes, Rescher (1993) reiterates Habermas' distinction between de facto consensus and rational consensus. De facto consensus occurs fortuitously or spontaneously as a result of the group interaction. These moments are useful because they provide clear direction for the group's efforts and can increase group cohesiveness as participants recognize that there are issues that unite them. Rational consensus results from either explicit institutional design or norms that emphasize conformity or discourage dissensus. This latter form of consensus flies in the face of pluralist thinking because it either presumes monism (i.e., the presence of a single, overriding value or a universally adhered to value hierarchy) or employs some form of pressure—either logical or social—that quiets competing viewpoints:

In various respects consensus is doubtless a good thing. The impetus to consensus unquestionably resonates to the human predicament: it reflects our penchant for conformity and our deep-rooted inclination to accept what others do, so as to achieve the comforts of solidarity and companionship. Moreover consensus can, in some conditions, provide us with the reassurance of being on the right track. But be this as it may, consensus is not something on which we should insist so strongly as to make it a pervasive imperative for current concern. A universal consensus fixed upon "the truth of the matter" or the optimal course of action is not a practical goal but merely a hopeful aspiration. It is one of those things the achievement of which we would doubtless welcome but the actual pursuit of which as a practical goal makes no real sense. (Rescher, 1993, p. 43)

Finally, Rescher (1993) argues that consensus is not an imperative; that is, rational minds can come to differing conclusions:

But must genuinely rational minds not ultimately reach agreement on meaningful issues? Does not the fact that rationality is inherently universalistic in its bearing—is objective and impersonal in its orientation—mean that rational people "have to" attain a consensus, so that rationality remains absent where disagreement prevails? Not necessarily! For while in characterizing a resolution as rational we are indeed staking a claim that is universal in its substantive bearing and intent, it is nevertheless perfectly conceivable that there might not actually be a universal consensus about the matter. (p. 8)

When applied to natural resource conflict management, Rescher's ideas generate a provocative challenge. It is a hugely complex task to craft institutions and processes that are as pragmatic and tolerant as pluralism demands. The demand for pragmatism comes from the need to have effective public policy— there is much work to be done, so let us get at it. We can ill afford to hold pressing policy decisions in abeyance as we immerse ourselves in long-winded or self-indulgent pluralist discourse. The tolerance that pluralism demands will, in turn, demand a large measure of civility and maturity from the participants. Many people will be challenged as they attempt to function effectively in processes that require (1) that they interact with people with differing worldviews, (2) that they articulate their values and goals persuasively, but not defensively, (3) that they craft solutions that represent quality public policy, and

(4) that they are sensitive to the impact of the decision on groups that will be negatively impacted by it or that were advocating for an alternative outcome. Few of us have much experience in processes that make these demands; in fact, in many countries, the more common models of policy formation are far more combative and confrontational than a pluralist approach would advise. So making progress in pluralist management of natural resource issues is not merely an issue of learning new skills—some old attitudes and assumptions will need to be unlearned as well.

Rescher's ideas raise doubts about the efficacy of consensus decisions to endure over time, particularly if diversity is not respected in all of its significant forms. When consensus becomes a "god term" in environmental conflict management, it risks evolving into dictated consensus, a decision-making process in which consensus is mandated by the decision authority or as a condition of participation.

A better alternative is emergent consensus, or consensus that grows out of collaborative interaction. As parties engage challenging environmental conflict situations through collaboration, they will discover those areas on which they can achieve consensus. Consensus agreements reached through collaboration are likely more genuine and enduring than dictated consensus because the parties generate agreements on their own. Collaborative Learning is a method that values emergent consensus. Through Collaborative Learning, parties can share concerns, develop improvements for managing the environmental conflict, and, where possible, reach consensus on those improvements.

CONCLUSION

At a July 1997 conference on "Communities, Land Use, and Conflict" in Catron County, New Mexico, Sam Burns from the Ponderosa Pine Partnership in southwest Colorado outlined 12 characteristics of successful, community-based collaborations. Among them he emphasized the "development of trust and confidence in the partnership's abilities to make real progress in achieving community ecosystem stewardship." He stressed the importance of "a planning process based in mutual education, learning, and increased social awareness among all partnership members." He called for "a commonly accepted set of trustworthy facts about the economy, natural resources, values and ways of life of the community that can form the basis of consent" (1997, p. 1). The characteristics of the partnership that Burns outlined correspond more with the features of collaboration than either consultation or consensus. As such, they reveal that the partnership is a process that is capturing the collaborative potential around the forestry issues in southwestern Colorado by integrating issues of relationships, procedures, and substance.

The Ponderosa Pine Partnership has responded to a natural resource management situation with significant collaborative potential and by its actions has increased and sustained that potential. It has done so by employing many of the key attributes of collaborative processes. The partnership experience reveals that communities can generate their own particular collaborative approach. As we explain and illustrate Collaborative Learning throughout this book, we do so in the hope that communities will not seek in it a collaboration recipe, but rather an inspiration for them to develop their own framework.

In a noteworthy book, E. Franklin Dukes (1996) of the University of Virginia Environmental Negotiation Institute sees an imperative for collaboration.

Beyond the practical need for agreement is the moral need to move beyond the type of fighting that characterizes so much of public conflict. This moral need has led to the search not only for common ground, but for *higher* ground: a ground for engagement of issues on terms such as fairness, integrity, openness, compassion, and responsibility. It is the search for forums and processes where individuals and organizations can be forceful advocates without being adversarial, where public officials can make effective decisions without being dictatorial, and where communities can come together rather than split apart when faced with tough problems and divisive conflicts. (p. 2)

Collaborative processes such as Collaborative Learning hold the potential to be processes on the higher ground of which Dukes writes. Collaborative approaches place significant importance on constructive, civic communication. As Dukes (1996) notes, processes for public conflict resolution must promote an engaged community, responsive governance, problem solving, and opportunities for building sustainable relationships. To make progress on all these goals, constructive, civil discourse is critical: honest, responsible, public talk. As Barber (1984) observes, "Talk has the power to make the 'I' of private self-interest into a 'we' that makes possible civility and common public action" (p. 189).

Public policy conflicts, Dukes (1996) observes, are "socially constructed, dynamic organisms, whose actors, issues, and consequences are invariably shaped and transformed by the means available and used to contest them" (p. 9). Collaborative Learning and other collaborative methods can foster a social reconstruction, away from the divisiveness of natural resource conflict and toward the development of sound environmental conflict management, decision making, and the building of sustainable communities. In the next chapter we focus on the importance of working through environmental policy conflicts via learning.

NOTE

1. We use the term "collaboration," in this chapter, throughout the book, and in the phrase "Collaborative Learning," in a manner different from some historical uses of the term. We want to acknowledge that, in recent European history, "collaboration" has meant something very negative and tragic. During the Second World War, for example, "collaboration" meant giving aid and comfort to the enemy. Our use of collaboration as a positive, constructive term should in no way diminish the importance of understanding the term as negative in certain historical contexts.

Chapter 5

Learning as a Foundation
for Good Decisions

> Knowing is a process, not a product.
>
> —Jerome Bruner
> *Toward a Theory of Instruction*

This chapter is based on a simple concept: decision quality is linked directly to learning. Stated another way, better decision processes result from better learning. Certainly, there are some decisions, mostly routine ones, where learning does not play a prominent role. But there are other decisions where learning plays a crucial role in the process. These are often complex decisions with ambiguous processes and uncertain outcomes. Collaborative Learning is designed to deal with these complex decisions through activities that maximize learning opportunities for the participants. A Collaborative Learning process also arranges the activities in a sequence that is consistent with the order through which people learn most readily. As a result, Collaborative Learning feels natural and comfortable; it may feel more like common sense than like a "technique."

Many organizations use the concept of "analysis teams." Certainly, federal natural resource agencies such as the USDI-Bureau of Land Management and the USDA-Forest Service use interdisciplinary analysis teams to meet their analysis requirements pursuant to NEPA. Despite the dominance of "analysis" as an organizational mind-set, the term has limitations. Analysis has a rather static tone, as if all of the transcendent issues about the decision have been settled, and the questions at hand are not particularly fluid or dynamic. It is almost as if the ingredients to the decision are sitting on the shelf, and the analysts can concoct a decision by merely combining them in a relatively predictable—almost rote—manner. This term also assumes that the nature of the situation is not going to change before the analysis is done. But some tasks are not as well understood or stable, and in these cases "analysis" may not be the best approach. In these situations a learning orientation may be preferable.

Learning begins with the admission that you don't know everything. It is a better mind-set to adopt when you face situations that are not routine. When there are multiple ways to view a situation, when cause-and-effect relationships are uncertain, or when the purpose and need for action are unclear, then it is better to *expect* to be surprised by the process of moving toward a decision as well as in implementing it. Decision processes based on a learning philosophy are more fluid, improvisational, and resilient in the face of change than those based on an analysis mind-set.

So the questions that Collaborative Learning conveners, designers, and facilitators need to ask about learning begin to emerge at this point:

- How do people learn?
- Do teams learn differently than individuals?
- What different activities are part of learning?
- How can Collaborative Learning activities be designed to promote learning?

This chapter provides some answers to these questions. But step-by-step instructions on creating rich learning environments are probably not entirely possible. Collaborative Learning applications are truly learning opportunities for the facilitators as well as for the participants. It would be both hypocritical and untrue to suggest that agency managers and citizens should adopt an inquisitive, exploratory, learning-based orientation and at the same time imply that Collaborative Learning facilitators have all the answers. Collaborative Learning facilitators need to be open to new ways of understanding adult learning and new ways to design deliberative processes that enhance learning.

THE LEARNING FOUNDATIONS OF COLLABORATIVE LEARNING

Collaborative Learning is based on several premises, with one being that decision quality flows, at least in part, from the learning that occurs as part of the decision process. Moreover, learning becomes more difficult as decisions become more complex but simultaneously becomes more important in shaping the outcome. Consider some of the large decisions in life: choosing a life partner, selecting a college, switching careers, buying a house (or worse yet, building one). In each of these situations, the learning process may have taken weeks or months. Now consider the enormity of the learning task associated with some public policy decisions. Decision makers must face issues as confounding as conserving endangered species, lowering teen pregnancy rates, planning transportation systems, and so forth. The premium that society places on high-quality public decisions requires that public officials thoroughly learn their way through the complexity of the tasks that they face. Arbitrary and capricious decisions are both socially unacceptable and legally indefensible. Thoroughness—a hard look—is the prevailing standard for evaluating the adequacy of agency decision making.

If one goal of collaborative public discourse is to somehow improve agency and community decisions, then that discourse should both focus on promoting learning and also be enriched by learning. How does learning theory inform the design of collaborative processes? Collaborative Learning is grounded in two topics in learning theory: adult learning and experiential learning. Research shows clearly that adults do not learn well in the kinds of environments that are typical of K–12 classrooms (scholars of learning are realizing that many children do not flourish in those environments either, but that is another issue). Adults bring more experience, less patience, and little tolerance for being "taught"; they want to learn actively while they are working on the issues important to them. They need to be co-learners much more than pupils. Adult learning theorists have provided a strong foundation for understanding the unique challenges and opportunities of working with adults in Collaborative Learning settings; if we go to the effort to incorporate their thinking in our facilitation efforts, then our collaborations can be more effective and the participants more satisfied.

The second part of learning theory that is particularly useful in Collaborative Learning is the experiential learning model of David Kolb (1984). It is, in turn, grounded in the work of other scholars such as Dewy, Lewin, and Piaget, and focuses on the process of *learning by doing*. Kolb's conclusion is that experiential learning processes go through four distinct stages, each a different combination of either action or passivity, real experience or abstraction. The Kolb model is used in Collaborative Learning processes to provide a rough road map of the stages the process goes through and the order in which they should occur.

ADULT LEARNING THEORY

Malcolm Knowles has popularized the concept of andragogy, or the art and science of facilitating adult learning, as distinct from pedagogy, which is the art and science of facilitating children's learning (Davenport, 1993). The basic tenets of this position, according to Knowles (1980, pp. 44–45), are as follows:

Four crucial assumptions about the characteristics of the learners are different from the assumptions upon which traditional pedagogy is premised. These are the assumptions that as individuals mature: 1) their self-concept moves from one of being a dependent personality toward being a self-directed human being; 2) they accumulate a growing reservoir of experience that becomes an increasingly rich resource for learning; 3) their readiness to learn becomes oriented increasingly to the developmental tasks of their social roles; and 4) their time perspective changes from one of postponed application of knowledge to immediacy of application, and accordingly, their orientation toward learning shifts from one of subject-centredness to one of performance-centredness.

Knowles ultimately added a fifth assumption to his model: that adults are motivated to learn more by internal than external factors (Knowles et al., 1984, p. 12). Knowles deeply influenced adult education theory and practice through his extensive writings on andragogy. As Merriam (1993, p. 1) explains it,

"Andragogy is arguably the best known set of principles explaining learning in adulthood, or, more accurately, characteristics of adult learners." Prevailing thought among educational scholars is that andragogy and pedagogy are more a continuum than a dichotomy. Both contextual factors and the learning styles of individuals mean that some adults can benefit from activities that are characteristically pedagogic, while some children can flourish in a learner-centered environment that is usually associated with andragogy. In either case, it is undeniable that adults bring a particular set of attributes to a learning environment, and the match between those attributes and the environment will affect the effectiveness of their learning.

Vella's 12 Fundamental Principles of Adult Learning

Jane Vella, a protégé of Knowles, has 40 years of professional experience designing and conducting adult education programs around the world. Her notion is that the essential feature to adult learning is *dialogue*, which seeks to close the gap between expert and client. Her 1994 book extends Knowles' assumptions into a set of 12 principles of effective adult learning:

- Needs assessment
- Safety
- Sound relationships
- Sequence and reinforcement
- Praxis: Action with reflection
- Respect for learners as subjects of their own learning
- Cognitive, affective, and psychomotor aspects
- Immediacy of the learning
- Clear roles and role development
- Teamwork: using small groups
- Engagement of learners in what they are learning
- Accountability

Our contention is straightforward: the more a deliberative process is grounded in these principles, the better the chance of contributing to good decisions and satisfied participants. At first glance these principles are so simple as to appear basic, perhaps trivial. We prefer to think of them as fundamental because even though they can be stated in simple terms, their impact is anything but trivial.   Not all of these are particularly crucial to the function of collaborative inquiry in the policy arena; many of them are more important in traditional skill-building settings. Some, such as safety, praxis, and immediacy, are central to creating environments in which collaborative behaviors can productively flourish. But the cumulative effect of all 12 principles working in consort—not just 1 or 2 of them in isolation—that allows dialogue to flourish:

A significant problem in the education of adults is the perceived distance between teacher and student: between doctor and patient, between lawyer and client, between social worker and troubled parents, between judge and accused, between professor and adult learner. Until this distance is closed, the dialogue limps. The twelve stories in this book demonstrate the efficacy of closing that distance—of searching for means of honest dialogue across cultures, genders, classes, and ages. All of the principles are indeed means to close that gap and develop that dialogue. (1994, p. xiv)

Vella's perspective on the power of dialogue to close the expert-client gap has relevance to public policy situations. Many of our policy processes create and reinforce a distinction between experts and officials, on one side, and citizens, on the other. This gap, this disconnect between the governed and governance, is at the core of the criticisms of Mathews, Reich, and Yankelovich that were discussed in Chapter 1. As long as the procedures and rhetoric of policy processes continue to keep the participants separated, the learning by all parties will be diminished.

Needs Assessment. The task of needs assessment occurs during stage 1 of Collaborative Learning. Several techniques help identify key stakeholder groups and understand what their issues and concerns might be. Focus groups, semistructured interviews based on chain-referral sampling, and rapid rural appraisal are all potentially applicable. Another useful activity in Collaborative Learning processes has been stakeholder meetings prior to beginning the Collaborative Learning meetings to inform key individuals and groups about the upcoming process and to solicit their design suggestions. But whatever technique one uses, it is important to listen for the important themes in peoples' comments, as well as for the specific concerns, because it is through understanding the themes that fundamental improvement in the situations becomes possible.

Safety. This is a crucial consideration with several dimensions:

1. Physical safety. There is potential for both verbal and physical assaults in uncontrolled public meetings related to controversial issues. Do not conduct meetings if physical safety cannot be reasonably assured.
2. Interactional safety. You can remove people from their social comfort zone by asking them to interact in unfamiliar ways or with unfamiliar people. A whole range of activities might be appropriate in some settings but would not be useful in a tense, potentially contentious public meeting with diverse participants. One convention that we have adopted is to never force people to work with someone they don't know. We encourage mixing among the participants but do not force it. (Pay particular attention to older couples; we have seen situations where a wife appeared to have been compensating for the husband's low literacy level. If we had separated them, they may not have been comfortable enough to participate.)
3. Epistemic safety. Some environments discourage raising doubts or asking questions. Learning requires risk, and if the participants do not feel that they can take those risks, then they probably cannot learn. The ways in which a safe learning environment can be effected are both obvious (how much of the meeting time is devoted to interaction among participants) and subtle (the body language and responses of the facilitators). Questioning and skepticism are important parts of learning, and if the process cannot make it valid for people to display those behaviors, then their learning will not be as spontaneous and natural as it otherwise could be. Diminishing the participants' opportunity to ask tough questions doesn't aid the process; even if the process restricts doubt-raising, those doubts are still

there. They merely surface at breaks, during the participants' discussions while driving home, and so on.

In all of these dimensions of safety, your design goal should be to *moderate* the degree of risk-taking that you are asking of the participants. If they perceive the process as violating their safety, then they are likely to do one of the following: leave, reduce their active participation, or lash out. These behaviors are all defensive strategies to provide the sense of safety that they feel the process has not provided. Participants must feel comfortable for a learning environment to be constructive. But by the same token, it is neither possible nor desirable to completely eliminate the interpersonal risk, because conflict between individuals and among choices provides a large part of the motivation for the participants' involvement and learning.

Sound Relationships. The keys here are authenticity and respect. Much of the conflict resolution literature addresses these issues, so they are discussed more thoroughly in Chapters 3 and 7. A major conclusion is that relationships depend, in large measure, on the maturity with which people interact. There are countless signals that we send about the respect that we have for one another. A typical consideration is whether agency personnel should wear uniforms in a public meeting. (Agencies such as the USDA-Forest Service and the USDI-Bureau of Land Management and National Park Service have "ranger-type" uniforms.) How will various stakeholders view the uniforms? As an indicator of an us-versus-them attitude? As a display of power or control?

Sequence and Reinforcement. The chronological order in which issues are addressed is central to the effectiveness of learning. The progression that appears the most appropriate to us is the Kolb learning cycle, which is discussed in the second part of this chapter. But the Kolb model does not focus on the importance of reinforcement as a specific part of adult learning and organizational change. To the extent that a goal of Collaborative Learning is to enable long-term change in how agencies and citizens interact over complex issues, then the Collaborative Learning approach will need to be used repeatedly. Using it once will not create the desired behavioral or attitudinal changes, at least not permanently.

Praxis: Action with Reflection. This is the concept of learning by doing, with the added dimension of self-reflection. Active learning has been shown to be more effective than passive learning, and that is particularly true with adult learners. Collaborative decision processes are rich environments for praxis; the participants are learning in order to do something; they are not just learning for its own sake. That is necessarily an active, problem-oriented environment. By the same token, the multiparty discursive nature of the process creates the opportunity for reflective thought—as other people state their positions and preferences, the participants are forced to examine their own.

Respect for Learners as Subjects of Their Own Learning. This principle demands that the conveners of a collaborative process respect the abilities and experience that the participants bring to the process. They are not subjects in an agency-directed process, nor are they uninformed people who would agree with the agency if they only understood the science better, nor are they data that agency can incorporate into its decision algorithm. They are citizens, many of whom may be decision makers in their own professional lives. If they are treated as less than that, then some potential benefits of their participation may be overlooked.

Cognitive, Affective, and Psychomotor Aspects. Lewin (1951) noted that little substantive learning occurs without involving all three domains. Too often public policy situations are defined in largely cognitive terms (what do I think about this situation?), when, in fact, there are important affective considerations (what do I feel about it?). In addition, there are more active (psychomotor) ways to involve people than we tend to use. The quintessential example from the natural resources arena is the field trip: discourse and interaction are far different when participants are out of the meeting room and in the woods.

Immediacy of the Learning. Adults must find relevance in an issue in order to invest their time in learning about it. The potential for this relevance and immediacy is very high in public policy learning situations, but not universally so. While agencies must do a certain amount of "planning," the immediacy of these processes is not always clear to the public. The advisability of convening a collaborative group to assist with planning is therefore less clear than in situations with more obvious payoffs. Certainly, project-related decisions that quickly lead to tangible results are more amenable to collaboration. Planning efforts tend to be longer, more abstract, and with less visible impact on people's lives; for all of these reasons, they tend to try everyone's endurance. The principle of immediacy explains part of that dynamic. The reader may note that this principle directly reiterates one of the concepts in Knowles' definition of effective adult learning.

Clear Roles and Role Development. In the adult education literature, this concept generally refers to the roles in the teacher–student relationship. The important recognition in adult learning is that the role distinction between teacher and student is much more complex and dynamic than is typically the case in the K–12 environment. Adult learners often take more responsibility and demand more autonomy than do children. In multiparty collaborations, the roles are even more varied, and the importance of role clarity is perhaps more important. Who are the decision makers? What is the decision space? Are agency employees impartial subject experts or participants who necessarily bring a value-laden aspect to their participation? Is the facilitator of the meeting expected to be impartial?

Roles should also be allowed to shift and evolve as a Collaborative Learning process unfolds. Such change in the relationships is both inevitable and desirable. The facilitator may need to take a leadership role in establishing ground rules and appropriate behavior in the early stages, but control over the discourse may also shift as the participants and the process mature. Different people may be the relevant subject experts as the focus of the discussion shifts. Some individuals may be able to exert intellectual leadership when the learning tasks are comfortable but will also hold back at other times.

Teamwork: Using Small Groups. Team learning has proven its value in virtually every educational setting. A collaborative process is necessarily a team activity, and it is possible to design small-group activities that enhance the group nature of the process. Embedding such activities in a Collaborative Learning process has a number of safety and conflict management advantages that, in turn, amplify the learning value of small-group activities.

Engagement of Learners in What They Are Learning. Engagement is related to immediacy in some fundamental ways. With adult learners, it is particularly important to engage in the complexity of the situation both immediately and directly—to jump right into it. Rather than hold a series of meetings about issues that might be part of the situation and delay substantive discussion of "the problem" until that foundation is laid, adult learners prefer to reverse that sequence: engage in the situation and learn subject material as it becomes meaningful in their understanding of it. When adults take the time to learn about complex issues, they are more often motivated because they see the learning as an intermediate step in improving their current situation, rather than as a relatively academic activity that may pay future dividends. The learning is the means to an end, not vice versa.

Accountability. The participants must define for themselves whether they are satisfied with the results. They must feel comfortable challenging both the facilitators and decision makers with their doubts. They must also be able to pursue their preferred outcomes through other processes (administrative appeals, litigation, legislation, etc.) if they are not satisfied with the progress achieved through the collaboration. The decision makers who control the outcome of the process must clearly state what amount of power sharing they can accept and then be consistent in that position as the process unfolds. Individuals must be accountable for their own behavior.

Situational Cognition

In addition to the andragogic concepts of Knowles and Vella, the notion of situational cognition is useful in the design of Collaborative Learning processes. Situational cognition is a simpler concept than it seems: People's thinking is shaped by the context within which they are operating. With adults, more so than with children, the ability to do complex cognitive tasks is linked to the context in which the tasks are to be performed. For example, adults have a much lower error rate on mathematics as they do their grocery shopping than they do on a pencil-and-paper test (Lave, 1988). A general rule might be that the more abstract the setting (i.e., the less context it provides) the lower the cognitive performance. Knowledge and learning have to be understood as inextricably integrated with the setting in which they occur; consequently, adult learning can be understood as "fundamentally situated" (Brown et al., 1989, p. 32). As Wilson (1993, p. 73) explains the concept:

What does it mean to be "fundamentally situated"? It means that "context is an integral aspect of cognitive events, not a nuisance variable" (Rogoff, 1984, p. 3). Learning is thus an everyday event that is social in nature because it occurs with other people; it is "tool dependent" because the setting provides mechanisms (computers, maps, measuring cups) that aid, and more important, structure the cognitive process; and, finally it is the interaction with the setting itself in relation to its social and tool-dependent nature that determines the learning. Thus, learning is a recursive process in which adults act in and interact with context. (Lave, 1988; Rogoff, 1984)

These notions of situational cognition argue strongly for bringing together learning theory and collaborative practice. Collaborations are, by definition, the kind of social interaction that Wilson (1993) refers to. Also, collaborations typically focus a particular sphere of shared interest, and the problems that need to be addressed define the learning needs. The procedural informality of collaborations also can respond to the tool-dependent nature of situational cognition because the participants can apply tools to the task as they see fit. If they feel that they need special maps, various forms of biophysical data, financial projections, or expert presentations, they are free to acquire them.

A collaborative process can therefore function as a learning incubator because it can include activities that are situationally defined, tool-dependent, and socially interactive. It is here that collaboration begins to depart from the traditional public participation tasks such as hearings. As Mathews contends:

The standard public hearings that bring citizens and officials together are probably the most counterproductive mechanism of all. People report, "I have been to too many public meetings wondering if I'm wasting my time." Or they confess, "When I come home from work I think, 'Why should I attend a public meeting since it won't change anything?'" Comments like these are common. People think that hearings don't work because little hearing goes on. Officials usually make presentations or get lectured to by some outraged individual. Little two-way communication occurs. And with no feedback, people don't think they have been heard. The prevailing sense is that a decision was reached long before the hearing was scheduled. (1994, p. 23)

This representation is perhaps overly harsh, but it does remind us that public hearings can lack all three dimensions of a learning environment, or at least that's how participants can perceive them. First, they are not situationally defined because there is no authentic decision space within which the participants can operate: the decision is perceived to have been reached prior to the meeting. Second, the tool dependence is often low because the hearing involves just testimony by individuals and little working with maps, models, or data. Finally, the typical social interaction in hearings is antithetical to learning: it is tightly constrained by time and rules, and the communication is intended to convince rather than explore.

In the realm of situational cognition collaborations offer some profound, but largely untapped, potential. Much of the writing on collaboration has a "field of dreams" notion about the value of meetings: "convene it and they will agree." Social psychological research explains that agreements are more likely in group settings because as people interact, they feel some degree of social attachment that makes them less likely to openly contradict each other (e.g., Fiske & Taylor, 1991). But while the benefit of the community-building value of collaboration is not to be underestimated, there is also value in going well beyond it. As Jarvis noted, "Learning is not just a psychological process that happens in splendid isolation from the world in which the learner lives, but . . . it is intimately related to the world and affected by it" (1987, p. 11). To the extent that collaboration can reinforce the learning of the participants, it creates a self-perpetuating environment: as the process reinforces the learning by individuals, it helps create a social context in which learning is a safe and valued behavior. That will then allow others to ask questions and raise doubts as they, in turn, learn about the situation at hand and the social context within which they are operating. Through these activities the deliberative processes referred to in Chapter 1— Yankelovich's "working through" and Reich's "social learning"—become tangible.

The demand for subtle and thoughtful process increases as situations become more complex and as the controversies are more easily ignited. There may be no more solid foundation for that design than the notions of situational cognition and Vella's 12 principles. They provide an opportunity to ground one's design choices in a set of questions that are rarely included in public participation or collaboration primers.

EXPERIENTIAL LEARNING

Vella contends that the order in which learning occurs is essential to its effectiveness. We propose a corollary: the more complex the situation, the more sensitive the learning to issues of order. In order for Collaborative Learning processes to enhance learning, they should sequence activities in the order that learning theory indicates. But in what sequence of steps do people learn? To use Yankelovich's term, how do we "work through" a complex issue?

David Kolb (1984) has presented a model of experiential learning that is directly applicable to collaborative decision processes. His work begins with a synthesis of the learning theories of Dewey, Lewin, and Piaget. The resulting model (Figure 5.1) goes through four distinct stages: reflective observation, abstract conceptualization, active experimentation, and concrete experience.

Reflective observation (RO) is the process of understanding the world and asking questions about it. When people ask "why?," they have begun to reflectively observe the world around them. (If you have ever spent much time with a two- or three-year-old child, you know the importance of "why" as an early learning activity.) The key notion is that the learner is beginning to become grounded in reality, and is identifying aspects that either invoke curiosity or appear somehow problematic.

The next stage, *abstract conceptualization* (AC), is the process of developing an abstract model of the situation. It can be paraphrased as the "what" question. The difference between abstract conceptualization and reflective observation is that cognitive processing has begun: the learner is putting an order to the situation as an initial step in explaining the "why" question that started the learning.

Once the learner has developed a mental model of the situation, he or she applies it to the situation, either to determine its accuracy at explaining the world or its efficacy in improving a problematic situation. He or she asks a series of "how" questions that evaluate the various alternative explanations. This *active experimentation* (AE) takes the abstract model that the learner has developed and ground-truths it against reality. The final stage of active experimentation occurs as the learner decides if one of the possible explanations adequately explains the situation.

Figure 5.1
Kolb's Model of the Learning Cycle

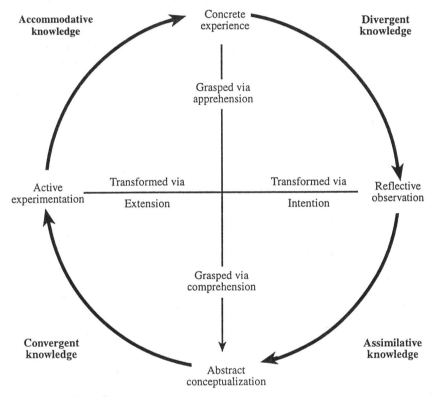

Source: Kolb (1984).

The final step of experiential learning is *concrete experience* (CE), or the actual application of the explanation that the learner has been developing. These field applications amount to "what if" questions into the adequacy of both the abstract conceptualization and the possible explanations that emerged from the abstract model of the situation. In many ways, application is the purpose of the entire learning process; the learner wanted a better understanding of the world or a better approach to a problematic situation.

A useful aspect of Kolb's model flows directly from Dewey's (1938) concept of recursive learning. As a person finishes a process of experiential learning, the Kolb model argues that the learner has moved back into real experience, in a situation that is very similar to the one that gave rise to the initial "why" question. Regardless of how successful the first iteration of experiential learning might have been, the learner will still have "why" questions to address. If the first learning effort was fruitless, then the learner will address a re-framed version of the initial question. If the first learning effort succeeded, then the learner can move to a second level of questions that is more advanced and is grounded in the understanding garnered by the first iteration. But in either case, experiential learning never stops; we continually perceive, model, test, and apply as we learn through our lives.

Several key features of Kolb's model are relevant to Collaborative Learning:

- Learning styles exist, and vary among individuals.
- Learning is best conceived of as a process, rather than in terms of outcomes.
- Learning is a continuous process grounded in experience.
- Learning is motivated by conflicts.
- Learning is a holistic process of adaptation to the world.

Learning Styles Exist and Vary Among Individuals.   According to Kolb, learning through experience involves transactions among the four adaptive modes: concrete experience, reflective observation, abstract conceptualization, and active experimentation. These modes combine to form learning dialectics. The abstract/dialectic consists of two opposite prehensions: comprehension (conceptual interpretation and symbolic representation) and apprehension (felt qualities of immediate experience). The active/reflective dialectic is made up of two contrasting transformations: intention (figurative representation of experience) and extension (active, external manipulation of the external world). These modes and dialectics combine to form four different forms of knowledge: divergent, assimilative, convergent, and accommodative. In explaining his model, Kolb remarks:

The central idea here is that learning, and therefore knowing, require both a grasp or figurative representation of experience (prehension) and some transformation of that representation. Either the figurative grasp or the operative transformation alone is not sufficient. The simple perception of experience is not sufficient for learning; something must be done with it. Similarly, transformation alone cannot represent learning, for there must be something transformed, some state or experience that is being acted upon. (1984, p. 42)

In other words, experiential learning is both grounded and dynamic. It is grounded because it begins and ends with one's understanding and experiences of the world. It is dynamic because it involves change in the learner's beliefs and understanding of the world but also can generate activity that can alter the learner's environment.

Each person is most comfortable in particular parts of the learning cycle; each of us has our unique approach to learning. *Divergent learners* are very creative and grounded in values and feelings. They are able to embrace ambiguity, look for patterns, and generate alternatives. *Assimilative learners* are comfortable putting order to information by classifying and defining. They are able to construct theories and models to test alternatives. *Convergent learners* are innovative solution-generators. They set goals and criteria, make decisions, and are personally involved as leaders and/or facilitators. *Accommodative learners* immerse themselves in situations by taking action. They seek opportunities to implement solutions.

No individual has a learning style that exhibits only one of these four learning types, and each of us is able to exhibit all four to a greater or lesser extent. But some people find some of these activities and ways of learning to be easy and some to be more of a struggle. As a result, we tend to de-emphasize those ways of learning that are difficult and dwell on those in which we are more comfortable. The result is our preferred learning style: how we tend to approach the learning tasks in our lives.

The notion of preferred learning styles provides important motivation for using *learning teams* but includes considerations in their use. Because no one individual is equally strong in all of the learning styles, learning teams can be more effective than any individual. Teams can create a composite learning style that is better balanced than any individual's style. But there are two considerations to bear in mind regarding learning teams. First, if a learning team is to be effective, that effectiveness will come not from the *similarity* in learning types among the participants but from the *differences*. In many ways, the ideal learning team is four individuals, each with well-developed abilities in one of the four different learning styles. But the downside of joining together such unidimensional learners is that they might not know how to interact with each other. Their learning styles might be so narrow that they would not know how to value the contributions of the other participants or understand the learning styles that they bring to the team.

This raises the second consideration in the use of learning teams: the intellectual leadership in the team must circulate around the team. Different learning styles are more important at different stages in the learning process, and as such, people make their greatest contributions during those stages that require the learning styles that are their strength. The convergent learner should play a prominent role when convergent learning is the crucial activity, and so forth. As the learning progresses, different team members should be encouraged to assume some real intellectual leadership and bring their full creativity, orderliness, decisiveness, or committed leadership to the task. But it is a rare team, in our experience, that can share the intellectual leadership in the kind of authentic way that this learning styles argument would call for. Personalities, power differentials, and time constraints all conspire to prevent it. If team learning can happen at this fundamental level, it would seem to be a thing of organizational beauty.

Learning Is Best Conceived of as a Process, Rather Than in Terms of Outcomes. In his essay entitled El Dorado, Robert Louis Stevenson wrote that the true value of any quest was not in arriving at one's destination, but in the journey itself. This observation is as true in learning quests as it is in searching for lost cities. A focus on outcomes rather than learning processes prevents one from observing all that happens en route. As Kolb notes:

When viewed from the perspective of experiential learning, the tendency to define learning in terms of outcomes can become a definition of non-learning, in the process sense that the failure to modify ideas and habits as a result of experience is maladaptive. The clearest example of this irony lies in the behaviourist axiom that the strength of a habit can be measured by its resistance to extinction. That is, the more I have "learned" a given habit, the longer I will persist in behaving that way when it is no longer rewarded. Similarly, there are those who feel that the orientations that conceive of learning in terms of outcomes as opposed to a process of adaptation have had a negative effect on the educational system. Jerome Bruner, in his influential book, *Toward a Theory of Instruction* (1966), makes the point that the purpose of education is to stimulate enquiry and skill in the process of knowledge getting, not to memorize a body of knowledge. (1993, p. 144)

Learning Is a Continuous Process Grounded in Experience. Kolb's model codifies something that many adult educators echo: adults are constantly learning in their capacities as parents, voters, consumers, and professionals. It is, in many ways, how we move through life. It is not always an elegant process, and it is often constrained by factors such as cultural predispositions, power differentials in society, time limitations, and the amount of our formal education. Even so, we are fundamentally "on-the-job" learners, and the job is being an adult. For example, Schön (1983, 1987) researched how professionals "know-in-action." Learning occurs as professionals engage in the very activity of their practice in the everyday world, although there are substantial differences between the preferred systematic approaches of technical rationality and the actual, tacit theories-in-use of practicing professionals. Stated another way, practitioners do not apply well-constructed theoretical approaches to well-understood problems with easily predicted results. They are far more adaptive and improvisational in their application of general principles. Professional practice is therefore not "instrumental problem solving made rigorous by the application of scientific theory and technique" (Schön, 1983, p. 21). It is more an extemporaneous response to the situation at hand, with the professional's choices grounded in the principles that define his or her field of expertise.

It is therefore crucial that anyone trying to lead adult learners bear in mind that he or she is dealing with mature adults who have long been experiential learners. This is as true in Collaborative Learning processes as in the traditional courses that were Kolb's focus:

How easy and tempting it is in designing a course to think of the learner's mind as being as blank as the paper on which we scratch our outline. Yet this is not the case. Everyone enters every learning situation with more or less articulate ideas about the topic at hand. We are all psychologists, historians, and atomic physicists. It is just that some of our theories are more crude and incorrect than others. But to focus solely on the refinement and validity of these theories misses the point. The important point is that the people we teach have held these beliefs whatever their quality and that until now they have used them whenever the situation called for them to be atomic physicists, historians, or whatever. (1993, pp. 145–46)

Learning Is Motivated by Conflict. There are a number of levels at which conflict and learning are interwoven. At the individual level, conflict not only provides the motivation for learning but also shapes the learning at a fundamental level. Internal cognitive dissonance (disagreement in perceptions of the world or a gap between aspirations and reality) motivates much of our perceived need to learn, and the learning itself can be characterized as a series of conflicts between different ways of knowing. The theoretical models upon which Kolb based his efforts

suggest the idea that learning is by its very nature a tension- and conflict-filled process. New knowledge, skills, or attitudes are achieved through confrontation among four modes of experiential learning . . . .In addition, the *way* in which the conflict among the dialectically opposed modes of adaptation gets resolved determines the level of learning that results. If conflicts are resolved by the suppression of one mode and/or dominance by another, learning tends to be specialized around the dominant mode and limited in areas controlled by the dominated mode. (1993, pp. 147–48)

The relationship between the manner of conflict resolution and the quality of learning has analogues at the interpersonal level. In any multi-party collaboration or interdisciplinary team there are inevitably individuals whose preferred learning styles differ, and as a result they will tend to view the situation in some very different ways. They may also have little patience for some learning activities, even though others in the group may want to spend time on those activities. If the differences in preferred learning styles among individuals are resolved by suppressing either activities or individuals, then the learning process of the entire group is diminished. The facilitator of a learning team must be able to use a range of techniques that honor different learning styles and not just assume that everyone's learning preferences are similar. This provides an important additional new dimension to the facilitator's credo to "be inclusive." The notion of inclusivity normally refers to individuals, but it should be broadened to include the range of individual learning styles that the participants bring as well.

Learning Is a Holistic Process of Adaptation to the World. Learning does not involve just a part of the person; rather, it involves cognitive, emotional, psychomotor, and social aspects simultaneously. It does so as part of a fundamental process of human growth and adaptation, where views of one's self, of other, and of the world around us can be variously tested, changed, and reinforced. To quote Kolb:

Learning is *the* major process of human adaptation. This concept of learning is considerably broader than that commonly associated with the school classroom. It occurs in all human settings, from schools to the workplace, from the research laboratory to the management board room, in personal relationships and the aisles of the local grocery. It encompasses all life-stages, from childhood to adolescence, to middle and old age. Therefore it encompasses other, more limited adaptive concepts such as creativity, problem solving, decision-making, and attitude change that focus heavily on one or another of the basic aspects of adaptation. Thus, creativity research has tended to focus on the divergent (concrete and reflective) factors in adaptation such as tolerance for ambiguity, metaphorical thinking, and flexibility, whereas research on decision-making has emphasized more convergent (abstract and active) adaptive factors such as the rational evaluation of solution alternatives. (1993, p. 149).

Learning is therefore a powerful foundation upon which to build collaborative processes. It is such an integral part of our lives and the decisions that we make that it often goes unexamined. Perhaps learning receives so little explicit thought because it will happen no matter what choices are made. Learning occurs even in the most impersonal exchange of letters or in the most rule-bound public hearing. But often that learning is not about the issues at hand but about how little the stakeholders care about each other's point of view.

It should be possible to design an entire range of public involvement and conflict management strategies that are grounded in learning theory and therefore have enhanced deliberative power. Four attributes appear to be fundamental to that process: (1) the recognition of the "adultness" of the participants, (2) an authentic desire to mutually learn about the situation at hand, (3) sufficient time to design learning-based activities, and (4) the persistence and organization needed to competently conduct the activities. None of these should be an insurmountable challenge to agency personnel, elected officials, or citizen organizers.

A perennial concern, however, is that a collaborative, mutual learning approach will be expensive and time-consuming. In an era of organizational downsizing and fiscal accountability, that concern is justifiable. There are two different responses to the concern. First, learning-based collaborative processes are likely to be more expensive in the short term, but it is considerably less certain that they are more expensive in the long run, if the costs of procedural delays, litigation, and resource values are included. In addition, as agency personnel and their stakeholders become more familiar with deliberative approaches, collaboration will likely become more efficient as their skills, trust, and confidence increase. The first generation of mutual learning efforts could be more expensive than conventional approaches would have been, but the additional cost would probably decrease as the participants moved up the learning curve. The additional costs associated with collaboration might never disappear, but efficiency would increase with experience. Second, even though a learning approach is likely to take longer than a more arbitrary decision process, the costs of adding the public to the process are not the significant increment. Taking the time needed to learn one's way to a decision inevitably involves more up-front cost than a "snap" judgment. Collaborative Learning is based on the assumption that there is a set of complex public policy decisions in which such an abbreviated decision process is insufficient. In those cases, a learning approach of some kind is called for, and the questions are if and how to involve the public in it. All of the additional cost of the learning-based approach should not be blamed on public involvement, however.

OTHER APPLICATIONS OF LEARNING THEORY

There are many learning theories and techniques with potential relevance to agency decision-making processes and public involvement. The integration of learning concepts into Collaborative Learning merely scratches the surface and begins to reveal the potential benefits in incorporating an educational/psychological perspective into our procedural choices. In particular, two other perspectives on the importance of learning need to be included in a discussion of Collaborative Learning; one is the work by Kai Lee in adaptive management, and the other is the work by Peter Senge on learning organizations. These are both important because they provide additional support for one of the underlying assumptions of Collaborative Learning—that learning is central to our ability to make decisions about environmental systems in the policy arena.

Adaptive management is a philosophy about the management of large, complex systems that has been developed by ecologists (e.g., Holling, 1978; Walters, 1986; Walters & Holling, 1990 [see Nega, 1998 for a literature review]). The essential notion of adaptive management is that we will never understand large systems as much as we might like because it is impossible to conduct controlled or replicated experiments upon them. They are too large to either control or replicate. In addition, they are sufficiently dynamic that the measurements from last year may not be relevant to the situation this year. Too make matters even more complicated, there may be a substantial lag—measured in years or even decades—between our management actions and their eventual effects. Therefore our management choices are always based on incomplete knowledge, and our actions are implicitly field experiments of the prevailing understanding of what the system is, how it operates, and how it is likely to respond to our manipulations. We should expect to be surprised when large systems respond in unexpected ways when we disturb them, and we need to view those surprises not so much as policy failures but as opportunities to learn about the systems and update our understanding of them. An adaptive management approach is one that is designed from the outset to test clearly formulated hypotheses about how the system is likely to respond to our actions.

While Kai Lee is not one of the originators of the adaptive management approach, his book *Compass and Gyroscope* (1993) is relevant to Collaborative Learning because it attempts to explain how to take adaptive management concepts into the policy arena. He calls for the development of "civic science," where science and technology are the compass, and democratic politics is the gyroscope. The goal is to move management decisions out of the realm of applied science and into the sociopolitical realm more than perhaps has been the case. This will necessarily require the learning aspects inherent in adaptive management to be located in the public sphere, hence the term "civic science."

Managing large ecosystems should rely not merely on science, but *civic* science; it should be irreducibly public in the way responsibilities are exercised, intrinsically technical, and open to learning from errors and profiting from successes. Policies to learn must persist from times of biological significance, and they must affect human action on the scale of ecosystems. These are demanding conditions, difficult to assure even if governments had unlimited resources and needed only vision and will. In fact, of course, the degree of control and the magnitude of resources available are always scarce. The strategy I urge—

to be idealistic about science and pragmatic about politics—is meant to respond to these real conditions. (Lee, 1993, p. 161)

Lee also acknowledges the extent to which a learning-based policy model would depart from our more common approaches, which implicitly assume a degree of certainty and predictability that the systems thinkers now tell us is probably not attainable.

An emphasis on learning is an unconventional way to think about public policy. Most policies hum with the tension between efficiency and fairness—between maximizing some objective and sharing its benefits equitably. Learning may not lead to the most efficient or most equitable result, because fairness and equity are not enough to define good policy when knowledge is sparse. Face with ignorance, one can ignore it, or hope to learn enough by trial and error to muddle through, or try to overcome it. Although learning can sometime be deferred, the cost of information can never be evaded. (1993, p. 185)

While Lee's focus is on policy formation and the management of large ecosystems, Peter Senge addresses the business world. Senge is perhaps the most widely known writer in the topic of organizational learning (Senge, 1990; Senge et al., 1994). His focus is primarily on for-profit businesses, but his arguments are readily transferable to public or private nongovernmental organizations. Despite the different areas of interest, both Lee and Senge come to essentially the same conclusion, that quality learning is a key to sustainability. Lee is interested in sustaining the natural world and the human communities that rely on it. Senge is interested in a far less grandiose (but no less important) topic: sustaining companies in times of fierce competition and rapid change. His thesis is that the essential challenge of organizational effectiveness is to be a learning organization—one that learns quickly and reliably in order to adapt to a changing world. Put in a business context, a company cannot merely decide to be either the low-cost producer or the high-quality producer or the most responsive or the most thorough. It must variously exhibit all of those traits and more. In order to meet the needs of rapidly changing world markets and exploding technological options, the key to being competitive in the long term is to be a better learner than one's competitors. The learning organization will be exploring new options, dropping ventures when they appear to be dry holes, and reflecting on its mission and structure. To quote Senge:

As *Fortune* magazine recently said, "Forget your tired old ideas about leadership. The most successful corporation in the 1990s will be something called a learning organization." "The ability to learn faster than your competitors," said Arie De Geus, head of planning for Royal Dutch/Shell, "may be the only sustainable competitive advantage." As the world becomes more interconnected and business becomes more complex and dynamic, work must become more "learningful." It is no longer sufficient to have one person learning for the organization, a Ford or a Sloan or a Watson. It's just not possible any longer to "figure it out" from the top and have everyone else following the orders of the "grand strategist." The organizations that will truly excel in the future will be the organizations that discover how to tap people's commitment and capacity to learn at *all* levels in an organization. (1990, p. 4)

CONCLUSION

Learning is part of all decision processes. Because it is such an inherent part of both adult life and policy processes, formal models of decision making and public participation have often left it unexamined. Learning has received little attention in the context of policy processes because of implicit assumptions that it is pervasive, that it just naturally happens, and that it cannot be affected to any considerable extent. The purpose of this chapter is to illustrate that although learning is both pervasive and natural, it is not necessarily easy or omnipresent. It is certainly possible to design processes that preclude any authentic learning: make them passive, constrain the time so that the participants are rushed and tired, avoid participant-to-participant interaction by channeling communication through an official, vacillate about the bounds of the decision space, and so on.

The learning theories presented in this chapter provide four fundamental insights. First, Knowles' concepts remind us that adult learning should be active, respectful, and pragmatic. Second, Vella's principles of effective adult education offer a checklist of issues that the conveners and facilitators of collaborative discussions should bear in mind. Third, the notions of situational cognition show that collaborations create a powerful social setting that can potentially enhance the participants' learning. Finally, Kolb's model of experiential learning reminds us that the kinds of learning that occur in collaborations follow a fairly predictable pattern, from concrete experiences through reflective observation, abstract conceptualization, and active experimentation. This pattern becomes a rough template that Collaborative Learning processes can be built upon.

Chapter 6

Systems Thinking

> The idea of the adaptive whole is a very general idea, but it has also
> turned out to be a very powerful one, suggesting that the world is
> characterized by complex structure and much connectivity. This at least
> matches our intuitive feeling that the world is probably more like a
> dense privet hedge than a glass of water or a handful of marbles.
>
> —Peter Checkland and Jim Scholes,
> *Soft Systems Methodology in Action*

APPLICATIONS OF SYSTEMS THINKING

This chapter describes the way that Collaborative Learning uses systems thinking
and begins by considering the range of situations in which systems thinking is
useful. Three broad applications of systems thinking relate directly to
Collaborative Learning: organizational learning, community-level planning, and
natural resource management.

Organizational Learning

We ended Chapter 5 by introducing the Peter Senge's key ideas about the
learning organization. Senge (1990) contends that five disciplines are necessary
and sufficient to create a learning organization. Four of these are equally
important: personal mastery, mental models, building a shared vision, and team
learning. But a fifth discipline stands above the others and serves a more
integrative function; *systems thinking* is the *sine qua non* of organizational learning.
Senge asserts that systems thinking provides real leverage in organizational
thinking. The essence of systems thinking, according to Senge, is seeing

interrelationships rather than linear cause-effect chains, and processes of change rather than "snapshots."

The practice of systems thinking starts with understanding a simple concept called "feedback" that shows how actions can reinforce or counteract (balance) each other. *It builds to learning to recognize types of "structures" that recur again and again:* the arms race is a generic or archetypal pattern of escalation, at its heart no different from turf warfare between two street gangs, the demise of a marriage, or the advertising battles of two consumer goods companies fighting for market share. Eventually, systems thinking forms a rich language for describing a vast array of interrelationships and patterns of change. (Senge, 1990, p.73)

Community-level Planning

While Senge applies systems to formal organizations, systems thinking can equally important in understanding informally organized systems as well as situations that mix formal and informal structures. There is perhaps no better illustration of a mixed formal/informal situation than a town. A town has formal governance: laws, elected officials, procedures, and so on. It also has a physical structure: size, layout, location, and infrastructure. We think of many of its aspects as systems: water and sewer systems, transportation systems, electrical systems, school systems, and so on.

But towns are not merely physical or political entities; they are also communities. For our purposes, we can define community as a series of social interrelationships and structures. The social aspects of community start to involve the various organizations (clubs, churches, etc.), kinship groups, and social networks.

With this mental model of a town as an intermingling of formal municipality dimensions and more informal community dimensions, imagine some aspect of the town that the residents regard as a problem. The major employer in town might be reducing operations and laying people off, or the new subdivisions are straining public services and reducing the quality of life for longtime residents, or there may be high rates of drug use or pregnancy among teenagers. Whatever the problem, it will invariably involve more than one dimension of the town. Any event that occurs (employers come and go, new laws are passed by the state legislature, a natural disaster ensues) will have effects that ripple throughout the town's various formal and informal systems. By the same token, any ideas for improvement that are generated from within the community will have their own ripple effects across the systems that make the town what it is. Therefore, an evaluation of "better" cannot stop at the specific effects that the proponents might have intended on any one system but must consider the full range of intended and unintended consequences of the action.

Yet it often seems that our governmental structures and political processes are established with little regard for the systemic nature of the towns that we are trying to manage. Our school systems, public safety providers, revenue planners, and land planning departments have few formal lines of communication between them, but the pattern of land development in a town would surely affect them all and be affected by them as well. But without communication among the various systems, citizens lack the means to either anticipate or control the ripple effects that decisions in a particular aspect of the town have elsewhere.

If Senge is correct about the important role that learning plays in effective organizations and about the importance of systems thinking in organizational learning, then systems thinking has a central role to play in the continued improvement of our public decision making. This is true at all of the various scales, from an elementary school Parent Teacher Association through local and state government, and into the realm of international negotiation.

Natural Resource Management

Systems thinking plays an integral role in how we think about the environment, natural resources and their management. The concept of ecosystems—interconnected networks of climate, land, and biotic inhabitants—is a cornerstone of twentieth century biology. Much of ecosystem science can be traced back to the same systems theorists who provide the intellectual foundation for organizational thinkers such as Senge. In addition, the management paradigm *de jour* in natural resource management is "ecosystem management," which explicitly attempts to base management decisions on ecosystem principles. As such, it demands an organizational ability to think in systems terms, so as to understand the natural systems at issue and how the effects of any management action would ripple through these systems.

Despite the applicability of systems thinking to natural resource management, at least two major forces conspire to constrain it. First, virtually all natural resource managers have some measure of formal university education, particularly those in public agencies and corporations. This education includes a traditional philosophy based on ideas of reductionism developed by René Descartes that the way to solve complex problems is to reduce them into their component parts and solve each part in isolation. This approach has become so ingrained in education and scientific knowledge that its implications go unrecognized. As Checkland has noted:

The lesson (of reductionism) has been well learned, and the idea is deeply embodied not only in scientists, for whom the idea is central, but in anyone who has a Western-style education. Systems thinking, however, starts from noticing the unquestioned Cartesian assumption: namely, that a component part is the same when separated out as it is when part of a whole. This makes finding out about systems thinking very different from finding out about, say, Renaissance literature, the politics of the Middle East, or natural selection in the fruit fly. (1981, p. 12)

The second constraint on systems thinking in natural resource management and environmental policy making is that many of the management and regulatory organizations are organized in ways antithetical to a systemic approach. Environmental and natural resource agencies and companies use hierarchical organization, divide responsibilities along disciplinary lines that reinforce the effects of Cartesian reductionism, and parse administrative authority along political boundaries that often ignore ecological processes that transcend the politically drawn lines on the map. Numerous efforts to eliminate each of these barriers have sprung up in recent years as agencies and organizations attempt to "reinvent" themselves in order to pursue ecosystem management (Knight & Landres, 1998). Even so, the effects of these and other organizational constraints will not be easily or quickly overcome.

CONTRASTING LINEAR, NONLINEAR, AND SYSTEMS THINKING

Systems thinking is a way of seeing the world, a process of organizing information in order to understand its complexity. But it is not the only way of organizing information; two of the other common ways are known as linear and nonlinear thinking. We can better understand systems thinking by comparing and contrasting all three approaches. Table 6.1 presents lists of attributes for these different ways of organizing our thoughts. Many of us use predominantly linear thinking; certainly it is the dominant thinking approach embedded in Western (i.e., Eurocentric) education, science, and technology. It forms the basis for Newtonian physics and shapes our understanding of the world around us at a fundamental level. Nonlinear thinking, on the other hand, assumes that causality is not the simple "A causes B" model implicit in linear thinking. Rather it is possible for events to be caused by precursors so seemingly distant and removed as to be almost beyond comprehension. For example, a common metaphor among nonlinear thinkers is that a butterfly beating its wings in Asia could change the next month's weather in New York (Gleick, 1987). Instead of relying on a Newtonian view of the world, nonlinear thinkers can accommodate more ambiguity than can linear thinkers.[1] Nonlinear thinkers must learn to accept that some problems are not solvable, but the possibility of unsolvable problems is rarely acknowledged in science.

The solvable systems are the ones shown in the textbooks. They behave. Confronted with a nonlinear system, scientists would have to substitute linear approximations or find some other uncertain backdoor approach. Textbooks showed students only the rare nonlinear systems that could give way to such techniques. They did not display sensitive dependence on initial conditions.[2] Nonlinear systems with real chaos were rarely taught and rarely learned. When people stumbled across such things—and people did—all their training argued for dismissing them as aberrations. Only a few were able to remember that the solvable, orderly, linear systems were the aberrations. Only a few, that is, understood how nonlinear nature is in its soul. (Gleick, 1987, p. 68)

Systems thinking is yet a third way of organizing information, and focuses on networks of relationships and causality perhaps more than either linear or nonlinear thinking tend to do. As Checkland has observed:

Cursory inspection of the world suggests that it is a giant complex with dense connections between its parts. We cannot cope with it in that form and are forced to reduce it to some separate areas which we can examine separately. Our knowledge of the world is thus necessarily divided into different "subjects" or "disciplines", and in the course of history these change as our knowledge changes. Because our education is from the start conducted in terms of this division into distinct subjects, it is not easy to remember that the divisions are man-made and are arbitrary. It is not nature which divides itself up into physics, biology, psychology, sociology, etc., it is we who impose these divisions on nature; and they become so ingrained in our thinking that we find it hard to see the unity which underlies the divisions. (1981, p. 60)

Table 6.1
Comparing Linear, Nonlinear, and Systems Thinking

Linear Thinking	Nonlinear Thinking	Systems Thinking
Structure	Chaos	Relationships
Problem solving	Order without predictability	Associations
Hypothesis testing	Randomness	Unpredictability
Cause and effect	Infinite Complexity	Qualitative
Reductionist	Multi-directional	Quantitative
Rational Actor	Iteration	Emergence
Quantitative	Qualitative	Multi-directional
Comparison	Fractals	Iterative
		Transformation
		Feedback

The key point when comparing different thinking styles is that one style is not "bad" and another "good." Indeed, each offers us a way of understanding the world that the others do not. Any way of seeing is also a way of not seeing. We arguably would not have made technological progress without the rigor that the demand for reductionism, repeatability, and refutation has brought to linear thinking and the scientific method. But we might also not have the range of environmental problems to deal with if we had used a systems approach to anticipate that our technological advances might create unintended, negative consequences. In addition, the scientific method and Newtonian physics cannot cope with the sorts of problems that emerged in the wake of Einstein's work on relativity. Most complex situations probably require all three thinking styles—linear, nonlinear, and systems—and the most versatile thinkers can use them all. It is important to be able to match one's intellectual approach to the attributes of the situation at hand.

FUNDAMENTALS OF SYSTEMS THINKING

What, then, are the core notions of systems thinking? As noted earlier, systems thinking begins with seeing interrelationships rather than linear cause-effect chains and seeing processes of change rather than snapshots (Senge, 1990). While this provides a good start, we must certainly go well beyond these initial notions. It is important to recognize at the outset that since systems thinking is a way of organizing information, the systems representations that result are intellectual abstractions—human constructs. They offer a means of understanding the world by looking for relationships and interactions. Still, they are not "real" in the same way that many of their component parts are. In fact, much of their value flows from this abstract nature, because skillful systems thinkers can change their models of the system and think through the implications of those changes. But, especially in the ecological sciences, there is a tendency to reify the systems model—to regard it as being as "real" as its components.

Scale and System Models

A well-regarded text in forest ecology notes that "the term ecosystem is more of a concept than a real physical entity—a concept with six major attributes" (Kimmins, 1987, p. 26):

- Structure
- Function
- Complexity
- Interaction and interdependency
- Temporal change
- No inherent definition of spatial scale

Referring to the absence of any inherent spatial scale, Kimmins reinforces the notion that an ecosystem is less tangible than its parts:

An individual organism is a tangible entity. It has a clearly defined physical size. Populations and communities are also spatially defined entities, although their size may sometimes be rather difficult to define. A flock of birds or a school of fish constitute easily identifiable populations, but their spatial boundaries may be difficult to establish because the space they occupy may change periodically. Similarly, identification of a population of spruce trees in the northern boreal spruce forest or of a biotic community in the open ocean may require a somewhat arbitrary definition of spatial boundaries. However, in spite of these problems, the focus of attention in the terms *population* and *community* is clearly on a real physical entity that often can be defined quite easily. The biotic community of a clearcut or of a wet valley bottom can be readily observed and its spatial limits described. The term *ecosystem*, on the other hand, focuses on the structure, the complexity of organization, the interaction and interdependency, and the functioning of the system, and not on the geographical boundaries of the systems. (1987, p. 26)

Clearly, Kimmins' notion is that ecosystem concepts allow us to develop and use conceptual models of biotic and abiotic processes to better understand the world around us. The admonition in this passage is that ecological thinkers need the ability to think about ecological processes occurring over whatever spatial scale is relevant and to be willing to change one's scale of resolution in order to see what new understanding emerges as a result. If our notion of ecosystem becomes too rigid, too static, then we may lose some of our ability to ask

---

interesting questions and recognize previously unnoticed interrelationships. Our models may begin to become more "real" to us than the trees, streams, and mountains that they are intended to help us understand.

Classes of Systems

In his 1981 book, Checkland presents a classification scheme of general types of systems. The different classes of systems are:

- Natural
- Designed Physical
- Designed Abstract
- Human Activity
- Transcendent

For our purposes, it is useful to delete one of Checkland's classes, but add another. Transcendent systems refer to "systems beyond knowledge" (Checkland, 1981, p. 111), and while that is an intriguing intellectual category, it offers little practical value in Collaborative Learning projects. On the other hand, an addition to Checkland's list that has proven useful to us is the *designed natural system*, which is a useful category for understanding natural resource management.

Natural Systems. These are the systems on which the biologists and ecologists focus. The various scales of natural systems range from the subcellular to the global. Chemical processes, organismic functions, population dynamics, disturbance ecology, plant succession, nutrient cycling, hydrology, and countless other natural processes and structures can be understood as natural systems.

Designed Natural Systems. These are the domain of the farmer, rancher, and forester. In many ways, designed natural systems are intermediate between natural and designed physical systems. They are purposive human attempts to create goods or services from nature or in some way control natural processes. Managed forests, farms, and fish hatcheries all exemplify types of operations that are clearly designed and managed to meet objectives, but those objectives must be informed by the attributes and capabilities of the natural system, as well as by human preferences.

Designed Physical Systems. These systems we see around us every day: buildings, suspension bridges, electrical power grids, etc. They are designed purposively by people, but they have inert components rather than the living components found in designed natural systems. They are the domain of the engineer and builder.

Designed Abstract Systems. These systems are human constructs, but they are abstract in that the rules are not derived from, or constrained by, either physical or natural processes. Poetry, mathematics, and music are abstract systems. Each is characterized by sets of rules and systemic relationships, but their definitions are always open to reinterpretation.

Human Activity Systems. Managers, bureaucrats, workers, and bosses populate these systems. Human activity systems are organizations (often designed, sometimes not), where the fundamental building block is people and whose primary reason for existence is some form of activity to achieve some change. Companies, agencies, schools, and hospitals are all obvious illustrations. Social structures can similarly be thought of as human activity systems, in the sense that they provide a level of mutual defense or productive ability that individuals alone could not.

What Is a Farm?

From a systems perspective, what is a farm? It is a complex system that co-mingles at least three of Checkland's types: designed natural, designed physical, and human activity systems. It is a designed natural system because the fields and pastures are purposeful manipulations of natural processes; it is a designed physical system because of the engineered roads, buildings, and irrigation systems; and it is a human activity system because the organized efforts of people make it function.

We can use these different systems ideas to help us understand how we can think about the operation of the farm. Suppose that the farmer, her banker, and a crop specialist meet because the farm is not producing a profit, and their goal is to find a solution. If the farmer focuses on equipment effectiveness (a designed physical systems view), the banker on labor and insurance costs (a human activity systems view), and the crop specialist on the latest hybrid or planting technique (a designed natural systems view), they may talk right past one another. If they are going to generate different management ideas that offer the potential for authentic improvements which can save the farm from insolvency, then their ideas are going to have to be valid in all three domains of the farm. It does the farmer no good to dream of new equipment or to have the crop specialist offer some exciting new hybrid if the banker cannot get the financial numbers to pencil out. It likewise does no good for the banker to suggest cost-saving ideas that are not feasible given either existing technology or the productivity of the farm's soil.

One of the major values of clarifying these different system classes is that they are often interwoven at a fundamental level, and the failure to 'untangle' them can lead to unclear thinking. We have seen situations were people were trying to "fix" a situation, but they all saw different "problems" because they had different systems models in their heads. For people are going to collaborate effectively in a complex situation, at the very least they should engage the situation as the same systems type—they need to share the systems view. If some participants insist on viewing it only as one type of system, and others steadfastly view it as another, there will be a huge cognitive and rhetorical chasm that can impede both communication and progress.

Components of Systems

Moving beyond *types* of systems, it is possible to consider the *attributes* of systems; their building blocks, if you will. As Figure 6.1 illustrates, there are six core components in systems modeling:

- Elements
- Relationships
- Boundaries
- Environment
- Inputs
- Outputs

Elements. These are the "things," the nouns, of the system model. Whether they are cells, workers, computers, plants, and so on, they are the tangible items that we think of as constituting the system.

Relationships. These are the linkages among the elements in the systems model. They are the connections that allow the system to function dynamically, rather than merely be a hodgepodge of unrelated elements. Because relationships are typically active, they tend to be verbs: constrain, communicate, transport, transform, assemble, store, and so on.

Boundaries. These establish the edge of the system being modeled. Boundaries distinguish between elements and relationships within the system from material outside the system.

Environment. This is everything beyond the boundary. Like a boundary, this is an arbitrary choice because as the system modeler varies the boundary, elements and relationships can cross in and out of the system/environment threshold.

Inputs. These are things that flow from the environment into the system. These can be energy, water, money, raw materials, authority, and so on. Inputs are things that the system utilizes but does not provide for itself.

Outputs. These are the things that flow from the system into the environment. They may be both intentional (finished products, information, etc.), or they may be unintended or undesirable (waste, pollution, etc.).

Note that the systems modeler's choices in defining boundaries, environment, inputs, and outputs are interrelated. Returning to Kimmins' notion that ecosystems have no inherent boundary, we see that the modeler can establish at whatever point seems appropriate to the learning task at hand. The bounds placed on a system are inevitably arbitrary, because the system is connected in some way to other systems. The modeler's choice of where to put the line reveals how she or he *is* thinking about the situation, and in turn affects how she or he *can* think about it. The boundary is an explicit statement of what aspects of the real world the modeler views as outside the system and which aspects the model is designed to emphasize. Wherever the boundary is set, however, there will still be aspects of the real world—which are essential to the function of the system— that lie outside of this particular model. The result is that inputs (what the system employs) are conceived as *flowing into the system* and that outputs (what results from the system) are conceived as *flowing out of it*. But if the boundary is expanded, what might have previously been either inputs or outputs may now be entirely within the system. The definitions of environment, input, and output are all contingent upon the definition of boundary.

Figure 6.1
A System and Its Components

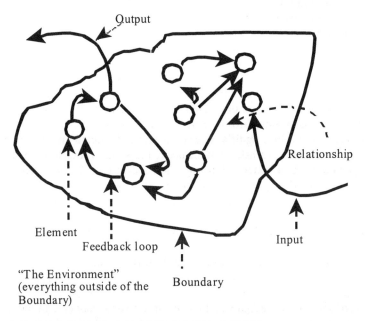

Source: Wallace Institute for Alternative Agriculture, Greenbelt, MD.

The act of setting the boundaries and how doing so affects one's thinking comprise a significant issue in systems thinking. Increasingly, business and organizational theorists have called on corporate leaders to see systems innovatively and openly (e.g., Ackoff, 1999; Scott, 1998; Sherman, 2000). They have recognized that companies should not necessarily view themselves as systems where both suppliers and customers lie outside the system, with raw material flowing in from the suppliers and finished goods shipped to consumers. Putting the bounds of a mental model of the system coincident with the formal definition of the company makes both the behavior of suppliers and the preferences of consumers exogenous to the company's own decisions. They are constraints that must be considered but cannot be affected by the company. As business theorists increasingly reject that notion, they argue that companies must form strategic alliances with suppliers and consumers to create more cost-effective, high-quality, zero-defect products with responsive service. They argue that we should strive to understand business as a seamless web of activity that runs from suppliers, through the company, into consumers. They are essentially asking managers to revise their mental models, to move the boundary out so that suppliers and consumers are no longer considerations in the environment, but are viewed as part of the system.

Common Systems Features

There are three defining dynamics to systems that provide much of their power in explaining complex situations. These are:

- Transformation
- Feedback loops
- Emergent properties

Transformation. In the systems literature, there are two different notions of transformations in systems. The first is that the system transforms other things. That is to say, systems are dynamic—they do things. At the core level, transformation is the concept of converting the inputs into the outputs. But that view merely considers transformations that are visible at the boundary of the system. As part of achieving that system-level outcome, there may be a myriad of smaller or intermediate transformations occurring within the system. Part of the challenge and value of systems thinking is to deconstruct the simple "inputs into output" notion of the system into its component intermediate transformations. Understanding them and their interactions is a big step in understanding the entire system.

The second notion of the transformative nature of systems is that *the systems themselves* have the ability to be transformed. This involves thinking about the dynamic nature of systems not only as doers but also as internal evolvers. Thus we need to be able to think about the structure and processes of systems dynamically, not as rigid monoliths.

Feedback Loops. A feedback loop is a familiar concept to many of us. It is when a system or part of one repeats a pattern of activity, often in a manner that continues to reinforce itself. All of us have heard the squeal of electronic feedback when a microphone is placed too close to a speaker (the feedback occurs when the microphone picks up sound from the speaker and transmits it back through the speaker). Systems thinkers have identified two different kinds of feedback: reinforcing (the feedback increases the initial behavior) and counteracting (the feedback reduces or negates the initial behavior), as well as a variant known as *feedforward* loops (when the anticipation of a future reaction changes current behavior).

Emergent Properties. While most people are familiar with the concept of feedback loops, the notion of emergent properties is less commonly understood. Emergent properties are scale-dependent because they are properties of systems that occur (or are apparent) only at the scale of the entire system. An attention to emergence in systems thinking flows directly from an attention to holism, and the presumption that the whole may, in fact, be more than the sum of the parts. In Checkland's terms, the principle of emergence is "that whole entities exhibit properties which are meaningful only when attributed to the whole, not to its parts . . . . Every model of a human activity system exhibits properties as a whole entity which derive from its component activities and their structure, but cannot be reduced to them" (1981, p. 314). Cartesian reductionism cannot recognize these emergent properties because when the system is reduced into its component parts as the first step in understanding it, the emergent property disappears.

One example of an emergent property is human health. If you try to figure out where health comes from, you will likely become frustrated. It does not "come from" some part of the system; it emerges from the system as a whole. This frustration will be particularly pronounced if you choose to intellectually "chop the system up" and say that the health comes only from diet or exercise or genetics. All may contribute at some level, but at another level, each is also individually insufficient. It may even be that health cannot even be adequately understood if we restrict our understanding to the physical realm. Social and spiritual issues may be just as integral to a complete understanding of health. Understanding health, because it is an emergent property, requires a holistic understanding of "human."

The notion of emergent properties flows directly from the ability to organize complexity at different hierarchical levels:

It is the concept of organized complexity which became the subject matter of the new discipline "systems"; and the general model of organized complexity is that there exists a hierarchy of levels of organization, each more complex than the one below, a level being characterized by emergent properties which do not exist at the lower level. Indeed, more than the fact that they "do not exist" at the lower level, emergent properties are *meaningless* in the language appropriate to the lower level. "The shape of an apple", although the result of processes which comprise apple trees, and although, we hope, eventually explicable in terms of those processes, *has no meaning* at the lower levels of description. The processes at those levels result in an outcome which signals the existence of a new stable level of complexity—that of the whole apple itself—which has emergent properties, one of them being the apple's shape. (Checkland, 1981, p. 78)

Emergent properties may be one of the reasons that systems thinking has an important role in natural resource management and public policy. If the world consisted entirely of situations in which their complexity was reducible—they could be adequately studied as component parts—then a more discipline-based, compartmentalized, and reductionist approach would solve all of the management problems. But we presume that the world has another set of problems—those in which an important part of the complexity arises at the systems level—then an additional set of intellectual tools is necessary. Indeed, when we think about a number of vexing public policy problems, we see that they are arising as emergent properties. In the natural resource arena, biodiversity, species conservation, and habitat effectiveness are all emergent properties of a set of effects among biotic, abiotic, and human systems. The efficient functioning of financial markets is increasingly an emergent property that arises at the global scale as a result of interaction between central banks, private investors, and regulators. Whether we turn our attention to health care, education, or communication, emergent properties are often the policy "stumpers." We may well be challenged to understand and manage these systems because we are constrained by a culturally ingrained tendency to try to simplify them, rather than to embrace their complexity. But if Checkland is correct, any attempt to reduce their intellectual complexity will dissipate rather than enhance our ability to manage the emergent properties.

Systems Thinking and Dog Training

The socialization of animals involves subtle yet powerful forms of feedback. The distinction between reinforcing and counterbalancing feedback explains why some dogs develop into calm family dogs, and others become more aggressive. If people are calm around a puppy, and reinforce appropriate behaviors with affectionate, positive behaviors, then a dog feels good about itself and its relationship to the humans. It wants to please, and that, in turn, makes it easier for the humans to display loving and gentle behavior toward the dog. Negative reinforcement, when used sparingly, can function as counteracting feedback that interrupts episodes of inappropriate behavior. But it is entirely possible, on the other hand, for the relationship to take a negatively oriented approach. Instead of reinforcing positive behavior, some humans send feedback only when the dog behaves inappropriately (i.e., they only exert discipline). Then the dog understands the humans more as defining what not to do, and it learns to avoid inappropriate behaviors out of fear of the consequences. This fear- and discipline-based relationship can be as self-perpetuating as the more positively focused approach: both are based on the notion of feedback. In both cases, behaviors of the dog generate reactions from the people that tend to reinforce the pattern of behavior of the dog.

Dynamic and Detail Complexity

While Senge does not use the term "emergent property" in his writing, he makes a similar distinction that is equally powerful. He differentiates between *detail complexity* and *dynamic complexity*, with the difference being that detail complexity refers to the nature of the components (and hence would be reducible), but dynamic complexity refers to the nature of the system as a whole (and hence would not be reducible). Situations that are dynamically complex have emergent properties; therefore Senge concludes that our analytical approaches need to accommodate dynamic complexity:

Why then have these supposed tools for dealing with complexity not empowered us to escape the illogic of the arms race?

The answer lies in the same reason that sophisticated tools of forecasting and business analysis, as well as elegant strategic plans, usually fail to produce dramatic breakthroughs in managing a business. They are all designed to handle the sort of complexity in which there are many variables: *detail complexity. But there are two types of complexity.* The second type is *dynamic complexity*, situations where cause and effect are subtle, and where effects over time of interventions are not obvious . . . When an action has one set of consequences locally and a very different set of consequences in another part of the system, there is dynamic complexity. When obvious interventions produce non-obvious consequences, there is dynamic complexity. (1990, p. 71)

Senge contends that we often confuse dynamic with detail complexity, and fundamentally misperceive the problem at hand:

The real leverage in most management situations lies in understanding dynamic complexity, not detail complexity . . . Unfortunately, most "systems analyses" focus on detail complexity not dynamic complexity. Simulations with thousands of variables and complex arrays of details can actually distract us from seeing patterns and major interrelationships. In fact, sadly, for most people "systems thinking" means "fighting complexity with complexity," devising increasingly "complex" (we should really say "detailed") solutions to increasingly "complex" problems. In fact, this is the antithesis of real systems thinking. (1990, p. 72).

SOFT SYSTEMS METHODS

The branch of systems thinking that forms the foundation of Collaborative Learning is *soft systems methodology* (SSM), which begins by categorizing systems into "soft" and "hard" types. Whether a systems situation is referred to as either soft or hard depends on the nature of the objective function—the goal or purpose—of the system. When a system has a clearly defined objective function, then the system is referred to as "hard." But if the objective function cannot be clearly defined, or there are competing notions of what the appropriate objective function ought to be, or there are multiple objective functions, then the problem is referred to as "soft" (Checkland, 1981). Hard problems can be delegated to specialists in operations research, systems analysis or systems engineering with the confidence that they will be able to derive solutions that achieve the objective. But they will not know how to begin if you give them a soft problem because the goals or ends are problematic—what are they trying to model, or simulate, or optimize?

Indeed, the purpose of Checkland's efforts throughout the 1970's and 1980's concentrated of the elaboration of systems notions for soft problems. As he explained in his 1981 book:

The next two chapters describe a research programme which aimed at developing ways in which systems ideas could be used in tackling soft, ill-structured problems. The programme assumed that the concept of a human activity system could be relevant to such problems, and hence its aims also included that of finding out more about descriptions of this kind. Its method was to tackle actual problems facing real-world managers; its criterion of success was that the people concerned feel that the problem had been "solved" or that the problem situation had been "improved" or that insights had been gained. (p. 146)

Checkland's efforts were driven out of a desire to see to what extent hard systems ideas could be applied to the somewhat more "fuzzy problems that managers face and to social problems which are even less well defined" (p. 150). Checkland:

did not imagine that the methods suitable for tackling 'hard' engineering problems would survive unscathed their transfer to 'soft' problem situations . . . A main outcome of the work is a way of using systems ideas in problem-solving which is very different from goal-directed methodology. It emerges from the research experiences as a systems-based means of *structuring a debate*, rather than as a recipe for guaranteed efficient achievement . . . (1981, p. 150)

Public policy problems often are a mix of soft and hard systems. Because public policy is redistributive, it is inevitably political. Much political debate is over the appropriate objectives of policies, and that debate is fueled by a complex mix of self-interest and deeply held values. The kinds of policy problems that we must therefore figure out how to engage are the soft ones, those where there are still disagreements over what the fundamental objectives are. There are too many situations where it is unlikely that we will ever agree at a fundamental level or where the process of crafting such an agreement would be too tortuous. We must be able to apply systems thinking to those problems for which there is not yet consensus on the preferred outcome. But as that soft systems debate about the desirability and feasibility of improvements occurs, it may be essential at various points to utilize various hard programming techniques to evaluate alternatives. That is both an essential part of crafting technically competent policy and entirely consistent with soft systems. As Wilson and Morren explain:

Note that the proposed use of the soft systems approach in government should not be confused with the already established uses of *other* systems approaches, such as operations research, systems engineering, management science, and cost-benefit analysis. These are of the hard systems type discussed elsewhere in this book. In the present context, the problem with the use of these techniques is that *in practice* they involve *designed systems* rather than *mutual learning*. (1990, p. 263)

Perhaps more than any other factor, Collaborative Learning incorporates soft systems methods because we recognize a need to meaningfully address the multiple worldviews that arise in most environmental and natural resource public policy decisions. Moreover, those worldviews are based at least in part on deeply held values, suggesting they are not likely to change quickly or dramatically. Different constituencies invariably look at natural resources in fundamentally differing, but equally legitimate, ways. A river may be alternatively a source of water, a recreational resource, a placer mining opportunity, or habitat for endangered salmon. A forest may alternatively be a source of wood fiber, spiritual renewal, or biodiversity. Any natural resource-related facilitation approach faces a fundamental choice: It can either work to achieve value congruence among the participants or it can attempt to structure debate that generates implementable improvements even as differences in worldview persist. Producing value convergence can be the basis of consensus vision of what ought to be done, and "fixing the problem" can then be boiled down to a hard optimization task in pursuit of that vision. There are certainly "visioning-type" approaches that concentrate on generating value convergence.[3] We have chosen a different approach in Collaborative Learning, one that emphasizes learning about the different values and worldviews and does not attempt to have all of the participants share the same values or goals.

CONTRASTING THE FORMULATIONS OF SOFT SYSTEMS

While there is much to value in Checkland's efforts in soft systems, Collaborative Learning draws more directly from the subsequent efforts by Wilson and Morren (1990), for two primary reasons. First, Wilson and Morren address agriculture and natural resource management. Second, Wilson and Morren make a significant improvement over Checkland's conceptualization of the soft system process by integrating the experiential learning concepts of Kolb. That adds a measure of rigor to the logic of how the stages in soft systems inquiry are sequenced. Checkland's original work in soft systems predates Kolb's model; in many ways, his process has a more ad hoc arrangement that emerges more organically from the experiences in soft systems projects.

Checkland's formulation of soft systems methodology is presented graphically in Figure 6.2. Note that it flows in a generally counterclockwise direction, and that the activities are divided into real world and systems thinking by the dashed horizontal line. Contrast that with the Wilson and Morren formulation presented in Figure 6.3 which flows clockwise and now identifies four different intellectual kinds of activity that must occur: these are Kolb's four different learning styles (see Chapter 5). While Checkland continually refers to soft systems as an inquiry process, he does not explicitly ground it in any particular learning theory. Wilson and Morren intentionally marry his original ideas with Kolb's notions of experiential learning and create a stronger model in the process.

THE BASIC WILSON AND MORREN APPROACH

Stage 1: Understanding the System

This stage is characterized by what Kolb refers to as reflective observation: engaging the real world in order to perceive it, and not necessarily to understand or explain it. As Wilson and Morren describe:

To *reflectively observe* means to watch something and think about it without drawing conclusions. It is the learning activity that accompanies the question "What does this mean?" Reflective observation is a precursor of assimilation when we impose some kind of conceptualization. Thus, reflective observation leads to a preliminary ordering of elements, a tentative identification of objects, a proposed definition of relationships, and so on. (1990, p. 117)

The essential task in stage 1 is to observe the situation from the point of view of the different stakeholders. The goal is not to begin to focus on any one view of the "problem" or come up with the "solution"; time for those activities comes later.

Rather, the task of stage 1 is to understand the richness of the situation, and much of that complexity will come from the multiple worldviews of the situation.

Figure 6.2
Checkland's Model of Soft Systems Inquiry

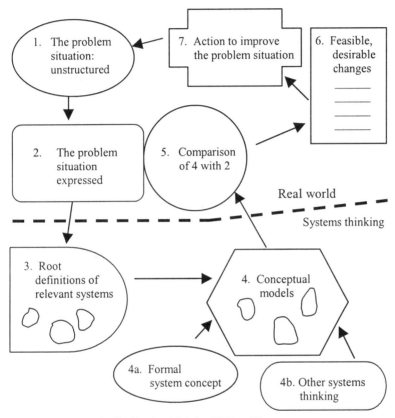

Sources: Checkland (1981); Checkland and Scholes (1990, p. 27).

Stage 1 is a "gathering" process; you collect people's accounts of what the situation is, and its history; stakeholders' opinions of other people and their perceived role in the situation; and their understanding technical issues involved in the situation. The task is not only to understand the various parties' views but to gather as much of the documentary information as practical: maps, charts, regulations, reports, newspaper stories, and so on. Understanding the situation includes both the parties and the context.

There are two inter-related challenges in this stage. First, there is a tendency to devote little time to this step or to even skip it entirely. The second is to cognitively anchor on the initial understanding that we develop of the situation and to remain intellectually wedded to that conceptualization of the situation. Often that conceptualization stems from our own disciplinary background: if we are engineers, then we see the situation as an engineering problem; if we are ecologists, then we see the situation as a natural phenomenon. Both of these tendencies should be resisted. The essential challenge of stage 1 is to avoid seizing an interpretation too quickly and to remain open to see the situation afresh, and with a minimum of preconceptions.

Figure 6.3
Wilson and Morren's Modification of Checkland's Soft System Model

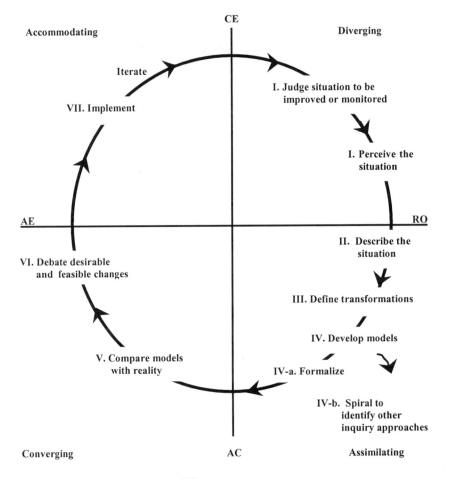

Source: Wilson and Morren (1990, p. 107).

Two analytic traditions offer important guidance in stage 1: qualitative sociology and Rapid Rural Appraisal. Qualitative sociology attempts to understand the nuances in people's lives and their social structures and processes. A common tool of qualitative sociology is semi-structured interviews or some other process by which the researcher can immerse himself or herself into the situation. The goal is to understand the situation as the research subjects understand it and to keep the influences of the researcher's own values to a minimum. It is a fundamental challenge to capture the full range of perspectives, not those that mirror our own or are held by people who resemble us (Erlandson et al., 1993; Lofland & Lofland, 1995; Wolcott, 1995).

Rapid Rural Appraisal (RRA) respects traditional knowledge. It assumes that rural people have valuable insights and information regarding the things that affect their lives. RRA has been defined as "a qualitative survey methodology using a multi-discipline team to formulate problems for agricultural research and development" (Dunn, 1994, p. 2). Dunn explains that "RRA has been particularly useful in the approach to complex problems, especially those in which 'people factors' are prominent" (1994, p. 2). RRA as a methodology emphasizes the present situation. As Dunn notes:

RRA embraces an holistic approach to the processes of defining a research context and selecting a team. Commonly RRA teams are multi-disciplinary, gender balanced and try to explore problems within their context. RRA is more "naturalistic" in its scientific approach. It does not attempt to control the research setting and is therefore not experimental or reductionist. (1994, p. 3)

Stage 2: Describing the Situation

The second stage of a soft systems approach, description, typically flows almost effortlessly out of the perception stage that begins the process. The task of stage 2 is to amalgamate the multiple perspectives that the researcher/analyst has just encountered into a single representation of the situation that accurately conveys the multiple worldviews of the stakeholders.

One of the more powerful techniques for this description stage is the construction of "situation maps": graphic representations of the complexity of the situation.[4] The details of how we use situation mapping are in the chapters on techniques (Chapter 8) and applications (Chapters 9 and 10). It is one of the few activities that we have used in virtually every situation we have facilitated, and we have more often been surprised than disappointed by its effectiveness.

As with the perception activities in stage 1, the challenge during this descriptive phase is to be both thorough and neutral. A good test of for these attributes is to ask if each of the stakeholders could see her or his own worldview reflected in the way in which the Collaborative Learning process is approaching the situation. The facilitator/analyst needs to be able to empathize with each of the worldviews, even though some will be quite different from the others and may in fact be at odds with her or his own perspective.

Stage 3: Developing Transformations

In this stage the user begins to convert his or her understanding of the real world into a more abstract representation. It begins the process of representing the complexity of the situation systemically. On Kolb's learning cycle diagram (see Figure 5.1), dropping below the horizontal axis represents this shift from the real world into the abstract. Stated in terms of Kolb's preferred learning styles, the shift is out of divergent learning and into assimilative learning. Assimilators' strengths are in reflective observation and abstract conceptualization. "They have particular strengths in inductive reasoning, formulating theory, and related activities such as modeling and concept building. As masters of induction, assimilators begin with various observations and logically arrive at a general statement explaining those observations" (Wilson & Morren, 1990, p. 39).

There are three essential tasks in stage 3, all of which begin to convert the relatively unorganized information gathered to this point into a systems understanding of the situation.

First, *transformation statements* are created, which designate basic features of an improved situation related to the themes of concern and primary tasks identified in stages 1 and 2. Second, each transformation statement is expanded . . . to become a *systems definition*, a blueprint for a conceptual model of the critical human activities envisioned to be in operation in a improved *future* statement. Third, conceptual models of *human activity systems* are formulated. (Wilson & Morren, 1990, p. 164)

Transformation Statements. As this explanation suggests, transformation statements are a key feature of SSM. Recall from earlier in this chapter that there are two different notions of transformation: transformations *by* the system of inputs into outputs, and transformations *of* the system into a different entity. A transformation statement that conveys both of these notions and follows this general form is: "This is a system to *change inputs* into *outputs*" or "This system creates *outputs* by *combining inputs*, subject to *environmental constraints*." A less generic illustration might be: "This farm is a system that grows winter wheat by combining the natural productivity of the land and climate with physical inputs (seed, equipment, fertilizer, etc.) and human inputs (hard work, knowledge, and risk)."

These transformation statements relate to the first notion of transformation, that is, transformation *by* the system. If we turn our attention to the second notion, transformation *of* the system, then the transformation statements begin to convey what the stakeholders think that they would like the system to be, not merely what it is now. Thus, the transformation statements can depart from mere description and begin to communicate values that the stakeholders have for the system

A compelling illustration of how transformation statements might differ, depending on the goals for a system, arose in the context of designing an undergraduate curriculum in horticulture. Within the faculty there were three distinctly different notions of what the essential transformation by the "horticulture education system" should be:

- It is a system to prepare entry level horticultural professionals to be competitive for jobs as soon as they graduate.
- It is a system to prepare students to succeed in the best graduate programs in horticulture or plant science.
- It is a system to generate the maximum number of student credit hours, with the minimum impact on faculty time.

Each of these three transformation statements would create an entirely different curriculum, and the conversion of the horticulture department from whatever it was at that time into one of these is transformation of the system itself.

The first transformation statement—to create entry-level professionals—would require a curriculum rich in the various pragmatic details that practicing horticulturists need on a day-to-day basis. This might range from cost accounting to the nuances of the latest pesticide application regulations, to knowledge of the policy processes that affect the agriculture industry. The second transformation statement—to create high-quality prospects for graduate schools—would require yet a different curriculum. The premium would be on more academic rigor in areas such as organic or analytical chemistry, statistics, and plant physiology; these are the foundations that would allow this educational system's graduates to prosper in graduate programs. The third transformation—to increase the size of the program with a minimum impact on the faculty—might seem cynical, but it is perhaps the most honest. The university from which this illustration is drawn, like many universities, used an accounting formula that allocated funding to departments based on the enrollments measured in terms of "student credit hours." Maximizing the student credit hours would therefore maximize the funding from the university to the program, and if the impacts on the faculty could be minimized, they would be able to pursue the various research and graduate training obligations that were also part of their academic obligations. A program that pursued this vision of a transformation statement might offer a number of well-designed, glitzy courses that appeal to students from across the university, as well as a major that was broadly appealing, and probably not too intellectually demanding.

But the important observation is that each of these transformations is based on a different vision for what the horticulture department might become. A faculty discussion of curriculum reform would consist of competing suggestions that represented each of these worldviews, although the worldviews might never be explicitly debated. The ability to allow the stakeholders to express and jointly evaluate multiple worldviews is a strength of soft systems that has been incorporated into the Collaborative Learning approach. It is neither productive nor respectful to engage in processes that convey to certain stakeholders that their worldview is invalid. If stakeholders receive that message, they may become defensive and exhibit behaviors ranging from aggression to passive non-communication or withdrawal.

The Importance of Multiple Transformation Statements

The acceptance of multiple worldviews and the exploration of the multiple transformation statements are one of the defining characteristics of soft systems methodology (SSM). Recall that "soft" problems are defined as those for which there is not agreement on the appropriate objectives for the system or even on the definition of the system. The generation of multiple transformation statements in stage 3 is the most tangible manifestation of SSM's willingness to explore multiple definitions of the situation.

As one traces this facet of the method back through Wilson and Morren (1990) and into Checkland (1981), the term that they associate with each of these different transformations is *Weltanschauung*, which we translate loosely from German as *worldview*. A person's worldview is the image—or mental construct—through which he or she interprets the world and assign values to different experiences, behaviors, and outcomes. It is therefore a multifaceted concept that includes notions such as values, goal, perceptions, and attitudes. Each transformation statement is a reflection of a particular worldview, which in turn reflects the stakeholders' aspirations and core values. Much of the psychological research on various facets of worldviews concludes that they become established in our youth, and there is relatively little change or updating of them as we age. (This is more so with core values such as the belief in right and wrong, and less true with attitudes toward specific events or behaviors.)

In recognizing the diversity of people, we must also recognize the diversity of their worldviews. Operating on the premise that worldviews are relatively inelastic psycho-social interpretations of the world, then it seems that a facilitation design that pursues value convergence is, in fact, embarking on a strategy that is contradictory to our understanding of the psychological factors that give rise to those worldviews. An alternative approach is to recognize that multiple worldviews exist, find ways to elicit them (which is the goal of stages 1 and 2), and then allow those multiple worldviews to coexist within the inquiry process as long as possible.

Expanding the Transformation Statement. While a set of transformation statements is a crucial beginning to a systems understanding, it is by no means sufficient. It is necessary to flesh out transformation statements into as much detail as is useful. Both Wilson and Morren (1990) and Checkland (1981) focus upon human activity systems, and both employ the mnemonic device of TACWOE (see below). The situations in which Collaborative Learning has been applied are not pure human activity systems—they involve designed physical or natural systems as well. Therefore, adequately expanding transformation statements may require other systems models in addition to a TACWOE-based discussion of the human activity system.

Stage 4: Modeling

This stage continues the convergent thinking that began in stage 3 by increasing the level of abstraction of the models. Because stages 3 and 4 are in the same quadrant of Kolb's learning diagram (Figure 5.1), they share the same learning tasks, and it can be difficult to tell precisely where one stage ends and the other begins. A key difference between them is that the modeling activities in stage 3 focus on the system that *is*; the modeling in stage 4 begins to examine the systems that *could be*.

A number of tasks can occur during stage 4:

- Clarify transformation statements.
- Develop subsystems.
- Define inputs and outputs.
- Define boundaries/resolve issues of scale.
- Develop measures of performance.
- Agree on decision processes.
- Clarify the effects of the environment on the system (Wilson & Morren, 1990).

Consistent with these tasks, a number of different kinds of modeling activities are appropriate in stage 4. If the system being studied is a human activity system, then the models can focus on developing an organizational system to fulfill the essential tasks. But this is also the point in the soft systems process when other models can be woven into the inquiry process. Many different forms of economic, ecological, and social modeling could be used to examine alternative futures. Benefit/cost analysis, geographic information systems, habitat viability models, and social impact assessment all exemplify the range of technologies that can be used to examine tradeoffs associated with the different strategies that stakeholders see as potentially improving the situation.

Components of the TACWOE Mnemonic Device

(T) Transformation. This refers to the defining task or purpose, of the system.

(A) Actors. These are the people responsible for performing the activities needed to make the system function. They are the human elements in the system, and can be defined in terms of the activities that they would carry out.

(C) Customers. These people are affected, either positively or negatively, by the function of the system. While this term includes customers in the traditional business sense, it can also refer to people with a number of other relationships to the system, for example, suppliers, partners, neighbors, and regulators. Identifying the customers is a particularly useful step when the transformation statement that you are expanding differs substantially from the current situation. If the situation was changed to reflect this new objective, there may well be both winners and losers in that process. Recognizing that eventuality and the potential political wrangling that it might engender is certainly useful.

(W) Worldview. As noted earlier, worldview refers to the values and assumptions of the stakeholders. What they prefer to be the system's function and why are important factors when expanding the transformation statement into a more complete expression of the system. Without it, the reason for the system and the motivation for any improvements to it are lacking.

(O) Owners. These people have power within the situation either to make a transformation occur or to veto it. In many ways, owners overlap with actors because both play an important role in the function of the system. The distinction is that owners have decision authority over the system. *"Owner* means those people or official positions that the designers of the system want to have enough influence, decision-making authority, and responsibility to be able to cause the proposed system to be altered; maintained under adverse, as well as normal, conditions; or cease to exist in an improved state of affairs." (Wilson & Morren, 1990, p. 171).

(E) Environment. This term refers to those factors outside the system being modeled. These factors can include both constraints and resources and need to be understood as exogenous to efforts to operate within the system or to improve it. Environmental factors can include economic parameters (interest rates, exchange rates, commodity prices, etc.), policy parameters (laws and regulations, procedural issues, and political environment, etc), and biophysical parameters (native species, soil productivity, climate, etc.).

Because of the time, effort, and expertise required to conduct the kinds of modeling activities conducted in stage 4 of the soft systems method, this is the point in Collaborative Learning when the emphasis on public participation is perhaps the least. In many of the Collaborative Learning projects we have conducted, this is a point when the process reverts back to conventional, expert-driven analysis activities. The key difference between Collaborative Learning and more conventional approaches is that the kinds of questions that the experts are modeling in a Collaborative Learning project have been informed by a dialogue process that is richer than typically occurs.

At the very least, stage 4 ends with at least two models: a model of the current situation that was developed in stage 3 and a model of an improved situation that can be achieved through the implementation of desirable and feasible changes. But because there may be multiple worldviews of the fundamental system objectives, it follows that multiple improved systems will emerge from this stage. The next two stages analyze and debate these different systems that could be adopted. In this feature there is a strong parallel between Collaborative Learning and rational comprehensive planning methods that develop a range of alternatives to analyze (e.g., planning pursuant to NEPA).

Stage 5: Analysis of the Models

The output from stage 4 is a set of models that systemically represent improved versions of the current situation. Each model and its notion of "improvement" correspond with one of the worldviews of the situation that were identified in stages 1 and 2. In turn, each model may consist of a set of models, where each describes one of the subsystems involved.

In Kolb's terminology, stage 5 marks the transition away from reflective observation (RO) into active experimentation (AE). It begins the part of the learning process known as convergence, which is loosely equivalent to beginning to "converge" on a strategy that can address the problematic dimensions of the current situation. Figure 6.3 illustrated this by moving to the left of the vertical axis.

In stage 5 of the soft systems approach, convergence is practiced when one or more conceptual models of human activity systems are compared to the situational summary or composite mind map of a problematical situation. The proposals for change that arise from matching conceptual models to the picture of reality stimulate discussion among participants. The comparison stage offers the analyst/facilitator and others involved an opportunity to determine the relevance of one or more conceptual models. At the least, comparing the fruits of conceptualization to the reality experienced in a situation can reveal new insights about what is problematical. (Vietor & Cralle, 1990, p. 213)

The primary task of stage 5 is to allow the participants in the process to understand the essential differences between the various conceptualizations of "desirable and feasible change" that have been developed up to this point. The efforts so far have been nonjudgmental, in the sense that each of the worldviews that were identified among the participants was expanded into a transformation statement and systems model, regardless of whether that worldview was either widely held or particularly practical.

Stage 6: Debating Desirability and Feasibility

This stage flows naturally out of stage 5 because it involves the debate of the different sets of improvements that have been developed thus far in the process. Indeed, stage 5 can be brief as the participants in the situation begin to juxtapose the relative strengths and liabilities of the different models, thereby making the transition into stage 6.

As we shall see in the chapters on Collaborative Learning applications, this is a stage when the management of the social environment is crucial. During this debate stage everything must "gel"; if good ideas are going to result from the Collaborative Learning effort, they must emerge here. But if old interaction patterns of positional discourse and personal attack are going to persist, they emerge here as well.

The debate during this phase is over the desirability and feasibility of improvements. Many public participation methods are able to elicit comments that primarily convey people's notions of desirability. Very few mechanisms also require that the public participants apply the test of feasibility to their comments.

As such, the comments that agencies receive are both internally inconsistent (for every comment that says "go right," there are also comments that say "go left"), and also impractical given biological, fiscal, or regulatory constraints. Thus, all of the feasibility burden falls on the "experts" in the process, who may never have the opportunity to explain directly to members of the public why the improvement they seek cannot be achieved, completely apart from any questions of its desirability.

But by the same token, both technical experts and officials are often trained to believe that they can, and should, keep their notions of desirability out of the process. That may not be possible to do, and even it were possible, it would rob the public discourse of some important information. In addition, if the values of the experts running the process are not allowed to be included overtly, then they may well be included covertly. Such a hidden agenda can do little to close the chasm of mistrust that exists between the governed and their government.

Flood and Jackson (1991) make an interesting point about the debate stage of soft systems. They contend that SSM seeks to generate improvements that are *systemically desirable* and *culturally feasible*. That is, they regard the test of desirability as applying not to culture so much as to the systemic attributes of the situation and regard feasibility as applying to cultural aspects of the situation. Although that may appear to reverse the logical structure of the task (when we initially used SSM, it seemed that the task was to achieve systemic feasibility and cultural desirability), the Flood and Jackson pairing is insightful and may be preferable:

The real point, Checkland would stress, is that the models are meant for generating meaningful debate where participants discuss potential improvements that are worthy of consideration. By this time, we have ensured that the models conform to systemic desirability (since they have emerged from the logic-based stream of enquiry) and we have some idea of whether they are culturally feasible (we have been carrying out cultural enquiry). The debate stages finally confirm which changes are indeed culturally feasible in this organization at this time. (Flood & Jackson, 1991, p.177)

Stage 7: Implementation

Of course a soft systems or Collaborative Learning process would be only so much talk if the ideas generated were not put into action. Stage 7 addresses that need.

The main tasks of the implementation stage are (1) to design an implementation plan, (2) to carry out the specific and highly varied actions of that plan, (3) to communicate the specifics to all affected parties, including, but not limited to, actors who have not previously been directly involved in the process, (4) to monitor performance and the environment and evaluate results, and (5) to modify aspects of the plan if information accrues requiring it. (Wilson & Morren, 1990, p. 282)

In terms of Kolb's model, we have moved out of the realm of abstraction, back into contact with the real world (above the horizontal axis in Figure 5.1). The learning that occurs during implementation results from concrete experience.

Because of the number of participants involved in a situation that requires a systems-based inquiry method such as Collaborative Learning, coordinating the efforts of all of the participants and ensuring timely and orderly implementation require a large measure of communication, leadership, and shared commitment. Many tools used in strategic planning are useful at this point, including performance criteria, timetables, needs-based budgets, clear lines of accountability and authority, and so on.

During this implementation stage the role for the facilitator/analyst begins to dissipate. The participants in the situation, not the facilitator/analyst, must implement the changes and live with the results. As Wilson and Morren note:

Hands off is the watchword. The more the people involved do for themselves, the better their learning. The analyst/facilitator's value is his or her ability (1) to offer advice, encouragement, and approval; (2) to cycle through the soft systems approach again if necessary, even reconvening a debate if some phases of implementation are seen to be seriously unraveling; and (3) to function as a resource person. (1990, p. 285)

THE NEED FOR A SYSTEMS APPROACH TO NATURAL RESOURCE AND ENVIRONMENTAL CONFLICTS

The situations in which we have applied Collaborative Learning have all been natural resource conflicts. Even though we feel that Collaborative Learning has applicability far beyond that particular sphere, we would like to focus briefly upon natural resource management. Specifically, we make the case for using systems-based inquiry processes in natural resource management. These ideas apply to the related environmental policy arena as well.

The overarching motivation for using systems-based inquiry is that natural resource management is increasingly characterized by a high degree of complexity. As the knowledge of natural systems increases, we attempt to craft management strategies that reflect that knowledge; hence they become increasingly complex. Moreover, that complexity does not reside within any particular discipline. Rather, it tends to be far more intellectually crosscutting as it combines elements from ecology, soil science, engineering, economics, and social psychology. The expansive nature of natural resource debates—where everything seems to be connected to everything else—would seem to be a ready-made situation for systems thinking.

As we consider the vexing questions in natural resource management, it appears that some of the most confounding issues can be explained by the systems concept of *emergent properties*. The cumulative effects clause from regulations pursuant to NEPA[6], the current emphasis on ecosystem management by the USDA-Forest Service and the USDI-Bureau of Land Management, and the challenges in the conservation of threatened species and the habitat upon which they depend all exemplify situations with a transcendent complexity that defies the kind of linear, reductionist thinking that comes so easily to both individuals and agencies.

Finally, consider what cognitive choice people face when they do not have a mental construct that is adequate to accommodate the complexity of the situation at hand. What are their options if they do not have a way of processing the complexity? There appear to be two: (1) give up and stop trying to be involved, or (2) simplify the mental model of the situation to create a manageable task. Neither outcome is particularly constructive. The first choice—withdrawal—is obviously not desirable when the goal is to construct a civic dialogue about policy. But the second—simplification—has some more subtle effects.

A particular simplification behavior has occurred sufficiently often in our projects that we have given it a name—single-devil bias. The behavior is fundamentally a simplification behavior; in an attempt to manage the complexity in the situation, individuals start constructing a mental story of the dynamics that have created the problems in the situation. More often than not, these stories explain the situation as involving a single precipitating party, behavior, or event that has created "the" problem. That single cause is what we refer to as the single devil. From a systems perspective, there are at least two flaws in simplifying the situation to such an extent. First, there is not just one notion of the problem because those features of the situation that someone finds problematic are grounded in her or his worldview. Second, none of the situations in which we have been involved have been created by a single devil; rather, they have resulted from a complex set of past decisions, natural events, and unintended consequences. Every situation is driven by multiple forces, and there are multiple points of leverage from which to affect it. But that ability is greatly diminished when the stakeholders are all operating on the basis of their own individually constructed single-devil biases, because each of these overly simplified stories would argue that the problem could be solved if only we attribute all of the blame and need to change to that single devil.

A Perspective on Systems Thinking

C. West Churchman was among the first generation of systems thinkers in the 1950s and 1960s. His thinking has certainly been influential in a number of branches of systems thinking, notably operations research and soft systems. Near the end of his book *The Systems Approach* (1968) he provides four propositions about the nature of systems thinking that we might all keep in mind:

- The systems approach begins when first you see the world through the eyes of another.
- The systems approach goes on to discover that every worldview is terribly restricted.
- There are no experts in the systems approach.
- The systems approach is not a bad idea

Taken together, these notions create a sense of humble optimism. The humility comes from the dual recognition that (1) any way of understanding the world is partial, and there are other equally valid ways of understanding it, and (2) we are unlikely, even using a systems approach, to fully understand it or to even fully master systems thinking as a way of understanding the complexities of the world around us. The optimism emerges from the understanding that once one recognizes the boundedness of any understanding, then having an incomplete or partial view of the world is easier to embrace.

There is no expectation of perfection in a systems thinking approach, and no implied expectation that the systems thinker can, and should, strive to create a perfect or exhaustive model. This attitude, a Zen-like acceptance of the reality that one cannot fully grasp or control, flows into Collaborative Learning; it frames the collaborative task as the search for incremental improvement rather than global solution. Solution is not an achievable goal if factors affecting systemic performance are outside the control of the participants. The appropriate metric of satisfaction is therefore improvement in the situation, where improvement is defined as desirable and feasible change. By the same token, our own personal development as systems thinkers and Collaborative Learning facilitators should be similarly incremental: always learning, always trying new things, and never presuming our own "expertness" is adequate. This notion is echoed by Senge:

If a learning organization were an engineering innovation, such as the airplane or the personal computer, the components would be called "technologies." For an innovation in human behavior, the components need to be seen as disciplines. By "discipline," I do not mean an"enforced order" or "means of punishment," but a body of theory and technique that must be studied and mastered to be put into practice. A discipline is a developmental path for acquiring certain skills or competencies. As with any discipline, from playing the piano to electrical engineering, some people have an innate "gift," but anyone can develop proficiency through practice.

To practice a discipline is to be a lifelong learner. You "never arrive"; you spend your life mastering disciplines. You can never say, "We are a learning organization," any more than you can say "I am an enlightened person." The more you learn, the more acutely aware you become of your ignorance. Thus, a corporation cannot be "excellent" in the sense of having arrived at a permanent excellence; it is always in the state of practicing the disciplines of learning, of becoming better or worse. (Senge, 1990, p. 10-11)

CONCLUSION

Although written accounts of systems inquiry can seem tedious and rigid, Collaborative Learning is in reality dynamic and flexible. In reflecting upon the Collaborative Learning projects behind us, we can confidently say that we have never gone through the process exactly the same way twice. Each situation offers different opportunities and obstacles, and our applications of both soft systems methodology and mediation theory have responded accordingly. This chapter's general discussion of soft system methodology does not intend to suggest that soft systems methods comprise a prescriptive approach. Certainly Flood and Jackson (1991) echo that notion:

Although we have described SSM as a somewhat rigid seven stage process, we must emphasize again that it is very rarely used that way. Each use of the methodology must be adapted to the context in which it is employed—it is this which makes SSM more than a technique. Different users will also bring their own flavour to the methodology. During any study employing SSM, it is as important to reflect upon the context of use (cultural enquiry) and the way the methodology is being used, as it is to go through the stages themselves. Every use of SSM tackles problem situations but should also involve reflection on the methodology and way it can be employed. So there is learning in the world about the problem situation, and also about the methodology itself. (p. 178)

Systems thinking is essential to active, social learning about complex and controversial situations. Drawing on work in soft systems, Collaborative Learning incorporates systems thinking as a significant component, in both philosophy and practice. Enacting systems thinking in the practice of Collaborative Learning relies on effective communication, the focus of the next chapter.

NOTES

1. Perhaps the most widely discussed book that applies non-linear thought to management is Wheatley (1992), which attempts to move beyond a Newtonian view of managing organizations by integrating concepts from quantum physics, self-organizing systems, and chaos theory.
2. This condition creates the butterfly effect referred to earlier.
3. Two popular methods for stakeholder visioning and value convergence is "future search" (Weisbord & Janoff, 1995) and "search conferencing" (Emery, 1982, 1983; Diemer & Alvarez, 1995).
4. The term in Wilson & Morren (1990) for these maps is "mind maps", drawn from Buzan's (1983) use of the term. Our Collaborative Learning projects have always involved a segment of people who were dubious of overly academic terms or "touchy-feely", "new age" approaches. We have substituted the phrase "situation map" for "mind map" because the former seems to be more content neutral and less problematic than the latter. See the section on situation mapping in Chapter 8 for a longer discussion of the issues related to sensitivity to this term.
5. The TACWOE mnemonic has appeared in various forms. Wilson and Morren (1990) present it as "CATWOE." The Wallace Institute for Alternative Agriculture's project on community visioning about food and agriculture policy employs "TACOWE." We have presented the framework as "TACOWE" for four reasons: (1) this format puts the improvement or "transformation" first, (2) the parties or stakeholders—actors, customers, and owners—are together, followed by their worldviews, (3) the environment—those factors that affect the system but are outside the system's boundary—comes last, and (4) TACOWE is easy to pronounce and remember (TACK and COW).
6. When considering the environmental impact of a proposed action, the cumulative impacts must be assessed. This is "the impact on the environment which results from the incremental impact of the action when added to the other past, present, and reasonably foreseeable future actions regardless of what agency (Federal or non-Federal) or person

undertakes such other actions. Cumulative impacts can result from individually minor but collectively significant actions taking place over a period of time". (40 CFR 1508.7)

Chapter 7

Collaborative Learning, Communication, and Culture

> It is the province of knowledge to speak and it is the privilege of wisdom to listen.
>
> — Oliver Wendell Holmes

We wrote this book in part because of requests from natural resource management professionals and citizens concerned about environmental issues. For several years we have worked with land management agencies and communities on natural resource management decisions. During the past decade we conducted numerous Collaborative Learning training programs for land management agency personnel and interest group leaders and facilitated many Collaborative Learning citizen workshops. In both the training programs and community meetings, we introduced people to systems thinking and conflict management via active, experiential learning. As we did so, we attempted to facilitate, model, and teach competent communication.

As we applied Collaborative Learning within agencies and communities, we were struck by people's need and desire to communicate well. Professionals from various agencies and nongovernmental organizations (NGOs) report in informal conversation that effective, clear communication is very important to the work that they do. They often remark that they regret not having taken communication courses in college. Citizens often express similar sentiments. Like agency staff, they comment that they know that good communication in natural resource management situations is essential. Citizens and agency staff alike note the need for "good communication with the government" or "good communication with the public," without necessarily clarifying what "good communication" might include.

This chapter draws upon these conversations in addressing "good communication" as part of Collaborative Learning. First, we offer a view of communication in the context of environmental conflicts. Second, we discuss the nature of communication competence. Third, we propose seven communication skills relevant to Collaborative Learning and collaboration in general. Fourth, we show how competent communication can foster meaningful dialogue between scientists and citizens. Finally, we explore the challenge of intercultural communication competence and how it can help us manage natural resource conflict effectively.

COMMUNICATION AND COLLABORATIVE LEARNING

As we outlined in Chapter 2, Collaborative Learning is a framework for conflict management, public participation, and decision making in public policy settings, particularly environmental and natural resource management situations. In each of these contexts, Collaborative Learning integrates and applies systems, learning, and conflict management through meaningful communication. In their classic work *Getting to Yes*, Fisher et al. emphasize that "there can be no negotiation without communication" (1991, p. 30). Similarly, there can be no Collaborative Learning without communication.

The Nature of Communication

Communication is a multidimensional concept. It refers to the transmission of a message, from some sender to some receiver. It can take place in many different settings, from interpersonal to group to public. Communication can occur via various channels, from face-to-face interaction to messages sent through some medium, such as television or the Internet. As James Carey notes, "Communication is a symbolic process whereby reality is produced, maintained, repaired, and transformed" (1989, p. 23).

Regardless of the context, communication is fundamentally about meaning. The recipients of messages interpret those messages, and in doing so, assign meaning to those messages. But people do not hold meanings in isolation; they share their interpretations with others. This sharing reveals that meanings are socially constructed, both individually and collectively.

A Social Construction Perspective

A social construction view regards communication as fundamentally a process of creating shared meanings. We send messages as objectively measurable statements, but as recipients we generate the *meanings* those messages convey. The meanings we assign to communication draw upon our knowledge and experience. Whether we interact in pairs, groups, organizations, or public settings, we generally have three options for interpreting a communicative act. First, we can accept in entirety the meaning and interpretation another party has generated. Second, we can attempt to impose our own meaning on the other party. But these options are neither viable nor likely in most communication situations. Hence, the third option:

we must negotiate shared meanings and interpretations with those of the other party. In so doing, the "persons-in-conversation co-construct their own social realities" (Griffin, 1997, p. 69). Proponents of this view include Pearce and Cronen (1981). They have theorized, in their "coordinated management of meaning" work, that joint discourse is the primary social process of human life, forming the "webs of social interaction in which we find ourselves and in which we live, move, and have our being" (Pearce, 1994, p. 19).

This negotiation is critical to the development of a shared understanding. People do not act in isolation; their actions occur within relationships, groups, and communities. Our communication is directed at others or affects others and is interpreted by others. A fundamental goal in communication is shared understanding, a goal acquired through coordinating our meanings and interpretations. As we listen to others explain their views on an issue, for example, we can relate our views to theirs. We can determine to what extent our meanings are similar, different, and possible to coordinate. Shared understanding is not synonymous with agreement. Rather, shared understanding denotes that, at some level, parties understand one another's views and interpretations. For example, two parties may hold fundamentally different views about what sustainability means (Peterson, 1997) or what government agencies should do about an endangered species such as the spotted owl (Moore, 1993; Lange, 1993). The parties achieve shared understanding when they understand one another's point of view and recognize that they will not likely ever reach agreement on the issue.

Furthermore, communication is reflexive. A "reflexive" process is one that reflects back upon, and changes itself. For example, your reflection in a mirror may cause you to alter your appearance, thus changing your image in the mirror. People tend to analyze their communication behavior after it has occurred (e.g., "I wish I had not said that"). Communication reflexivity means we can reflect upon our communication behavior and "metacommunicate," that is, "talk about our talk" or communicate about how we communicate. Similarly, we can analyze and reflect upon our communication behavior in anticipation of a communication situation.

COMMUNICATION AND COLLABORATIVE LEARNING: DIALOGUE AND DELIBERATION

Shared understanding and discovering areas of both agreement and disagreement are goals of Collaborative Learning. The generation of improvements—desirable and feasible actions or changes—hinges on constructive communication. Consistent with a social construction perspective, we consider communication to be human symbolic activity through which meanings are constructed and negotiated and some degree of understanding achieved.

Constructive communication is important throughout a Collaborative Learning process, but it takes on different forms at various stages in the Collaborative Learning cycle. In the early stages of Collaborative Learning, when understanding the situation, viewing the situation systemically, and identifying concerns and interests are the goals, communication emerges as dialogue. As participants in a

Collaborative Learning process begin to generate improvements, their dialogue evolves into deliberation.

Dialogue

Dialogue refers to communication interaction between parties that hold discovery, learning, and understanding as their primary goals. Dialogue draws its strength from both the commitment and skills of the participants. One of the foremost writers on dialogue, the late physicist David Bohm, explains that via dialogue:

A group of people can explore the individual and collective presuppositions, ideas, beliefs, and feelings that subtly control their interactions. It provides an opportunity to participate in a process that displays communication successes and failures. It can reveal the often puzzling patterns of incoherence that lead the group to avoid certain issues or, on the other hand, to insist, against all reason, on standing and defending opinions about particular issues. (Bohm et al., 1991/1998, p. 1)

Dialogue is open, nonjudgmental communication (Yankelovich, 2000). Participants in a dialogue listen intently, ask questions to learn and understand, and see tremendous worth in the collective wisdom of the participants. In *The Fifth Discipline,* Peter Senge writes that dialogue is essential to team learning. Citing Bohm's work, Senge notes the importance of "thought as a collective phenomenon" (1990, p. 240). Dialogue is important to Collaborative Learning; it is the form of communication that creates a shared understanding of the situation. Writers on dialogue make distinctions among "dialogue," "discussion," "debate," and "argument." We see these distinctions as somewhat artificial and contrived. We regard dialogue as a form of open, learning-oriented discussion. Dialogue is a form of discussion, a process in which parties communicate openly, constructively, and respectfully. In the early stages of Collaborative Learning, participants engage in dialogue as they seek to develop a shared understanding of the situation. As Collaborative Learning participants work through the stages of the CL process, their dialogue about concerns, interests, and possible improvements evolves into deliberation. As their conversation becomes increasingly deliberative, their decision-oriented discussion retains the qualities of their earlier dialogue.

Deliberation

The Dialogue Canada project offers an example of how dialogue can be valued and incorporated into society. In Collaborative Learning processes, dialogue is valued along with deliberation. As Collaborative Learning progresses through "situation understanding" and "situation improvement" stages, the parties' dialogue becomes increasingly decision oriented. As participants refine improvements, they deliberate about the desirability and feasibility of the actions or changes proposed.

The Dialogue Canada Project

Dialogue Canada is a non-profit, non-partisan, non-governmental association of individual citizens who are dedicated to encouraging communication among the diverse elements of Canadian society, whether linguistic, cultural, regional or ethnic. Its mission statement includes the following:

We believe that education, communication and participation are the components with which dialogue is established.

We believe that dialogue based on mutual respect is a key tool for the resolution of our problems and differences. Most important, we believe that ordinary citizens have a role to play in establishing dialogue and a responsibility to carry it out.
We believe that Canada is a model for the world in its demonstrated capacity for evolutionary compromise, in its respect for minority rights and its work for peace at home and abroad. But conflicts still exist. We want to be able to find new solutions as change raises new challenges. These solutions must be based on values shared and respected by all communities.

This activity emphasizes constructive, collaborative argument. Deliberation in Collaborative Learning is similar to "debating desirable and feasible change" in soft systems methodology (Wilson & Morren, 1990). In Collaborative Learning, participants experience both dialogue and deliberation; both are important communication orientations.

Dialogue provides a foundation for deliberation. Whereas dialogue emphasizes learning and understanding, deliberation builds upon that learning and understanding as parties begin to debate possible actions and philosophies. Deliberation emerges as parties discover the need to make a decision. This relationship can be viewed along a "discussion continuum" (Figure 7.1).

Figure 7.1
The Discussion Continuum

Dialogue	Deliberation
Learning-oriented	Decision-oriented

Inquiry and Advocacy

In *The Fifth Discipline*, Peter Senge distinguishes between "inquiry" and "advocacy." He writes that learning is the most productive when people combine skills in these two areas. "What is needed," Senge asserts, "is blending advocacy and inquiry to promote collaborative learning" (1990, p. 198). When inquiry and advocacy are combined, he explains, "the goal is no longer 'to win the argument' but to find the best argument" (1990, p. 199). According to Rick Ross and Charlotte Roberts of the Center for Organizational Learning, "When balancing advocacy and inquiry, we lay out our reasoning and thinking, and then encourage others to challenge us." We do so by stating: "Here is my view and here is how I have arrived at it. How does it sound to you? What makes sense to you and what doesn't? Do you see any ways I can improve it?" (Ross & Roberts, 1998, p. 1).

Communication interaction in Collaborative Learning, as it features both dialogue and deliberation, emphasizes inquiry and advocacy. Participants need to ask questions as they learn and understand. They also should have opportunities to voice their views as they propose and refine improvements designed to manage the conflict situation. Both inquiry and advocacy are important as discussion moves from dialogue to deliberation.

Balancing Inquiry and Advocacy

In *The Fifth Discipline*, Peter Senge distinguishes between "inquiry" and "advocacy" (1990, pp. 200–201).

When advocating your view:

- Make your own reasoning explicit (i.e., say how you arrived at your view and the "data" upon which it is based).
- Encourage others to explore your view (e.g., "Do you see gaps in my reasoning?").
- Encourage others to provide different views (i.e., "Do you have different evidence, data, conclusions, or interpretations?").
- Actively inquire into others' views that differ from your own (i.e., "What do you think?," "What are your views?," "How did you reach your conclusion?," "Are you basing your view on data I have not considered?").

When inquiring into others' views:

- If you are making assumptions about others' views, state your assumptions clearly and acknowledge them as such.
- State the evidence or "data" on which your assumptions are based.
- Do not bother asking questions if you are not genuinely interested in the other party's response and in learning from the other party (i.e., if you are only trying to be polite or show the other up).

When you arrive at an impasse (others no longer seem open to inquiries about there own views):

- Ask what evidence, data, or logic might modify their views.
- Ask if there is any way you might together to design a study (or some other inquiry activity) that might provide new information.

When you or others are reluctant to express your views or consider alternate ideas:

- Encourage them (or you) to think out loud about what might be making it difficult (i.e., "What is it about this situation, and about me or others, that is making the open exchange of ideas difficult?").
- If there is mutual desire to do so, design with others ways to overcome these barriers.

Civic Discovery

Collaborative Learning provides a framework for "civic discovery." Both dialogue and deliberation are important aspects of civic discovery. Civic discovery is citizen inquiry into controversial and challenging situations. It refers to activities and processes that provide opportunities for communities to debate their future and citizens to learn from one another. It is any citizen forum where "opinions can be revised, premises altered, and common interests discovered" (Reich, 1988, p. 144).

Public deliberation lies at the heart of civic discovery. It is civic discourse that features inquiry and advocacy; communication among citizens in which meanings converge and diverge, and collective or shared meanings and understandings emerge. Public deliberation is important to working through controversial and problematic situations, setting norms to describe and assess situations, and generating collective meanings and shared understandings about "the boundaries of the possible in public policy" (Majone, 1988, p. 164). Learning is critical to each of these tasks. Too often, though, government agencies control public deliberation in ways that thwart learning.

Communication Needs

For citizens, scientists, communities, and management agencies to deliberate and learn together as part of creating natural resource management policy, they need to communicate competently about various matters, including:

- The technical, legal, and financial issues at hand
- Procedural issues
- Perceptions, concerns, and values of other participants
- Their own goals and those of others
- Personalities
- Communication styles
- Their own set of options
- Relative benefits of different strategies
- Individual and collective meanings and interpretations

For example, the new natural resource management orientations, such as ecosystem-based management, emphasize deliberative communication akin to "civic science" (Lee, 1993). In confronting the inevitable tensions between science and politics in order to manage ecosystems well, natural resource professionals must be both "idealistic about science and pragmatic about politics" (Lee, 1993, p. 161). In ecosystem-based management, science and politics are forever wedded; "ecosystem-scale science requires political support to be done" (Lee, 1993, p. 165). Political support hinges, in part, on involving the public in meaningful ways. Effective public participation, though, is more than simply encouraging "citizen dialogue" or "good communication." It depends on communication competence; that is, parties communicating appropriately and effectively (Lustig & Koester, 1993; Cupach & Canary, 1997). Public participation efforts need to be structured to emphasize collaborative communication, dialogue, learning, and opportunities to work through differing viewpoints. Public involvement approaches that are philosophically consistent with ecosystem-based management stress learning, competent communication, dialogue, and deliberation as features of structured discussion that include both scientific/technical and local knowledge.

Constructive communication in Collaborative Learning, whether as dialogue or deliberation, requires commitment and effort. Participants in a Collaborative Learning process ideally want to and will work toward communicating well.

COMPETENCE IN COMMUNICATION

During the past two decades "competence" has become a seminal term in communication. More than 20 years ago, Bochner and Kelly (1974) characterized interpersonal competence as "(1) the ability to formulate and achieve objectives; (2) the ability to collaborate effectively with others; i.e., to be interdependent; and (3) the ability to adapt appropriately to situational and environmental variations" (p. 288). Similarly, Wiemann (1977) described communication competence as "the ability of an interactant to choose among available communication behavior in order that he may successfully accomplish his own interpersonal goals during an encounter while maintaining the face and line of his fellow interactants within the constraints of the situation" (p. 198). Hammer et al. (1978) identified three competence factors in interculturally experienced people: (1) the ability to deal with psychological stress; (2) the ability to communicate effectively; and (3) the ability to establish interpersonal relationships.

Encouraged by these and other works on competence, numerous scholars have, in recent years, devoted significant attention to "communication competence," examining it in varied communication settings or contexts.   Consequently, scholarship has emerged concerning interpersonal communication competence in various areas of human interaction. But the intercultural communication scholars have arguably devoted the most time, particularly in recent years, in theoretical and research work on communication competence.   Their work stresses that communication competence "characteristics" are ultimately intertwined with determinants of competence. What people judge as competent affects what people try to do to be competent, in conflict and other communication situations. People's impressions and judgments of a communicator's competence are critical. Impressions may be of oneself or the other; parties judge the appropriateness and effectiveness of their own message behavior as well as the message behavior of other interactants (Spitzberg, 1991; Collier, 1996; Cupach & Canary, 1997).

What is Communication Competence?

Communication competence has three dimensions:

- Adaptability: Competent communicators assess situations and when necessary adapt their expectations and behaviors accordingly.
- Appropriateness: Competence means employing communication behaviors that both you and others judge to be appropriate to the situation.
- Effectiveness: Competent communication behaviors, as evaluated by oneself and others, is effective in achieving one's communication goals.

The key point is that appropriateness and effectiveness are evaluated by others as well as by oneself. Other's judgments of your communication behavior are critical to determining your communication competence.

Communication Competence Skills

In collaborative public participation venues, communication competence is not a phase but rather ideally permeates the entire public participation experience. Such competence is fostered through the development and implementation of discourse and interaction guidelines (e.g., "ground rules" that value diversity), facilitation, and taking stock, a point we address later.

As noted earlier, competent communication has been defined as communication activity that is perceived as effective in achieving certain objectives while being appropriate to the context in which the activity occurs (Spitzberg,

1988).   The components of communication competence include context, impressions of appropriateness and effectiveness, and adaptability based on knowledge and motivation, and actions.   Both the individual and others in a particular setting judge the individual's communication competence in that setting. The individual's coorientation skill (ability to orient one's actions with another person) helps align one's own impression with the judgments of others. Based on our work in the natural resource policy arena, we have identified a number of communication "skill" areas that reflect the need for adaptation, appropriateness, and effectiveness in public participation.   Collaborative Learning strives to encourage competent communication and quality discourse by emphasizing these interrelated communication "skill" areas, areas that can be viewed as part of a collaborative communication competence "system."   All these skill areas are presumed to occur within a broader framework of cultural sensitivity, respect, and commitment to understanding. The skill areas include:

Listening. That listening is a skill of collaboration seems obvious. Critical, though, is the nature of listening. Parties must work to listen actively, even when arguments become quite heated.   Active listening involves a commitment to understanding the ideas of others, focusing on the essential message rather than detail, providing undivided attention, avoiding interruption, and paraphrasing to ensure understanding. This requires patience, particularly when working with and through language differences. Participants should withhold judgment until they are confident that they understand the other. Further, they should acknowledge the contributions of other parties, even during strong disagreements.

Key Features of Listening

- Commit to understanding—paraphrase and acknowledge.
- Focus on the essential message rather than detail.
- Provide undivided attention—avoid interruption.

Questioning and Clarification. Collaborative public participation processes emphasize learning (Walker & Daniels, 1997); questions are important to this task. Mediation, a similar albeit simpler collaborative process, values questions. Mediation experts emphasize the role of the mediator as questioner, particularly during the pre-negotiation interviews and information-gathering phases (see Moore, 1986; Keltner, 1987; Folberg & Taylor, 1984). Burrell (1990) studied mediators' question behavior in simulated roommate conflicts. She noted that the function of a question (information, restate, probe, social control, evaluate), more so than its form (open or closed), directly affects the type of disputant response. Questions, reframing, rephrasing, and the like foster evaluation of positions and identification of interests. Such questions and clarifications can serve as subtle, indirect argument and influence tactics that facilitate the transition from polarization and adversarial posturing to collaborative learning.

Key Features of Questioning

Questioning is both a way to learn and to empower others. Questions should be thoughtful and constructive:

- *Clarification*: Questions to better understand (e.g., "who," "what," "when")
- *Probing*: Questions to learn more (e.g., "why").
- *Hypothesis/scenario testing (e.g., alternatives)*: Questions to explore alternatives and introduce new perspectives (e.g., "what if").
- *Doubt raising*: Asking critical questions, exploring feasibility (e.g., "how," "what about").
- *Evaluation*: Questions to assess issues, ideas, and proposals.

Feedback. Collaboration encourages and is encouraged by constructive feedback. Feedback as constructive criticism can focus on matters of substance, relationships, or procedure. Such criticism addresses tangible and intangible concerns while "separating the people from the problem" (Fisher et al., 1991).

Key Features of Feedback

Parties need to provide regular, constructive feedback to one another. Specific communication techniques include:

- *"I" message feedback*: Use statements that begin with "I" (focus on yourself).
- *Appropriate, relevant self-disclosure*: Disclose information that is relevant to the present situation.
- *Description of feelings*: Try to describe your feeling with "I" messages rather than expressing them (e.g., "I get so frustrated when . . ." rather than "you are so inconsiderate when . . . ").
- *Perception check*: Check out the feelings, thoughts, intentions, and meanings you perceive rather than assuming them to be true. This may be particularly important when interpreting nonverbal behavior.
- *Behavior description*: Describe as accurately and objectively as possible the behavior you see that concerns you.
- *Specificity via indexing and dating*: Be specific about what occurred and when it occurred.

Feedback may address interactions and behaviors of public participation participants. Such feedback appears as relevant self-disclosure about feelings and thoughts concerning perceptions and observations. The feedback is communicated via "I" messages that provide specific information useful to the other party. The feedback is communicated as part of a "two-way street"; the person providing feedback invites feedback from the other.

Social Cognition/Self-monitoring. Collaboration can be advanced when participants maintain strong self-awareness of communication. Social cognition, or thought directed toward interaction (Roloff & Berger, 1982), involves a number of different elements. Communication-competent parties are sensitive to cultural, relational, and identity concerns of self and others, such as the desire to maintain respect, dignity, fairness, and face. Sensitivity toward language choice, meaning, and nonverbal display is part of highly competent self-monitoring. Similarly, competent communicators engage in perspective-taking (understanding the perspective, views, values, and concerns of others). They attempt to detect and accurately interpret behavioral cues and verbal communication (Sypher, 1984).

Key Features of Self-Monitoring

Communicating well includes a heightened awareness of our own behavior. We need to consider our own behavior in a number of areas:

- *Semantic sensitivity*: Monitoring the language that we use and being sensitive to the others' interpretations, the meanings that we intend, and the meanings that others construct.
- *Nonverbal sensitivity*: Monitoring our nonverbal behaviors and being sensitive to others' *interpretations* of those behaviors; welcoming others' concerns about our behaviors.
- *Face sensitivity*: Monitoring our verbal and nonverbal behaviors so we minimize threats to another party's "face."
- *Cultural sensitivity*: Monitoring our verbal and nonverbal behaviors so we respect and are sensitive to cultural norms, values, and meanings.
- *Personal identity sensitivity*: Monitoring our verbal and nonverbal behaviors so we minimize threats to another party's identity and sense of self.
- *Stress sensitivity*: Assessing the situation and monitoring our actions to be responsive to the stress and pressures that the other party is experiencing.
- *Time sensitivity*: Assessing the situation and monitoring our actions so that we time our confrontation, feedback, and intervention constructively and appropriately.

Dialogue. This skill area could be conceived of as the "umbrella" under which all the other communication competence skill areas reside. Dialogue is promoted via a norm of equality, in which parties have opportunities to share their ideas, to speak and be listened to (Eisenberg & Goodall, 1993).

Key Features of Dialogue

Competent communication interaction as dialogue emphasizes mutual learning, recognition, and empowerment. Dialogue permeates all the communication skill areas and is fostered through the following techniques:

- *Perspective taking*: Trying to understand the other person's point of view or experience thoughtfully (cognitively).
- *Empathy*: Trying to understand the other person's experience or viewpoint emotionally.
- *Bilateral focus, role reversal, and mirroring*: Techniques designed to promote perspective taking, empathy, and mutual learning.
- *Mutual-centeredness* (other and self-centeredness): Focusing on the interests of all primary parties.
- *Patience*: Giving people time to contemplate, speak, and respond.
- *Equal opportunity/time/turns*: Supporting everyone's opportunity to participate.
- *Acknowledgment and reinforcement*: Recognition for people's contributions and commitment.

Modeling. Competent communication in collaborative processes depends on people—modeling desirable, constructive communication behavior. Modeling involves a person engaging in particular behavior to serve as an example for others

---

Key Features of Modeling

We serve as models for others: spouses and partners, children, friends, coworkers, fellow community members, clients, etc. If we expect competent and collaborative communication behavior from others, we need to model that behavior ourselves.

- Demonstrate desired communication behavior.
- Invite feedback and criticism of your behavior.
- "Metacommunicate": Talk with one another about how well you are communicating and how communication can be improved.

to replicate (Johnson, 1990). Effective third-party intervenors, such as process consultants and mediators, demonstrate positive communication behavior they want disputants to display. This behavior can be accompanied by reinforcement and feedback.

Collaborative Argument. Some public participation analysts might associate argument only with traditional processes in which advocacy seems the preferred competence. In contrast, we think that argument is an essential dimension of communication competence in collaborative public participation. Constructive argument can be critical to a collaborative process' success. Parties must transcend traditional negative views of argument (usually related to arguers rather than argument per se). Participants see the promise of healthy argument, and work to debate issues collaboratively. This commitment includes valuing disagreement, a desire to learn, willingness to risk, open-mindedness, mutual respect, and acceptance of an ethical responsibility of fairness. Arguers agree to disagree, as both advocates and inquirers. They rely on fundamental argument skills, such as questioning, reason-giving and explanation, individual and joint case-building and modification, refutation and constructive criticism, explicit values discussion, and appraisal (Walker, 1991).

Key Features of Collaborative Argument

Collaborative argument requires both a constructive arguer orientation and particular arguer skills.

Arguer orientation:

- Valuing and respecting disagreement
- Desire to learn
- Willingness to risk
- Open-mindedness
- Distinguishing between arguers and arguments
- Positive regard for the other
- Ethical responsibility

Promoting Communication Competence

Communication competence is not a precondition of collaborative public participation such as Collaborative Learning; rather it is a process goal. To the extent that participants in collaborative activities can communicate well, the quality of their interaction, their degree of learning, and their contributions to the decision process are enhanced.

Skills of Inquiry and Advocacy

- Questions
- Reason giving and explanation
- Case building and modification; individual and joint
- Refutation and constructive criticism
- Values discussion
- Reflection

How do Collaborative Learning and similar collaborative processes foster communication competence? We see a number of ways, pertaining to both training activities and facilitation of collaborative processes.

Training. Improving communication competence in environmental policy public participation may begin with training agency members and interest group leaders. Training programs in Collaborative Learning, as noted in Chapter 2, include various key areas, such as systems thinking and conflict management. Constructive communication is critical to the effectiveness of any collaborative process (Walker & Daniels, 1996). Consequently, training programs in collaboration processes like Collaborative Learning should include material on communication competence relevant to the natural resource management context and opportunities for training program participants to experience constructive communication skills.

Process Design. Training programs can introduce communication competence skills to natural resource managers and community leaders. Citizens can be encouraged to communicate competently in collaborative public participation venues that build competence into their design. Communication activities, in pairs, small groups, and large group settings can provide citizens with opportunities to listen, to ask questions, to argue constructively, in short, to communicate well. In Collaborative Learning workshops, for example, participants work on controversial environmental and natural resource management issues in two-person and small group discussions (Daniels & Walker, 1996).

In addition to including activities to foster competent communication interaction, participants in collaborative public involvement processes can be encouraged to communicate well via procedural "guidelines" or "ground rules." A regular feature of mediation (Moore, 1996), ground rules remind participants what constitutes good communication. Ground rules allow facilitators to explicitly promote competent communication, even to subtly coach participants to interact capably.

Facilitation. Collaborative public participation processes like Collaborative Learning require skill, commitment, and perseverance. Stakeholders in a natural resource problem situation may not be able to progress beyond their disparate views and communicate competently without the help of a facilitator. In complex environmental controversies facilitation seems necessary to promote collaboration, particularly when empowerment of local communities is valued (Friedmann, 1992). Collaborative public involvement in general and participants' communication competence specifically are enhanced by facilitation that mixes mediation and process consultation strategies and tactics (Lewicki et al., 1995; Wilmot & Hocker, 1998). As they guide the public participation process, facilitators model the communication competence behaviors they are trying to encourage. Collaborative Learning processes in public settings need facilitation.

ILLUSTRATING COMMUNICATION COMPETENCE AND ENVIRONMENTAL CONFLICT: SCIENTIST AND CITIZEN INTERACTION

In Chapter 1 we discussed the fundamental paradox of public involvement that is an inevitable part of environmental policy conflicts. As we noted, a paradox exists between citizens' desire on one hand for the best available scientific and technical knowledge to be applied to any given environmental policy situation, and a simultaneous desire for inclusion in the policy decision-making process—a desire for meaningful voice. Environmental conflict resolution   seems to favor either technical expertise or an involved citizenry, when, in fact, both are important. A partial response to this paradox may reside in processes like Collaborative Learning that seek to provide techniques and forums for bringing together scientists and citizens, and integrating technical knowledge and traditional knowledge. Doing so begins with scientist and citizen communication competence (Walker & Daniels, 1999).

If scientists and members of the public are to interact well about environmental and natural resource management controversies, they must be willing to participate meaningfully in that interaction. Interaction and mutual learning as part of good decision making rely on a basic degree of communication competence. All parties must contribute constructively to the process and strive to communicate well.

Scientist Communication Competence

Constructive and substantive citizen–scientist dialogue begins with the scientific community. Citizens expect decision makers in natural resource management to base policy judgments on the best available knowledge, which includes the best available scientific and technical work. Citizens also want to contribute their local and indigenous knowledge of the situation and want to know that scientists and managers respect and are responsive to their local expertise. Scientists can foster citizen respect for their work and promote meaningful scientist–citizen dialogue by communicating competently. Scientific activity is fundamentally different from many other human endeavors (Keith, 1997), but scientific knowledge must be communicated well if it to influence policy. Influence relies on communication competence. This competence encompasses, but is not limited to, the following:

Assessing and adapting to the communication situation.   This includes analyzing the citizen as an "audience," that is, understanding what they know, what they want to contribute, what the scientist hopes to learn from them, and what the scientist would like them to learn (Collier, 1997).

Respecting cultural preferences in learning and knowing.   Cultural communities vary in the ways they learn and use their knowledge.

Employing clear language.   Scientists should minimize jargon and acronyms. Clarity does not mean "talking down" but rather relies on appropriate language frames, such as metaphors and illustrations.

Active, open-minded listening.   Scientists need to listen openly, taking notes on what citizens contribute.   Just as citizens question scientists about what they know, scientists should question citizens about their expertise and listen actively in order to understand local insights.

Patience.   Learning about complex natural resource situations takes time. Scientists need to be patient with citizens and with themselves as a mutual learning environment emerges.   Citizen understanding and scientist understanding of a situation are often different.   To learn, to make progress, and to discover points of agreement require a patience and tolerance to work through the issues that concern people.

Self-awareness and self-monitoring.   Scientists need to monitor their nonverbal and verbal behavior as they interact with citizens about natural resource management controversies.   Through self-monitoring, scientists can better model the communication competence behavior that promotes mutual learning and that they hope citizens will also exhibit.

Citizen Communication Competence

In a meaningful scientist–citizen dialogue, citizens also have a responsibility to communicate competently.   Citizens need to listen actively and be open to learning. Citizens can strive to understand the complexity and systemic nature of a situation. They need to accord scientists the appropriate opportunity to share their technical knowledge.   Citizens should employ clear language and be willing to provide evidence for the knowledge claims that they contribute.   Citizens, too, need to recognize that science is uncertain and that there is no scientific or technical "silver bullet" where complex natural resource management issues are concerned.   Citizen communication competence includes the ideas presented in the previous section.   In addition, citizen competence features:

Respect for technical expertise.   Scientists are sincere in their desire to contribute their knowledge to the natural resource management decision situation. Just as citizens want their ideas respected, they need to acknowledge the scientists' expertise.

Willingness to learn, willingness to study.   Technical expert material often appears in written documents and technical presentations.   While citizens should demand that these materials be understandable, they need to commit time to work with those materials in order to developing an understanding of the science of the situation.

Communicating traditional knowledge clearly. Citizens have much to contribute to environmental and natural resource conflict improvements. Their knowledge of a resource area may be insightful and detailed in ways different from that of the scientist, while just as relevant. Still, traditional knowledge needs to be communicated thoroughly so that traditional knowledge claims are explained and supported. This may occur in a workshop via maps or on the ground in a field trip setting. In either case, the citizen and scientist engage in meaningful dialogue in order to integrate traditional and technical knowledge and learn from one another.

COMMUNICATION COMPETENCE IN ENVIRONMENTAL CONFLICT: RESPONSIVENESS TO CULTURE

When we discussed the complexity of environmental conflicts in Chapter 3, we noted that sources of that complexity include cultural differences and deeply held values and worldviews. Collaborative Learning is designed to be responsive to the cultural and value-based diversity that is a part of environmental conflict situations. Competent communication, as noted earlier, includes sensitivity to culture and language. Just as Collaborative Learning draws upon diversity of learning styles, diversity of systems perspectives, and diversity of knowledge sources, it strives to be responsive to the diversity among the participants in any situation.

What Do We Mean by Culture?

A culture is a "system of socially created and learned standards for perceiving and acting, shared by members of an identity group" (Nadler et al., 1985, p. 89). A culture serves as a way to organize diversity (Hymes, 1962). Culture provides the primary foundation for our mental models and cognitive frames of other people. As Hall explains, "People cannot act or interact in any meaningful way except through the medium of culture" (1966, p. 177).

Communication competence in a Collaborative Learning process includes cultural competence. To the best of their ability, Collaborative Learning participants need to understand and respect the cultural diversity of the larger group. Understanding of cultures and communication competence are intertwined; in order to understand cultures, people need ways to talk about the similarities and differences between them (Gudykunst, 1994). Collaborative Learning activities strive to provide the means for such talk. Responsiveness to cultural diversity relies on understanding key variable dimensions of culture. These include variations in values, reasoning, context, and directness.

Values. Values are fundamental to both individual and group identity. Values are evaluative beliefs or judgments about right and wrong, good and bad, and so on, that guide individual behavior as well as community policy (Rokeach, 1979). Worldviews are comprehensive sets of values organized hierarchically that reflect cultural identity. Hofstede's (1980) comprehensive study of work-related values provides insights into values and worldviews of cultures. He has surveyed equivalent sample populations from organizations in more than 50 countries and has identified, through factor analysis, four value dimensions pertinent to national cultures, as follows.

Individualism versus collectivism features individual and group-related values. Of Hofstede's four cultural dimensions, this has received the most attention from scholars (Gudykunst & Matasumoto, 1996; Ting-Toomey & Chung, 1996; Ting-Toomey, 1999). Ting-Toomey and Chung, for example, see individualism and collectivism as different ways for people to conceptualize their sense of self and enact their identity. Members of individualistic cultures focus on themselves as individuals, finding meaning in life through individual achievement: accomplishing personal goals, meeting family needs, and succeeding competitively. People in collectivist cultures identify with the group or organization more than with themselves as individuals. A person's goals are typically those of the organization. Group achievement is valued above individual accomplishment. Collaboration with group members coupled with accommodating hierarchy are key to organizational effectiveness. Competition within the organization is shunned; competition with other organizations in order to benefit one's own group is accepted.

Power distance involves beliefs concerning power distribution, social inequality, and authority. It refers to the degree to which people accept status inequalities and power imbalances in organizational settings. Cultures high on the power distance continuum (e.g., Japan, South Korea) consider role and status hierarchy as normal. Cultures low in power distance (e.g., the United States, Sweden) favor equality and encourage parties in top positions to be egalitarian (Harrison, 1999).

Uncertainty avoidance refers to judgments designed to avoid threatening, vague, and tentative situations. Values pertaining to issues of life, death, conflict, and aggression reside within this dimension. These values come together to the degree that a culture accepts uncertainty. Cultures high on the uncertainty avoidance have little tolerance for ambiguity and need clarity on the key "life" values. Deviation from the norm (organizational and societal) is shunned. Members of high uncertainty avoidance cultures seek absolute truths and formal rules. Cultures low on the uncertainty avoidance continuum are more comfortable with ambiguity in the meaning of core values and rules governing behavior. Dissent and innovation are respected (Harrison, 1999).

Masculinity versus femininity illuminate such values as success, money, and material items in contrast to caring for others and concern for quality of life (Hofstede & Bond, 1984, pp. 419–420). Assertiveness and nurturance, terms that Hofstede (1980) associates with masculinity and femininity, respectively may be more appropriate than Hofstede's original gender-associated labels (p. 277). Assertive or masculine cultures generally value independence, ambition, performance, and achievement. Members of nurturing or feminine cultures consider quality of life and social relationships very important.

The U. S. and Japanese national cultures are frequently used to illustrate different points on the continua of these four dimensions. The U. S. national culture is generally high on individualism and masculinity and low on power distance and uncertainty avoidance. In contrast, Japanese national culture is considered high on collectivism and femininity and high on power distance and uncertainty avoidance.

Reasoning. Just as different people prefer different ways to learn, they prefer different patterns of reasoning. Reasoning, many scholars assert, varies across cultures. Glenn (1966), drawing upon the work of Pribram (1949), proposes universalism, particularism, and relationalism as reasoning patterns associated with national cultures. Reychler (1979) identifies "particularizer-generalizer" as a factor of diplomats' "analytic style", and asserts that diplomats from developing nations have a greater tendency to generalize—to reason deductively—than diplomats from developed nations (p. 186). Different patterns of reasoning become associated with national cultural negotiation styles (Binnendijk, 1987). Glenn et al. (1977) present factual-inductive, axiomatic-deductive, and intuitive-affective reasoning patterns as part of "cultural styles of persuasion" (Walker, 1987, 1990).

Context. Anthropologist Edward Hall's (1966, 1976) seminal work on culture presents context as the organizing conceptual framework for understanding cultural differences. Context "is the information that surrounds an event" (Hall & Hall, 1998, p. 200). Understanding messages depends on the cultural context in which they occur (Hall, 1976). Context varies on a continuum from high to low. As Hall explains:

High context people pay special attention to the concrete world around them. Everything in the physical setting communicates something subtle but significant: the atmosphere of the room, sounds, smells, expressions on people's faces, and body language. High context people tend to remember people's names and details and events. The subtle cues in a real-life setting intuitively but intentionally communicate important information. Low-context people, on the other hand, pay special attention to words, ideas, and concepts. They may remember a conversation about an important topic but not remember the names of the people in the conversation. The specific explicit words and ideas communicate more clearly than the implicit tone of voice. Low context learners enjoy analyzing and comparing ideas. (1976, p. 91)

People in high context cultures interpret messages, whether verbal or nonverbal, in part through the physical world within which the messages occur. High context people value the non-discursive world of sound, patterns, and displays. Members of low context cultures may pay little attention to the physical environment related to a message, preferring to focus on discursive symbols, that is, language.

In the United States there are both high and low context cultures. Many Native American cultures, for example, are high context: they place importance on their relationship to the natural world—the land, the water, the sky, and so on. In contrast, the American-European culture is low context: People of this ethnic origin separate themselves from the natural world, often seeing that world as conquerable through science and technology, both discursive enterprises.

As may be apparent from this discussion, Hall's conception of high and low context cultures corresponds with Hofstede's dimensions, particularly individualism and collectivism.

Directness and Indirectness.   As Hall's work reveals, high context cultures are generally less direct than low context cultures. Directness is often associated with low context and individualistic cultures, those that emphasize language over nonverbal cues, independence over interdependence, and self-interest over group or other interest.

In low context cultures such as the U. S. national culture, directness is valued. It is associated with strength and leadership. The U. S. national culture has embraced various phrases that feature directness, many of which are presented here.

Expressions of Directness in United States Euro-American Culture

- Tell it like it is.
- Don't beat around the bush.
- Put your cards on the table.
- Give it to me straight . . . I can handle it.
- Be up-front with me.
- Lay it on the line.
- Level with me.
- It's straight from the horse's mouth.
- Let's get it out in the open.

Source: Harrison (1999).

Cultures that emphasize directness generally consider indirectness to be inappropriate for solving problems and dealing with conflict. Direct cultures hold various assumptions about indirectness. If a person is not direct, members of low context cultures may assume that the person lacks the courage to confront the other party, is unwilling to deal with the issue, lacks commitment to address the problem, refuses to take responsibility for his or her actions, and is not concerned about the other party.

Many cultural communities value indirectness as the appropriate path for solving problems, particularly when status and role differences are present. To a westerner, indirectness in a conflict situation may seem to be avoidance, when the person being indirect may be seeking to resolve the conflict while accommodating status and position within the relationship. Indirectness, particularly within high context, collectivist cultures, is done for various reasons, as summarized here.

Reasons for Indirectness

- Saving and maintaining face, reputation, and honor.
- Deference to status or role.
- Harmony, in the relationship and context.
- Long-term benefit versus short-term gain.
- Generational expectations.
- Learned behavior (compliance with appropriate social norms).

Source: Harrison (1999).

Communication Competence and Collaborative Learning: Cultural Considerations

Collaborative Learning has been designed to be sensitive toward and responsive to cultural differences. The first step of the CL project, assessment, fosters learning about the cultural communities and contexts of an environmental conflict situation. A CL training program can include cultural matters to the extent appropriate in the given situation. CL workshop design varies according to the cultural issues and factors present in the situation. Facilitation teams, where pertinent, can be multicultural and multi-lingual. Overall, Collaborative Learning applications incorporate a number of cultural "considerations" that should be recognized by facilitators and participants alike (adapted from Harrison, 1997).

1. Include high and low context culture issues in the initial and ongoing assessment of an environmental conflict situation.
2. Be prepared for the fact that members of some cultural communities might openly deny that a particular problem situation exists, or at least play down the presence of conflict.
3. With some cultural communities, accept inaction as a probable form of displeasure and as a means of communicating indirectly.
4. Recognize the tactics of misdirection to shift personal blame to someone else.
5. Recognize face-saving tactics.
6. Do not expect a speedy decision or resolution. Be prepared to live with the conflict over a period of time.
7. If you expect a group to develop a consensus and agree on a decision, recognize that this consensus will often be influenced by the opinion of an older person or recognized leader.
8. Be comfortable with silence.
9. Be very careful about how you show strong displeasure.
10. Be careful to defer to age and/or position by using proper titles, greetings, and courteous manners.
11. Build a friendship with a person who can serve as a cultural bridge and informant.
12. Some cultural communities do not embrace "separating the people from the problem" (Fisher et al., 1991). With some cultural groups, do not separate the person from the person's words or acts. Criticizing a person's idea is often the same as criticizing or demeaning the person.

13. Try to ask nonjudgmental questions.
14. Be careful about evaluative or blaming statements. Consider using the following indirect methods:
15. Accept a "one-down" position: Grant the other party a "superior" place in the relationship (at least temporarily).
16. Tell a story or quote a proverb that indirectly deals with the problem situation.
17. Use inaction.
18. Use silence.

Three "Rules" for Dealing with Culture

- Golden Rule: "Do unto others as you would have them do unto you."
- Confucius' Rule: "Don't do unto others what you would not want done to you."
- Platinum Rule: "Do unto others as they would have done unto them."

Source: Harrison (1997).

CONCLUSION

Throughout the past decade natural resource management policies have been changing. Management philosophies have emerged such as ecosystem-based management, biodiversity, and sustainability. These recognize the importance of "people" aspects of natural resource decisions—the social, cultural, and political—than more traditional management orientations, such as "multiple use, sustained yield", which featured the physical, biological, and economic dimensions of natural resource situations. As management philosophies have evolved, the need for public participation processes sensitive to complexity, diversity, and systems has emerged. Collaborative Learning responds to this need.

Collaborative Learning relies on constructive communication for its success. Participants in Collaborative Learning have both the desire and the capacity to communicate well: to use communication competence skills that are appropriate to the natural resource policy situation. Training programs, Collaborative Learning process designs, and facilitation all contribute to participants becoming more competent communicators.

Traditional public participation activities will not ensure quality discourse and constructive civic dialogue. Collaborative public participation frameworks like Collaborative Learning, with communication competence as a recognized dimension, are necessary to provide citizens with meaningful opportunities to be a part of environmental conflict management and decision making. Such frameworks are responsive to the demand that government institutions "empower citizens rather than simply serving them" (Osborne & Gaebler, 1992, p.15). Collaborative Learning and similar processes, as they encourage competent communication as a part of constructive, substantive dialogue, will gain greater citizen commitment and provide forums for good science, good law, good politics, good economics, good culture, good communities, and, ultimately, good decisions.

Chapter 8

Techniques of Collaborative Learning

Learning implies a constant action. There is learning all the time. And the very act of learning is doing.

—J. Krishnamurti
You Are The World

This chapter provides various "how-to" ideas related to conducting Collaborative Learning projects. Perhaps the most important message to communicate in this chapter is that these ideas are presented to aid in the creative application of Collaborative Learning and are by no means presented as *the* Collaborative Learning approach. Certainly, our intent is not to constrain readers' creativity as they tailor Collaborative Learning to their specific needs, because one of the strengths of Collaborative Learning is that it can be readily adapted to accommodate the unique challenges of each new situation. There is no standard design for a Collaborative Learning project or meeting; we have rarely, if ever, done exactly the same thing twice. The purpose of the theory chapters in this book (Chapters 3 through 6) is to provide grounding upon which to make choices. To the extent that readers understand the defining attributes of their situation and are comfortable with the theoretical foundations of Collaborative Learning, then they are the best judges of what will or will not work in any given situation. There may therefore be as many ideas in this applied chapter that these readers ignore as there are ideas that they adopt.

In Chapter 2 we noted that a comprehensive application of Collaborative Learning includes five interrelated steps: assessment, training, design, implementation/facilitation, and evaluation. In light of the communication competence issues we addressed in Chapter 7, we discuss Collaborative Learning tools and techniques in these five areas.

ASSESSMENT

Conflict management processes employed in environmental and natural resource policy situations need to be appropriate for, and responsive to, the complex, diverse, and systemic nature of those situations. Developing an appropriate and responsive process relies on assessment—a substantive understanding of the situation. Based on that understanding, a conflict management, public participation, or decision-making process like Collaborative Learning can be designed that values inclusiveness, flexibility, and learning. Writing about public policy situations, mediators Susan Carpenter and W.J.D. Kennedy posit that a "thorough understanding of the situation leads to a management strategy designed for the specifics of a dispute and, in turn, lasting solutions" (1988, p. 71). We discuss two related assessment tasks: assessing the environmental conflict situation and assessing parties' or stakeholders' roles.

Assessing the Conflict Situation

Collaborative Learning and other methods for collaboration (e.g., search conferencing [Emery, 1982, 1993; Diemer & Alvarez, 1995]; participatory decision making [Sirmon et al., 1995]; constructive confrontation [Burgess & Burgess, 1996]) are appropriate for complex environmental conflict situations, in part, because they are comprehensive. The tools and techniques of Collaborative Learning emerge from understanding Collaborative Learning's philosophy of conflict management and decision making as a process of improvement and from comprehending the theoretical bases of Collaborative Learning: systems, learning, and conflict management.

A Collaborative Learning project begins with assessment of the environmental conflict situation. This assessment is essential to determine the collaborative potential of the situation. Collaborative potential, a concept we introduced in Chapter 4, refers to the extent to which an environmental conflict situation can be addressed collaboratively in terms of both process and outcome. Process collaborative potential features the capacity for parties to interact constructively, substantively, respectfully, and fairly. Outcome collaborative potential considers opportunities for decisions that the parties consider mutually beneficial.

Assessing the collaborative potential of a situation is important for two reasons. First, the assessment reveals if collaboration makes sense in the particular environmental conflict situation. If collaborative potential is low, any collaborative method may be counterproductive. Second, if some parties believe collaboration is necessary even though collaborative potential is low, the assessment will identify areas in which collaborative potential can be increased.

For example, if trust among the parties is low, activities can be pursued to increase trust (e.g., field trips, informal dialogues, social functions, back-channel interactions).

Assessment Frameworks

Assessment of an environmental or natural resource policy conflict situation should occur according to an appropriate framework. This could be a framework that an agency, community organization, or interest group constructs, or it may follow some published approach that has been developed for understanding diverse and complex natural resource management situations. These frameworks typically provide a series of questions and activities for gathering and analyzing information. "Conflict assessment," we should note, differs from "social assessment" and "social impact assessment." Social assessment typically refers to an evaluation of the social, political, and cultural aspects of a planning situation generally and the social impacts of policy alternatives more specifically (Krannich et al., 1994). Social assessment work is often grounded in local communities (Little & Krannich, 1989), suggesting the importance of place-based values (Brandenburg & Carroll, 1995; Kemmis, 1990). Social assessment methods may be very useful as part of a conflict assessment effort (Krannich et al., 1994) but do not focus on the dynamics of the conflict situation. Consequently, social assessment can complement and inform conflict assessment but should not replace the evaluation of the dynamic complexity of the conflict situation.

A number of conflict assessment frameworks have been developed in recent years. Carpenter and Kennedy (1988), for example, have designed an assessment approach for public policy conflicts. Their Conflict Analysis Chart and Dynamics Continuum includes a grid featuring parties, issues, interests, the importance of issues, sources of power and influence, positions and options, and interest in working with other parties as components (pp. 85–92).

The Conflict Map, designed by sociologist Paul Wehr (1979), focuses on social and community conflicts. It consists of various important analytical areas: (1) summary description (of the conflict situation); (2) conflict history—origin and major events in the evolution of the conflict; (3) conflict context—scope and character of the context/setting in which the conflict occurs; (4) conflict parties—primary, secondary, and interested third parties; (5) issues, including facts-based, values-based, interests-based, and nonrealistic issues; (6) dynamics—precipitating events, issue emergence, transformation, proliferation, polarization and spiraling, stereotyping and mirror-imaging; (7) alternate routes to solution(s) to the problem(s); and (8) conflict regulation potential—internal and external limiting factors, interested or neutral third parties, and techniques of conflict management.

Wilmot and Hocker's (1998) Conflict Assessment Guide has been developed for understanding interpersonal and group conflict situations. It includes a number of important assessment areas, such as (1) orientation to the conflict—attitudes, perceptions, metaphors, culture, gender; (2) nature of the conflict—triggering events, history, assumptions, incompatibility, interdependence, scarcity, phases; (3) goals—clarification and framing, types, self versus other focus, individual versus system focus; (4) power—degree of openness, dependencies, internal and external currencies, degree of balance, sources; (5) styles and tactics—individual styles, perceptions of style, strategies and tactics; (6) assessment—repetitive patterns, microevents, tone; (7) personal intervention—options for change, conflict philosophy, self-regulation techniques, anger management; and (8) attempted solutions—management options, problematic solutions, third parties, resolution repetition.

The Progress Triangle Framework

We have developed and employed an assessment framework based on the conflict management Progress Triangle idea we presented in Chapter 3. We created the Progress Triangle Framework to help parties assess the collaborative potential of a situation, particularly in the environmental and natural resource policy arena.

As we highlighted in Chapter 3, we define "management" as the generation and implementation of tangible improvements in a conflict situation. Improvements in the ways we manage a conflict situation constitute progress. Therefore, environmental and natural resource conflict management can be thought of as "making progress." Conflict management involves making progress on the three fundamental dimensions of a conflict situation: substantive, procedural, and relationship. These dimensions can be viewed as part of a conflict management Progress Triangle, as presented in Figure 8.1.

Figure 8.1
The Progress Triangle

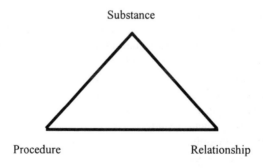

The Progress Triangle not only organizes visually and systemically the substantive, relationship, and procedural dimensions of conflict, but also provides parties with a cognitive frame that can transform their understanding of the conflict situation from a competitive, zero-sum orientation, to realizing the promise of collaborative interaction. This cognitive frame corresponds to using the Progress Triangle as a means for evaluating the collaborative potential of an environmental conflict situation.

The Progress Triangle Framework organizes assessment into three dimensions. The relationship dimension focuses on the parties, their relational histories, incentives, positions and interests, level of trust, sources of power, knowledge and skills, and their status, such as tribal sovereignty. The procedural dimension asks questions about decision space, sufficiency of resources (e.g., time, money), jurisdiction, timing, need for reducing tensions (cooling off), procedural history, procedural alternatives, and procedural preferences. The substantive dimension addresses tangible and symbolic issues, sources of tension, complexity, information needs, language and meaning concerns, and mutual gain options. In this section we examine the three areas of the Progress Triangle Framework—relationship, procedure, and substance—in more detail.

The Progress Triangle: The Relationship Dimension. While environmental and natural policy conflicts are overtly about substantive matters, progress on them often hinges on the quality of the relationships that exist among the conflict parties. Consequently, although assessment can begin at any one of the three triangle dimensions, in many cases examining relationship factors first may be insightful. The relationship dimension includes the parties in the conflict and their history with one another. It also includes the "intangibles" of any conflict situation, such as trust, respect, and legitimacy. Generally, the better the relationship among the parties, the greater the collaborative potential. The following questions may help in the assessment of the relationship dimension of a policy conflict. These questions do not cover all aspects of the relationship dimension that could be assessed but do identify areas that might warrant evaluation.

1. Who are the parties/stakeholders?
    *   Who are the primary parties?
    *   Who are the secondary parties?
    *   Is there media interest?
2. Do any parties have unique status (e.g., Indian tribes)?
3. What are the parties':
    *   Stated positions?
    *   Interests (concerns, fears, goals)?
    *   Worldviews and values?
4. What are the parties' relational histories?
5. What are the parties' incentives:
    *   To collaborate?
    *   To compete?
    *   To learn?

6.   What are the parties' BATNAs?
7.   Is trust sufficient? Can it be built?
8.   Can representatives/individuals work together?
     •   Are representatives available for the long term or likely to change?
     •   Are representatives restricted by constituents?
9.   Do the players have adequate knowledge and skills:
     •   To process information and think systemically?
     •   To communicate constructively and work through disagreements?
     •   To interact with acknowledgment and respect?

Assessing the relationship dimension typically begins by asking, Who are the parties? Stakeholder or party identification in the environmental conflict situation often includes distinguishing between primary and secondary parties. Primary parties are the key players in the conflict situation: those who want or need to be actively involved in conflict management decisions. Secondary parties are those who have a significant interest in how the conflict situation is managed but do not want to be directly involved in the process. Secondary parties may include parties who do not want to be involved but should be kept "in the loop," informed about progress made. Some interest groups may prefer to remain on the sidelines and not want to grant legitimacy to the collaborative process. Good collaborative projects keep the door open for these parties to later join the collaborative effort.

Once the parties have been identified, they can be examined in terms of their unique status (e.g., an Indian tribe with rights as a sovereign nation), positions, interests, goals, values, and concerns. The Wallace Institute for Alternative Agriculture's national Agriculture Policy Project provides an example of stakeholder analysis (Table 8.1). The project includes 15 local community agricultural policy community visioning workshops. Using a soft-systems/Collaborative Learning workshop design, facilitators instruct workshop participants (local citizens) to identify stakeholders and their concerns about an agricultural policy situation (e.g., loss of agricultural land, preservation of the family farm) and the extent to which those concerns are highly important, moderately important, or of low importance to the various stakeholders.

BATNA, or "best alternative to a negotiated agreement" (Fisher & Ury, 1981), is an important assessment issue that pertains to all three dimensions of the Progress Triangle Framework. We have included it in the relationship dimension because alternatives relate to interests and concerns. When assessing an environmental conflict situation, one should consider one's own and the other parties' alternatives to a collaborative conflict management or negotiation process. If a party's BATNA is more attractive than the outcome that they expect to receive through collaboration, that party has little incentive to engage in the collaborative process. Collaborative processes like Collaborative Learning need to be viable ways for parties to achieve their conflict management and policy goals.

Table 8.1
Wallace Institute Agricultural Policy Project Stakeholder Analysis.
Policy Situation: Loss of Agricultural Land in a Western Mountain Region

Concern Stakeholder	Land value	Scenic appeal	Profit-ability or income	Keep land in the family	Taxes and cost of regu-lations	Growth	Sustain-ability steward-ship
Ranchers	High	Medium	High	High	High	Medium	High
Farmers	High	Medium	High	High	High	Medium	High
Tourists	Low	High	Low	Low	Low	??	Low
Developers	High	High	High	Low	Medium	High	??
County Gov't	High	High	High	Medium	Medium	Medium	High

Source: Wallace Institute for Alternative Agriculture, Greenbelt, MD.

Other relationship questions to consider address the parties' prior experience with one another, their relational histories. If relationships between parties have been very strained in the past, trust may be low and require precollaboration work before a collaborative process is pursued. This prework may include information-gathering activities (e.g., field trips, science dialogues), social functions, and even venting sessions to improve the relational climate.

Relationship assessment should include evaluation of the parties' (both as organizations and as individuals) knowledge and skills. If improving parties' knowledge and skills will increase collaborative potential, training activities may be appropriate (an area we discuss later in this chapter).

The Progress Triangle: The Procedure Dimension. The procedure dimension of the triangle includes those elements that pertain to the ways in which conflicts are managed and decisions made. It also includes the rules, both regulative and generative, to which parties adhere in working through the conflict situation. Just as progress on the substance of a conflict relies, in part, on relationship factors, so, too, does it depend on procedures that parties regard as appropriate and fair. The following questions can guide assessment of the procedure dimension.

1. At what stage is the conflict?
   - Does the situation seem ripe for constructive action?
   - Is de-escalation needed first?
2. What are the legal constraints?
3. Who has jurisdiction?
4. What management approaches have been used in the past (procedural history)?
5. Is mutual learning desired?
6. What is the decision space?
   - How much can be shared with other parties?
   - Are key supervisors supportive?
7. Are resources sufficient (e.g., time, money, staff)?

8. What are the procedural alternatives?
    - How accessible are they?
    - How inclusive?
9. Are there needs for design and facilitation by an impartial party?

The first procedure dimension question addresses the intensity and ripeness of the conflict. This evaluation determines if intervention and collaboration are appropriate given the nature of the conflict at the present time. As Keltner notes in his "struggle spectrum," some conflicts escalate to a point of intractability, such that they cannot be managed constructively and collaboratively. Other scholars note that conflict management efforts need to be timed appropriately, and the methods used need to be relevant to the nature of the conflict (Wilmot & Hocker, 2001; Folger et al., 1997). The evaluator needs to assess whether de-escalation or intensity reduction (e.g., a cooling-off period) is needed before constructive conflict management strategies can be useful.

For example, some years ago we received a phone call from a USDA-Forest Service planner asking us to conduct Collaborative Learning workshops in communities that were a part of the national forest where he worked. As we began to assess the conflict situation, we learned that some citizens had broken through a road closure barrier, a Forest Service building had been vandalized, public demonstrations were occurring, and recent public meetings had been very volatile and heated. Given the escalation actions and intensity of the situation, we declined the invitation, deciding that the situation was not ripe for collaboration at that time.

Questions 2, 3, and 4 in our procedure dimension question sample focus on the critical issues of decision authority and decision space. Assessment needs to reveal who has jurisdiction in the environmental conflict situation, who has legal imperative to make or block a policy decision in that situation. Jurisdiction is related to decision authority—the individual or organization that has the legal or organizational duty to manage or regulate the situation.

Decision space stems from decision authority. Those parties with decision authority must clarify how much of the decision process and outcome they can share with other parties. The extent to which a decision authority can open up and share its decision-making process defines the decision space. For example, the Environmental Protection Agency (EPA), as a regulatory agency, enforces environmental laws such as the Clean Water Act and the Clean Air Act. The EPA can make decisions about clean water and clean air issues and impose those decisions on affected parties, or the EPA can invite affected and interested parties to work with the agency to determine how clean water and clean air standards can best be met. In the latter case, the EPA creates meaningful decision space while retaining its decision authority.

Other questions in this area of the Progress Triangle framework focus on procedural history, procedural alternatives, and resources. Understanding the procedures used in the past to deal with this conflict situation helps identify what may or may not work in the present. This relates to identifying the alternative procedures available to manage conflict and make decisions in the specific environmental conflict situation.

Procedural alternatives, such as traditional public participation activities (e.g., public hearings, open houses) and collaborative methods like Collaborative Learning, should be evaluated by criteria such as inclusivity, accessibility, and resource availability. Conveners and decision authorities should determine what procedures correspond best with their management goals and financial, staff, and time resources. Collaborative methods, for example, may require more time and staff training than consultative techniques.

The Progress Triangle: The Substance Dimension.   The third dimension of the Progress Triangle features the substance of the conflict situation. Substantive items are the tangible aspects of a conflict, such as the issues about which the disputants negotiate. Substance, though, also includes issues that parties may consider symbolic, such as "righting a past wrong." The following set of questions offers a framework for assessing substance.

1. What are the issues?
    *   What are the tangible issues?
    *   What are the symbolic issues?
2. What are the likely sources of tension over these issues (e.g., facts, culture, history, jurisdiction, values, interests, people)?
3. Are issues complex? Technical?
4. Is information needed? Is it available?
5. Are meanings, interpretations, and understandings quite varied?
6. Are learning opportunities available?
7. What are the mutual gain options (opportunities for mutually beneficial improvements), such as expanding the pie, nonspecific compensation, logrolling, bridging, fractionation, and cost cutting.

The most obvious area when assessing substance consists of the issues in the environmental conflict situation. As we have noted, issues can be substantive, symbolic, or both. Whether or not to designate a stand of timber for sale is a substantive issue. To some parties, such as those who have traditionally hunted in that timber stand, the sale issue may be quite personal and symbolic.

Once issues are identified, the evaluation can examine the "sources of tension" germane to those issues. As we noted in Chapter 3, sources of tension include (adapted from Wehr, 1979):

*   *Facts*: Disagreement over the "facts" of the issue, over what is true or accurate and what is "reality."
*   *Values*: Disagreement over what should be the determinants (criteria, bases, priorities) of a policy decision, a relationship, or some other issue in conflict.

- *Interests*: Disagreement over who will get what in the distribution of scarce resources, whether tangible or intangible (e.g., land, economic benefits, rights, privileges, control, respect).
- *Jurisdiction*: Disagreement over who has authority or jurisdiction concerning the problems and issues of the conflict and who has standing or legitimacy in the situation.
- *Persons/parties*: Disagreement pertaining to personal factors, such as interaction styles, idiosyncratic actions, personality-related behaviors, effects of the physical setting, and the like.
- *History*: Disagreement related to the history of the issue(s), the conflict, and the conflict relationship, as perceived by the parties in conflict.
- *Culture*: Disagreements that pertain to cultural orientations, worldviews, and identities. Parties' different cultural foundations, when not addressed, may contribute to misunderstanding.

Issues need to be evaluated according to their complexity. If issues are very technical, parties may need "content knowledge" learning opportunities. Information may need to be gathered and disseminated. If the issues are complex, systems thinking activities should help parties understand that complexity.

Analysis of the substantive dimension of the conflict should also focus on mutual gain opportunities. Collaborative Learning and other similar collaborative processes may not be helpful if the outcomes (improvements, agreements) do not benefit all the parties in some way. Various mutual gain outcomes may be relevant to a given environmental conflict situation. These include:

- *Expanding the pie*—Redefining the issues in the conflict so that more material is negotiable. The parties move from an "either-or" (zero-sum) to a "both-and" (variable-sum) perspective. Expanding the pie also occurs when more resources are added to the negotiation (Lewicki et al., 1994).
- *Non-specific compensation*—One party receives its objectives, while the other party is rewarded or compensated for yielding or accommodating. The first party, for example, might receive the desired immediate outcome while the second or other party will receive a benefit of similar value later on (Lewicki et al. 1994).
- *Logrolling*—Parties identify more than one issue in conflict and then identify priorities. Assuming priorities are different, the parties "trade off" these issues so each receives its top priority (Lewicki et al., 1994; Pruitt, 1981).
- *Cost cutting*—When parties or people experience conflict, any particular solutions may involve "costs" (economic cuts, inconvenience, suffering, harm, such as loss of face or reputation). By mutual agreement, a settlement might be found whereby one party achieves his or her objectives, and the other party gains reduced costs (Lewicki et al., 1994; Pruitt, 1983).

- *Bridging*—Parties understand one another's interests and invent new options that meet them. Bridging often requires fundamental reformulation of the problems in the conflict (Lewicki et al., 1994).

- *Fractionating the conflict*—Complex conflicts or issues can be broken up into smaller concerns. Dealing with the smaller, less significant issues first may build trust. Negotiators can employ a "salami tactic," moving ahead "one slice at a time" (Fisher, 1972).

- *Alternation*—If the conflict involves limited resources (a "fixed pie"), parties do not give up their preferred outcome but agree to gain it at a different time.

- *Unlinking*—Like fractionating, the negotiators divide issues. In doing so, they identify interests and positions that they are willing to concede. In order to achieve an integrative solution, parties may have to give up certain positions/demands or lower particular goals.

- *Intangible issue conversion*—Some issues in a dispute are tangible; definable, and reasonably objective, such as economic matters. Other issues are intangible, subjective, and abstract, such as respect, legitimacy, and face. Intangible issue concerns often override discussion of tangible issues and are difficult to negotiate in intangible form. Issues like face and respect need to be converted into something tangible, such as behaviors that can be negotiated. An issue like legitimacy might be converted into notification.

Using the Progress Triangle to Assess Collaborative Potential

Assessing a policy conflict situation in terms of the Progress Triangle's dimensions should help the analyst determine: (1) the current potential for collaboration and (2) the extent to which certain aspects of the situation need to be changed in order to establish good potential for collaboration. There is no formula for this assessment process. Rather, the analyst has to assess the situation as comprehensively as possible given available resources to do so, such as time, access to people for interviews, review of documents, and so on. In policy conflict situations, though, the parties' willingness to work together and the decision makers' willingness to share decision space are key factors. Still, the Progress Triangle can be a guide to developing preliminary assessment instruments that could be used to better understand various pressing conflicts and compare them. In a number of Collaborative Learning training programs, we have developed such an instrument, an example of which appears in Table 8.2.

Role Assessment. Related to the environmental conflict situation itself is the party's role in the conflict situation. Consequently, the role that a party or stakeholder plays in an environmental conflict situation is an important assessment area. An assessment process can begin with a party (individual, group, organization) identifying its probable role(s) in the environmental conflict situation. Each role that a party enacts in a given environmental policy conflict situation will influence that party's way of assessing and understanding the

Table 8.2
Progress Triangle Conflict Assessment Work Sheet

Instructions: Select a conflict or decision situation that is: (a) important to you, and (b) one in which you hope collaboration can occur. Assess that situation according to its relationship, procedure, and substance dimensions. The questions presented here are samples; you may want to modify them, replace them, or add to them.

Step One: Describe that Situation.

Step Two: Evaluate the Relationship Dimension of the Situation.
R1. Who are the major primary parties (i.e., directly involved) and their spokespersons?
R2. Are these parties willing to collaborate? To what extent? Can parties opposed to collaboration be persuaded to try?
R3. Who are the secondary parties and their access points?
R4. What is the history among the major parties?
R5. What is the degree of trust among the parties? How might it be improved?
R6. What power resources do the major parties have? What are the major parties' alternatives to collaboration?
R8. Who are the essential decision makers?
R8. Do any parties have face or identity concerns?
R9. Do parties have the capacity (e.g., time, skills) to work through the conflict collaboratively? Can capacity be improved?
R10. Are there any parties or individuals who have an incentive to be conflictual, or to impede progress?

Step Three: Evaluate the Procedure Dimension of the Situation.
P1. If not collaboration, what are the alternative methods or venues the major parties may use to pursue their goals (e.g., litigation, lobbying)?
P2. What is the "decision space" for the parties? What can parties contribute to the policy decision?
P3. What is the potential for a collaborative agreement to be "trumped" (blocked, overturned) by a decision authority outside the process?
P4. What are the constraints to applying collaboration to this conflict/decision situation?
    P4a. Are there legal restrictions on a party's participation?
    P4b. Are there deadlines?
    P4c. Are parties and interests diffuse geographically (e.g., local, regional, national)?
    P4d. Are there negative attitudes toward collaboration? From whom?

P5.   Is the collaborative process accessible?

P6.   Is the collaborative process inclusive?

P7.   Who is the best convener for the process?   Are multiple conveners desirable and possible?

P8.   Are external facilitators needed? Who provides facilitation?

Step Four: Evaluate the Substance Dimension of the Situation.

S1.   What are the issues important to this situation?

S2.   Do the issues vary among the parties?

S3.   Which of these issues are tangible?

S4.   Which of these issues are primarily symbolic?

S5.   Are there differences in how the major parties understand the situation, define the issues, and prioritize the issues?

S6.   What are the parties interests and concerns about these issues?

S7.   What policies or actions have been tried in the past to deal with this situation?

S8.   What are the key information needs (e.g., data) or information gaps that should be addressed as part of the process? Is information accessible and understandable?

Step Five: Connections.

C1.   What are the major connections among relationship, procedure, and substance factors you have identified?

C2.   What relationship, procedure, and substance factors can be improved to increase collaborative potential?

situation. In Chapter 3 we explained that a party may enact various roles in a conflict situation. The roles may affect the choice of strategies and tactics employed. Possible general role categories include (1) direct conflict party—in this role, the party interacts and negotiates for herself or himself; (2) conflict party as agent—in this role, the individual interacts or negotiates on behalf of someone else (e.g., an attorney); and (3) indirect conflict party—in this role, the individual uses a conflict agent; the conflict party advises the agent and may give the agent responsibility, while maintaining decision-making authority.

In an environmental conflict, there are more specific roles that a party can enact that correspond to these general role categories. They include:

- Participant: This party has an interest in the situation but no strong positions. A participant wants to be involved in the situation but is not a primary voice for a particular point of view or outcome.

- *Advocate:* This party holds a strong position on one or more of the major issues. An advocate is generally a primary stakeholder who is prepared to support a specific policy decision.
- *Representative:* This party participates or advocates on behalf of a group or organization. The representative may or may not have decision authority from the party that she or he represents.
- *Decision Maker:* This party has the authority to make and implement a decision. The decision maker establishes decision parameters and decision space.
- *Information Provider:* This party provides data or information pertaining to issues in the conflict situation. The information provider may see himself or herself as a "technical expert" or important source of local knowledge.
- *Initiator:* This party identifies the need for a process. The initiator may then become a convener or sponsor or seek parties to fulfill these roles.
- *Sponsor:* This party provides public support for the process. A sponsor may simply lend its name to the process or may also provide resources (money, a site, supplies, speaker, etc).
- *Convener:* This party brings parties together and provides a venue. The convener may also participate in the process design.
- *Designer:* This party designs decision-related processes appropriate for the conflict situation at hand.
- *Facilitator:* This party guides the process in an impartial manner. The facilitator may be internal to the situation (e.g., a member of an involved organization) or may be external (e.g., a consultant).
- *Evaluator:* This party evaluates whatever processes may be employed for working through the conflict situation.

A primary party in an environmental conflict should assess the role(s) that it prefers to enact in that conflict situation, as well as the role(s) that other parties will expect it to play. When considering roles, parties need to assess the extent to which other parties will see a new role as appropriate and credible. For example, if the Sierra Club wants to convene a diverse, multiparty collaborative process like Collaborative Learning, it needs to evaluate its ability to function in that role and evaluate the extent to which other parties will grant legitimacy to that role (Table 8.3).

The key roles in an environmental conflict situation seem to be participant, advocate, convener, and facilitator. When a party assumes more than one role, it should assess role compatibility. For example, a facilitator cannot likely assume any other role without compromising its impartiality. In contrast, a convener may also be able to interact as an advocate on some issues. Role assessment should include evaluation of an intended or desired role in a thoughtful, systematic way.

Table 8.3
Role Assessment Grid

Party	Intended Role	Expected Role	Goals	Interests

The following questions concerning the advocate, convener, and facilitator roles may prove helpful. An equivalent set of questions could be developed for other roles.

About Advocacy
- Do we (my party) have strong views and values on the issues?
- Do we want to share our knowledge of the situation?
- Do we have an action agenda we want to pursue? Do we have a solution in mind?
- Do we want to persuade others?
- Do others see us as an advocate/advocacy group?
- Do other parties?
- Do our own constituents?
- Does our staff?
- Can we shift roles depending on the situation?

About Convening
- Are we comfortable with the process moving in any direction?
- If necessary, can we accept a non-advocacy role?
- Are we satisfied with the process design?
- Are we viewed by parties as credible and fair?
- Are resources sufficient (staff time, physical facilities, budgets, etc.)?
- Do we want convening partners?

About Facilitation
- Do we (my party) want to manage the process?
- Do we have the necessary facilitation skills?
- Do we have sufficient content knowledge?
- Are we comfortable with not voicing our concerns and ideas about the situation?
- Can we remain impartial? Will the parties see us as fair?
- Do we need to involve outside facilitators?

As these questions reveal, the roles of advocate, convener, and facilitator are clearly different. The questions for the facilitator and advocate roles indicate the incompatibility of these two roles. Both roles are appropriate in an environmental conflict situation, but the party that attempts to be both advocate and facilitator will likely have little credibility in either role.

Understanding one's own role, the likely roles of other parties, and the expectations held about appropriate roles can be essential to understanding the collaborative potential of an environmental conflict situation. If parties enact incompatible roles or roles that others see as illegitimate, conflict management progress may be thwarted, and relationship issues could escalate. Furthermore, questions may arise about substantive and procedural issues as well. For example, if a party has convened a collaborative process that involves diverse participants, the convening party must consider the implications of also serving as a "technical expert" or "information provider" role. Even though enacting these dual roles may be possible, the convening party should be sensitive about how other parties will perceive the consistency and fairness of doing so.

TRAINING

The second component of a comprehensive Collaborative Learning project is training. Training provides people with the opportunity to learn about collaborative processes like Collaborative Learning and to determine if and where collaboration fits into their environmental conflict and decision work. Simply put, training helps people to learn and to decide if they want to "buy in" to the collaborative process.

When we first began to apply Collaborative Learning, we did not include a training component. Instead, we moved from assessment into design. Over time, we discovered that many people within the organization that convened the process had no idea what Collaborative Learning involved and why we did what we did. We learned that providing training to members of the convening organization(s) and interest group leaders was very important to the effectiveness of a Collaborative Learning project. Through Collaborative Learning training, key participants can learn about collaboration, Collaborative Learning, systems thinking, and conflict management in ways relevant to their environmental conflict and decision situations. After learning about Collaborative Learning— learning its principles and practicing some of its techniques—the participants can decide if and how Collaborative Learning should be applied to their situation.

When applied in external organizational settings (e.g., communication interaction between a management agency and interest groups), Collaborative Learning has the best prospects when the convening organization also uses collaboration internally. Training helps participants improve their collaboration skills within their organizations as well as in external, public settings.

A CL Activity: The "Best and Worst" Exercise

As we pointed out earlier, Collaborative Learning training programs should feature active learning tasks. One we have used in a number of trainings is the "best and worst" exercise. We have used this activity typically as an introductory task. Participants write out a description of a "best" experience they recall or a "best" future they envision pertinent to the training situation. They also write out a "worst" experience or "worst" future they foresee. As training program participants introduce themselves, they share their bests and/or worsts with one another. Through this exercise, participants are introduced to one another and learn about some meaningful experiences or predictions. Typical instructions are as follows:

Instructions: You have received an index card. On one side of the card, describe your *best memory* of a planning, public participation, or ID team experience. On the other side of the card, describe your *worst memory* of a planning, public participation, or ID team experience. Please label each side of your card "best" and "worst." You do not need to put your name on the card. You will be asked to share your "best" and/or "worst" with the group.

We strive to create training programs that emphasize the adult learning principles presented in Chapter 5. This is exemplified through our use of active learning. For example, our training courses devote significant time to systems thinking, an area that we teach, in part, through situation mapping. People learn how to foster systems thinking by practicing systems or situation mapping, an activity that we discuss later in the chapter under "Design." The *Fifth Discipline Fieldbook* (Senge et al., 1994) is an excellent source of systems thinking activities. Similarly, materials from the Structured Experiences series (Pfeffer & Jones, various years) may be useful for teaching conflict management principles and skills.

Collaborative Learning training programs vary in length, depending on the nature of the Collaborative Learning project, the needs of the convening organization(s), and scheduling constraints. We included some sample training outlines of varying lengths (Tables 8.4, 8.5).

Table 8.4
A Sample Two-Day Collaborative Learning Training Program

Day One: September 3
0900   Instructor introductions and workshop logistics
0915   Best and worst planning experiences (break follows)
1030   Why consider a collaborative learning approach?
        Traditional public involvement and collaboration
        Collaborative public participation
1115   The nature of Collaborative Learning (lunch follows)
1315   Systems and systems thinking
1330   An exercise in systems thinking (break follows)
1445   Group reports and systems improvement
1530   Application in planning situations: Assessing collaborative potential
1630   First day wrap-up

Day Two: September 4
0830   Assessing collaborative potential, continued.
        Application of CL to natural resource management situations
        Internal situations
        External situations (break follows)
1030   Group reports and discussion (lunch follows)
1300   A CL approach to public involvement: Design issues (break follows)
1445   A CL approach to collaborative stewardship
1600   Second day wrap up

Table 8.5
A Sample Three-Day Collaborative Learning Training Program

Day One: February 18
0830   Welcome and plan for the day
0915   The nature of environmental public policy conflict
        The Collaborative Learning approach (followed by a break)
1130   One leg of Collaborative Learning: systems thinking
        A systems thinking exercise (followed by lunch)
1315   Another leg of Collaborative Learning: Conflict management
        and negotiation . . . the Progress Triangle . . . and a conflict management
        exercise (followed by a break)
1445   A Collaborative Learning approach for community sustainability:
        An improvements perspective
1600   Identifying local controversies and assessing collaborative potential

Day Two: February 19
0900   Welcome and plan for the days ahead
0915   Introductions: "bests and worsts"
1000   Individual and collective objectives (followed by a break)
1030   What is Collaborative Learning?: A review
1045   Collaborative Learning: The importance of systems thinking
1115   A systems thinking activity (followed by lunch)
1330   Revisiting "bests and worsts": Collaborative Learning and assessing the
            situation (a break follows)
1445   Forest policy working groups
1630   Homework assignment

Day Three: February 20
0830   Doing Collaborative Learning: A workshop experience
0900   Issue presentations (followed by a break)
1015   A situation map discussion
1115   Concerns and interests (followed by lunch)
1330   Generating and discussing improvements (rolling break)
1530   Facilitating CL: Fundamental Skills
1615   Ideas for the future . . . pilot projects . . . and wrap-up

DESIGN

The third component to a comprehensive Collaborative Learning effort is design. Design refers generally to the overall plan—the strategy and tactics—for implementing a Collaborative Learning conflict management or decision-making approach. Design focuses on the "how to" of Collaborative Learning. Design issues can be organized along "journalistic" lines, that is, what, who, when, where, how, and how much. For the purposes of this discussion we use the term "convener" to refer to the party or parties responsible for designing the process. In many environmental conflict situations, the convener is the party with the management, regulatory, and/or decision-making responsibility.

The "What" of Design

This design issue is fundamental to a Collaborative Learning process. The conveners of a collaborative conflict management or decision-making process like Collaborative Learning need to identify their process and outcome goals. What outcomes or "products" do they hope a collaborative process will produce? The Progress Triangle can be a useful framework for identifying process and outcome goals. A collaborative process like CL can generate meaningful progress substantively, relationally, and procedurally.

The "what" of design also addresses constraints. Conveners need to consider time frames and resource needs. In order to achieve the identified goals, what timeline is appropriate? Are there relevant deadlines? Are organizational and community resources sufficient for goal attainment? Other questions are:

What are my (my party's) goals and objectives?
- What are my substantive goals?
- What tangible issues need to be addressed?
- Do I want implementation partners?

What are my (my party's) relationship goals?
- What relationship factors are important?
- Do I want to improve relationships among the parties?
- Do I hope that parties learn from each other?

What are my (my party's) procedural goals?
- What decisions need to be made?
- Do I want parties to have significant ownership of the process and outcome?
- What deadlines do I face?
- What staff and community resources are available?

The "Who" of Design

Once the convening party has identified his or her goals, he or she needs to address the "who" of process design. "Who" refers to "by whom, for whom, and with whom." "By whom" addresses who will be part of the process design. First, the convener should decide if it wants to be the sole designer of the process or bring in consultants to assist in the design. If the convening party has the process expertise (e.g., has staff who have gone through collaborative process training), he or she may be able to design a good process without assistance. Still, the use of external consultants may infuse new ideas and improve the process design.

A second "by whom" issue concerns process design "partners." At some point in the design work, the convener may invite other parties to help with the process design. For example, the convening party might develop a very tentative design and invite other parties to review and suggest improvements in that design. Doing so encourages other parties to invest in the design process and take some ownership of the final approach used. Furthermore, design partners can often provide information critical to good design work that the primary convener does not have on his or her own. For example, a federal agency might want to hold Collaborative Learning citizen workshops on recreation planning issues. By convening a design feedback meeting of interest group leaders, the convening agency can learn what technical presentations might be helpful, if the interest groups could recommend any workshop presenters, the days of the week and times of day citizens would most likely attend a workshop, and so on.

"For whom" focuses on who will benefit from the Collaborative Learning process. The designer (convener, consultant design team, convening partners) should clarify what primary and secondary parties will want to participate in, watch closely, and/or expect to benefit or believe they may be harmed by, the process and its outcomes. "For whom" factors relate to "role responsiveness," discussed in Chapter 3. As we noted then, related to a party's role in an environmental conflict situation, such as convener, is that party's responsiveness in that role (Druckman, 1977). In any given conflict situation, for example, the convening party must weigh and balance responsiveness and accountability to a number of parties. These include the convening party's responsiveness to itself (its own organization and staff, both vertically and horizontally); the convening party's responsiveness to the other direct conflict parties; the convening party's responsiveness to its own primary constituency; the convening party's responsiveness to secondary parties (those that influence it or other primary parties); the convening party's responsiveness to the public and community; the convening party's responsiveness to the media; and the conflict party's responsiveness to precedent and principle.

"With whom" asks the convener to consider whom it wants to be involved (to participate in) in the Collaborative Learning process. If the convener wants to include a select group of parties (e.g., invite some but not all parties), it needs to consider the tangible, symbolic, and legal implications of doing so. For example, if a federal agency designs a collaborative process for a select group of invited parties, it may need to comply with the Federal Advisory Committee Act (FACA).

"With whom" emphasizes issues of inclusivity and accessibility. In designing a Collaborative Learning process, the convener should consider the degree of inclusivity desired. Does the convener desire the broadest, most diverse participation possible? If so, the design needs to be responsive to the cultural, values, and interest diversity within and between relevant communities.

Sample questions concerning the "who" of design are:

Collaborative Learning by Whom?
- Do we (the convening party) design the process ourselves?
- Do we need to bring in consultants to lead a design team?
- Should we involve other parties in the design process?
- Should we seek cosponsors of all or some part of the process?
- Do we hope other parties will share ownership of the process?
- Who will facilitate the designed process? Should the facilitators be members of the convening party, local neutral facilitators, or external professional facilitators?

Collaborative Learning for Whom?
- Who wants a Collaborative Learning process to occur in this situation?
- Is there support within our own organization or group, vertically and horizontally?
- Who may be opposed to, or apathetic about, the Collaborative Learning process? Are these parties open to learning about CL and giving the process a chance?
- To whom do we (the convening party) need to be responsive?

Collaborative Learning with Whom?
- Who do we (the convening party) want involved in this process? How can we get them involved?
- How inclusive do we want the process? How can we achieve our inclusiveness goal?
- How accessible do we want the process? How can we achieve our accessibility goal?
- Are multiple methods for participation desirable and feasible?
- What parts of the design and design process are particularly symbolic, and for whom?
- Do we want to keep "sideline" parties informed? How can we do that?

Inclusivity is related to accessibility. The Collaborative Learning approach should benefit from, and be sensitive to, diversity, and diversity is fostered through making the collaborative process accessible. A half-day public meeting on a weekday/workday may be convenient for paid professionals (e.g., agency employees, interest group lobbyists, and lawyers) but may not be accessible for the interested citizen who cannot afford to take time off to attend.

The goals of inclusivity and accessibility can be met in a number of ways. First, conveners can devote time to outreach. Process conveners often include as one of their goals the substantive involvement of the greatest number and diversity of participants as possible. Design creativity can encourage moving beyond traditional participation process methods. Some groups may be willing to come to a multiparty gathering, for example, only after the conveners or decision makers have met with that group individually, at a place and time the group has determined. The collaborative process may need to be multifaceted, in terms of both method and place. Some citizens might prefer to participate privately, via a letter, phone call, or web site reply. Some parties might go to a Collaborative Learning meeting only in their own town and be reluctant to travel to a community 20 miles away. Many citizens may not see a meeting announcement published in the public notices section of the local newspaper but may learn about the meeting from a church bulletin, broadcast public service announcement, newsletter, or posting on the grocery store or laundromat bulletin board.

Second, inclusion and access are fostered through sensitivity to the symbolism of design. The design and implementation of a collaborative process like Collaborative Learning are important both tangibly and symbolically. Tangibly, the collaborative process should be responsive to concerns about inclusivity, accessibility, psychological and physical safety, and comfort. Symbolically, design choices communicate powerful messages to parties about their standing and legitimacy in the situation. For example, the decision to hold a Collaborative Learning workshop on a weekday may communicate to citizens that they are unimportant because they must take time off work to attend. Conducting a field trip in English only may discourage non-English or non-native English speakers from participating and communicate to them that their ideas are not valued as much as those of English speakers.

Third, some parties may be very skeptical about a Collaborative Learning approach to a particular environmental conflict situation. They may choose to maintain their distance or "stay on the sidelines" and not get involved, even though the convener wants them to participate and has encouraged them to do so. The convener needs to design the process such that it keeps the door open for the "sideline" parties to participate at some future point (Ury, 1992). Collaborative processes are frequently ongoing, with parties and their representatives changing and with opportunities for new parties to join the process at various points. The Collaborative Learning approach can be designed to keep "sideline" parties informed about collaborative progress, so that if and when Collaborative Learning becomes an attractive alternative, "sideline" parties can become direct participants.

The "When, Where, and How" of Design

"When, where, and how" issues grow out of the convener's assessment of the situation and choices about what and whom. "When and where" matters relate to "with whom" factors of accessibility and inclusion. Choices about when and where design events occur depend on time of year, available resources, and planning timelines as well as the ripeness of the conflict situation and whom the convener wants involved in the process. A common Collaborative Learning event is a meeting, such as a CL citizen workshop. Consequently, the "when, where, and how" of design can focus on planning a meeting.

IMPLEMENTATION AND FACILITATION

After the Collaborative Learning approach has been designed, it is ready to be implemented. Effective implementation relies on competent design and facilitation.

Implementing Effective Meetings

There are myriad details involved in conducting effective meetings, ranging from room layout, to scheduling, to agenda, to refreshments. It is certainly possible to become entirely bogged down in these minutiae; in fact, some facilitator training sessions that we have reviewed put much of their focus on these issues. But at a larger level, Collaborative Learning meetings inevitably seem to be juggling two questions: what are our core learning/communication goals, and what are our constraints? The design choices must further the learning tasks that the meeting, workshop, or field trip is intended to promote. These learning goals define what is desirable in terms of an ideal process, and the ideal format for Collaborative Learning meetings changes substantially as the process progresses around Kolb's learning cycle (Kolb, 1984). But that ideal can rarely (if ever) be completely achieved because of constraints to the process. Certainly, in the venues in which we have worked—which typically are smaller towns—the availability of meeting rooms has forced us to adapt. We have conducted meetings in a wide variety of spaces, from grange halls, to high schools, to city council chambers. In addition, there is no single locale or time of the day or week that works for all of the potentially relevant stakeholders. Any meeting choice constrains their participation. But the learning goals are our touchstone as we make decisions in response to these challenges.

A well-run meeting is not unlike a fine restaurant, in that the surroundings should add to the experience, not detract from it. A meeting should be comfortable for the participants, and the notion of comfort is multifaceted. It should be held at a place that does not intimidate them. For example, we rarely hold meetings in Forest Service buildings, and we dissuade Forest Service employees from wearing their official uniforms.

The room should provide sensory comfort; not too loud, dark, hot, bright, stuffy, and so on. The pace of the meeting should not be exhausting, because we must always remember that the people who choose to attend a meeting are voluntarily donating their time and no doubt have busy and tiring lives. Evening meetings are particularly problematic in this regard; if we expect people to go home from work, grab a quick dinner, and then go to our meeting, we have an obligation to make it as pleasant as possible. The facilitation should use time efficiently, but not leave the workshop participants feeling rushed.

The physical layout of the room is another aspect of meeting design where choices flow directly out of the learning goals. The key is to employ a layout that facilitates the kinds of communication that promote the learning activities. In some stages of Collaborative Learning, the primary communication flow is from a presenter to a listening audience. This kind of learning can be accommodated quite nicely by a lecture-style room layout. But more often in Collaborative Learning, the learning tasks are occurring *among* the participants, and this is best served by small tables where they can interact. There are other situations where the learning is related to specific topics, and then a workshop design where people circulate to different "stations" to learn about the different topics might be preferable. It can also be quite useful to have a variety of maps on the walls where the workshop participants can either gather information or make spatially specific comments by writing directly on a map. Moreover, it is possible to alter the room layout in the course of a long workshop as the learning tasks change. We have, for instance, used lecture-style seating in the morning and discussion tables in the afternoon. There are even times when a "meeting" (i.e., people interacting in a room) is not compatible with the learning goal and a field trip or some other learning opportunity is called for.

There are also activities that are commonly part of planning team or public involvement meetings that are rarely used in Collaborative Learning meetings because they have low learning value or may even reduce learning. A prime example is the "go-around," where people introduce themselves and state their affiliation ("Hi, I am Bob, and I am with the South Hills Conservation Alliance"). Social cognition research clearly shows that when we label people as belonging to a particular group, we begin to interpret what they say through a filter of our own attitudes toward that group (e.g., Fiske & Taylor, 1991). If we belong to that group or feel allied to it, then we will be more favorably disposed to the comments. But to the extent that we feel ourselves opposed to that group, then it will be quite hard to accurately hear and evaluate those statements. In many ways, a "go-around" can reinforce group-based stereotypes and perceptions, which is contrary to the learning goals that are at the core of Collaborative Learning.

Facilitation Defined

Facilitation refers to an impartial third party's providing procedural guidance to group participants to promote constructive communication, information exchange, learning, and collaborative negotiation. Facilitation can be provided by members of the convening party, facilitators obtained locally, or professional facilitators who may be outside the local community. The choice of facilitators should be based on the related factors of impartiality, fairness, and credibility. Regardless of who facilitates (internal, local, external), Collaborative Learning participants need to view the facilitators as impartial on the issues, parties, and possible improvements; fair toward the parties and the process; and credible as skilled facilitators who understand something about the parties and the situation.

Facilitation involves an impartial third party's providing procedural guidance to group participants to promote constructive communication, information exchange, learning, and collaborative negotiation. The facilitator could be a member of the discussion group but needs to play only the facilitator role (wear only one hat). Facilitation requires skills designed to help parties communicate constructively and competently in challenging situations. According to Kiser (1998), a skilled facilitator is adept at removing barriers to performance, engineering effective and empowering change efforts, aiding a group to improve as a team, guiding parties as they work through a conflict, and assisting a team to develop a strategic plan as they work through a conflict. The facilitator emphasizes the process so that parties can work together well. Reaching agreement is not a primary goal.

In contrast, mediation is an intervention by a neutral and impartial third party into an existing dispute in order to facilitate joint decision-making (integrative) negotiation. The mediator does not resolve conflict for the parties, has no authority to make decisions for, or control the actions of, the parties, and can work effectively only when all parties participate willingly in the mediation. Facilitators use many of the same techniques as mediators, but in mediation processes agreement is a primary goal.

Facilitation and Collaborative Learning

Collaborative Learning activities are generally facilitated, although the facilitation need not be done by someone outside the group, organization, or community. Regardless of the environmental conflict situation, there are some general features of Collaborative Learning facilitation. These include:

- *Do assessment work.* We have emphasized throughout this chapter the importance of assessment. This applies to the facilitators as well as conveners. The facilitators need to develop a fundamental understanding of the environmental conflict situation. This likely includes general knowledge of the substantive issues of the situation.
- *Consider participant needs, room settings, and media resources.* As we noted in the design section of this chapter, participants in a collaborative process benefit from a comfortable, appropriate work setting.
- *Plan for contingencies.* Anticipate challenging behaviors and develop responses to them. Cranky people and difficult behaviors can be managed best by anticipating them and what one may do as a facilitator if they appear.
- *Whenever possible, work as part of a facilitation team.* Given the complexity of environmental conflict situations, a facilitation team can better direct a Collaborative Learning process than an individual facilitator. Workshops may include many different parties, and discussion groups may be large. If an individual becomes difficult, one facilitator can talk with that person individually while the other facilitator continues to direct the process.
- *Maintain flexibility in the process.* Adjust such things as work sheet time and discussion group size based on the situation.

There is an extensive body of literature on facilitator skills. Recent works by Hunter et al. (1995), Kaner et al. (1996), Kiser (1998), Weaver and Farrell (1997), and Webne-Behrman (1998) provide numerous useful ideas on how to facilitate, particularly in group and organizational settings. Many of these authors' ideas may be relevant to facilitating collaborative public participation processes in environmental conflict situations.

Key Collaborative Learning Facilitation Skills

A CL facilitator should possess and employ skills that facilitators use in conflict, team-building, and decision-making situations. Still, there are some skills we believe are extremely important to a Collaborative Learning process. Essential facilitation skills include:

Patience. As we have noted throughout this book, environmental conflicts are complex. Among complexity factors are the many parties involved and the strong values they hold about environmental issues generally and the matters of the specific conflict situation. Consequently, participants in a Collaborative Learning process will be coming to that process from different directions and often with skepticism. Facilitators need to be responsive to participants' skepticism about, and hesitation to engage, the collaborative process. Furthermore, by exhibiting patience, facilitators communicate respect for people who are working through issues in ways they have likely done before, with a diverse group they may not typically encounter.

Active, supportive listening. Listening is a fundamental and often overlooked communication skill (Adler & Towne, 1998). Facilitators need to both practice and foster active listening. Participants, via Collaborative Learning process guidelines and facilitator guidance, can listen to others actively and respectfully. They can be encouraged to withhold judgments until they understand the other party's ideas, to not interrupt, to ask clarifying questions, and to listen for the essential message rather than just the detail.

Keeping personal views and substantive knowledge in check. Earlier we stated that Collaborative Learning facilitators need to have a basic knowledge of the substantive or content issues of the environmental conflict situation. Such knowledge improves the facilitator's credibility and her or his ability to develop situation maps and track parties' conversations about the issues at hand. At the same time, the facilitator should avoid becoming a content provider or issue advocate in the Collaborative Learning process. Like mediators, Collaborative Learning facilitators may ask questions to encourage parties to identify their interests, clarify and assess their improvements, and consider alternatives. But CL facilitators should not debate the participants' ideas, unless they are willing to permanently leave their facilitator role so that they can be advocates.

Continual monitoring. During our discussion of communication competence in Chapter 7, we featured "self-monitoring." Facilitators need to monitor their own behaviors during the Collaborative Learning process, but they need to monitor participant actions as well. For example, CL facilitators should move among CL discussion groups to evaluate the progress that groups are making and if parties are interacting constructively and respectfully. Facilitators should be aware of the potential for participants to be angry or upset about the environmental conflict situation. Such participants may need opportunities to vent or may need more facilitation attention so that their behaviors remain constructive.

Modeling behaviors. Modeling can be an important part of competent communication interaction and conflict management (Johnson, 1990). CL facilitators should recognize that they are models for the communication competence and conflict management behaviors that they hope CL participants will exhibit.

Acknowledgment and recognition. In their groundbreaking book *The Promise of Mediation*, Bush and Folger (1994) emphasize that effective mediation should do more than simply try to gain an agreement among disputants. Bush and Folger advocate a mediation process that empowers disputants to assert themselves and recognizes disputants when they make constructive contributions and interact well. Similarly, CL facilitators should acknowledge the contributions of CL participants and recognize them for their investment in the process as well as their good ideas.

Facilitation Tools

Collaborative Learning processes, such as citizen participation workshops, respect strategic behaviors, self-interest, and competitive incentives. Many CL participants may view the specific environmental conflict situation competitively. Therefore, a challenge that the CL facilitator may face concerns converting competitive orientations and behaviors into collaboration. Drawing from a number of sources (Lewicki et al., 1994; Rubin et al., 1991; Wilmot & Hocker, 1998; Gray, 1989; Fisher et al., 1991; Folger et al., 1997; Ury, 1993), we have assembled this set of tools for doing so.

1. *Propose a "learning" perspective.* Conflicts and disputes are often challenging to work through. A benefit to the challenge is the learning that can occur about the issues, the parties, and the relationship. If disputants see the conflict interaction as a mutual or joint learning opportunity, they may be more inclined to collaborate.

2. *Make trust an overt issue.* Some reasonable level of trust is critical to collaboration. You can build trust by discussing why parties may not trust one another and what parties can do to earn and display trust. You can begin by asking others to express concerns about the degree of trust in the situation and their own trustworthiness as parties.

3. *Encourage sharing information.* Sharing information can build confidence in the process and trust among the parties. Guide parties to focus on interests and concerns and to model interest-disclosing behavior. Use questions to discover underlying interests and to reduce ambiguity and uncertainty.

4. *Foster metacommunication, or "talk about talk."* Parties can communicate about the dispute settlement and interaction process. Take stock from time to time about the collaborative process you are using and how well it is working (Tjosvold, 1991).

Parties can discuss how well they are communicating and what they are learning from one another.

5. *Ask CL participants to commit to constructive, competent communication.* This can be done as part of the CL process "ground rules" (see later discussion) as well as throughout the CL process. Help parties practice the following communication behaviors:

    a. Active listening (including paraphrasing). This includes withholding judgments until one understands the other's positions and interests.

    b. Relevant self-disclosure of information and reactions.

    c. Checking one's perceptions rather than assuming one knows what another party means or intends.

    d. Describe behavior and indicate how one is reacting to that behavior.

    e. Use "I" messages. Parties can keep their messages focused on themselves ("I am frustrated by this road closure") rather than labeling or accusing ("You closed the road and must not care about the local community").

    f. Criticize and evaluate constructively.

6. *Encourage sensitivity to language and definition.* Anticipate possible meanings and interpretations. Reframe parties' statements to promote clear understanding. Reframe issues, interests, and concerns in order to transcend differences and locate some common ground. For example, "conflict resolution" may be reframed as conflict "management" or "situation improvement."

7. *Recognize disagreement and encourage parties who disagree to argue collaboratively and constructively.* Acknowledge and foster respect for diversity of opinions. Encourage inquiry and disagreements that stem from interests. Keep arguments focused on issues rather than on people. Support "raising doubts" and "constructive skepticism."

8. *Ask parties to try to understand the views of others.* CL facilitators can use questions and discussion tasks to encourage:

    a. Role reversal—Examining and attempting to understand the issues from the other party's/parties' perspective.

    b. Bilateral focus—A variation of role reversal; parties share with one another perceptions about what the other is feeling, thinking, interpreting, and thinking.

    c. Imaging—Each party indicates how it see itself, how it sees the other, how it thinks the other party would describe it, and how it thinks the other party views itself. The information is shared.

    d. Mirroring—A third party (e.g., the facilitator or another member of the CL process) interviews the conflicting parties about the difficulties of working together, shares this information in a joint session, and facilitates discussion.

9. *Help parties identify and arrange consequences.* CL participants can negotiate outcomes that will occur if someone violates the ground rules, withdraws from the CL process, breaks an agreement, or moves away from a collaborative strategy. Consequences may be stipulated in a protective contract (Druckman, 1977). Such a prenegotiation agreement clarifying consequences may establish a foundation for collaboration.

10. *Monitor and model behavior*. Provide feedback to parties and ask them to take stock of the appropriateness and effectiveness of their party's and others' behaviors.

11. *Reduce tension*. Unproductive conflicts and disputes often become highly emotional and personal. Parties become angry, frustrated, and upset. They display strong commitments to positions and argue strenuously for their side, and rigidity increases. When discussion turns into personal attack, little promise remains for a productive outcome. Tensions can be addressed via the following:

    a. Tension release or "venting"—allow a party to vent emotion (a cathartic release). This may be accomplished via "open microphone time" (see later discussion). Emphasize the importance of recognizing that feelings are authentic and legitimate; encourage parties to respect and acknowledge other parties' feelings and concerns. The parties may discuss feelings without counseling one another; they can be guided to engage in appropriate self-disclosure.

    b. Call for a break of an appropriate length (e.g., a recess) in the process to give parties time to be away from one another.

    c. Where feasible, separate the parties and employ a caucus to meet with parties individually (Moore, 1988).

12. *Coordinate de-escalation*. You could encourage synchronized de-escalation, GRIT (Graduated Reciprocation and Tension Reduction, sometimes referred to as graduated reduction in tension). This refers to intentional concession-making to promote reciprocal concessions (taking turns).

13. *Use a "single negotiating text,"* or "draft discussion text" as a starting point for dialogue (Raiffa, 1982).

14. *"Deconstruct" or take apart the dispute*; "fractionating" or unlinking can reduce a large, complex problem into smaller parts (Fisher, 1972). Techniques include:

    a. Reduce the number of parties on each side (this is very risky in some public policy disputes, because those parties excluded may pursue unilateral BATNAs). A good way to manage party numbers is to promote "self-nomination" or selection, while requiring a strong, demonstrated, literal commitment to the collaboration process.

    b. Control the number of physical, tangible issues involved.

    c. Have parties state issues in concrete terms rather than as principles. If a principle or policy seems to loom as a hidden agenda, then parties should discuss concerns over principles; separate concrete issues from them.

    d. Parties can focus on exceptions to a principle that do not negate the principle.

    e. Parties can be urged to restrict the precedents involved—both procedural and substantive—such that single issues do not become major questions of precedent.

    f. Big issues can be divided into smaller issues: by time, by application, and so on.

    g. Issues should be depersonalized. As Fisher et al. (1991) urge, "Separate the people from the problem."

    h. Parties can distinguish between short-term and long-term concerns. Common ground may be easier to find on long-term concerns. Once that common ground is discovered, parties can back up from the long view to the short term, seeing what common ground might exist along the way.

15. *Help parties establish commonalities.* Escalated conflicts and disputes tend to magnify perceived differences and minimize perceived similarities. The search for common ground seeks to increase similarities.

   a. Superordinate goals—parties look for, and find, common ground among their short-term and/or long-term goals and reframe their description of the situation and these shared interests into superordinate goals.

   b. Common enemies—the parties in conflict find a common enemy, a third party who will gain if the disputants do not reach agreement. Perhaps the enemy is the problem itself or those who will make the decision if the conflict parties do not reach a settlement or generate meaningful improvements.

   c. Agreement on the rules, procedures, timetables, agendas, and so on. Parties can negotiate collaboratively about the process. Parties may modify the Collaborative Learning approach to best meet their needs and the situation.

   d. Identify and create long-term visions of the future.

16. *Recognize each party's legitimacy in the collaboration process.* Maintain sensitivity to face and identity concerns. Intervene actively if significant face concerns arise.

17. *Acknowledge sharing power.* Insofar as possible, support parties' as decision makers, owners of both process and outcome. Possibly raise the issue of developing ongoing collaborative management groups.

18. *Help parties make their preferred options more desirable to the other party.* Techniques include:

   a. A party provides its counterparts with a "yesable" proposal (Fisher & Ury, 1981). A party can create an option (make an offer) on some issue that the other parties will find acceptable.

   b. Parties can ask for a different decision or reformulation of the situation. Help parties revise and refine their demands or needs: rephrase, reformulate, repackage, reorganize. Urge parties to think creatively and invent options for mutual gain.

   c. Parties can sweeten the proposed improvements rather than intensify threats. Encourage the use of positive frames. Rewards are often more enticing than threats.

   d. Parties can generate objective, agreed-upon standards for evaluating alternative solutions or improvements.

19. *If tensions are high, facilitators might help the parties communicate indirectly.* In some situations, direct communication may be difficult or may not be trusted. Indirect and covert tactics may be necessary, such as:

   a. "Trial balloon" ideas and options from one party to another to gauge reaction and get feedback.

   b. Back-channel contacts. Parties might hold informal discussions that are not part of a formal, public process. A "walk in the woods" or an informal dinner meeting at a restaurant can provide parties with safe, relaxed settings to test out ideas.

   c. Parties may communicate through an intermediary (likely a messenger). The facilitator might be the intermediary.

   d. Parties can send conciliatory signals: some symbolic move to indicate a willingness to collaborate and negotiate in good faith. Cards and gifts may symbolize a desire to work through the conflict situation.

While these tools can be useful in facilitating a Collaborative Learning process, we want to feature in depth two that we have used in a number of Collaborative Learning applications.

Ground Rules

The notion of ground rules simply refers to a set of behavioral standards, or rules of conduct, that the workshop participants agree to comply with. The use of ground rules is a common part of mediation or multiparty facilitation (e.g., Carpenter & Kennedy, 1988, distinguish between behavioral, procedural, and substantive ground rules [p. 119]), and it is widely acknowledged among practitioners that the participants in any process must agree to the validity of the ground rules as a precondition to their voluntary compliance with them. A common technique for achieving this commitment to the ground rules is to have the participants generate the rules for themselves, perhaps with a draft list provided by the facilitators as an initial step.

Although Collaborative Learning projects have always used ground rules, we have not undertaken the step of working with the workshop participants to generate the list. Rather, we present a list at the beginning of each workshop and ask if there are any modifications that the workshop participants might prefer. A typical list is provided later. We have adopted this abbreviated strategy because we typically conduct public meetings with no control over the participant list rather than a multi-meeting process with a stable set of participants. Generating a set of ground rules can take several hours, which exceeds the time for the typical evening meeting. If we were working with a finite group of stakeholders who had to work closely together for a long period of time, then the time spent on a participant-generated set of ground rules would be well spent. But since the participant mix changes in each of the public meetings that we have run, a new set of ground rules would need to be generated at each session, which would largely preclude progress on other issues. By providing a set of ground rules, discussing what they mean, and offering the opportunity for modification, we believe that much of the value of ground rules has been achieved but that much less time has been required. Some sample ground rules are:

- Listen openly and actively.
- Withhold judgment until the other person's view is understood.
- Ask questions for understanding before responding.
- Give everyone equal opportunity to speak.
- Focus on concerns and interests rather than positions.
- Examine future improvements rather than dwelling on the past.
- Emphasize the situation rather than the people.
- Value disagreement and constructive argument.
- Look for ways to achieve mutual gain.
- Regard one another's views as legitimate and deserving respect.

- Commit to giving the Collaborative Learning workshop process a chance to succeed.

Open Microphone Time

Despite the use of ground rules, some people may choose to disrupt the orderly progression through the prepared agenda for the workshop. It is a challenge to deal with these behaviors constructively because there is a fine line between being permissive and being autocratic. If the facilitators permit one or more individuals to move the agenda of the meeting according to their wishes, then the needs of the other participants are being largely overlooked. But if the facilitators are excessively heavy-handed in rigidly adhering to a predetermined focus, then that behavior is contrary to the kind of inquisitive experiential learning environment that Collaborative Learning attempts to foster.

In our experience, disruptive behaviors emerge because a workshop participant has an issue or concern that does not appear to fit into the agenda of the meeting, but that participant feels strongly that the issue should be surfaced. The issue may be only tangentially related to the stated purpose of the meeting. At one of the Oregon Dunes National Recreation Area planning meetings held in 1993, a person came to one of our all-day workshops *determined* to discuss the recent Forest Service decision to temporarily suspend commercial mushroom picking in the area. That topic had little to do with the presumed focus of our workshop; ours was just the first Forest Service meeting to be held since the decision was announced, and this mushroom picker was determined to use the workshop that we were facilitating as a means to let the agency know how furious he was with the decision.

The question, then, is to find a means by which people such as this mushroom harvester have time to voice their concerns but also not to allow the meeting to be derailed. The technique that we have adopted in our Collaborative Learning meetings is referred to as "open mic" time because it allows for some unscheduled time for participant comments about issues of their choice, much like "open mic" time on talk radio. While we do not announce it or describe it in any written agendas unless needed, we are prepared to redirect the last portion of the meeting—perhaps 15 to 30 minutes—to "open mic" time. If there appear to be workshop participants with a particular ax to grind, then we will insert the "open mic" time into the schedule, encourage them to participate in the workshop process until that point, and then use the "open mic" time to address their needs.

This strategy seems to meet the needs of most workshop participants, and often by the time the meeting has largely concluded, the initial rancor that made us schedule the open mic time has largely dissipated. One explanation is that the workshop participants may have been able to use other activities such as the work sheets to voice their concerns. (Another, less elegant explanation may be that by the end of the day they are just tired.)

TECHNIQUES TO PROMOTE SYSTEMS THINKING

Situation Mapping

Situation mapping is perhaps the most useful single technique that Collaborative Learning employs in the early stages of the process. Situation maps are identical to the *mind maps* that Wilson and Morren (1990) discuss and that they, in turn, attribute the concept to Buzan (1983). Our shift in the terminology does not denote a change in emphasis or technique; rather, we feel that "mind mapping" is an overly esoteric term for many of the settings in which we have applied Collaborative Learning. Mapping the situation, on the other hand, does not seem to be an odd or contrived activity for the participants in the sessions we have conducted. Particularly in the natural resource arena, people have a high level of comfort with the notion of different kinds of maps to convey different kinds of information. But if we found ourselves facilitating a Collaborative Learning project in a different field of endeavor—say, health care or education policy—the concept of "mapping" might not be as comfortable to those participants as it has proven to be in the natural resources arena. We would try to devise another term that seemed to more appropriately match the sensitivities embedded in that new situation, probably one linked to how the participants were used to thinking about information. The key is to not allow the jargon of Collaborative Learning or soft systems to become an impediment to either communication or learning.

Situation mapping is the process of graphically representing a situation in order to create a shared and systemic understanding of it (see Figure 8.2). The graphic, or spatial, depiction of the situation allows a far more relational understanding than could be developed through other means. It is quite a flexible technique; perhaps the only "rules" are to (1) put verbs on lines to convey the dynamic relationships and put nouns at the nodes of the lines to convey the elements in the system and to (2) start in the middle of the page. It is also very useful to bound the system in one's mind as you develop the situation map; in the absence of boundaries the scope of the map can become unwieldy. This activity is a surprisingly powerful way to create a learning team environment, and there may be no way to convey in this chapter how useful situation mapping has been in our applications of Collaborative Learning. It is equally at home in public meetings and interdisciplinary team settings, but there are different facilitation sensitivities in each of those environments. The goal is to engage all of the participants in building a shared understanding of the situation, one that is larger that the perspective of any individual or interest group but that reflects each of the more individualistic worldviews. It is the dialogue and the exploratory thinking among the participants that the facilitator must strive to generate, reinforce, and capture through the situation mapping.

The Fundamental Features of Situation Mapping

Be creative, not evaluative. The appropriate time to use situation mapping is near the beginning of the Collaborative Learning process, in stages 1 and 2 of Wilson and Morren's soft system model or, equivalently, during the divergent learning portion of Kolb's experiential learning model. Accordingly, the purpose of situation mapping is to understand the situation, not to jump to generating improvements or debating potential changes. It is an activity that falls into the general category of brainstorming activities, and the general rule of thumb during brainstorming is that ideas are to be generated, not critiqued. All of the choices that need to be made in terms of technique or timing should be decided so as to increase the comfort level of the participants so that they are able to wrestle with the inherent complexity of the situation in as effective a manner as possible.

Create a situation map that represents a single worldview, but also create shared worldview maps as well. Situation maps inevitably depict the worldviews of their authors. As such, the depiction of the situation will be as narrow or as broad as the spectrum of people generating it. It is entirely possible and appropriate to develop a situation map that represents the particular worldview of the situation that is held by only one stakeholder group (the agency view, or the environmentalist view, or the neighbor's view, etc.). In fact, each of these may be an important step for grounding the facilitator/analyst in the situation. But it is equally possible and probably more important from a Collaborative Learning perspective to develop a situation map that represents a composite worldview. None of the participants would be expected to necessarily hold that composite worldview, but they should be able to see their particular worldview represented in it.

Strive for dynamic complexity, not detail complexity. Both the challenge and value in systems thinking lie in understanding the big picture, not the myriad details that constitute it. It is more important that the participants in a Collaborative Learning process understand the dynamics that have given rise to the current situation than to have encyclopedic knowledge of the minutiae that constitute it. Situation maps should seek to portray the fundamental forces that drive, reinforce, and constrain the choices that the stakeholders might be interested in pursuing. This will necessarily mean that some of the things that the analyst/facilitator might know about the situation might not appear on the situation map that they use to prompt discussion.

Specific Collaborative Learning Tactics

Create a discussion chassis based on interviews of stakeholders and other background research. Generating a situation map can be both frustrating and time-consuming. It is rare that your first draft of a situation map will show the complexity of the situation as elegantly as subsequent versions are able to do. In addition, starting a situation map from a stark, blank piece of paper can create "mapper's block," even among those experienced with the technique.

To address these challenges, we typically present "discussion chassis" situation maps in our public workshops as a starting point for discussion (see Figure 8.2 for an example). Doing so has several advantages: it saves valuable meeting time, it gives the participants a tangible point of departure, and it ensures that a range of issues will be engaged from a systems perspective.

The situation maps that we prepare are the result of interviews we conduct with agency personnel and other stakeholders, as well as other forms of research into the situation (i.e., the stage 1 activities). The task in a public meeting is to briefly explain the situation map and then engage the participants in an editing/revision process that allows them to refine and embellish upon our rough draft. Our experience is that the participants universally add considerable detail and richness to the chassis we provide (see Figure 8.3, which shows the detail that the participants in a particular meeting added to map shown in Fig. 8.2), and to date we have not had a group take major exception with the rough draft or rebel against the exercise in its entirety.

Even so, there are some risks to this rough draft approach. First, there is a chance that the draft will not reflect the stakeholders' understanding of the situation with sufficient accuracy that they can begin to modify it productively. Second, they may feel that the draft is being used to somehow control the agenda by constraining or prescribing the issues to be discussed. The facilitators should be confident in their presentation of the situation map, but not defensive about the particular way in which it represents the situation. The key is to generate creativity, not conformity.

Use two layers of situation maps; start with a core/fragment to get people thinking in those terms before they are exposed to the larger situation. As Figure 8.3 shows, there is a lot of complexity in a realistic situation map, even in a rough draft that does not attempt to capture every issue. When the situation map is presented for the first time, there tends to be a collective gasp/chuckle about it. As a technique to introduce the situation map more gradually, we have begun to present a partial map of the situation that depicts a subset of the issues in order to ease people into graphic representations of the situation. Figures 8.4 and 8.5 present a pair of situation maps from the Wenatchee fire recovery project; Figure 8.4 shows the dynamic complexity in only the fire ecology of the forests in this particular region, and Figure 8.5 shows the ways in which fire links to other issues. Note that Figure 8.4 reappears as the central portion of Figure 8.5. If the former is introduced initially, participants have an opportunity to develop a comfort level with it. When the latter is introduced, they have already begun to think about the situation in spatial and relational terms. As a result, they find the transition to the more complete situation map less abrupt and a more natural extension to how they already understand the situation.

Figure 8.2
ODNRA Situation Map

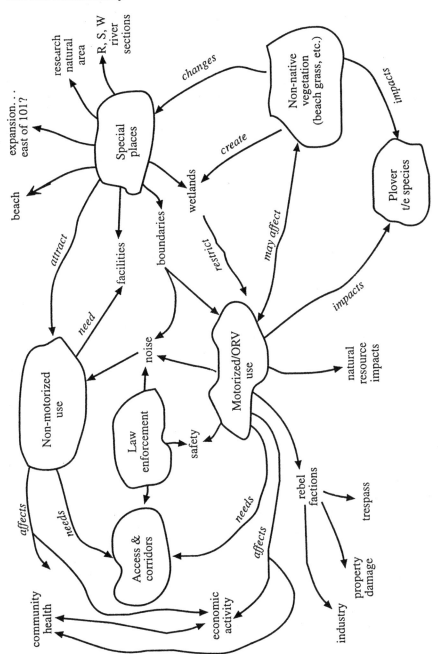

Figure 8.3
ODNRA Situation Map – Florence Workshop
Revision

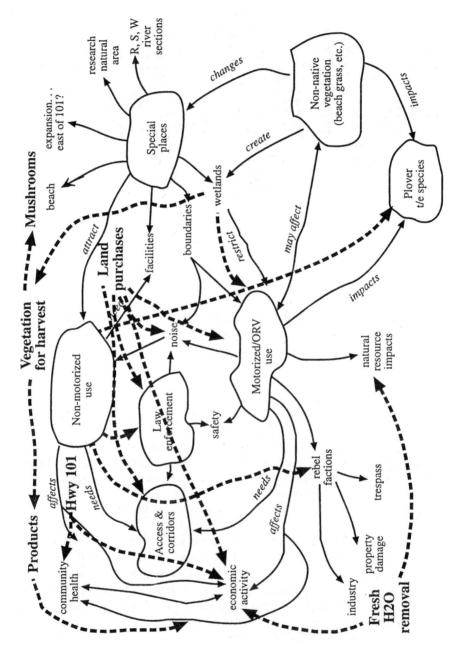

Figure 8.4
Fire Ecology Situation Map

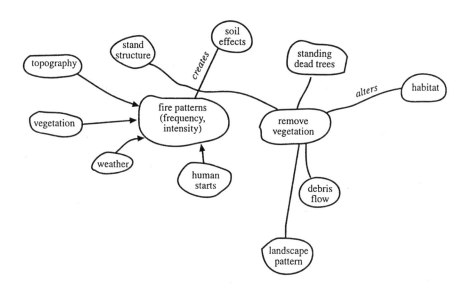

Wilson and Morren (1990) also suggest this incremental approach as an important way to foster systems thinking: They present a technique called "progressive disclosure" that emphasizes parts of the system building on one another.

One useful communication technique is called *progressive disclosure*. Make a series of overheads, flip charts, or drawings on a chalkboard, each having only a part of the model on it so a particular feature can be discussed without the other information being revealed. Progressively uncover and present elements of your model. Use the same order of discussion as you used originally to develop the model. If transparencies are used, then eventually all features can be laid on top of each other, and the entire system can be seen as a whole. How detailed you get in describing each property of the system must be judged in terms of your audience and the time available. (pp. 192, 195)

Involve participants in editing/adding to the situation map. The rough draft situation map need not be overly complete; rather, it should just be a starting point. The purpose of this exercise is not to demonstrate how capable the *facilitators* are at situation mapping or how thoroughly they understand the situation but to help the *participants* to generate a complex understanding of the situation and one another. Even if the facilitators could develop a map that is somehow   more   "correct"   (whatever   that   means,   for   a

Figure 8.5
Fire Recovery Situation Map

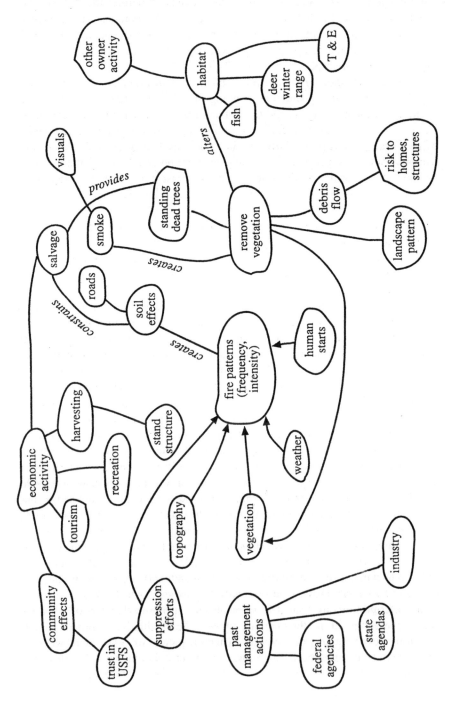

necessarily arbitrary way of representing a necessarily subjective world), it is more important that the workshop participants generate their own. The discussion, the careful thought, and the unexpected observations are the goals of this activity. The output, in a very real sense, is not the map that ultimately emerges. Rather, the mapping and the learning that the participants experience together are important.

Use a facilitation approach that values all contributions to the map. The key to effectively using situation mapping in a group setting is to engage the creativity of the participants and to get them playing off each other's comments and perspectives. Making a comment in a group setting is always a risk-taking behavior, and that is particularly true in an activity that is new (which situation mapping is, to most people) or in settings that are potentially contentious (which Collaborative Learning applications are, in most cases). It is therefore incumbent for the facilitators to create an environment that reduces the risk of venturing an idea.

Our approach has been to reinforce all of the participants' efforts to amend or elaborate on the situation map. These efforts can be verbally reinforced but also tangibly reinforced in the way in which the comment is reflected on the situation map. The goal should be to find a way to reflect all comments on the situation map in some manner.

If controversial linkages are proposed, denote them with a question mark. If a tangential or cross-cutting comment is made, add it to the margin of the map, perhaps without connections to any particular issue. When in doubt about how to represent an issue on the map, it is always useful to ask the workshop participant how to best display their idea. The specifics of what the facilitator chooses to do are less important that the bigger need to create an authentically supportive environment that honors the diversity of worldviews and helps the participants understand the situation more broadly than perhaps they had done before.

In some contentious situations, it may be important to deflect attempts to make particularly adversarial changes to the situation map. We have certainly encountered situations where someone in a Collaborative Learning meeting attempted to make a change to a situation map that was an overt challenge to the worldview or goals of another group. It is necessary to acknowledge that perspective and to find a way to reflect it on the situation map but do so in a way that prevents an escalatory spiral. Situation mapping occurs very early in the Collaborative Learning process, when the participants may have spent relatively little time working through the systemic complexity of the situation and have little understanding of the other parties and their goals. People may attend an introductory Collaborative Learning workshop expecting to forcefully advocate their preferred outcome, but it is premature to engage in that sort of debate at such an early point in the learning cycle. The facilitative approach should therefore acknowledge and record different points of view and ways of understanding the situation. But those differences should not be explored in detail, nor should there be any attempt to resolve them at this stage in the process.

Use a hand-drawn, nonhierarchical map. Some important symbolic messages are conveyed by the style of the situation map that is presented in Collaborative Learning workshops. We rely on hand-drawn (albeit neat and clear) maps rather than more slick graphics that could be produced using any of a number of computer programs. If it looks professionally prepared, it no longer conveys the message that at this point the situation map is a work in progress, a first draft that requires their modifications and enhancement.

In addition, we are forever being asked rather suspicious questions about the nuances of the map. Typically, someone will approach us at the first break after the map has been presented and ask, "Why is their issue in a circle, and ours isn't?" or "Why is this issue capitalized?" or "Why is their issue above ours?" All of these questions show that the participants are looking carefully at the behavior of the facilitators for any evidence of bias. This, in turn, reinforces the need for an informal representation of the situation that presents a casual, rather than sinister, environment. It also argues for a nonhierarchical representation of the situation, rather than one that places issues in any kind of ranking or tiered arrangement to one another. A notable example of a hierarchical systems diagram is the fishbone, a diagram which represents the issues flowing off one another as smaller bones flow off the spine of a fish. Our experience leads us to conclude that such a cause-and-effect representation will not generate constructive learning because it necessarily states that some issues are more important than others. Indeed, much of what divides groups seems to be their different notions of causality. While a shared understanding of the cause-and-effect linkages in the system may be a hugely important accomplishment for the participants in a Collaborative Learning process, it is not consistent with Kolb's notions of experiential learning to jump to that point prematurely.

A Final Note on Situation Mapping

We would not have predicted that situation mapping would be as effective as it actually is. To be perfectly honest, our first few attempts to use situation mapping in public meeting settings were anxious moments. Our doubts about the technique turned out to be unfounded. There is only one instance out of the dozens of times that we have used situation mapping where it did not connect well with the workshop participants. Far more often, the surprises we experience in situation mapping are positive surprises: it accomplished more than we would have anticipated. A number of impromptu comments that workshop participants have made over the years convince us that situation mapping improves people's system grasp of the situation: "This tells me that we can't really 'manage' this situation because there is too much going on" or "Everything is connected to everything else" or "We are all in this together." Each of these comments provides evidence that workshop participants are beginning to move beyond the single-issue focus that might have initially motivated their involvement.

Because situation mapping is an activity that involves divergent learning, the people who prefer that learning style are the most natural situation mappers. There are also other people for whom situation mapping is a struggle. It is useful to anticipate that different people are going to react to this activity in different ways, and to develop strategies that allow the divergent learners to exert some intellectual leadership at this point so that all of the participants can benefit from the creativity that learning style engenders.

From Situation Mapping to Concerns and Improvements

In a Collaborative Learning process, whether as part of planning team interaction or as a public participation strategy, participants articulate their concerns about the environmental conflict or policy decision situation. They do so as they develop a shared understanding of the environmental conflict situation, via the first three stages of Collaborative Learning cycle (see Chapter 2). After participants have worked with a situation map as a group, they work individually on their concerns about the environmental conflict situation they have just "mapped." Following a small group discussion of their concerns, participants individually and in groups develop ideas to improve the management of the situation. These improvements—actions, activities, projects, management plans, etc.—are part of the fourth and fifth stages of the Collaborative Learning process cycle. A one-day Collaborative Learning citizen workshop typically culminates in participants writing about and sharing their ideas for improving the situation. An important tool for articulating concerns about the situation and developing improvements is the work sheet.

Work Sheets

One challenge in public involvement processes of all kinds is to collect the thoughts and recommendations of the participants. A particular challenge in Collaborative Learning is to give the participants enough time to adequately express the complexity of their ideas. Recall that a goal of Collaborative Learning is to allow the participants to generate a complex understanding of the cause-and-effect relationships in the situation; if there is no means for them to convey that complexity in their comments, then much of that achievement is essentially lost. It is therefore incumbent upon the designers of Collaborative Learning processes to help the participants develop and convey their ideas with enough clarity and depth that they are useful to the decision maker(s).

A technique that we have used to promote thoughtful comments is to provide the participants with work sheets for recording their ideas, as well as ample time for them to both write down their ideas and also refine them based on the comments of other workshop participants. Two formats for these work sheets are presented as Tables 8.6 and 8.7. We have learned a number of lessons regarding the use of work sheets such as these.

Ask the participants to sign the work sheets and include their phone numbers. There are a number of reasons that these work sheets should not be an anonymous activity. First, Collaborative Learning is trying to get participants to take ownership of the ideas that they are generating. There may be no more tangible symbolic form of that ownership than signing your own suggestions. Signing one's work sheet also may reduce the likelihood of extreme or stridently positional comments (although we have no particular empirical evidence regarding this proposition). But there are two far more pragmatic reasons. Most of the Collaborative Learning processes that we have run involve at least two work sheets; having the names on them allows them to be collated by participant. There have also been times when a planning team or decision maker wanted to follow up with a workshop participant based on an idea that was presented on the work sheet. Without the name and phone number, continuing the dialogue after the workshop would probably not be possible.

Use a sequence of questions and work sheets that allow the participants to work their way through the systemic complexity. As Tables 8.6 and 8.7 show, the work sheets provide a series of questions that steer the participants through the task. Rather than provide a blank sheet of paper and expect a fully developed and clearly articulated comment, the questions parse the task into a series of substeps that collectively provide a coherent response to the task. Breaking up the task into more manageable components aids the participants and keeps them on task.

In addition to using a sequence of questions on work sheets, we have used a sequence of work sheets. The early stages of soft systems focus on identifying themes of concern, which can then be organized into improvements. Tables 8.6 and 8.7 are typical of the work sheets that we have developed to assist the workshop participants with each of these activities. One lesson about the value of this sequence came from an experience where we did not follow it. We designed a three-hour evening workshop format to assist a Forest Service planning team with a landscape-level assessment. In order to compress the activities into three hours, we elected to omit the "concerns" work sheet and proceed directly to the "improvements" work sheet. Upon reviewing the comments that were provided on the "improvements" work sheets, they appeared to have been largely unsuccessful because participants devised improvements that were generally vague and unfocused. In many ways, they resembled the kinds of comments that are more typically provided on the "concerns" work sheets. It may well be that participants need the iterative process of defining their concerns and then generating improvements. Skipping the "concerns" step appears to have had an unfortunate effect on the quality of the improvements that were proposed.

Table 8.6
Sample Themes of Concern Work Sheet (space condensed)

_____Workshop

Name_____

Phone_____

Concerns and Interests

Think about the current _____ situation, as portrayed by the map we have just discussed. Look at the areas of that Situation Map that are important to you.

1. What part of the Situation Map is particularly important to you? What issues are involved?

2. What are your specific concerns and interests about these issues? Why are these issues important to you?

3. What other parts and issues of the Marys Peak situation must be considered when designing improvements related to this part of the Situation Map?

4. What people or views must be considered when designing improvements related to this issue or area?

Use progressive discussion to allow the participants to discuss their comments. After the participants have completed their work sheets, we ask that they discuss their comments with one other participant for approximately 10–15 minutes. As this conversation winds down, we then ask them to form somewhat larger groups around the table and continue the discussion. This format allows everyone to discuss his or her ideas, as well as get the comments of other workshop participants. Another name for this activity is "2-4-8" (referring to the increasing group size), and there are a number of reasons that we prefer it to more commonly used techniques for Collaborative Learning workshops. Perhaps the most notable of these is that it allows everyone—not just the rhetorically assertive—to be actively advocating for his or her ideas. It is a far more natural communication activity than large-group formats where one person speaks at a time, and the remaining 30 or 40 people listen.

Table 8.7
Sample Improvements Work Sheet (space condensed)

_____Workshop

Name_____Phone_____

          Improving the_____ Situation

Think about the areas and issues of concern that you have just written about. With
your concerns and interests in mind, identify an improvement in the
_____ situation. An improvement may be an action, project, or
management approach that you think would be both desirable and feasible.

1.   How could the _____ situation be improved? Is this a short-term
     or a long-term improvement? Describe the improvement; be as specific as
     possible.

2.   Why is this improvement desirable?

3.   How is this improvement feasible? For example, who might be responsible
     for implementation? How might your improvement be funded? Be as specific
     as possible.

4.   What obstacles currently stand in the way of making this improvement? How
     might those obstacles be overcome?

5.   How does this improvement relate to other parts and issues of the
     _____ situation?

These table discussions generate the kind of participant-to-participant
communication that is conducive to active learning. As part of this learning, it
can be useful to encourage the workshop participants to interact with people they
do not know or with someone whose views on the issue are perhaps different
from their own. When we urge workshop participants to mix, some people take
advantage of the opportunity, but, typically, more do not. Our facilitation style
has never been to use the meeting design to force the participants to mingle. As
noted in Chapter 5, in adult learning we want to create a safe and comfortable
learning environment, as well as be sensitive to the literacy level of our
workshop participants. Forced interaction with relative strangers or political
opponents has seemed to be a more aggressive facilitation tactic that we have
chosen not to employ.

A variation on the "concerns–improvements" work sheet approach includes "critical concerns analysis" and structured "improvements analysis." Both of these activities would follow participants' individual efforts on concerns and improvements work sheets. Critical concerns analysis adds a step between concerns and improvements.

The "critical concerns" activity asks participants, in small groups, to share their individual concerns. Following that, the group selects a set of the concerns (e.g., three or four) they deem most important or critical. The group then conducts a critical concerns analysis in order to further their understanding of the situation. An example of a critical concerns analysis grid or framework that focuses on policy improvements appears in Table 8.8.

Table 8.8
Critical Concerns Analysis Grid (space condensed)

Critical Concern	Parties or stakeholders who have concern	Policies that relate to the critical concern	Effects of those policies	Parties or stakeholder goals	Possible policy improve- ments or changes

Source: Wallace Institute for Alternative Agriculture, Greenbelt, MD.

Similarly, Collaborative Learning workshop parties could refine the improvements they have generated individually by participating in an "improvements analysis." The improvements analysis task begins with group members sharing their individual improvements. The group then selects one or more of those improvements to refine according to the improvements analysis areas presented in Table 8.9. Improvements can be generated individually via the work sheet format presented in Table 8.7, or via the "critical concerns–improvements" work sheet that is included in Table 8.10.

As Table 8.10 illustrates, developing improvements can take more than one form. The Wallace Institute for Alternative Agriculture's project on community visioning about food and agriculture policy used the "improvements analysis grid" to help citizens evaluate improvements in their community's local food and agriculture policy and practices. This work preceded an "action planning" step which was critical to implementing change.

Table 8.9
Critical Concerns Improvements (space condensed)

Improving the _____ Situation
Critical Concern(s)_____ Think about the critical concern(s) your group has selected. Identify up to three improvements that deal with this critical concern. An improvement is an action, a project, or management approach that you think would be both desirable and feasible. As a policy change, an improvement can either add to, or subtract from, the present situation (e.g., building a road, removing or closing a road). A policy improvement could also be the extension or refinement of a current policy. What improvements address your group's critical concern(s)? Describe each improvement. Improvement One: Improvement Two: Improvement Three:

Source: Wallace Institute for Alternative Agriculture, Greenbelt, MD.

EVALUATION

The fifth and final step in a comprehensive Collaborative Learning application is evaluation. Collaborative Learning activities should be evaluated by those who participate in, convene, design, and facilitate them. We have organized our discussion of evaluating Collaborative Learning projects into a series of questions.

Who should evaluate a Collaborative Learning process? Ideally, a Collaborative Learning project is evaluated by someone who has not been a part of the process but is familiar with Collaborative Learning. When feasible, conveners should retain individuals with methodological expertise to design and administer an evaluation protocol. University researchers, for example, may be willing to evaluate a collaborative process if they can use the data beyond preparing a report for the conveners, such as publishing the data in an academic paper. The convener might discuss with a similar organization (e.g., one federal agency contacting another) the possibility of one or more of its members conducting the evaluation. If retaining an external evaluator is not feasible, the convener may designate a project evaluator from within one's own organization.

Table 8.10

Improvements Analysis Grid (space condensed)

Implementers	Affected Parties	Key Players	Values and Beliefs – Mind Sets	Outside Forces
Analyzing Improvements. Consider your team's set or system of improvements (selected from the improvements you and other group members have generated on the Improvements Work sheets) and analyze in the following areas:				
Who will implement (operate, manage) your improvements? Who will be the administrators? What people, groups, organizations?	What people, groups, or organizations will benefit from your improve- ments? What people, groups, or organizations believe they will be hurt by or lose from improve- ments?	Who are potential Blockers? What parties may have the desire and/or power to block your improve- ments? Who are potential Supporters? What parties can provide key support for your improve- ments?	What mind sets, values, and beliefs are impotant to consider when implementing the improve- ments?	What factors should be considered as "givens" in the situation that pertain to your improvements but seem outside or external to your set or system?

Source: Wallace Institute for Alternative Agriculture, Greenbelt, MD.

Arrangements for the evaluator or evaluation team should be made relatively early in the overall Collaborative Learning project, at least prior to the implementation phase.

There could be significant benefit to securing the evaluator before Collaborative Learning training, so that the evaluator could participate in all or part of the training in order to be familiar with Collaborative Learning.

What and who should be evaluated? A comprehensive Collaborative Learning project should include evaluation of training and implementation.

Collaborative Learning training participants should assess the training program, indicating what content material and activities they found useful and ways in which the training program should be improved. Collaborative Learning activities, such as citizen workshops, scientist–citizen dialogues, and field trips need to be evaluated to determine their effectiveness. Participants in these activities can be asked questions that pertain to the substantive, procedural, and relationship progress made.

When and how should Collaborative Learning evaluation take place? Evaluation needs to be as thoughtful as the design of a Collaborative Learning process itself. The conveners and designers need to work with evaluators to determine what evaluation methods best fit the situation. For example, if a Collaborative Learning process includes members of high-context cultural communities, qualitative evaluation procedures such as open-ended or semi-structured interviews may generate more useful feedback and a better response rate than more structured, quantitative techniques such as multi-item surveys. Given the potential diversity of Collaborative Learning process participants and the variability of applications, Collaborative Learning evaluators should consider a multiple-method approach that incorporates a variety of research techniques, such as observation, interviews, and surveys.

Collaborative Learning process evaluation can take place at various points in the overall application. For example, the Wenatchee National Forest Fire Recovery Project described in the next chapter included a survey instrument distributed at the start of full-day Collaborative Learning citizen workshops, a second survey instrument that participants completed at the end of the daylong workshop, and follow-up surveys sent to workshop participants six months later. Whether pretests, posttests, interviews, surveys, and the like are employed, evaluators need to work with conveners and process designers to ensure that the evaluation methods are appropriate for the participants, the setting, and the conveners' goals.

CONCLUSION

As we noted in Chapter 2, Collaborative Learning can be envisioned on two levels, as a content-focused process that fosters collaborative interaction via a number of stages and as a context-focused project framework that includes phases of assessment, training, design, implementation/facilitation, and evaluation. At the project level, the training, design, and implementation phases are points at which Collaborative Learning process activities are important. In training, people learn about Collaborative Learning concepts and techniques. Through training, members of the convening organization can experience aspects of Collaborative Learning and decide if, when, and how Collaborative Learning processes may beneficially apply to the environmental conflict and decision situations they face.

In design, conveners and their design team consider their assessment of the environmental conflict situation and develop Collaborative Learning activities that meet the decision or management needs of that situation. For example, a federal agency considering a management or regulatory action compliant with the National Environmental Policy Act (NEPA) can determine what public participation activities should foster collaboration and mutual learning. A Collaborative Learning citizen workshop is obviously structured much differently than a public hearing and fosters distinctly different communication behaviors. Arguably, very little, if any, mutual learning occurs at a public hearing, while Collaborative Learning activities emphasize learning about stakeholders.

Design and implementation both feature Collaborative Learning activities that foster systems thinking and the development of desirable and feasible improvements in the management situation. Generally, Collaborative Learning techniques are directed by an impartial party, a facilitator, who understands the Collaborative Learning process well. Facilitation is particularly important as the complexity of the Collaborative Learning activity increases. For example, an organization planning team (such as a federal agency interdisciplinary team) with members who have gone through Collaborative Learning training can employ techniques such as situation mapping without facilitation. In contrast, a public workshop using Collaborative Learning techniques relies on facilitators whom the workshop participants consider credible and impartial.

In this chapter we have presented various Collaborative Learning activities and techniques. They need to be applied in ways that respect the unique features of the particular environmental conflict situation. In the next two chapters, we illustrate this point as we describe cases in which we have applied Collaborative Learning.

Chapter 9

The Practice of Collaborative Learning: Citizens, Scientists, and Foresters in Fire Recovery Planning

> It is more trouble to consult the public than to ignore them, but that is what you are hired for . . . Public support of acts affecting public rights is absolutely required.

> —Gifford Pinchot
> First Chief of the Forest Service

In Chapters 1 through 7 we provided the theoretical and conceptual foundation of Collaborative Learning. In Chapter 8 we turned our attention to practice, presenting a project framework and a number of techniques that we have developed and applied as part of Collaborative Learning work. In the next two chapters, we describe various cases in which we have applied Collaborative Learning. This chapter features one case, fire recovery planning on the Wenatchee National Forest of central Washington in the Pacific Northwest. This case represents the most comprehensive application of Collaborative Learning that we have attempted.

BACKGROUND: FIRE ON THE WENATCHEE

Forests and rangeland burn each summer in the Western United States. During the summer of 2000, for example, more than 800,000 acres of land in Montana and Idaho alone were engulfed by fire. Many of the western summer fires occur on public land, managed by state agencies or by the federal agencies of the USDA-Forest Service or the USDI-Bureau of Land Management.

For Forest Service personnel on the Wenatchee National Forest in central Washington, the summer of 1994 started out as a typical season. With its proximity to the Puget Sound area, recreation activity in the forest was high.

Wenatchee National Forest employees looked forward to the summer, the "project season," when they could do much of their work out on the ground. By the end of the summer of 1994, "out on the ground" had taken on a much different meaning.

Fire risk throughout the forests of central Washington had been building for many years. Fire suppression had been a forest management priority throughout much of the twentieth century, and many stands of trees that might have been thinned naturally through fire had become thick with younger trees. Slash piles from fires in the early 1970s remained on the ground. Fuel loadings in the Wenatchee National Forest were high, and with another summer of hot weather and drought conditions, forest managers were concerned. Not only was the fire risk genuine, but throughout the 1980s and early 1990s an increasing number of people had built primary or secondary residences in or on the edge of the forest. A fire, Forest Service officials feared, would potentially destroy property and could put people's lives in danger.

Their fears were realized in the summer of 1994. On Sunday evening, 24 July, a lightning storm moved east across the Cascade Mountain range of central Washington. The storm followed in the wake of record-breaking summer temperatures and came upon forests suffering from years of droughtlike conditions. It ignited numerous fires, 41 in the Wenatchee National Forest alone.

The fires thrived because of a number of factors. In addition to the unusually dry forest conditions and large volume of natural fuels, the fire burned in steep terrain, stoked by strong winds with gusts up to 50 miles per hour. When the fires broke out, few local fire-fighting resources were available. Fire-fighting equipment based in the Pacific Northwest, for example, was being employed to fight fires in the Rocky Mountains. During the first few days of the fires, extreme, unpredictable fire behavior hindered containment efforts. Many seasoned firefighters encountered wildfire activity atypical to what they expected. Some reported that fires made dramatic, rapid runs down valleys, consuming over 1,000 acres in a two-hour period (Wenatchee National Forest, 1994, p. 1).

By late July, four significant fires were burning simultaneously in the Chelan County portion of the Wenatchee National Forest: the Tyee Creek fire northwest of Entiat and southwest of Chelan, the Rat Creek (which was human-caused) and Hatchery Creek fires around Leavenworth, and the Round Mountain fire near Lake Wenatchee. Collectively, the fires burned over 181,000 acres on parts of four ranger districts, temporarily closed major highways, destroyed 37 homes, involved over 8,000 firefighting personnel from 25 states, and cost almost $70 million to suppress (Wenatchee National Forest, 1994, p. 2). Although the fires were generally contained by mid-August, some high-country areas continued to burn through September (Figure 9.1).

In late August the Wenatchee National Forest launched a short-term rehabilitation effort to thwart erosion, reduce the risk of floods, and maintain public safety. Some forest areas were closed to the public. Burned hillsides were seeded and fertilized. Drainages were shored up with hay, gravel, and log walls.

Figure 9.1
The Wenatchee National Forest and Its Ranger Districts

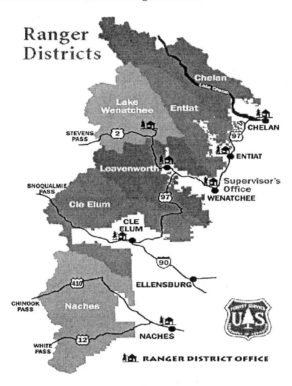

Source: Wenatchee National Forest Web site (http://www.fs.fed.us/r6/wenatchee).

Burned trees were cut as part of a contour felling process. Roads were modified to provide for manageable water flows during winter snowmelt and spring rains.

As short-term rehabilitation efforts proceeded, forest-level and ranger district management began to plan for the long-term health of the forests. They realized that rehabilitating the forests required a comprehensive fire recovery planning effort. This effort needed to be grounded in ecosystem-based management (ESBM), combining the best available scientific knowledge with thorough public involvement. To draw upon the best available science, the forest leadership supported the development of a science team organized by the Wenatchee Lab of the USDA Forest Service Pacific Northwest Research Station. The science team would incorporate data from these and previous fires to determine management scenarios that would maintain forest ecosystem health.

The forest supervisor, the forest rehabilitation director, and district rangers decided that the fire recovery public involvement situation offered an opportunity for innovation. They recognized that forest restoration activities could be controversial and that different views about fire recovery and forest health provided the potential for conflict. Consequently, they decided to employ a collaborative approach and solicited the participation of the authors to do so.

Ecosystem-based Management

The decision to use Collaborative Learning and its overall application design were grounded in the importance of ecosystem-based management and community. The Wenatchee National Forest Leadership team wanted to implement fire recovery projects within a broader planning effort that emphasized ecosystem-based management and forest health. Ecosystem-based management represents a natural resource management philosophy of sustainability and sustainable development (Salwasser, 1994). The concept of ecosystem-based management, Salwasser explains, emphasizes that "knowledge and technology can be used in actions to encourage desired conditions of ecosystems for environmental, economic, and social benefits, for now and for future generations" (1994, p. 7). In a similar vein, Jensen and Everett note that the primary objective of an ecosystem management philosophy is "to sustain the integrity of ecosystems (i.e., their function, composition, and structure) for future generations while providing immediate goods and services to an increasingly diverse public." They add that "sociological, ecological, technological, and economic information must be integrated to identify optimal land uses and to describe the spatial relations of commodities and values across the landscape" (1994, p. 6).

ESBM strives to integrate the science, culture, and politics of natural resource management. This is not easy to do, given temporal differences in scientific, community, and policy systems. The complexity of ecosystems prolongs the data-gathering process, which, in turn, often complicates and confounds the policy decision-making process (Stanfield, 1988; Cortner & Moote, 1998). Still, ecosystem-based management must not compromise its commitment to incorporating the best scientific information available. As Salwasser observes, "If ecosystem management is to work, people will need a common understanding of what ecosystems are" (1994, p. 7). Similarly, land managers will need to understand people's concerns about ecosystems.

While one of the principal bases of ESBM is the use of the best available science and technology, with the best science comes uncertainty. Science cannot provide absolute, enduring answers to natural resource management questions that are fundamentally ambiguous. The management of land does not lend itself easily to controlled experiments, and the results of investigations conducted on complex ecosystems are rarely unequivocal (Stanfield, 1988). Within a framework of ESBM, such ambiguity should provide promise rather than pessimism. As Kai Lee notes, "Experiments often bring surprises, but if resource management is recognized to be inherently uncertain, the surprises become opportunities to learn rather than failure to predict" (1993, p. 56).

We addressed this emphasis on the best available science in Chapter 1. Ecosystem-based management, though, needs to incorporate more than just scientific knowledge. It needs knowledge from a number of perspectives, including local and indigenous knowledge. Long-term residents and users of an area likely have intimate knowledge of that area and insights different from those of the agency scientist, who probably has spent less time on the ground than they have. In many parts of the West, members of Native American tribes know much about a landscape, stand of trees, meadow, or watershed, knowledge often underutilized in public lands management. Ecosystems maintain physical, biological, economic, social, and cultural values, and ecosystem-based management occurs in a political context. ESBM, therefore, needs to be responsive to all these dimensions, as illustrated by Figure 9.2.

Figure 9.2
The Ecosystem-Based Management Hexagon

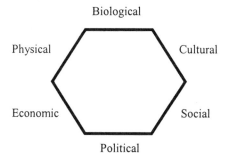

Both the natural science and the social science of ESBM provide numerous opportunities to learn. Just as natural science experiments are typically continual as landscapes change, the public involvement activities that they include should be ongoing and deliberative as communities and social systems change.

Community

Wenatchee National Forest managers also wanted fire recovery planning to draw strength from the forest's communities. Communities provide meaningful opportunities for working through the paradox of technical expertise and inclusiveness that we presented in Chapter 1, a paradox that is apparent in fire recovery planning. This paradox is confronted well by thinking and planning for ecosystem health as sustainability: the sustainability of the natural resources in conjunction with the sustainability of communities connected to those natural resources.

When developing management policies for natural resource sustainability, our sense of community needs to be clear, while recognizing that communities may be defined differently for different purposes (Wilkinson, 1992). Julie Gorte of the Office of Technology Assessment (1993) asserts that "a community is one of those things that defies precise description, but we usually know when we are looking at one" (p. 296). Communities can be viewed as administrative: a town, a city, a state, or a nation are all communities (Gorte, 1993). Communities may be defined by identity (Carroll & Lee, 1989) or by place (Kemmis, 1990; Brandenburg & Carroll, 1995; Cantrill, 1998). Another way of defining community is by interest: an environmental community, an industrial community, a religious community, a professional community, and others that span administrative boundaries (Gorte, 1993). Communities, too, "can be seen as collections of people and groups with different sustainability preferences" (Gale & Cordray, 1994, p. 328).

A national forest is important, for example, to different types of communities. It is essential to place-based communities such as towns whose economic sustainability is connected to that forest. It is meaningful as well to interest-based communities: people whose recreational and spiritual activities, values, and worldviews hold the forest dear.

Arguably, communities of place are among the most essential communities to the practice of ecosystem-based management. They have a significant stake in the ESBM activities consistent with both natural resource and community sustainability. Members of communities with an attachment to place possess local knowledge. At best, public participation components of ecosystem management and sustainability will involve citizens meaningfully, in ways that respect indigenous knowledge and value mutual learning. "Long-term residents who have managed or worked the land are reservoirs of practical experience," natural resource sociologist Robert Lee surmises, and "these wise people are often precisely those who know most about how to implement sustainable practices" (1994, pp. 173–174).

The Wenatchee National Forest has been a meaningful place to many people, a place to work and to enjoy recreation activities. The Wenatchee National Forest fire recovery situation included identity, place, and interest dimensions of community. Many people in forest-adjacent communities felt a personal and symbolic—and for some, even spiritual—attachment to Wenatchee National Forest lands. When fire burned places in the forest they considered special, they felt that they had lost a part of themselves. Lastly, members of different organizations with varied interests were concerned about the fire recovery issue. People with environmental interests feared that salvaging dead and dying trees in the burn areas would be more disruptive than helpful to forest health. People affiliated with forest products industries worried that salvage would not occur soon enough to be economically feasible. People in tourist businesses pondered how the fires might affect tourism in Chelan County.

COLLABORATIVE LEARNING AND WENATCHEE NATIONAL FOREST FIRE RECOVERY PLANNING

The "Fire Recovery Collaborative Learning Project," or FRCL, was implemented via the five phases that we highlighted in Chapter 8. These phases were iterative, each building upon the work and learning that had occurred earlier. We think that the overall Collaborative Learning application that occurred with the Wenatchee National Forest can serve as a model for how Collaborative Learning might be systematically applied to other complex environmental policy situations.

The Assessment Phase

The FRCL began with a phone call to the first author from the Wenatchee National Forest (WNF) fire rehabilitation director. In the spring of 1994 the rehabilitation director and the ranger of one of the WNF districts impacted by the fires had heard a presentation on Collaborative Learning by the authors at an ecosystem management conference (Daniels & Walker, 1995b). Based on that talk and support of a Pacific Northwest Research Station Wenatchee Lab senior scientist, the fire rehabilitation director recommended to the Wenatchee Forest Leadership team that Collaborative Learning be considered as the basis for the WNF's fire recovery planning public involvement work. The district ranger concurred. The first author traveled to Wenatchee, Washington, for meetings with the WNF's senior leadership, including the forest supervisor. During this trip, the first author participated in a field trip into some of the burn areas and talked to members of the Wenatchee National Forest's senior staff. Shortly thereafter, both authors met with the Wenatchee National Forest's senior leadership team and agreed to conduct Collaborative Learning as a significant component of fire recovery planning.

We decided to work with the Wenatchee National Forest for a number of reasons. First, we learned during our initial assessment that the Wenatchee National Forest's senior leadership team was committed to innovation in its public involvement activities. Team members saw in the fire recovery planning effort an opportunity to "do things differently," to involve citizens collaboratively in the fire recovery process. Second, WNF leaders identified in the fire recovery planning effort a significant amount of decision space. In other words, while the WNF leadership team maintained decision authority, the forest supervisor and district rangers were receptive to citizen concerns and ideas about what and how fire recovery activities should be conducted. Third, a key senior scientist of the Forest Service's Wenatchee Pacific Northwest Research Station backed the project. He saw a direct link between a Collaborative Learning approach to public involvement and the work of the fire recovery science team that he directed.

As we noted in Chapter 8, assessment is an essential component of any Collaborative Learning application. The more thorough the assessment, the greater the likelihood that the collaboration strategy will manage the conflicts in the situation and make meaningful progress (Carpenter & Kennedy, 1988). Assessment in this project needed to be more substantial than the authors' initial project evaluation and the Wenatchee National Forest leadership staff commitment to use Collaborative Learning.

Consequently, following the commitment of the Wenatchee National Forest leadership team, we began work to comprehensively assess the fire recovery situation. We needed to understand the situation as well as we could to determine if and how Collaborative Learning would apply to the situation. The assessment work included two tracks: one of community social assessment and one of assessing the appropriateness of Collaborative Learning activities.

The first track linked us to the Fire Recovery Science Team. Two colleagues from another Pacific Northwest university and we constituted the Social Science Research Group (SSRG), a component of the Fire Recovery Science Team. The SSRG's responsibilities were twofold: to conduct a social/community assessment related to the fire rehabilitation and recovery effort, and to evaluate the Collaborative Learning workshop process. This latter task is discussed later in this chapter.

To accomplish the first task, SSRG faculty placed two graduate student research assistants into communities that had experienced the summer fires. The students were trained and observed by faculty members of the SSRG. The research assistants conducted ethnographic interviews with more than 120 residents in the Leavenworth area, Chelan area, and Entiat valley. The interviewee sample relied on chain referral to cover the broad spectrum of groups and interests in Chelan County. Interviews were held with environmentalists, orchardists, public officials, property rights advocates, residents who had lost their homes in the fires, loggers, and so on. The data generated from these interviews were used both as a component of a Science Team report and as background for designing the Collaborative Learning workshops (Findley, 1996; Carroll et al., 2000).

We took responsibility for the second track, assessing the appropriateness of Collaborative Learning activities. We made several trips to the Wenatchee National Forest, met informally with citizens and Forest Service personnel, interviewed county commissioners and news media representatives, reviewed newspaper coverage of the summer fires, and participated in field trips into the burned areas. Based on this appraisal and the social assessment data generated by the ethnographic interviews, we determined that Collaborative Learning was appropriate for the fire recovery situation.

Orientation and Training

This phase featured the education of appropriate Wenatchee National Forest personnel. Some of this occurred during our frequent visits to the Wenatchee National Forest shortly after the fires, visits that included meeting ranger district personnel, making presentations about the project, and participating in field trips into the burned areas.

We believe that Collaborative Learning can be useful in a variety of environmental and natural resource management situations, both internally within groups and organizations and externally when organizations work with citizens. Organizational effectiveness is dual in nature, pertaining to both internal and external relationships and procedures (Kreps, 1990). The FRCL project included work to improve the Wenatchee National Forest's ability to collaborate internally, such as within interdisciplinary (ID) planning teams, and collaborate externally with citizens, interest groups, organizations, and other agencies.

Based on our knowledge of the forest, the fires, and affected communities, we designed and conducted a two-day Collaborative Learning Training Course for Wenatchee National Forest personnel. FRCL project success depended, in part, on Wenatchee Forest staff, particularly the district-level interdisciplinary teams' understanding, respecting, and accepting the Collaborative Learning process. The 25 participants in the training did not necessarily need to identify areas in which they would use Collaborative Learning (although many did). They did, though, need to be supportive of the forest's CL effort. Consequently, we encouraged constructive skepticism as we took participants through the training segments. We emphasized the importance of a learning organization approach to CL (Senge, 1990). The training course included presentations on soft systems methodology, mind mapping, learning, and communication competence. It employed small group activities to teach participants about stages of the Collaborative Learning framework. These small group activities included ID team members from specific ranger districts working on decision-making situations, such as adaptive management area planning, watershed assessment planning, and a recreation area construction project conflict.

Design and Implementation

Based on the two-dimensional assessment, we designed and implemented fire recovery citizen workshops that employed some stages and techniques of Collaborative Learning. Given how closely intertwined the design and implementation phases were, we discuss them together here.

A key component of the FRCL project was a series of citizen workshops, the first set of which was part of the Wenatchee National Forest's "preproject" effort. As such, the ID teams sought public input before developing specific fire recovery projects that would be subject to National Environmental Policy Act (NEPA) review. The workshops were constructed to emphasize both scientific expertise and citizen involvement. The project included four full-day workshops: two in Leavenworth, Washington; one in Entiat, Washington; and one in the greater Seattle area (Lynnwood, Washington).

Workshop Design Issues. Consistent with the tenets of Collaborative Learning, the Wenatchee National Forest leadership and we wanted the workshops to be accessible to citizens and inclusive of diverse viewpoints, ideas, and concerns. We wanted accessibility and inclusivity to be compatible with the workshop emphasis on substantive, mutual learning. The district rangers, and the ID teams from Leavenworth and Entiat—the two most fire-affected ranger districts—and we hoped that the workshops would provide people with the opportunity to learn from one another, to express their concerns about fire recovery planning, and to share their ideas about how the Wenatchee National

---

Collaborative Learning and Local Knowledge

At the first "issue presentation" evening program, in Leavenworth, we met a local logger. He had worked in the area woods for several years, making his living as a "gyppo" logger. When the fires began, he was one of the first to respond, fighting the summer fires on the front lines. As he fought the fires, he took pictures and put together an impressive set of slide photographs. After the evening program ended, he stayed an extra hour (until 11 P.M.) and showed his slides to the first author (Daniels). Based on that conversation, we recommended to WNF staff that this local logger give a presentation on the fires at the upcoming issue presentation programs scheduled for Wenatchee, Entiat, and Chelan. WNF personnel agreed, and we invited the local logger. He accepted our invitation and gave an excellent talk at each of the issue presentation programs. He participated in both the full day Collaborative Learning workshops in Leavenworth.

Forest could recover from the fires. Furthermore, we sought to design a workshop process that would draw upon both local and technical expert knowledge.

Toward this end, we met with Leavenworth and Entiat ID teams, district rangers, the WNF fire rehabilitation director, and the WNF public affairs officer. While we were the primary designers, we viewed the Leavenworth and Entiat ID teams and district rangers as our consultative team. We asked them questions and listened to their concerns and ideas. We discussed options and made recommendations to them. Even though we were the trainers, designers, and facilitators, Wenatchee National Forest staff members were the conveners of the process and the fire recovery policy decision makers.

Using a decision-making team approach to design issues, we asked the WNF personnel a number of interrelated workshop design questions:

1. *How much did citizens know about the WNF fires, fire ecology, forest health, and forest rehabilitation?* If there was inadequate information or misinformation about the fire situation, time should be devoted to presenting material in a traditional educational format, with presentations followed by a question-and-answer period. After discussion of options, we recommended that the Wenatchee National Forest sponsor a number of "issue presentations" evening programs. These two-and-one-half-hour programs featured presentations on the summer fires, fire ecology, ecosystem (fish, wildlife, water, vegetation) impacts, Collaborative Learning, and the decision-making process. The presentations included slides and overheads. Usually, agency personnel gave the presentations, although WNF staff were receptive to including a local, nonagency presenter.

2. *Were WNF planning personnel concerned more with number of participants or quality of participation?* If WNF staff wanted a lot of participants in the public involvement process, a more traditional open house or public hearing format could be preferable to a Collaborative Learning approach. We explained that the Collaborative Learning workshop process functions best in a full-day format but can be adapted to a four- to five-hour period. The WNF staff hoped the process design would draw a lot of citizens, while fostering good discussion and learning. We recommended a full-day workshop format.

3. *Where should workshops be held?* The fires burned primarily in two ranger districts: Leavenworth and Entiat. These two communities are 25 miles west and 40 miles northwest, respectively, of Wenatchee, the largest city in Chelan County, the county seat, and site of the Wenatchee National Forest headquarters. WNF staff pointed out that many recreation users in the Wenatchee National Forest come from the Puget Sound area, and the fires were well covered in the Seattle and Tacoma area media. WNF staff and we decided to hold Fire Recovery Collaborative Learning Workshops in Leavenworth, Entiat, and the Seattle area.

4. *When in the planning process should workshops occur?* The fires were contained in August and simmered in the high country into early October. Yet even as some areas of the forest still smoldered, the Wenatchee National Forest implemented a comprehensive, short-term forest rehabilitation effort. During September through December 1994, contractors and crews were brought in to seed burned areas with wheat to stabilize the ground and to remove debris from streams to prevent impoundments and flooding. The fire recovery ID teams were initiating their planning work in early 1995. We asked WNF staff when they wanted citizen participation: at the beginning of the planning process, sometime during the more formal NEPA process, or both. From the community assessment interviews we had learned that people experienced the fires personally and significantly. Based on this knowledge, discussion of the immediacy of the fires, and awareness of seasonal demands for salvage, WNF staff and we decided that the citizen workshops should occur at the beginning of the planning process, as pre-NEPA activity. Citizens, like agency planners, were involved in the fire recovery planning process on the ground floor.

5. *When during the week should workshops take place?* Once the WNF staff made the commitment to full-day workshops early in the planning process, the WNF staff and we discussed which day of the week would be preferable for each site. A weekday workshop would attract people who could participate as part of their job (staff members of interest groups, agency personnel, business and industry employees) but would not be accessible to the citizen who worked during the week. A Saturday workshop would fit in best with citizens' work schedules, but might not appeal to agency and industry employees and others who had weekend commitments. WNF staff were most concerned about involving concerned citizens in the fire recovery workshops. Since interest in fire recovery planning seemed greatest in the Leavenworth area (and since Leavenworth was accessible to Wenatchee), we recommended that two identical full-day workshops occur in Leavenworth: one on a Friday and a second the next day on Saturday. Two weeks later a Saturday workshop

was held in Entiat, followed by a full-day Saturday workshop in Lynnwood, Washington, two weeks after that.

6. *Who should convene and sponsor the workshops?* Collaborative Learning workshops may appeal to more citizens when more than one organization sponsors them. As we noted in Chapter 3, there are many roles that individuals and organizations can play in a collaborative process. A varied group of sponsors may communicate to citizens procedure fairness and the significance of the event. Even though the Wenatchee National Forest was convening and funding the workshops, we recommended that Leavenworth and Entiat ranger district staff solicit cosponsoring organizations, at no cost to those organizations. Some cosponsors signed on, including the Leavenworth City Council and Leavenworth Chamber of Commerce for the Leavenworth workshops.

7. *Who from the Wenatchee National Forest should participate in the workshops?* An important part of the fire recovery workshops was mutual learning between scientists and citizens and interaction between scientific knowledge and local knowledge.   This would occur only if agency scientists participated actively throughout the workshops, just as other citizens would. We stressed that Wenatchee National Forest staff needed to engage the workshops as they hoped any other citizen would, in their dual roles as agency professional and citizen who lived in the area and was concerned about forest health and forest management. At more traditional public meetings we have seen agency professionals display the "back of the room" syndrome, standing aside from other citizens and not getting involved. We not only insisted that agency scientists be involved and participate fully in all the workshop tasks, but asked them to join different tables during the small group discussions. We were concerned, though, about how many WNF staff would participate. If too many agency personnel participated and outnumbered citizens, the workshop process would be less effective. Consequently, we identified for each workshop WNF staff who were essential and those who were on "standby." Citizen turnout was strong, so all attending WNF staff participated.

Publicizing the Workshops.   Once workshop design issues had been addressed, we focused on another design and implementation activity: publicity. Given the accessibility and inclusivity goals, we wanted to publicize the meetings broadly. We advised WNF staff to go beyond the standard mailing and public notice announcements. We encouraged district rangers to make personal phone calls to people they wanted to attend a workshop. The district rangers were interviewed on local radio about the workshops. Articles and advertisements about the workshops appeared in local newspapers. Public service announcements appeared on radio and cable television. Flyers were posted at community grocery stores, minimarts, and laundromats. Interest groups received invitations and announcements to include in their newsletters.

The Step I Workshops.   The initial workshops began with the assumption that people need a common base of knowledge about fire recovery issues. To that end, the workshops were preceded by "issue presentation evenings," meetings at which the public could learn about issues such as fire ecology and fire effects on wildlife, fish, vegetation, recreation, tourism, and so on. Presenters came from federal and state agencies and the local area (non-agency).

The subsequent day-long Collaborative Learning workshops emphasized informal discussion more than formal presentation. As noted earlier, these workshops were open to the public and publicized widely. Their goal was the identification of public concerns and the generation of management improvements that the ID teams could use as part of their fire recovery project development work.

To achieve this goal, the workshops employed a number of CL techniques presented in the previous chapter. The daylong workshops began with the best and worst views exercise. At the Leavenworth and Entiat workshops, the relevant district ranger and ID team leader gave short presentations that summarized the talks given at the evening issue presentation meetings. Since no issue presentation evening was held in the Seattle area, the Lynnwood workshop included issue presentations during the first two hours.

As we discussed in the previous chapter, situation mapping is a powerful Collaborative Learning activity. As typically used in CL workshops, it is the first large-group discussion exercise. It is designed to encourage a number of key learning activities, including systems thinking and understanding the diversity of stakeholder interests in the situation.

Our development of the fire recovery situation map relied on the community assessment work, our library work, and conversations with agency personnel. Based on our understanding of the fire recovery situation, we prepared a draft situation map. Following the issue presentation summaries, we distributed copies of the situation map to each workshop participant, placed a transparency copy on an overhead projector, and with overhead pens in hand, asked workshop participants to improve the map. The original map and the citizen-amended version appear in Figures 8.4 and 8.5. Figure 9.3 presents one of the revised versions.

Situation mapping and individual and small group tasks that focused on concerns, interests, and the generation of improvements all related to the fire recovery management situation (see Daniels & Walker, 1996; and Daniels et al., 1996 for discussions of these techniques). These activities loosely paralleled "issue identification" in traditional problem solving and "focusing on interests" in mutual gains negotiation (Fisher et al., 1991). Participants identified concerns and improvements individually, and then discussed them initially in pairs, followed by groups of four to eight.

Situation mapping, an activity described in Chapter 8, proved to be one of the more provocative Collaborative Learning techniques used in the FRCL effort. This activity attempted to create a collective understanding of the fire recovery situation. Its purpose was to create a visual representation or "rich picture" (Wilson & Morren, 1990) of the fire recovery situation. The map included enough material so that all participants could see their interests and concerns satisfactorily represented. A common behavior when dealing with situations as complex as the fire recovery situation is to choose a single cause and attribute all of the negative features of the situation to it ("it's all due to bad fire suppression management"; "it's all due too much fuel material"; "the forest will be harmed if salvaged"). A properly constructed situation map can show that there are many possible causes and thus many possible changes that could be undertaken. It presents a "systems" view of the problem situation, encouraging participants to think systemically about concerns, interests, needs, and situation improvements. By doing so, workshop participants learn about the situation as a dynamic, open system (Roberts, 1999). The systems thinking fostered by situation mapping helps parties address and work through the complexity of the situation rather than be overwhelmed by it (Senge, 1990).

Step II: ID Team Planning. The four initial CL workshops produced, via collaborative discussions, numerous statements of concerns/interests and more than 100 improvements related to management of the fire recovery situation. Brief summaries of all the improvements were sent along with thank-you letters to all workshop participants. Consequently, workshop parties got to see the improvements generated at the workshops they did not attend. These concerns/interests and improvements were subsequently reviewed as part of fire recovery project planning. The fire recovery ID teams, working out of the Leavenworth and Entiat Ranger Districts, developed specific short-term and long-term projects. Project areas included trail rehabilitation, sensitive plant protection, wildlife habitat restoration, salvage, fuels reduction, reforestation, public safety, and forest product development. Consistent with NEPA requirements, the ID teams prepared draft environmental assessments (EAs) for specific projects.

The Second Public Involvement Step (Step III Workshops). As draft EAs were being developed, the Leavenworth and Entiat Ranger Districts assessed the value of continuing to use CL workshops for NEPA-related public involvement. The Entiat ID team decided to employ a more traditional approach, holding "open houses" to generate comments on its proposed fire recovery actions.

In contrast, the Leavenworth Ranger District ID team chose to continue a CL approach. Consequently, about three months after the initial CL workshops, the Leavenworth Ranger District sponsored a second round of CL workshops. At these advanced-stage workshops, designed and facilitated by the authors, participants received texts of proposed fire recovery actions, such as a possible timber salvage project. Working with these texts and detailed maps, participants engaged in both dialogue and debate as they deliberated ways in which the proposed actions could be modified and improved. In so doing, they considered whether the projects represented desirable and feasible change. Included in these discussions were questions about whether some of the projects should occur at all.

Step IV: Project Development. Following the advanced-stage CL workshops, the Leavenworth ID teams revised their proposed actions, released draft and final environmental assessments on those actions, and invited public comment on them in the form of letters. Following the appropriate comment

Figure 9.3
Revised Fire Recovery Situation Map

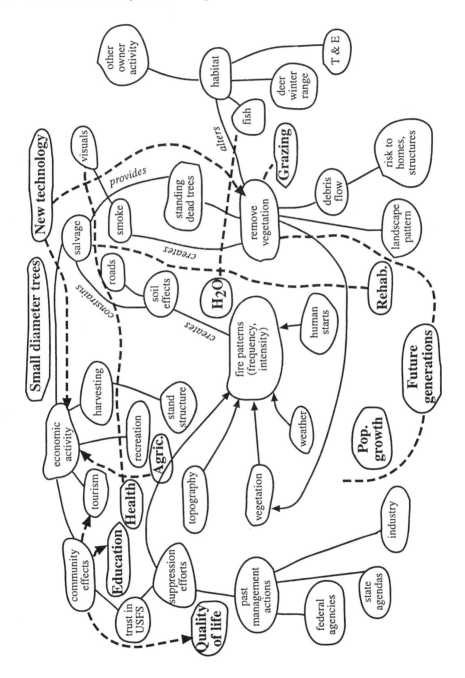

period, a record of decision was reached on proposed actions. Projects were finalized and initiated on the ground.

Other Actions. As part of this overall project, Collaborative Learning was applied to other Wenatchee National Forest planning activities. In three ranger districts some CL techniques were used as part of watershed assessments. One ranger district held a CL workshop to deal with organizational development issues.

Evaluation

A comprehensive Collaborative Learning application includes project evaluation. To accomplish this, the SSRG (Social Science Research Group) of the Science Team designed survey instruments to be administered to participants in the Collaborative Learning citizen workshops before, immediately following, and six months after the workshops (Blatner, 1997).

The FRCL project provided an opportunity to bring Collaborative Learning into a substantial ecosystem-based management situation. Through Collaborative Learning, the Wenatchee National Forest, the relevant natural resource management agency, was able to engage communities in meaningful ways. Initial project evaluations from both agency and nonagency workshop participants were favorable and constructive (Blatner, 1997). Citizens have reported that they felt listened to and that their knowledge was respected. Workshop participants seem to have valued the workshops' emphases on learning, constructive communication, and the generation of specific management improvements. Citizens have appreciated the opportunity to interact individually and in groups with Forest Service personnel, and Forest Service employees have welcomed the opportunity to participate in these workshops as citizens.

CONCLUSION

The FRCL project was an attempt to involve the public innovatively and to confront directly the policy paradox of expertise and inclusion presented in Chapter 1. The fire recovery project was comprehensive, including assessment, training, design, implementation, and evaluation phases. The CL citizen workshops were designed to feature learning—citizens to citizen, agency to citizen, citizen to agency, and agency to agency. This learning provided the basis for dialogue and deliberation. The workshop process respected diversity of views and, in so doing, tried to provide opportunities for people to express their views and test ideas in constructive ways.

What the long-term effects of the FRCL project will be is uncertain, and the impact will likely be different from one community to another and one ranger district to another. The Leavenworth district ranger reported to us that her district uses a Collaborative Learning approach for all of its significant public involvement work and that the fire recovery ID team leader has become very competent at leading these CL efforts. She has told us that her community's citizens now expect collaborative public involvement activities and value mutual learning opportunities. In 1997 the Wenatchee National Forest received a national "Showcase" award from the U.S. Department of Agriculture for its public involvement work as part of fire recovery planning. The Leavenworth Ranger District and Wenatchee National Forest remained committed to collaborative public involvement, even as the salvage rider legislation was implemented.

As we have noted throughout this book, natural resource conflicts are about matters of substance, procedure, and relationships. Collaborative Learning specifically addresses issues of substance through fair, accessible, and inclusive procedures. In so doing, the potential exists for relationships among parties to improve. Such change may be subtle and incremental, but Collaborative Learning as a process of civic discovery offers people an opportunity to interact about natural resource management issues that concern them. As the *Wenatchee World* reported about one of the Leavenworth workshops:

Participants were encouraged to get into small groups and discuss their ideas with people who may have differing views.

Longtime Leavenworth logger Grant Gibbs said one thing he would most like to see as a result of the fires was more logging of trees—especially the burned trees—and the removal of debris from the forest floor.

Across the table, Liz Tanke, a member of the Western Ancient Forest Campaign, listened intently. Afterwards, she asked Gibbs more about his ideas but said she felt that more dead trees should be left standing for birds.

"I may disagree with what you are saying and you might not agree with me," she said, "but I think we should wait to see what [U.S. Forest Service scientist] Rich Everett and his group [the Science Team] come up with before we make any judgments." (Partridge, 1995, p. 10)

Collaborative Learning is one of many innovative approaches that may meet the needs for effective public participation in ESBM better than traditional activities. The approach is particularly applicable for ecosystem-based management situations because it has been designed specifically to address the policy challenges of public lands. The Wenatchee National Forest application illustrates four features that make it well suited to ecosystem-based management situations like fire recovery: (1) it explicitly adopts a systems approach to the situation and works to improve the participants' systems understanding; (2) it is more modest in its expectations for progress than the more frequently used rational-comprehensive models that seek solutions; (3) it expects and attempts to accommodate a wide range of worldviews about land management and the strategic behaviors that those worldviews are likely to generate in controversial situations; and (4) it emphasizes constructive communication through dialogue, argument, and negotiation—the core of public deliberation and civic discovery.

Chapter 10
_____

The Practice of Collaborative Learning: Other Applications

> Man shapes himself through decisions that shape his environment.
>
> — Rene Dubos

The previous chapter described one of our most comprehensive applications of Collaborative Learning: the Wenatchee National Forest fire recovery planning process. We believe that Collaborative Learning, both conceptually and methodologically, is potentially relevant to a variety of environmental and natural resource conflicts and decisions. The applications we present in this chapter illustrate this varied applicability. We present these applications according to project phases described in Chapter 8—assessment, training, design, implementation, and evaluation. We also include background on each application and discussion of the challenges that we perceived and the lessons that we learned. Every environmental and natural resource conflict situation is challenging, with opportunities to handle conflict effectively and make good decisions.

THE OREGON DUNES NATIONAL RECREATION AREA[1]

The Oregon Dunes National Recreation Area (ODNRA) management situation represents one of the first comprehensive applications of Collaborative Learning (Daniels & Walker, 1996). This project included four of the five stages of a Collaborative Learning project: assessment, design, implementation, and evaluation. We did not provide a training component, a point we will address later.

Background

In April 1993 we received a call from the supervisor of the Siuslaw National Forest about holding Collaborative Learning workshops as part of the Siuslaw

National Forest's public participation aspect of its new ODNRA draft management plan. The ODNRA management process had been under way for more than two years, culminating in a Draft Environmental Impact Statement (DEIS) of alternative management strategies that was released to the public in April 1993. Before this release, the Siuslaw National Forest held a public comment period during which it received letters and sponsored open houses on the DEIS alternatives. Many letters were critical of the DEIS preferred alternative, and the open houses drew a lot of citizens who were upset with the Siuslaw National Forest's tentative plans. The ODNRA and Siuslaw National Forest leadership thought a series of Collaborative Learning workshops might generate constructive citizen involvement and feedback in ways that other public participation activities did not. After a preliminary assessment of the situation, we decided to develop a Collaborative Learning project.

Figure 10.1
Oregon Dunes National Recreation Area (ODNRA)

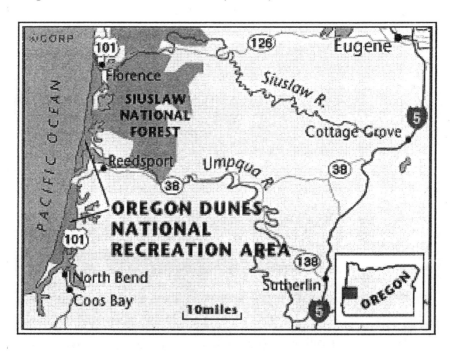

Source: ODNRA Web site (http://www.fs.fed.us/r6/siuslaw/oregondunes).

The Oregon Dunes National Recreation Area consists of a strip of land approximately 40 miles long and on average 1.5 miles wide on the central Oregon coast between Florence in the north and North Bend-Coos Bay in the south (see Figure 10.1). There are 31,500 acres within the ODNRA boundary. The dunes system within the ODNRA has been part of the Siuslaw National Forest since 1908, when the Forest was established. By an act of Congress, the dunes became a national recreation area in 1972. The legislation states that the area is to be administered by the USDA-Forest Service for the purposes of "public outdoor recreation use and enjoyment . . . and the conservation of scenic, scientific, historic and other values contributing to the public enjoyment of such land and waters . . . " (Siuslaw National Forest, 1993, p. I-1).

The ODNRA is a multiple-resource, multiple-use area. Major issue areas addressed in the planning process included off-road vehicle (ORV) management (e.g., access, noise, safety), nonmotorized recreation activities (e.g., hiking, camping, interpretation), vegetation (particularly non-native European beach grass), threatened/endangered species (e.g., the western snowy plover), wetlands, wild/scenic river designation, user population management, and local community impacts (particularly economic). Of these, the presence of ORVs in the ODNRA was the most contentious. Before the planning process, approximately 48 percent of the ODNRA was open to ORVs. The ORV community wanted more of the Dunes open to motorized recreation. The dominant environmental organization in Oregon wanted ORVs excluded from the ODNRA.

Table 10.1
ODNRA Collaborative Learning Project Timeline

April 1993	ODNRA Draft Environmental Impact Statement (DEIS) released
April 1993	Meeting with ODNRA and Siuslaw National Forest leaders to discuss the possibility of Collaborative Learning Workshops
April 1993	Forest Service open houses held about the ODNRA DEIS plans
May 1993	Siuslaw Leadership Team field trip through the Oregon Dunes
May 1993	Assessment interviews and trips to ODNRA
May-June 1993	Public comment period (letters) about ODNRA DEIS plans
June 1993	Stage 1 Meeting
July 1993	Content analysis of public comment letters
July 1993	Stage 2 workshops in Florence, North Bend/Coos Bay, and Eugene/Springfield
August 1993	Consultants' analysis of stage 2 workshop improvements
August 1993	Summary list of stage 2 workshop improvements and invitation to stage 3 meeting mailed to all stage 2 workshop participants
August 1993	Mail survey of all stage 2 workshop participants
September 1993	Stage 3 workshop stage 1 meeting
December 1993	Consultants' report to ODNRA and Siuslaw National Forest staff
February 1994	ODNRA Final Environmental Impact Statement (FEIS) released
Feb.-March 1994	Public comment period (letters) about ODNRA FEIS plan
April 1994	Siuslaw National Forest ODNRA management plan Record of Decision

The first ODNRA management plan was prepared during the late 1970s and adopted in 1979. In 1990 the Siuslaw National Forest leadership decided that the management plan needed revision. The National Forest Management Act (NFMA) of 1976 and the National Environmental Policy Act (NEPA) of 1969 require preparation of an Environmental Impact Statement (EIS) when a management plan is revised. Public involvement is a significant part of EIS development and the planning process, as directed by NFMA and NEPA.

Public involvement in the ODNRA planning process began in March 1991. Initial activities included scoping sessions and a newsletter survey. In January 1992 five draft management alternatives were presented to the public via open houses and a newsletter. Based on public response, three more management alternatives were developed. In April 1993 a Draft Environmental Impact Statement (DEIS) was published for public review and comment via open houses and letters. The Siuslaw National Forest received approximately 4,200 letters during the 90-day comment period.

Assessment

Assessment included several activities. First, we first read the 200 plus page Draft Environmental Impact Statement, which included the various management alternatives. Second, we obtained from ODNRA and Siuslaw National Forest headquarters staff the names and phone numbers of people with strong interest in the ODNRA management situation. We called many of these people, interviewing them over the phone about their Oregon Dunes management concerns.

As we talked with people we discovered how deeply people felt about the Oregon Dunes; it was a special place to many. We decided that we needed to meet people face-to-face, so we traveled to the Oregon Dunes National Recreation Area, once as part of a Siuslaw National Forest leadership team field trip and some times on our own. We had both been on the Dunes before, as hikers. Consequently, on one of our trips we rented motorized off-road vehicles so that we could experience motorized recreation on the Oregon Dunes.

Third, we organized a six-member group of graduate students to help us with a content analysis of letters received during the DEIS public comment period. We developed a content analysis framework, trained the graduate students, and with them worked through a 1,220-letter sample from the set of 4,200 letters.

The content analytic procedure was designed specifically for the ODNRA workshop project. Team members were instructed to read each letter and analyze it according to the following categories: support/opposition to ORVs; distributive/integrative view of ODNRA conflict situation; and reactions versus recommendations. We also coded letters in terms of reference to specific DEIS alternatives, and evaluated detailed comment letters in terms of ODNRA issues addressed. Results of the content analysis were presented at the Collaborative Learning workshops (stage 2 meetings).

Training

This project did not include a training phase. In retrospect, we wish it had. Given the timing of our Collaborative Learning project intervention and the

Siuslaw National Forest's decision time line, we decided to forgo training. We will address this issue later when we discuss "lessons learned."

Design and Facilitation

Collaborative Learning Workshops were conducted during the summer of 1993 as a supplement to the formal comment period. "The workshops were intended to provide a public forum, involving people with varied interests, in which [participants could] test ideas and develop collaborative suggestions for improvement of several planning issues at the [OD]NRA" (Siuslaw National Forest, 1994, p. 20).

Working with the ODNRA interdisciplinary team, we developed objectives for the project. They were:

Supplement the ongoing public participation process pursuant to NEPA. Other ODNRA public involvement activities, such as open houses and letter-writing, were generally structured in ways that featured question-answer-comment sessions or individual statements. While these activities were very important, CL meetings allowed people to talk with one another about concerns, issues, and improvements. Through face-to-face discussions, people could learn about and test the ideas and views that could not be expressed in letters or in large, formal public meetings. Workshop discussions encouraged people to go beyond competitive positions and attempt to find areas on which they could collaborate. The Collaborative Learning project was not a substitute for other NEPA public participation activities related to the Oregon Dunes National Recreation Area Management Plan DEIS.

Provide a forum for innovation and collaboration regarding the management of the ODNRA. Public views about the ODNRA were appearing in the form of positions in opposition to one another. Citizens attempted to convince the decision maker, the Forest Service, to favor their particular "side." This type of communication, as we have noted earlier in the book, was asking the decision maker to "arbitrate" the conflict, the result of which could have been a "compromise" that no one would want. The workshops were designed for collaborative discussions and decisions: to learn about the views of others, to locate areas of common ground, to generate improvements with diverse support, and to identify issues on which agreement did not seem likely.

Within the design phase, the ODNRA Collaborative Learning project included a number of major events:

- Inform stakeholder groups and involve them in process design.
- Provide a common base of knowledge about major Dunes issues.
- Identify concerns about ODNRA management.
- Generate suggested improvements.
- Organize the improvements based on different strategic visions for the ODNRA.
- Debate the improvement sets.
- Report to the USDA-Forest Service and publics.

These events related to a series of ODNRA Collaborative Learning project meetings.

Stage 1 Meeting.[2] The stage 1 meeting had two goals. First, the meeting introduced the project team to influential members of the public who were important to the ODNRA planning process. Second, the meeting provided an opportunity for influential citizens to provide input into the preliminary designs for the stage 2 workshops.

This meeting was publicized, and participants were encouraged to attend via invitation. No one, though, who asked to attend was turned away. The meeting was designed to work with a small group (fewer than 20 participants) who could learn about and provide feedback concerning the general Collaborative Learning project design. The initial list of participants was drawn from names provided by the Forest Service of: (1) past participants in ODNRA meetings, (2) people who had expressed interest in the land management planning process, (3) people with specific expertise or knowledge that might be relevant to this project, (4) people who represented an organization, governmental body, or agency that should be involved. Seventeen people participated in this half-day meeting, held in Florence, a coastal community adjacent to the ODNRA.

Stage 2 Meetings. Approximately one month after the stage 1 meeting, we held three "stage 2" citizen meetings/workshops, two in communities adjacent to the ODNRA and one in a large urban area of the Willamette Valley, about 80 miles east of the ODNRA. Attendance varied at the three meetings. The Oregon coast community workshops drew 30 and 41 people; the Willamette valley community meeting involved 32 people. Attendees included both preregistrants and walk-ins. No one who expressed any interest in the stage 2 meetings (or any other meeting, for that matter) was discouraged or excluded in any manner.

We used the following methods to publicize the workshops:

Flyer/poster. Six hundred copies of a one-page flyer were printed. Multiple copies were distributed to the Chambers of Commerce in Florence, Reedsport, Eugene, Coos Bay, and Springfield; the ODNRA Headquarters in Reedsport; the city of Reedsport; and Oregon Motor Sports in Portland. A mailing list of over 150 individuals, associations, and organizations was prepared, and copies of the flyer were sent to them. Names of individuals came from a list of participants in previous ODNRA public meetings; organization addresses came from the Oregon Directory of Forest Interest Groups (Oregon State University Extension Service, 1993). Organizations represented diverse interests, ranging from Caveman 4-Wheelers of Grants Pass and the Pacific NW 4-Wheel Drive Association to the OSU Extension Service offices in Lane, Douglas, and Coos counties to the Audubon societies in Corvallis and North Bend.

Newspaper advertisements. We ran a 1" by 6" display advertisement in the following newspapers in the two weeks before the meetings: *Siuslaw News,* Florence; *Eugene Register Guard*; *Coos Bay World*; *Medford Mail Tribune*; *Reedsport Courier*; *Corvallis Gazette-Times*; *Albany Democrat-Herald*; and *Newport News Tribune.* In addition, copies of the flyer were sent to the suburban desk of *The Oregonian* and the city desk of the *Salem Statesman Journal.* The workshops were mentioned in the community happenings/meetings calendars for both these papers and in some of the ones with advertising.

Public service announcements (PSAs). We sent 15-second and 30-second PSAs to fourteen radio and four cable television stations in Florence, Coos Bay, North Bend, Reedsport, and Eugene/Springfield.

Stage 2 Meeting Format. The stage 2 workshops all followed the same format. The mornings were devoted to issue presentations and a panel discussion, and the afternoons to Collaborative Learning activities to identify concerns and generate improvements. They were designed to provide members of the public with similar systemic views of the ODNRA situation, and then allow the participants to suggest improvements to the Dunes situation, based both on this systemic perspective and on the comments of other participants. Stage 2 workshop activities included:

Issue presentations. The first portion of each workshop featured issue presentations that addressed scientific and legal dimensions of ODNRA management. Talks were given on the snowy plover (a threatened species), European beach grass (a non-native vegetation that is taking over the sand dunes), wetlands legislation, off-road vehicle legislation, and recreation use. Each presentation included a question-and-answer session. The topics varied somewhat depending on the location of the workshop. For example, the Eugene meeting included a presentation on recreation, while the Coos Bay/North Bend meeting provided a presentation on economic development. Presentations were given by Forest Service personnel as well as local citizens with relevant expertise. For example, a talk on Oregon Dunes geology was presented by a Florence ice cream shop owner, an avowed "amateur" geologist.

Panel discussions. Following the issue presentations, each workshop included a panel discussion. Panelists represented critical stakeholder groups. For example, the Florence panel consisted of a leader of the ORV community, a prominent homeowner with property adjacent to the dunes, and a local environmentalist (affiliated with a statewide or national organization). Panelists at the other workshops included a county commissioner, a Chamber of Commerce officer, and a local economic development expert. Each panelist talked for a few minutes about his viewpoints and concerns or those of the group he represented. The panelists then engaged the workshop participants and one another in a question-answer-comment session.

Best and worst views and situation mapping. In addition to the issue presentations and panel discussions, two active learning tasks were used to create a common understanding of the ODNRA situation. When participants arrived at the stage 2 workshop, they were given blank cards and asked to write down their best and worst imaginable futures for the ODNRA. Workshop assistants transferred these "bests" and "worsts" to newsprint and displayed them on walls for all participants to see. This activity demonstrated that most people's interests in the ODNRA situation were far more compatible than either their prior expectations or positions may have indicated.

The second method for creating a collective understanding of the ODNRA situation was building a mind map of the situation (called "situation map" in the workshops), a technique we described in Chapter 8. Its purpose was to create a visual representation or "rich picture" (Wilson & Morren, 1990) of the ODNRA situation that included enough material so that all participants could see their interests and concerns satisfactorily represented. Many letter writers and open house participants focused on a single cause and attributed all of the negative features of the situation to it ("it's all due to ORVs"; "it's all due to beach grass"; "it's all due to radical environmentalists"). Based on our understanding of the ODNRA situation, we constructed a situation map to show that there were many possible causes and thus many possible changes that could be undertaken. It presented a "systems" view of the problem: encouraging participants to think systemically about concerns, interests, needs, and situation improvements.

Individual and small group tasks. A participant-centered active learning task provided a transition from common understanding to action, identifying themes of concern and interests (drawing upon CL stages 4 and 5). The participants selected aspects of the ODNRA situation, as shown on the situation map, that concerned them or that they thought could be improved. As we noted in Chapter 8, this activity paralleled "issue identification" in traditional problem solving and "focusing on interests" in mutual gains negotiation (Fisher & Ury, 1981). Participants identified concerns individually and then discussed them initially in pairs, followed by groups of six to eight. Concerns emerging from the groups were recorded on overhead transparencies and presented to the entire workshop.

The next activity took the discussion from concerns to improvements (Collaborative Learning stages 4, 5, and 6). Based on their themes of concern and interests, participants generated ideas that they considered to be desirable, feasible improvements to the current ODNRA management situation or its preferred alternative. They developed improvements individually and discussed them in pairs, then in larger groups. Participants engaged in some preliminary debate about the desirability and feasibility of improvements, although they primarily talked about the details of and need for the improvements.

Improvement Analysis. Following the stage 2 workshops, the consultants (this book's authors) examined the concerns and improvements work sheets that workshop participants developed. The ODNRA stage 2 workshops produced, via collaborative discussions, numerous statements of concerns/interests and a set of improvements for management of the ODNRA situation. As facilitators, we reviewed the workshops' proposed improvements. A list of the improvements from all three stage 2 workshops was mailed to each stage 2 workshop participant. Consequently, a participant at one workshop (e.g., Florence) learned about improvements generated at the other workshops as well as his own. In addition, as facilitators and consultants, we prepared a content analysis of the stage 2 workshop improvements (Table 10.2).

A total of 76 improvements sheets were generated (21 at Florence, 24 at Eugene/Springfield, and 31 at North Bend/Coos Bay). Many of the improvements sheets contained more than 1 improvement, however. The 76 sheets provide a total of 133 separate improvements (average of 1.75). The most common number of improvements per sheet was 1, but it ranged as high as 6.

Table 10.2
Content Analysis of ODNRA Improvements

Improvement topic	Number	Percent (N=133)
European beach grass, non-native vegetation	35	26.3
Off-road vehicle (ORV) noise	18	13.5
ORV regulations enforcement and education	17	12.8
ORV curfew	10	07.5
Improve facilities (e.g., campgrounds)	10	07.5
Enhance ORV access to the Oregon Dunes	5	03.8
Conduct long-range planning	5	03.8
Snowy plover management and habitat	5	03.8
Use of volunteers	4	03.0
Restrict ORV access to the Oregon Dunes	3	02.3
Biological diversity/nature	3	02.3
Economic development	3	02.3
Historical interpretation	3	02.3
Maximize Research Natural Area (RNA)	2	01.5
Disabled access to the Oregon Dunes	2	01.5
Minimize RNAs	1	00.8
DEIS alternative A or C	1	00.8
Other	6	04.5

We can make two important observations from the improvements sheets. The first is that the level of integrative thinking probably exceeds what can be captured in frequency counts or in the average number of issues per improvements sheet. Even those improvements sheets that focused on one issue often selected an issue that cut across a number of other issues or gave a rationale for their suggestion in terms of impacts/improvements for other issues. There appears to have been considerable integrative thinking embedded in the improvements generated at the workshops, which is the intent of the Collaborative Learning method in general and of the situation mapping/improvement generating in specific.

The second observation regarding the improvements sheets is that beach grass control/eradication cuts across many of the issues and points of view regarding the ODNRA. The improvements can be broadly clustered into two sets: those addressing human enjoyment/conflict or those addressing biological protection/diversity. Beach grass management, more than any other single issue, cuts across both of these clusters and is an issue for which there is broad consensus regarding desired management philosophy. Regardless of other values, many if not most improvement sheet respondents want a more aggressive beach grass eradication/control emphasis on the ODNRA.

Stage 3 Meeting. About six weeks after the last stage 2 workshop, a "stage 3" meeting took place to discuss the ODNRA management improvements that stage 2 workshop participants had generated. This meeting provided participants with the opportunity to debate (discuss and argue constructively) sets of changes that had been prepared by the project team, based on the suggestions provided at the stage 2 meetings.

Twenty-six people participated in the stage 3 workshop. Like the stage 1 meeting, the invitations to participate were to specific people, most (but not all) of whom had attended one of the stage 2 workshops. The ODNRA staff and the project team prepared a list of potential invitees. The goal of the stage 3 meeting task—debating desirability and feasibility of improvements in the ODNRA management plan—would be best accomplished through a smaller, rather than larger, group of participants, people knowledgeable about the issues and willing to engage one another collaboratively. These factors combined to make a by-invitation format more appropriate than a widely publicized open public meeting. Still, attendance was not limited to people who attended one of the stage 2 workshops; anyone who wanted to participate was welcome. Of the 26 stage 3 participants, 3 had not attended a stage 2 meeting.

The content analysis of the improvements was the basis of a number of "draft improvement texts," much like single-negotiating texts (Raiffa, 1982), which were distributed to participants in the stage 3 meeting. Three stage 2 participants were solicited to develop their own "improvement texts" on the issues of ORV management, beach grass control, and economic/community development. These, too, were distributed to stage 3 parties. After discussion of "ground rules," stage 3 participants organized themselves into issue-centered work groups (e.g., beach grass, ORV management, and economic development). Following is the stage 3 tentative workshop agenda.

0900	Welcome and introduction to the workshop.
0930	"Big pictures" of the ODNRA. (break follows)
1015	Issues team discussions: Developing ODNRA improvements (lunch follows)
1300	Issues team reports
1345	Evaluation teams discussions: Refining ODNRA improvements (break follows)
1530	Implementing improvements
1700	The end . . . and thank you

Workshop participants discussed and debated the improvement texts, suggesting changes, additions, modifications, and deletions (CL stages 7 and 8). An example of a "draft improvement text" appears in Table 10.3.

Table 10.3
Sample Excerpt of an ODNRA Draft Improvement Text

PROPOSED IMPROVEMENT: Off-Highway Vehicle Management (OHV) *GENERAL IMPROVEMENT AREA*: Enhancing the management of OHV use on the ODNRA. DEIS REFERENCE: II, 39-42 *WHAT IS THE GOAL*? Implement efforts that deal with the following management issues:	
OUR DRAFT	YOUR IMPROVEMENTS

OUR DRAFT

NOISE ENFORCEMENT
(1) Implement a "flag system" using flags that indicate the noise class of each machine on the ODNRA. Allow different machines to operate in different areas, at different times, and in different manners depending on the noise class.
(2) Develop an OHV-user managed noise measurement, flagging, and education system.
(3) Collaborate with manufacturers and vendors to work on the technical feasibility of gradually dropping noise levels on the ODNRA, with an eventual goal in the low 90 db range.

ACCESS
(1) Designate a night riding corridor, preferably to the beach, where there would be no curfew.
(2) Distinguish between areas that are for wide open OHV use "joy riding," and other areas that are designated for touring at lower speeds and with quieter machines.
(3) Examine land allocations in Alternative F to identify those areas proposed to be closed to OHV use that would be suitable for a touring designation.
(4) Increase the level of signing of closed areas.

DISABLED ACCESS
(1) Indicate the machines of disabled riders with a light blue flag in addition to the orange one.
(2) Disabled riders can go anywhere hikers can go on the ODNRA, except where strictly prohibited.
(3) Carefully monitor level of disabled use to determine if adverse impacts are occurring.

After the stage 3 meeting the facilitators prepared final versions of the various draft improvement texts. These were presented to the leadership teams of the Siuslaw National Forest and Oregon Dunes National Recreation Area. Both the Final Environmental Impact Statement and the Record of Decision incorporated aspects of the improvements generated and refined at the stage 2 and stage 3 meetings. Table 10.4 presents a portion of a draft improvement text presented to the ODNRA and Siuslaw National Forest leadership staff, as modified by the stage 3 workshop participants. As this discussion suggests, many of these Collaborative Learning design steps, implemented as part of the ODNRA public involvement process, corresponded to selected aspects of the overall nine-phase CL framework (see Table 10.5). The first stage featured learning about the Collaborative Learning process. This was the focus of the stage 1 meeting and the beginning of each stage 2 meeting. At each stage 2 workshop, the facilitators (authors) outlined the Collaborative Learning process and the "ground rules" for interaction. The "ground rules" emphasized various aspects of Collaborative Learning communication competence, particularly listening and collaborative argument areas.

Table 10.4
ODNRA Draft Improvement Text Excerpt, as Modified by Workshop Participants

PROPOSED IMPROVEMENT: Off-Highway Vehicle Management (OHV) *GENERAL IMPROVEMENT AREA*: Enhancing the management of OHV use on the ODNRA. DEIS REFERENCE: II, 39-42 *WHAT IS THE GOAL?* Implement efforts that deal with the following management issues:	

OUR DRAFT	YOUR IMPROVEMENTS
NOISE ENFORCEMENT (1) Implement a "flag system" using flags that indicate the noise class of each machine on the ODNRA. Allow different machines to operate in different areas, at different times, and in different manners depending on the noise class. (2) Develop an OHV-user managed noise measurement, flagging, and education system. (3) Collaborate with manufacturers and vendors to work on the technical feasibility of gradually dropping noise levels on the ODNRA, with an eventual goal in the low 90 db range.	Establish a noise level of 95 decibels (db) by 1 January 1996. Reevaluate that goal of a lower level in 1996, with an eventual goal in the low 90 db range by the year 2000.
ACCESS (1) Designate a night riding corridor, preferably to the beach, where there would be no curfew. (2) Distinguish between areas that are for wide open OHV use "joy riding," and	Establish a flexible curfew and night riding policy, adapted to each area (selectively imposed). *10 P.M. curfew in the Florence area. *11 P.M. curfew at Horsfall, Memorial Day to Labor Day.

other areas that are designated for touring at lower speeds and with quieter machines. (3) Examine land allocations in Alternative F to identify those areas proposed to be closed to OHV use that would be suitable for a touring designation. (4) Increase the level of signing of closed areas.

*10 P.M. curfew at Bluebill.
*Allow night riding out of Hauser and Winchester.
*Consider the possibility of night riding boundary markers north of Horsfall.

DISABLED ACCESS
(1) Indicate the machines of disabled riders with a light blue flag in addition to the orange one.
(2) Disabled riders can go anywhere hikers can go on the ODNRA, except where strictly prohibited.
(3) Carefully monitor level of disabled use to determine if adverse impacts are occurring.

The ODNRA needs to reinforce its commitment to provide handicap access in usable areas.
*Implement a blue flag system.
*Allow disabled riders to be accompanied by a companion rider.

Table 10.5
Collaborative Learning Stages at the ODNRA Workshops

CL Stage	Meeting Stage	CL Workshop Activity
I. Learning about the CL Process	1, 2, 3	Meeting introductions and CL "lecture"
II. Creating Common Knowledge and Understanding	2	Issue presentations Panel discussions Best and worst futures Situation map
III. Generating Themes of Concern/Interests	2	Tie to situation map 1-2-6: Finding common and distinct concerns
IV. Generating, Developing, and Discussing Improvements	2	Short-term improvements Long-term improvements 1-2-6: Testing improvements
V. Debating and Refining Improvements	3	Issue-centered work groups Draft improvement texts Collaborative argument about feasibility and desirability Implementability

The steps of the project, presented earlier, corresponded to various Collaborative Learning stages:

- Inform stakeholder groups and involve them in process design (stage 1 meeting)
- Provide a common base of knowledge about major Dunes issues (stage 2 meeting
- Identify concerns about ODNRA management (stage 2 meeting)
- Generate suggested improvements (stage 2 meeting)
- Organize the improvements based on different strategic visions for the ODNRA
- Preparation for the stage 3 meeting
- Debate the improvement sets (stage 3 meeting)
- Report to the USDA-Forest Service and publics

Presentation to the USDA-Forest Service. Seven weeks after the stage 3 workshop, we met with the ODNRA and Siuslaw National Forest leadership staff to present a draft final report on the project. We discussed specific findings and recommendations for future collaborative activities.

Evaluation

The final component of the ODNRA Collaborative Learning project was evaluation. While informal observation and post-workshop discussion suggested that the ODNRA workshops contributed positively to the ODNRA planning process, ODNRA staff and we sought more concrete feedback. The ODNRA workshop project included the development and distribution of a post-workshop survey. We created the survey to assess attitudes about ODNRA management processes and to measure perceptions of the workshops themselves.

In mid-August, we mailed surveys to the people who had participated in one or more of the July workshops in Florence, Eugene/Springfield, or North Bend/Coos Bay. By mid-September 39 surveys had been returned. A second mailing resulted in 15 more surveys. Overall, the workshop survey obtained a 54% response rate. Of the 54 survey respondents, 38 participated in the entire day of a full-day workshop. The remainder attended either the morning or afternoon session only. The results of this survey reported here have appeared earlier in the journal *Environmental Impact Assessment Review* (Daniels & Walker, 1996).

Survey Design. The survey included both open-ended questions and a number of statements to which individuals responded using Likert (bipolar) scales. The Likert scale items constituted the majority of the post-survey. Answers to the survey's open-ended questions have been reviewed and are generally consistent with the survey's quantitative results. The Likert scale items allowed responses ranging from 1 to 5 or 1 to 7. The accompanying tables present mean values (averages) for these responses. In all cases, the higher the mean value (the closer to 5 or 7), the more favorable the response.

Survey Results. Survey statements address the following areas:

- Perceptions of the ODNRA management situation.
- Factors contributing to the usefulness of the Workshop.
- Judgments concerning the ODNRA workshop process.
- Assessment of specific workshop activities.
- Effect of the workshop on participants' views of ODNRA parties.
- Preferences concerning processes for achieving ODNRA goals.

Perceptions of the ODNRA management situation. Five statements on the survey asked respondents to evaluate various aspects of the ODNRA management situation, with "5" representing "strongly agree" (see Table 10.6). Responses were very strong regarding the desire for a flexible and adaptive management plan ($\bar{x}$ = 4.47) and for management activities that involve the public ($\bar{x}$= 4.72).

Survey participants also responded favorably to statements about constructive communication about ODNRA issues and understanding of ODNRA views, although these results were not particularly strong. On all the management situation items, all-day workshop participants responded much more positively than morning-only participants did.

Table 10.6
Perceptions of the ODNRA Management Situation
(1=strongly disagree; 5=strongly agree)

Statement	Respondents	$\bar{x}$	s.d.	n
Constructive communication is occurring on ODNRA issues.	*total group*	*3.78*	*1.01*	*51*
	attended all day	3.89	0.89	38
	attended morning	3.36	1.29	11
	attended afternoon	4.00	1.41	2
At present ODNRA parties understand one another's ODNRA views.	*total group*	*3.20*	*1.06*	*51*
	attended all day	3.37	1.00	38
	attended morning	2.64	1.21	11
	attended afternoon	3.00	0.00	2
ODNRA views and concerns of other parties are as important as yours or those of your party.	*total group*	*3.49*	*1.65*	*53*
	attended all day	3.56	1.65	39
	attended morning	3.00	1.65	12
	attended afternoon	5.00	0.00	2
ODNRA management process should view the ODNRA management plan as flexible and adaptive to change.	*total group*	*4.47*	*0.89*	*49*
	attended all day	4.59	0.69	37
	attended morning	3.90	1.37	10
	attended afternoon	5.00	0.00	2
ODNRA management process should include activities that will involve the public as openly and completely as possible.	*total group*	*4.72*	*0.54*	*50*
	attended all day	4.76	0.49	37
	attended morning	4.64	0.67	11
	attended afternoon	4.50	0.71	2

Factors contributing to ODNRA workshops. Three statements addressed the contributions of various factors to the ODNRA workshops, with "5" indicating "highly important." As Table 10.7 shows, there was support for using outside facilitators ($\bar{x}$= 4.17) in the workshop process. Respondents agreed very highly ($\bar{x}$= 4.82) that the willingness of USDA Forest Service and other agency personnel participate in the workshops was important to their success. Data also indicated that workshop participants believed that the collaborative learning process used during the afternoon of the workshop contributed positively to the discussions ($\bar{x}$ = 4.31).

Table 10.7
Assessment of ODNRA Workshop Factors
(1=not important; 5=highly important)

Components	Respondents	$\bar{x}$	s.d.	n
Willingness of USDA-Forest Service and other agency employees to participate in the ODNRA workshops	*total group*	*4.82*	*0.43*	*51*
	attended all day	4.82	0.46	38
	attended morning	4.91	0.30	11
	attended afternoon	4.50	0.71	2
Collaborative learning process during the afternoon of the ODNRA workshops.	*total group*	*4.31*	*0.87*	*45*
	attended all day	4.29	0.90	38
	attended morning	4.40	0.89	5
	attended afternoon	4.50	0.71	2
The use of outside facilitators.	*total group*	*4.17*	*1.29*	*48*
	attended all day	4.33	1.17	36
	attended morning	3.70	1.57	10
	attended afternoon	3.50	2.12	2

ODNRA workshop accomplishments. The survey included 12 Likert scale statements that asked for respondents' judgments about the ODNRA workshop process. Mean scores for these items appear in Table 10.8, with "5" representing "strongly agree." Many items in the survey were presented as "accomplished" statements: the workshop "allowed" "encouraged," "contributed," and so on. General uniformity appears in the responses to these statements: the mean scores vary from 3.38 to 4.33. These results indicate general agreement that the ODNRA workshop process created a positive climate for discussing ODNRA management issues, despite the many obstacles that the workshops faced. In this section of the survey, respondents reacted most strongly that the workshops provided parties with an opportunity to generate ideas about the ODNRA ($\bar{x} = 4.33$). On every item, all-day participants responded much more favorably than morning-only participants; mean value differences frequently approached or exceeded one full point. The data indicated that all-day participation was important to viewing the workshop as a success. Given that the morning sessions of the workshops involved presentations and a panel discussion, morning-only participants may have felt "talked at." Participants who remained for the afternoon (all-day) participated in Collaborative Learning activities that involved face-to-face discussion.

Assessment of specific workshop activities. One question set (Table 10.9) asked workshop participants to evaluate specific workshop activities, with "5" indicating "helped greatly." With the exception of the morning panel discussion, they assessed the tasks favorably. Three activities—issue presentations, identifying concerns and interests, and developing ODNRA situation improvements—generated mean value responses of about 4, indicating that participants found these tasks helpful.

Table 10.8
Oregon Dunes NRA Workshop Accomplishments
(1=strongly disagree; 5=strongly agree)

Statement	Respondents	x̄	s.d.	n
ODNRA workshops were open and accessible to all interested people.	*total group*	*4.17*	*1.19*	*51*
	attended all day	4.34	1.07	38
	attended morning	3.55	1.44	11
	attended afternoon	4.00	1.41	2
ODNRA workshops provided parties with the opportunity to generate ideas about the ODNRA.	*total group*	*4.33*	*0.86*	*51*
	attended all day	4.53	0.73	38
	attended morning	3.73	1.10	11
	attended afternoon	4.00	0.00	2
ODNRA workshops allowed every party's ODNRA interests to be considered.	*total group*	*3.88*	*1.06*	*49*
	attended all day	4.03	1.03	38
	attended morning	3.22	1.09	9
	attended afternoon	4.00	0.00	2
ODNRA workshops encouraged open discussion and evaluation of ideas.	*total group*	*3.96*	*1.03*	*48*
	attended all day	4.13	0.96	38
	attended morning	3.25	1.17	8
	attended afternoon	3.50	0.71	2
ODNRA workshops promoted the development of coordinated improvements.	*total group*	*3.77*	*1.15*	*47*
	attended all day	3.89	1.12	36
	attended morning	3.11	1.17	9
	attended afternoon	4.50	0.71	2
ODNRA workshops helped parties understand aspects of and perspectives on ODNRA issues.	*total group*	*4.04*	*0.98*	*49*
	attended all day	4.29	0.77	38
	attended morning	3.00	1.22	9
	attended afternoon	4.00	0.00	2
ODNRA workshops led to the development of an ongoing, organized approach to coordinate progress on ODNRA matters.	*total group*	*3.38*	*1.09*	*45*
	attended all day	3.63	1.03	35
	attended morning	2.50	0.93	8
	attended afternoon	2.50	0.71	2
ODNRA workshops encouraged joint decision making.	*total group*	*3.55*	*1.29*	*49*
	attended all day	3.78	1.27	37
	attended morning	2.70	1.16	10
	attended afternoon	3.50	0.71	2
ODNRA workshops involved the public in ways different from other public meetings.	*total group*	*3.96*	*1.15*	*46*
	attended all day	4.08	1.05	36
	attended morning	3.25	1.49	10
	attended afternoon	4.50	0.71	2
ODNRA workshops included participants from all affected parties and interests.	*total group*	*4.10*	*1.01*	*49*
	attended all day	4.38	0.68	36
	attended morning	3.20	1.32	9
	attended afternoon	3.50	2.12	2

ODNRA workshops promoted learning and common understanding about Dunes issues and how they are interrelated.	total group	3.81	1.15	47
	attended all day	4.03	1.13	36
	attended morning	3.00	1.00	9
	attended afternoon	3.50	0.71	2
ODNRA workshops included opportunities for participants to argue constructively about issues, concerns, and recommendations.	total group	3.74	1.15	47
	attended all day	3.97	1.03	36
	attended morning	3.11	1.36	9
	attended afternoon	2.50	0.71	2

Effect of the workshops on participants' views of ODNRA parties. An ever-present risk in potentially contentious intergroup meetings is the chance that relationships could be damaged during such a meeting, when a principal goal is to achieve the opposite. The survey asked if the workshops affected the participants' views of groups represented at the meeting (Table 10.10). The response scale for this question ranged from 1 (more negative view) to 7 (more positive view), with 4 representing no change.

The results show limited effect on views of ODNRA parties, but if there is any change, it is positive. There is consistency in the mean scores, which range from improved perceptions of off-road vehicle users, off-road vehicle businesspeople, and the USDA-Forest Service, to a more neutral mean response for environmentalists. Worth noting is the mean response of 4.48 for the USDA-Forest Service, corroborating the finding reported earlier that the agency members' behavior contributed positively to the discussion. These results show that the workshops did not hurt views, and may have achieved a modest relationship change.

It is probably unrealistic to expect a one-day meeting to significantly alter relationships and views that have developed over many years and have been hardened by previous natural resource disputes. Further, any facilitation that relies on relational progress as a precursor to substantive progress many have a reduced chance of progress of any kind. The approach employed by the ODNRA workshops emphasized substantive or conflict matters rather than relational concerns.

Preferences concerning processes for achieving ODNRA goals. The final statement set on the survey addressed peoples' preferences about different processes or methods for achieving their goals related to the management of the ODNRA (Table 10.11). "5" represented "strongly preferred." Six alternative processes were presented. Only one, litigation, generated opposition ($\bar{x} = 2.50$). The process judged the most favorably was collaborative discussion ($\bar{x} = 4.38$). In a moderately preferred or supported range were organizing alliances and coalitions and lobbying ODNRA management staff. The interesting aspect to these results is that people prefer face-to-face discussions and dislike litigation, even though it is currently a common mechanism for addressing natural resource disputes.

Survey Results Viewed in Total. The results from the quantitative portions of the survey were encouraging regarding the workshops and the prospects for coordination and collaboration with the public as part of ODNRA management.

Table 10.9
Assessment of ODNRA Workshop Activities
(1=did not help; 5=helped greatly)

Task	Respondents	$\bar{x}$	s.d.	n
Issue Presentations	*total group*	*4.04*	*1.04*	*47*
	attended all day	4.19	0.92	36
	attended morning	3.55	1.29	11
	attended afternoon	----	----	--
Panel Discussion	*total group*	*2.98*	*1.20*	*45*
	attended all day	2.92	1.15	36
	attended morning	3.22	1.39	9
	attended afternoon	----	----	--
Creating a Situation Map	*total group*	*3.26*	*1.33*	*38*
	attended all day	3.25	1.36	36
	attended morning	----	----	--
	attended afternoon	3.50	0.71	2
Identifying concerns and interests about ODNRA issues	*total group*	*3.92*	*1.06*	*39*
	attended all day	3.89	1.07	37
	attended morning	----	----	--
	attended afternoon	4.50	0.71	2
Developing ODNRA situation improvements	*total group*	*4.09*	*0.98*	*35*
	attended all day	4.09	1.01	33
	attended morning	----	----	--
	attended afternoon	4.00	0.00	2

The survey showed that people regarded collaborative discussion as the best means for meeting their ODNRA objectives. These processes promote face-to-face talk: information sharing, learning, problem solving, and compromising. More importantly, through these methods parties maintain some investment in the management planning process.

Respondents not only supported collaborative discussion; but also supported strongly the involvement of the USDA-Forest Service and other relevant agencies. Such support seemed to value government agencies, not as mediators, but as fellow stakeholders. ODNRA participants appreciated the opportunity to work with agency representatives, learning from them and teaching them through such interaction. The facilitators and facilitator assistants observed that participants responded well to the ground rules for the meetings, including those that emphasized constructive communication. Participants interacted well and with respect.

The survey data indicated that agency involvement and collaborative discussion were promoted through the workshop process. Participants considered the workshop design constructive. Issue presentations and Collaborative Learning via situation map, themes of concern, and situation improvement activities were important parts of an effort to respond effectively to the complex ODNRA management. Parties concerned about the ODNRA wanted to be involved in an effort with, not against, government agencies and other stakeholder groups.

Table 10.10
Assessment of the Extent to Which the ODNRA Workshops Changed Participants'
Views of ODNRA Parties
(1=more negative view; 7=more positive view; 4=no change)

Party	Respondents	x̄	s.d.	n
USDA-Forest Service	total group	4.48	1.46	50
	attended all day	4.55	1.35	38
	attended morning	4.30	2.00	10
	attended afternoon	4.00	0.00	2
Environmentalists	total group	3.98	1.31	49
	attended all day	4.16	1.28	37
	attended morning	3.60	1.17	10
	attended afternoon	2.50	2.12	2
Off-Road Vehicle Users	total group	4.88	1.17	50
	attended all day	4.76	1.17	38
	attended morning	5.30	1.16	10
	attended afternoon	5.00	0.41	2
Off-Road Vehicle Businesspeople	total group	4.61	1.26	49
	attended all day	4.36	1.17	36
	attended morning	5.27	1.35	11
	attended afternoon	5.50	0.71	2
Nonmotorized Recreation Users	total group	4.17	1.10	48
	attended all day	4.47	0.88	36
	attended morning	3.40	1.08	10
	attended afternoon	2.50	2.12	2

The ODNRA Collaborative Learning workshops fostered that involvement. In doing so, they contributed to the development and maintenance of a constructive approach to dealing with the ODNRA situation.

Lessons Learned

The ODNRA Collaborative Learning project was, in 1993, the most comprehensive application of Collaborative Learning that we had attempted. The results of this application indicated that a Collaborative Learning framework could help parties make progress on a problem situation. The evaluations of the ODNRA project indicated that, through Collaborative Learning:

- Participants' understanding of the situation is broadened.
- Concerns are expressed and meaningfully discussed.
- Improvements have been developed and implemented.
- Strategic behaviors persist.
- Relationships improve.

Through Collaborative Learning activities such as mapping, parties saw the situation as a complex system of issues. Doing so broadened their understanding

Table 10.11
Preferences Concerning Processes for Achieving ODNRA Goals
(1=strongly opposed; 5=strongly preferred)

Method	Respondents	$\bar{x}$	s.d.	n
Organizing alliances or coalitions	total group	3.60	1.07	48
	attended all day	3.56	1.16	36
	attended morning	3.80	0.78	10
	attended afternoon	3.50	0.71	2
Collaborative discussions	total group	4.38	0.77	47
	attended all day	4.60	0.60	35
	attended morning	3.70	0.95	10
	attended afternoon	4.00	0.00	2
Litigation	total group	2.50	1.56	48
	attended all day	2.36	1.61	36
	attended morning	3.20	1.32	10
	attended afternoon	1.50	0.71	2
Letter writing	total group	3.15	1.18	48
	attended all day	3.00	1.26	36
	attended morning	3.70	0.67	10
	attended afternoon	3.00	1.41	2
Use of media	total group	3.15	1.24	48
	attended all day	3.17	1.25	36
	attended morning	3.30	1.25	10
	attended afternoon	2.00	0.00	2
Lobbying ODNRA management staff	total group	3.21	1.35	47
	attended all day	3.11	1.41	36
	attended morning	3.78	0.83	9
	attended afternoon	2.50	2.12	2

of the situation. Collaborative Learning promoted discussion of stakeholders' concerns. From these concerns, parties developed tangible improvements that reflected their understanding of the particular situation as a system. As we reflected upon this application, we recognized some important "lessons" we had learned.

Training. We realized that subsequent applications should include a training component to teach people about Collaborative Learning and orient them to the specific project design. Although we had a stage 1 meeting for interest group leaders and concerned citizens, we did not hold one for ODNRA and Siuslaw National Forest staff. We provided citizens with an opportunity to learn about, and help design, the CL application but did not do so with agency personnel. Consequently, many agency staff who attended stage 2 workshops did not know what to expect or what was expected of them.

Timing of the Intervention. We first met with Forest Service staff on the day that the ODNRA Draft Environmental Impact Statement was released to the public. At that point, the ODNRA planning process had been going on for over two years.

Many citizens were skeptical of some new "collaborative" process or were so burned out that they did not want to participate in anything else. Representatives of a leading environmental group told us that they were not interested in more meetings; they had their response strategy in place (appeals and, if necessary, litigation). Furthermore, we held the public workshops on Saturdays in July on the Oregon coast, thereby asking people to give up a Saturday during the best summer recreation weather.

Evaluation by Facilitators. While we designed a valid survey approach, we realized that evaluation of CL projects is best handled by parties other than those who design and facilitate the process. Consequently, Wenatchee (Chapter 9) and subsequent applications have included external evaluators.

Working as a Design and Facilitation Team. Given the complexity and comprehensiveness of the project, we included a project administrator and graduate students as members of the project team. The project administrator's coordination of publicity and local site arrangements were particularly valuable.

FOREST PLAN REVISION AND THE CHUGACH NATIONAL FOREST, ALASKA

A more recent application—in fact, one that is still occurring as this book goes to press—addresses public participation in the forest plan revision process. The specific project site is the Chugach National Forest of south-central Alaska. The Chugach National Forest, with headquarters in Anchorage, is the second largest national forest in the United States, second in size to only the Tongass National Forest, also in Alaska. The Chugach National Forest covers over 5.6 million acres, including much of the land around Prince William Sound.

Background

Forest plans set broad general direction for managing the national forests. They can be thought of as zoning documents that identify where and under what conditions an activity or project could occur. Normally, they do not make site-specific decisions on particular projects. By law under the National Forest Management Act of 1976 (NFMA), each national forest has a forest plan. Most forest plans were adopted initially between 1978 and 1986, with the idea that they would be revised every 10 years.

The Chugach Forest Plan was signed in 1984. Since that time there have been many changes in society's needs and environmental conditions that have made the original plan out of date. Examples include the *Exxon Valdez* oil spill, the rapid spread of the spruce bark beetle on the Kenai Peninsula, and the increase in recreation and tourism in Alaska. In addition, the plan must incorporate new information about species such as brown bears.

Figure 10.2
The Chugach National Forest, Alaska

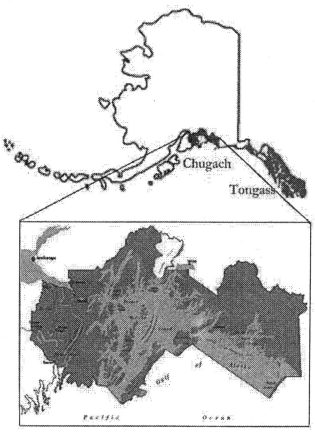

Source: Chugach National Forest Web site (http://www.fs.fed.us/r10/chugach).

A forest plan features various uses, including the following:

- The forestwide, multiple-use goals and objectives.
- The forestwide management requirements (standards and guidelines).
- Boundaries of management areas and prescriptions for management areas for applying future activities in a management area.
- Identification of land that is suitable for the production of timber.
- Identification of a maximum amount of timber appropriate for sale.
- Procedures and techniques required to monitor and evaluate the effectiveness of forest management actions.
- Roadless areas recommended for study to determine if they might become part of the National Wilderness Preservation System.
- Rivers and streams recommended as suitable and eligible to include in the Wild and Scenic Rivers System.

The forest planning procedures on the Chugach include a number of steps.

Notice of Intent and Scoping. The forest plan revision process formally began in April 1997, when Chugach National Forest planning staff published in the *Federal Register* a notice of intent to revise the forest plan. In spring 1997 the staff mailed letters and newsletters to interested individuals and groups, held workshops in various communities, and the met with interested groups and individuals.

Collaborative Learning workshops were conducted as part of this scoping process. Concerns and improvements generated by citizens at the CL workshops along with letters and newsletter responses were entered into a database and analyzed to identify conflicts and interests. The Chugach National Forest interdisciplinary planning (ID) team subsequently developed problem statements and interest statements that they tied to goals and objectives for the revised forest plan to address. The ID team reviewed these problem statements and interest statements with the public before developing any draft alternatives.

Analysis of the Management Situation. Along with scoping activities to communicate with citizens and interest groups, the forest plan revision ID team prepared a report: "Analysis of the Management Situation" (AMS). The AMS contains reports on the current conditions of the resources, preliminary supply and demand analysis, need for change items, preliminary list of issues, summary of forest plan amendments, review of forestwide standards and guidelines, social assessment, and land allocations outside the forest plan decision process.

Alternatives. The ID team planning schedule called for formulating forest plan management alternatives during spring and summer of 1999 (Forest Plan Revision Timeline, 1999). This led to the development of a variety of draft alternatives, by both the ID team and stakeholders (e.g., interest groups). Nine alternatives were developed in detail, with seven selected for analysis in the draft environmental impact statement (DEIS). The DEIS, which also included a preferred alternative, was released for public review in July, 2000. Following an extensive public comment period, a final decision on the revised forest plan should be made during winter 2000-2001 (DeLapp, 2000).

Public input consistent with a Collaborative Learning philosophy has been an important part of the planning process, including citizen comments on alternatives. On its Web site, the ID team explained that:

The main reason for formulating alternatives is to find the best way to provide the greatest good for the greatest number of people through our management of the national forests. Alternatives will provide different ways to address the problem statements and interests we have identified during the plan revision process. We intend to take the draft alternatives out to the public before completing a draft Forest Plan. (Summary of the General Procedures, 2000).

Environmental Impact Statement and Record of Decision. In a forest plan revision process, the forest plan revision ID team provides an analysis of the alternatives in a Draft Environmental Impact Statement (DEIS). The DEIS presents estimates of the social, economic, physical, and biological effects of implementing each alternative. The DEIS includes a preferred alternative along with the other alternatives that the ID team has considered. The DEIS is distributed to all interested parties and available for a 90-day review and comment period.

After the ID team receives and reviews comments, it prepares the Final Environmental Impact Statement (FEIS). This document, too, is open to public comment. Following review of the FEIS, the forest supervisor prepares a Record of Decision. The Record of Decision formally makes public the selection of an alternative the Forest Service will implement. It also contains the analysis that lead to that decision and the reasoning that went into it. This final decision is the responsibility of the regional forester.

Chugach Forest Plan revision activity, as noted earlier, entered into the DEIS stage of the overall process during summer, 2000. At this stage, as with prior stages, the ID team continued its commitment to an "open public process" based on Collaborative Learning principles (Revision Update, 2000).

Collaborative Learning and Chugach Forest Plan Revision

As referenced previously, Collaborative Learning workshops have been conducted as part of the Chugach forest revision ID team's scoping work. The initial workshops occurred after we had conducted two training sessions and had completed a modest degree of assessment work.

Initial Contact. In October 1996 we conducted a week-long Collaborative Learning project in Petersburg, Alaska. Staff from the Stikine Area and Petersburg Ranger District of the Tongass National Forest had asked us to help them apply Collaborative Learning ideas to their landscape-level planning work. Our week in Petersburg included two days of assessment work, four days of training, and design and facilitation of a Collaborative Learning citizen workshop about Kupreanof Island, the focus of the landscape planning effort.

One participant in the four-day training was the staff social scientist from the Chugach National Forest in Anchorage. He found the training useful and envisioned Chugach National Forest projects where Collaborative Learning techniques might be applicable. The staff social scientist kept in touch with us after the training. A few months later, in May 1997, the second author was in Anchorage on other business and called on the social scientist, who assembled the available members of the forest plan revision ID team to meet with the second author. As a result of this half-day meeting, the ID team decided tentatively to incorporate Collaborative Learning ideas and activities into its forest plan revision public participation work.

Assessment and Orientation. Following the May meeting, we proposed to the Chugach planning team that assessment and training occur in two steps. First, we would travel to Anchorage in August 1997 to conduct initial assessment work and present a half-day CL orientation program for members of the Chugach National Forest leadership team, including the forest's three district rangers.

Based on prior experience, we knew that line officer support was important to the success of a Collaborative Learning effort. The Chugach National Forest includes four line officers, management personnel who have the legal authority to sign a Record of Decision: the forest supervisor in Anchorage, and district rangers in Cordova, Girdwood, and Seward. None of the line officers are members of the forest plan revision ID team. As the forest's chief management officers, though, their support for the forest plan revision is essential. As deciding officers, they have the authority to review and propose changes in the plan revision. Consequently, we knew that their support for the public participation strategy was important. The Collaborative Learning half-day program that we presented to the line officers and other members of the forest's leadership team gave key people the opportunity to learn about the Collaborative Learning approach, raise questions about its applicability, and discuss if and how it might be used as part of forest plan revision. Through this orientation session the ID team and we could discover if any line officer opposed the use of CL. None did. Still, the orientation session revealed that the CL project leadership would come from ID team members rather than line officers.

The orientation session also served as an assessment opportunity. During this session we met key members of the Chugach National Forest staff and heard their concerns about the project and CL's relevance to it. Through this interaction, we better understood the forest plan revision situation. We also devoted time to reviewing the Chugach National Forest's media files, which helped us understand the environmental and natural resource policy context of southcentral Alaska.

Based on our August work, the ID team and forest leadership staff decided to make Collaborative Learning workshops a significant component of their initial public participation efforts, within the scoping face of the forest plan revision process. Collaborative Learning workshops took place during November and December 1997 in Anchorage, Cordova, Seward, and Valdez. In response to citizen requests, additional workshops were held in Soldotna and Whittier. The November 1997 Chugach National Forest Collaborative Learning assessment, training, and workshop schedule was as follows:

Monday, 10 November	Arrive in Anchorage
Tuesday, 11 November	Interview stakeholders: interest group leaders, business and community leaders, and so on
Wednesday, 12 November	Collaborative Learning training for ID team members,
Thursday, 13 November	line officers, other relevant Forest Service personnel, other agency representatives, and key interest group leaders
Friday, 14 November	Full day (900-1700) Collaborative Learning Workshops
Saturday, 15 November	on Forest Plan Revision issues
Monday, 16 November	CL training third day follow-up and depart Anchorage

We traveled to Anchorage in November 1997 to work eight days with forest staff and local citizens. Our first full day featured assessment. We interviewed interest group and business leaders, learning about concerns regarding the management of the Chugach National Forest. Our 10 hours of interviews—with snowmobilers, cross-country skiers, environmentalists, oil and timber industry employees, and miners—revealed varied positions and interests but a shared, strong attachment to the forest. Many people we talked with envisioned different uses of the forest but all wanted it to be a healthy, sustainable ecosystem.

Training. Following the day of assessment interviews, we presented a two-day Collaborative Learning training program. Participants included ID team members, line officers, forest leadership team members, and two members from the local community (one from Alaska Nature Conservancy and a local mediator). The training program reviewed some of the ideas presented at the earlier August Collaborative Learning orientation, but placed importance on both conflict management and systems thinking aspects of the CL process. Following is an outline of the training program.

Day One: 12 November
0900   Instructor introductions and workshop logistics
0915   Best and worst planning experiences (break follows)
1030   Learning teams, learning organizations
1100   Why consider a Collaborative Learning approach?
         • Traditional public involvement and collaboration
         • The nature of Collaborative Learning (lunch follows)
1300   Systems and systems thinking
1330   An exercise in systems thinking (break follows)
1445   Assessing collaborative potential
1530   Collaborative Learning and natural resource management: An exercise
1630   First day wrap-up

Day Two: 13 November
0830   Continue working on management situations
0930   Group reports (break follows)
1035   Reassessing collaborative potential
1100   Applying Collaborative Learning to public meetings: design issues (lunch follows)
1300   A conflict exercise and discussion (break follows)
1435   Conflict management skills
1600   Second day wrap-up

The training occurred on a Wednesday and Thursday. There were two full-day Forest Plan Revision Collaborative Learning workshops in Anchorage on the subsequent two days. The design for each day was the same so that citizens could attend either Friday or Saturday. Training participants were encouraged to attend and be involved in one of the Collaborative Learning workshops, to serve as participant-observers. Trainees took part in the workshops as citizens and agency personnel and learned about the Collaborative Learning workshop process by experiencing it.

On the Monday following the two Anchorage workshops, we held a third training day. This day featured a discussion of the Collaborative Learning workshop process, with trainees sharing their questions, observations, and insights. The discussion employed a workshop "debriefing" guide:

To do list
         • "Thank you" letters to cosponsoring organizations
         • Mailing to participants—transcribe list of improvements
         • Plans for other meetings: facilitators, agendas, issue presentations

Review of process
         • Specific questions about what we did

- Reactions to outcome

Larger questions
- How to build a base of support inside the CNF—the ranger districts, the supervisor's office, and the regional office
- Who at the district, forest, or region level may be potential champions of the collaborative process?
- How can awareness and support be generated among the public?
- What links can be made to other agencies? How?
- What links can be made to other collaborative projects, for example, the Kenai Watershed Forum and Alaska Audubon Society's efforts regarding brown bears?

Major process steps
- Organizing work sheets into themes of concern, which lead to alternative development
- Enhancing learning team aspects of interdisciplinary team (IDT) behavior

Following that conversation, we worked with a number of the trainees, principally the ID team, to design subsequent Forest Plan Revision CL workshops that would take place in Cordova, Valdez, and Seward. These workshops were shorter than those in Anchorage, either half-day or evening. They would be facilitated by Chugach National Forest staff who had participated in both the CL training and Anchorage workshop process.

Design and Facilitation. About 90 people participated in the two Anchorage workshops, 55 on Friday and 35 on Saturday. Many of the Friday participants were professionals representing interest groups, nonprofit organizations, and businesses. The majority of the Saturday participants were citizens not formally affiliated with or representing specific groups or organizations.

The Anchorage workshops consisted of issue presentations, situation map discussion, and group interaction about concerns and improvements. Both concerns and improvements discussions were grounded in work sheets that each citizen prepared. Following is the 14 and 15 November 1997 Anchorage workshop design.

0830	Continental breakfast and registration
0900	Welcome, Gary Lehnhausen
	Plan for the day, Gregg Walker and Steve Daniels
0910	Issue Presentations

- Forest plan revision process, Ken Rice
- Spruce bark beetle, Beth Schulz
- Recreation issues, Susan Rutherford (break follows)

1030	The Collaborative Learning workshop process, Steve Daniels and Gregg Walker
1045	Mapping the Chugach NF management situation (lunch follows)
1245	Chugach NF management: interests and concerns (break follows)
1400	Chugach NF management improvements
1530	Summarizing the improvements
1545	Organizing for the future
1630	Call it a day . . . and thank you

Issue presentation topics and speakers were selected by ID team members, in consultation with the authors as project consultants. We met with each presenter and provided guidelines for the presentation, such as purpose and time constraints. We reviewed each speaker's presentation and encouraged speakers to be focused, informative, and audience-centered without being too technical. We did not want presentations that were "watered down" to the point of compromising important scientific or procedural information (e.g., laws pertaining to forest plan revision). We did want material communicated clearly, so that laypeople could understand the science and policy of forest plan revision, as well as the place and role of these workshops within the overall forest plan revision process.

In the month following the Anchorage workshops, Chugach National Forest Staff facilitated Collaborative Learning workshops in Cordova, Seward, Valdez, Soldotna, and Whittier. Citizen participation ranged from 15 in Whittier and Soldotna to 35 in Cordova. Taken together, about 210 citizens took part in one of the seven CL forest plan revision citizen workshops.

The workshops outside Anchorage followed the Anchorage design, abbreviated to fit into half-day or evening schedules. Chugach National Forest staff who had participated in the Collaborative Learning training facilitated the workshops, including presentation of the situation map. The situation map used at the Anchorage workshops was employed at all the subsequent workshops. Similarly, the concerns and improvements work sheet forms used at the Anchorage meetings were employed at the workshops in the smaller communities.

Evaluation and Follow-up. As of this writing, the forest plan revision process continues. The ID team has reviewed citizen comments and specialist data as part of its development of forest plan management revision alternatives. The ID released the Draft Environmental Impact Statement (DEIS) in summer 2000 and has planned activities for citizens to comment on the DEIS alternatives. Consistent with the revision project's emphasis on collaboration, citizens can learn about and suggest improvements in the draft alternatives.

As part of the evaluation process, the second author read the concerns and interests work sheets and the situation improvements work sheets that citizens developed at the seven Collaborative Learning forest plan revision workshops. The second author presented a report on this matter to the ID team in April 1998.

Lessons Learned

The Chugach National Forest's forest plan revision process is both comprehensive and ongoing. It represents an ambitious attempt to make collaborative participation a key part of the overall planning process. As we have worked with the Chugach National Forest plan revision ID team, we have learned a number of lessons about applying Collaborative Learning to something as comprehensive as forest plan revision.

Institutional Support—Vertical and Horizontal. In this as well as in other applications, we discovered the importance of internal institutional support for Collaborative Learning. When we first met with members of the Chugach Forest

Concerns and Improvements Analysis
Report to the Forest Plan Revision ID Team

General reactions

1. In a significant number of cases, I did not find a great distinction between an individual's "concerns and interests" and "improvements." For some citizens, particularly at the Valdez, Soldotna, Anchorage, and Seward workshops, "improvement" sheets communicated values, world views, and management orientations more than specific management actions. This in understandable given when these workshops have occurred in the forest plan revision planning process and is very consistent with other CL workshops held early in a planning process. When a CL workshop occurs in a "pre-scoping" period, we have found that citizens are as likely to communicate their hopes, fears, desires, goals, and cautions (interests and concerns) as they are specific management ideas.

2. In contrast, I saw several specific improvements generated at the Cordova and Whittier workshops. A number of Cordova participants were concerns about ORV use and access. Some referred to access to specific islands, for example, Montague Island. Others focused on specific Copper River road points. Similarly, Whittier participants often addressed impacts of the Whittier road, and the need for recreation infrastructure (e.g., campgrounds, trails) to support the expected significant increase in use.

3. A number of people commented on processes: that they wanted to continue to interact and communicate with Chugach National Forest Staff. From reading the concerns and interests (CI) and situation improvements (SI) work sheets, I got the impression that people felt reasonably comfortable with a collaborative public involvement philosophy generally and collaborative workshop activities specifically.

4. Participants' comments revealed, to varying degrees, a systems perspective. Some people did so quite explicitly. Many people, by answering the work sheet questions, related their issue(s) to other issues in the land management plan revision management situation.

5. On their SI work sheets, many participants did not address the feasibility question well. Many of the feasibility comments were very general. For example, a citizen might propose a significant action and state that it was quite feasible and would not cost anything. This suggests to me that the Chugach National Forest (CNF) faces a challenge: to educate citizens about feasibility, regarding both the laws that the CNF has to follow and the resources (budget, staff, time) the CNF has. People are asking the CNF to do more and more, even though CNF resources are diminishing.

6. Overall, a good number of people participated. But I wonder if the

planning team is satisfied with the number of participants. I am curious to learn, too, how planning teams will increase participation (if that is a desired goal) at future collaborative workshops. I am also interested in the planning teams' thoughts on the variable workshop format (i.e., full-day workshops in Anchorage and Cordova; two- to four-hour workshops in Valdez, Seward, Whittier, and Soldotna).

Specific Issue Reactions

1. *Access.* This issue appeared in a lot of participant comments, both on CI and SI sheets. People who seemingly held different worldviews seemed to agree via their written comments that the Forest Plan Revision needed to address access in a meaningful way.

A. *Designation.* Many people writing about access advocated some sort of designation plan; some people even called for "zones" established for particular uses. Many of the access/designation ideas focused on motorized and nonmotorized recreation activities. This issue appeared at most of the workshops (I do not recall it being a significant issue in Soldotna) and seemed particularly important to people in Cordova and Anchorage. For some, motorized recreation meant snow machines. For others (particularly in Cordova), motorized recreation meant ORVs.

The nonmotorized recreationists emphasized "quiet" as part of their national forest experience. They would like to ensure that "natural quiet" areas are available and accessible for low-impact recreation activities. These citizens seemed to accept and respect the idea that motorized recreationists deserved their place/space as well.

Seasonal designations were addressed occasionally, but did not stand out as an important component of people's access and designation ideas.

Overall, the comments on this issue suggested that many citizens, reflecting diversity, would accept some kind of area designation system responsive to a "multiple use" recreation perspective.

B. *Fees.* Some (although not a large number) of people writing about "access" supported the idea of access fees, beyond current levels. I do not recall anyone explicitly opposing any and all fees.

2. *Wilderness area designation.* Several people referred specifically to the College Fjord/Nellie Juan Wilderness Study Area. Some people proposed permanent designation as their improvement. Even those who did not see wilderness designation as necessary seemed willing to accept the idea as long as other areas of the CNF were designated for their use.

3. *Habitat.* Many people commented on habitat (although not as often as recreation access was mentioned). The comments emphasized habitat quality and wildlife values. Not surprisingly, people from Seward and

Soldotna (and some from Anchorage) are concerned about brown bear. People do not want CNF actions that might compromise habitat.

4. ***Management orientation.*** Several people referred to specific management orientations or themes. Ecosystem management, biodiversity, and multiple use were the most notable.

5. ***Prince William Sound.*** Some workshop participants, particularly at the Whittier and Valdez meetings, expressed concerns about human activity in Prince William Sound. A number of people were interested in a strong CNF presence and more active management.

6. ***Local influence.*** Particularly in Cordova, but at other workshops as well, citizens commented on the importance of local input into CNF decisions. Some people expressed strongly that they did not want outsiders (lower 48, beltway, Anchorage) to assert more influence over the management process than local interests.

Plan Revision ID team, we perceived that understanding of, commitment to, and enthusiasm for Collaborative Learning varied. We decided that an orientation program was necessary so that Chugach personnel, including members of the ID team, could learn enough about Collaborative Learning to decide if they wanted to incorporate it into their forest plan revision process.

We also recognized that support from supervisors or decision makers was essential to the success of the project. In the Forest Service, key supervisors are "line officers," management staff (forest supervisors and district rangers) who have the authority to make management policy decisions. Line officers are considered the institutional leaders of the agency. When we began to work with Chugach staff, we discovered that the forest supervisor was retiring and consequently did not get involved. The district rangers were skeptical, in part, because the initiative for Collaborative Learning came from the staff social scientist and public affairs officer, both people who worked in the headquarters office in Anchorage. The district rangers had heard a lot about collaboration activities in general and were concerned that Collaborative Learning might be just some new "fad." The orientation and training sessions welcomed their skepticism and provided them with opportunities to ask questions and voice their concerns.

Local Leadership. In all Collaborative Learning projects we have conducted, the sustainability of the Collaborative Learning effort has depended, in part, on local leadership. External consultants can get the Collaborative Learning project started, but someone from a local agency or the local community must carry it forward. In the Chugach project, key members of the forest plan revision ID team provided that leadership. As they learned about, experienced, and facilitated Collaborative Learning workshops, they discovered the power and value of collaborative public participation. ID team members learned both the language and procedural substance of Collaborative Learning, so that CL ideas have permeated much their public interactions. They have experimented with new ways of public involvement, such as holding open, public ID staff meetings.

Continuity. The Chugach National Forest application also reveals the importance of continuity and consistency among different public participation efforts. The forest plan revision ID team maintains a web site and distributes a newsletter that symbolize the ID team's and Forest Leadership staff's commitment to collaboration. Newsletters have often included columns written by members of interest groups who want to be part of the forest plan revision dialogue.

Workshop Preparation. Although the issue presentations constituted less than 30 percent of the Collaborative Learning forest plan revision workshop agenda, we knew that these presentations would be important to the workshops' success. Consequently, we worked closely with the ID team to select topics. ID team members chose the speakers, people with whom we worked to ensure excellent presentations. The presenters gave admirable talks, presentations that were clear, informative, and engaging. Each presenter supported his ideas with a slide or multimedia presentation.

MARYS PEAK RECREATION MANAGEMENT PLANNING

In contrast to the broad, comprehensive, and somewhat abstract forest plan revision process on the Chugach National Forest, in late 1997 and early 1998 we applied Collaborative Learning to a specific, clearly defined planning area: recreation management on Marys Peak.

Background

Marys Peak, just west of Corvallis, Oregon, is an area managed primarily by the Alsea-Waldport Ranger District of the Siuslaw National Forest. The highest point in the Coast Range at 4,097 feet, Marys Peak offers panoramic views of the Cascades, Willamette Valley and the Coast Range. On a clear day you might see as far as the Pacific Ocean. There are several picnicking areas, more than 10 miles of hiking trails (some open to mountain bikes), and a small seasonal campground. Unique plant communities add to the interest of the area; including stands of noble fir and alpine meadows. With its proximity to the communities of the mid-Willamette valley, Marys Peak is a very popular recreation site.

Before European settlement in the Willamette Valley, local Indian tribes regularly held vision quests on Marys Peak. Various species of plants and insects clung to dear life there after the Ice Age. Early settlers grazed their flocks of sheep and goats. Today, thousands of visitors come to Marys Peak annually for sightseeing, cross-country skiing, hiking, bird watching, picnicking, or scientific research. Marys Peak offers an array of natural scenic delights and varied activities.

According to Andrew Hagestedt of the Oregon Offbeat(s) Network:

The Marys Peak experience begins with Marys Peak Road: The winding, twisting, nine-mile route that leads to the summit. Filled with dramatic scenic surprises at every turn, it yields forested bluff after forested bluff, eventually turning into awesome viewpoints and waysides where you suddenly realize you have driven above the clouds. Along the way are entrances to three of the four trails that crisscross the park, and a few gentle waterfalls from which to grab a handful of clear, pure mountain water.

In the winter, the road is generally snow plowed and skiing becomes a favorite activity in the higher elevations. During the summer, it is hiking and viewing that provide the biggest pleasures. East Ridge, Meadow Ridge, North Ridge and Tie trails all offer different treks through a variety of stunning environments. Camping is an option, too, although only six spots are available on a first-come basis. The peak is a haven for stargazers and is extremely popular during such stellar events as a lunar eclipse or meteor shower . . .

Because of its height, a myriad of rare plant species grow there which occur only in certain climates, and in some cases, are indigenous to the mountain. Marys Peak allows certain kind of fir trees, insects, flowers and grasses to thrive because its habitat changes so drastically: Different climates exist in bands from one altitude to the next. An extremely rare species of Caddis fly was discovered there within the past 40 years, and numerous kinds of plants grow in small colonies, sometimes only within a few acres. Many plant species exist mainly in dry, desert-like conditions that only occur on the peak at certain elevations and on slopes where wind, temperature and sun conditions are just right. (Hagestedt, 1999)

As this "Oregon Offbeat(s) Network" report suggests, many people in western Oregon consider Marys Peak to be a special place. As such, it experiences heavy human use. In recent years some of that use has been destructive. Marys Peak facilities (e.g., the campground and the parking lot bathrooms) have been the sites of vandalism. In light of the heavy recreation use and the publicity surrounding the Marys Peak vandalism, the leadership of the Alsea-Waldport Ranger District and the Siuslaw National Forest decided to collaborate with citizens about the management of human activity, particularly recreation, on Marys Peak. Many of the senior staff, including the forest supervisor, had worked with the authors on the Oregon Dunes Collaborative Learning project a few years earlier. Consequently, forest leaders contacted the authors about using a Collaborative Learning approach for public involvement concerning the Marys Peak recreation management situation.

Assessment and Training

In this Collaborative Learning project, assessment and training were closely intertwined. At the time of this project, both authors lived in the Marys Peak region and had spent time on the peak. Both authors had followed news stories pertaining to Marys Peak, including reports of vandalism that appeared in the *Corvallis Gazette-Times*. The authors had worked with a number of the Siuslaw National Forest staff on the Oregon Dunes project a few years earlier. Consequently, the authors were reasonably familiar with the Marys Peak management situation.

Still, the authors received from the Alsea-Waldport District planning team and Siuslaw National Forest public affairs office personnel the names of local environmentalists who had expressed concerns to the Forest Service about Marys Peak issues. The authors interviewed a number of these local citizens and asked the Siuslaw National Forest staff to invite them to the two-day Collaborative Learning training. Some local environmentalists participated in the training.

The authors also encouraged Siuslaw National Forest personnel to invite key Bureau of Land Management (BLM) staff to participate in the training. Although most of Marys Peak is managed by the Siuslaw National Forest, part of the peak area is under the jurisdiction of the BLM. The training included a number of staff from the Salem District office of the BLM.

The training program corresponded to the general design used at a number of earlier Collaborative Learning applications. The first day featured discussion of collaborative processes generally and Collaborative Learning specifically and how these processes compared with traditional public participation approaches. Training participants also learned about and practiced systems thinking. During the second day participants examined their current projects and workplace conflicts in terms of their collaborative potential and systems features. Consequently, on day 2 they applied CL ideas to their particular work situations, including the management of Marys Peak. The Siuslaw National Forest/Marys Peak two-day training agenda serves as the two-day training example in Chapter 8 (Table 8.4).

As has been the case in other CL training programs, the Marys Peak training included a workbook of handouts, activities guides, and overhead masters. The Marys Peak CL training booklet table of contents (topics and page numbers) follows.

Design, Implementation, and Evaluation

The Marys Peak application included three Collaborative Learning workshops. In October 1997 two "Concerns and Improvements" CL workshops were held, one as a four-hour evening meeting and one as a seven-hour Saturday meeting. These workshops were designed to be duplicates, with the evening meeting a condensed version of the Saturday event. Almost 60 people attended the evening workshop; about 20 people participated in the subsequent full-day workshop.

The October workshops featured issue presentations, concerns work sheets and discussions, and improvements work sheets and discussions. The workshops culminated with each person summarizing her or his improvement for the large group. The two workshops generated about 90 improvements, with some participants developing more than one.

The first author, the Siuslaw National Forest planning team, and a group of Oregon State University forest recreation students analyzed the concerns and improvements work sheets. Based, in part, on these analyses, the planning team (which included the Alsea-Waldport District Ranger) decided to hold a follow-up workshop in January 1998.

The January meeting was designed such that participants would work with, organize, and refine ideas generated at the October meetings. Consequently, the January workshop corresponded to latter stages of the Collaborative Learning cycle, providing people with an opportunity to develop sets of improvements and consider their desirability and feasibility. About 35 people attended the January workshop, 20 of whom had participated in one of the October meetings. The workshop schedule follows.

0830   Registration and continental breakfast
0900   Welcome: Introduction to the workshop and plan for the day -- Steve
        Daniels and Gregg Walker
0920   Reviewing the improvements and the Marys Peak recreation planning
        process -- Doris Tai
0945   Developing action strategies (working break)
1045   Action strategies, goals, and objectives
1145   Assessing and refining action strategies: Selecting and synthesizing
        (working lunch)
1300   Discussing preferred action strategies: What is feasible?
1345   Wrap up for the day . . . and thanks for your participation!

The primary focus of the January workshop was the development of "action strategies." After the Alsea-Waldport District Ranger reviewed the October improvements and the planning process, participants were asked to prepare an "action strategy"—a set of improvements that need to be, and can be, done in the short term to improve the management situation. Workshop participants developed their action strategies according to questions on an action strategy worksheet (Table 10.12).

Participants shared their action strategies with the entire workshop, with key points recorded on a flip chart. Based on this information, participants joined with others who identified similar improvements to form working groups. For example, a number of participants prepared improvements pertaining to the creation of a citizen organization, the Friends of Marys Peak. This working group integrated and refined various improvements and in doing so, provided a foundation for such an organization and gained commitment from citizens to participate in it.

This Collaborative Learning application did not include formal evaluation. The formation and evolution of the Friends of Marys Peak organization has provided some anecdotal evidence of the CL workshops' contributions, but individual workshop participants were not surveyed.

Lessons Learned

As has been the case in all of our Collaborative Learning applications, we learned some new lessons from the Marys Peak project.

Consistency in Duplicate Workshops.   Offering a four-hour version of a seven-hour workshop before that daylong workshop provides citizens with an incentive to attend the shorter option. We hoped for a large turnout at the full day workshop. We knew that the full-day version would give citizens the opportunity to more fully engage Marys Peak management issues. When the number of participants in the full day workshop was comparatively small, we realized that holding the evening version first was a more attractive option for citizens. They did not know that a CL workshop was quite different from typical public meetings and had no reason to chose seven hours over four.

Follow-up.   Citizens want follow-up opportunities to develop tangible actions. The January workshop seemed essential to build upon the good work done by citizens at the October meetings. The January workshop was well integrated with the October meetings and produced desirable and feasible short-term improvements.

OTHER APPLICATIONS AND LESSONS LEARNED

Collaborative Learning has been applied to a number of other natural resource management situations, and from each we have discovered additional important lessons. We highlight these here.

Clarify decision space.   In one application, we worked closely with the interdisciplinary team at the ranger district level. We never met the supervisor of the particular national forest in which this Collaborative Learning project occurred. Forest Service personnel and citizens worked collaboratively for months, developing a community-based management alternative for an area. The forest supervisor, who knew little or nothing about Collaborative Learning, rejected the management alternative because it did not achieve, from his view, adequate timber harvest levels. Unfortunately, he had never communicated a minimum level of timber harvesting that the Collaborative Learning project was supposed to reach, and therefore the participants in the process could not realistically have been expected to meet that goal.

Table 10.12
Action Strategy Work Sheet (space condensed)

Marys Peak Workshop
Name_____   Phone_____

Action Strategy
At the October 1997 Marys Peak Workshops, participants proposed policies and actions designed to improve the Marys Peak recreation management situation. These "improvements" were changes intended to be both "desirable" (a good idea) and "feasible" (something that was possible to implement). Doris Tai, the Alsea-Waldport District Ranger, has just reviewed these improvements and the management themes that emerged from them. With these improvements in mind, develop an ACTION STRATEGY. An action strategy is a set of improvements that you think need to be and can be done in the short term to improve recreation management on Marys Peak. Develop your action strategy according to the following questions:

1. What improvements need to be done in the short-term? You may want to identify three or more, drawing from the improvements lists.

2. How do these improvements relate to each other? How do they form a coherent package of improvements?

3. Why is this set of improvements desirable?

4. How can this set of improvements be implemented?
   - Who needs to be involved (what people, groups, organizations)?
   - What is a suitable time line for implementing these improvements? Is there an order to these improvements?
   - What resources are needed to implement this set of improvements? Are these resources available? Where? How can these resources be acquired? Who has them?

5. What are the costs or trade-offs of doing this set of improvements?

6. What are the costs or consequences of *not* doing this set of improvements?

7. State the purpose of these improvements by completing the following:
The objective of these changes is:
_____
_____

Additional comments:

Assess the internal organizational situation as well as the external situation. In a particular Collaborative Learning application on a western national forest, we did a significant amount of assessment through local media and interviews with interest group leaders. Our assessment did not focus substantially on organizational and interpersonal issues within the particular national forest. During the Collaborative Learning training, staff persons talked to us privately and often about problems within the national forest as an organization. We learned that national forest staff members were not working together collaboratively and trust levels were very low. Before conducting meaningful collaboration with citizens, the forest leadership needed to foster collaboration among employees.

Cultivate local champions. For a collaborative effort to be sustainable, there needs to be good local organizational leadership. Those Collaborative Learning applications that have endured have done so primarily because of local leadership who are committed to citizen collaboration. Collaborative Learning applications should devote attention to developing local leaders or "champions" who are capable of, and interested in, maintaining the collaborative approach.

CONCLUSION

This chapter has presented the details of selected Collaborative Learning project applications. These applications have varied in their focus, scope, and comprehensiveness. Yet all have adhered generally to the five-phase design featured throughout this book: assessment, training, design, implementation, and evaluation.

Any Collaborative Learning application begins with a fundamental understanding of the situation. Conveners need to determine the collaborative potential of the environmental or natural resource conflict situation. Based on that evaluation, conveners can consider the appropriateness of a Collaborative Learning approach. If Collaborative Learning is used, its overall framework needs to be adapted to the features of the specific environmental policy situation.

Chapter 8 featured the techniques of Collaborative Learning. Chapter 9 and this chapter described several situations in which the Collaborative Learning approach has been applied. Each application has differed somewhat from the others, reflecting our belief that while the philosophy of Collaborative Learning remains constant across applications, we must fit the "tool (or technique) to the task."

NOTES

1. Much of the Oregon Dunes discussion originally appeared in *Environmental Assessment Review* (Daniels & Walker, 1996). Reprinted with permission.
2. The activities in the Wenatchee and Oregon Dunes projects were not organized into strictly comparable phases. In order to illustrate that distinction, the Wenatchee phases are referred to as "Steps" in chapter 9 and the Oregon Dunes phases are referred to as "Stages" in this chapter.

Chapter 11

Persistent Challenges and Future Directions

> Systems problems require systems thinkers who can work across disciplines and be imaginative and integrative, flexible and adaptive. We need managers who are passionate about interdependent as well as independent thinking.
>
> — R. Edward Grumbine
> *Reflections on "what is ecosystem management?"*

This chapter has three goals: to summarize the important messages that run through this book, to anticipate the projects and innovations that might shape the evolution of Collaborative Learning, and to reflect on Collaborative Learning in the larger context of community-based collaboration. Recapping the important themes in the book integrates them into a whole rather than discussing them as separate topics. Turning our attention forward is equally important because it may embolden the reader to experiment with Collaborative Learning and may enhance the rate at which the Collaborative Learning principles and techniques are tested and refined. Finally, it is important to view Collaborative Learning within the milieu of community-based collaboration, which is an international phenomenon.

RECURRING THEMES

Collaborative Learning as a Behavioral Model

We believe that Collaborative Learning represents a distinct step in the evolution of participatory decision making. Part of the innovation in Collaborative Learning comes from the fact that it reframes the fundamental *purpose* of public participation. To a greater extent than perhaps any other technique, Collaborative Learning stresses the potential for *mutual learning through public involvement activities*. The emphasis on learning and systems thinking distinguishes

Collaborative Learning from traditional public participation. This emphasis also makes Collaborative Learning consistent with notions of action learning, which seems essential to how we deal with an uncertain and turbulent future.

Action learning transforms management from the traditional function of control to one in which the main concern is facilitating the colearning process (Morgan, 1982). It stresses doing rather than simply observing. Action learning recognizes that how confront the unpredictable, turbulent future is increasingly important in terms of what we value and what we do (Ramirez, 1983).

In the Collaborative Learning framework, the purpose of public involvement is not one-way communication from the decision-making agency to potentially affected public. Nor is it a hearings-type process where citizens provide testimony in a quasi-judicial format. Neither of these models—both of which are commonly used in natural resource decisions—has design features that make it likely that significant learning will occur. If fact, if learning does occur, it arises in spite of these methods rather than because of them.

But by the same token, Collaborative Learning moves beyond reliance on collaborative consensus as the logical successor to traditional NEPA-style public involvement. Even though we recognize that consensus approaches are being widely touted as the wave of the future in natural resource decision making, we do not demand consensus as a precondition to making management decisions. Collaborative Learning acknowledges that even in situations that provide very high quality learning about the complexity of natural resource management, well-meaning and well-informed people can hold differing opinions about the best way to proceed. It may be just as important for citizens to learn why they disagree and still find ways to work together, than to assume the only issues on which they can move forward are those where there is consensus.

Collaborative Learning Is Not a Formulaic Process

Every chapter in this book includes the admonition not to view Collaborative Learning as a rigid, apply-it-by-the-book approach. The disciplines that are the foundation of Collaborative Learning do not lend themselves to formulaic application. The calls for situation-specific responsiveness that you hear from scholars of systems thinking, conflict management, and adult education are amplified when all three disciplines are integrated into a Collaborative Learning approach to managing environmental conflict.

Certainly, Checkland argues against a standardized approach to soft systems as he explores the concept of soft systems as a "methodology":

My sense of the word here is that the outcome of the research is not *a method* but a set of *principles of method* which in any particular situation have to be reduced to a method uniquely suitable to that particular situation. I believe this point to be an important one and am prepared to labour it. In attempting to work in the real-world we face an astounding variety and richness. If "soft" systems thinking is reduced to method (or technique) then I believe it will fail because it will eliminate too much of the munificent variety we find in real life, just as the generalized algorithms of management science have tended to lose contact with the uniqueness of each individual management problem. (1980, pp. 161-162)

Barbara Gray concludes her 1989 book on collaboration with a series of recommendations for changes that she feels would enhance the prospects for collaborative approaches in the public policy arena. One of her recommendations is for the institutionalization of collaboration—making it a formal and legitimate option in the policy process. But even in the midst of her call for institutionalization, she notes that flexibility must be preserved as well.

A final thought on institutionalization is that the under-organized character of many collaborations and their success in constructively transforming the domain of necessity require the maintenance of open, permeable, and flexible methods of organizing throughout the three phases of collaboration. Nurturing redundancy (Ackoff, 1974) and loose coupling (Weick, 1976) within the domain enhance the prospects for longevity and wider adoption of innovations. This may suggest that continued experimentation with different institutional forums for collaboration is preferable at this time to a more standardized arrangement. (pp. 278-279)

And finally, educational theorists have recognized the need to move beyond a one-size-fits-all model of instructional systems design. In their recent book on adult learning, Tennant and Pogson contend that teachers must be willing to draw from disparate traditions, rather than rely largely on a single disciplinary construct:

The task for the teacher is to build on the capacity for theory to enhance experience and for experience to enhance theory. This is particularly difficult for someone coming from a strong disciplinary background with its own internal logic and rational sequential development. Furthermore, any discipline by itself is rarely likely to be sufficient to inform current experience—experience does not respect disciplinary boundaries. If the discipline is seen as paramount, current experiences mainly serve to help understand the theory. If the link with experience is paramount, theoretical constructs mainly serve to illuminate current experiences. In the best scenario, the discipline is introduced in the context of shared experiences and both outcomes are achieved: theory illuminates practice and practice illuminates theory. (1995, p. 156)

If the best thinkers in the disciplines that guide Collaborative Learning feel that site-specific responsiveness and flexibility are central to high quality work, then our destiny as Collaborative Learning designers and facilitators encompasses accepting ambiguity, rejecting disciplinary rigidity, and enacting adaptability. Perhaps a major danger sign would be to hear someone say "A Collaborative Learning approach must do Y," because that is not true. There are no "must" aspects of Collaborative Learning; the demands of situation always drive the choices.

Complexity Prevents Solution but Assures Improvement

Natural resource decisions can appear paralyzingly complex. The range of values and stakeholders, the layers of laws and reams of regulations, and the complicated scientific concepts all interact to create an apparently overwhelming context. But despite this complexity, tough and important environmental decisions must be made on an on-going basis. They are part of the fabric of our everyday civic lives, and we can ill afford to be immobilized by gridlock.

The way that Collaborative Learning approaches this complexity is to seek improvement rather than solution. The very aspects of contemporary environmental decision making that render solutions perhaps unattainable make improvements virtually assured. In complex situations, there are always things that could be done to improve the situation, just as there is probably no set of improvements that "solve" the problem to everyone's satisfaction. The multiple facets of a wickedly complex situation create many ways in which the situation can be improved, and once our minds are freed from the Sisyphean task of solving the problem in its entirety, those improvements can readily be identified.

Assessment as a Foundation for Strategic Choice

Anyone who contemplates convening or participating in a collaborative effort must thoroughly diagnose the domain-level dynamics, including the history of the problem and prior relationships between the stakeholders. Failure to conduct a thorough and frank assessment creates various risks, ranging from applying collaboration to situations that have low collaborative potential, to conducting a project that is beyond one's skills, to damaging people's willingness to engage in collaboration because they or their acquaintances have had bad experiences. Conveners need to learn the extent to which each stakeholder is either affected by the problem, has access to other alternatives, and/or has the power to advance or block a negotiated solution. Effective diagnosis involves prudent analysis of the nature and strength of the underlying interdependencies and the power dynamics among the stakeholders (Gray, 1985). Domains in which one or more key stakeholders discount their dependence on other stakeholders and overestimate their individual capability to influence outcomes affecting the domain may be unlikely candidates for collaboration unless a convener or mediator can reframe their perceptions (Gray, 1989).

INTEGRATING OTHER APPROACHES

The second figure in this book shows how Collaborative Learning has been crafted by integrating the ideas from systems thinking, adult learning and conflict management (Figure 2.2). We contend that this intellectual integration is a fundamental strength of the approach because it allows us to rely on the most useful insights from a number of fields—to pick and choose in order to create a rich learning environment. As we lead future Collaborative Learning projects, we will continue to integrate more ideas into the approach when they offer some potential enhancements. By the same token, as other people apply Collaborative Learning in various situations, there is even more opportunity for additional techniques to be integrated. It is also likely that Collaborative Learning concepts and methods can be integrated into other techniques to enhance them.

TECHNOLOGY

Technology has the potential to enhance the practice of Collaborative Learning in two significant ways. First, it can address a fundamental limitation of any meeting-based decision process: to a limited extent, technology can overcome the reality of space and time. Whenever and wherever one chooses to hold a meeting, whether for Collaborative Learning or any other group discussion, some people will be unable to attend because of logistical limitations. The constraint may come from scheduling; as anyone who has tried to arrange meetings knows, there is no time when everyone can attend. The constraint may also come from geography; there is no one place that everyone can feasibly reach.[1]

Second, technology has the ability to help us deal with complexity. High-quality decisions about natural resource and environmental issues require good science. The kinds of issues to which Collaborative Learning has been applied include so many factors beyond human control, so much scientific uncertainty, and so much technical complexity, that we could too easily shrug our shoulders and wait for the experts to fix them. But decisions in a participatory democracy must be grounded in the body politic, and that means the science must be grounded there as well. Fortunately, a number of technologies can be used to help analysts and citizens alike wrestle with the intellectual complexity of natural resource decision making. These technologies therefore have direct applicability in Collaborative Learning projects.

Technology to Aid Communication

A wide range of communication technologies has the potential to mitigate the effects of space and time by offering means of information flow through virtual discussions. The Internet seems the most obvious way to of achieve asynchronous, ageographic communication, through sites where interested members of the public can learn about projects and provide input via electronic mail. This form of interaction lacks any type of deliberation or stakeholder-to-stakeholder communication, however, and it is a technological version of traditional consultative public involvement: the agency produces a plan, and the public comments on that plan. The only innovation is that the communication is now electronic rather than paper-based.

An entire field of inquiry known as "computer-supported collaborative learning" (CSCL) has emerged in recent years to explore the application of technology in assisting group learning processes. Much of CSCL's attention is on learning in traditional instructional settings (primary, secondary, university, and professional development), but the related technologies have exciting potential for fruitful application in innovative public involvement approaches. Like many fields in communication and computing technology, the capacity of CSCL technologies (both hardware and software) are exploding[2]. A more interactive model of virtual public involvement would use techniques that allow the participants to interact with one another through bulletin boards and chat rooms. In a more advanced model parties could interact to construct a shared understanding of a situation by jointly working through an aspect of a Collaborative Learning project. For example, Inspiration Software offers a program, Inspiration, that allows electronic construction of a situation map (their term is "concept map"). As the company's Web site reports: "Inspiration integrates dynamic diagramming and outlining environments to help you organize ideas and information. [You can] easily create and modify concept maps, webs and other graphical organizers using Inspiration's Diagram view" (www.inspiration.com). This software allows several people to simultaneously contribute to the construction of a situation map from different locations.

Technology to Aid Our Understanding of Complexity

A variety of technologies could constructively be used to help people think their way through complex environmental decisions. Rather than try to provide a laundry list or categorization scheme of these potentially useful tools, we prefer to describe one—geographic information systems—which has considerable power in helping people visualize and manipulate complex information.

Geographic Information Systems. The use of geographic information systems (GIS) has been growing in the natural resource and environmental professions in the last two decades. Various technologies are integrated into a GIS: data acquisition from remote sensing or on-the-ground measurements (often augmented with global positioning capabilities), software that converts the data into manipulatable files and provides analytical capability, and output capabilities, typically mapping processes that can display the information in a graphic form (Aronoff, 1989). GIS offers two fundamental capabilities: the ability to ask analytical questions of spatial data (e.g., how many acres of mixed conifer forests are within 30 meters of perennial streams in this watershed?), and to create visual representations of conceptual relationships (e.g, where are the high phosphate concentrations in the ground water relative to agricultural acreage?). GIS capabilities not only can describe what is, but can also display what could be. GIS can be linked to other kinds of models to allow us to project how conditions may change in the future and to understand how those impacts are likely to be distributed across the landscape.

The analytical capabilities of a GIS are a source of considerable power in Collaborative Learning as we attempt to learn our way through complex decisions. But the potential that GIS represents can be captured only if the analysts realize that it must aid the learning of *all* of the participants and not merely buttress the views of a particular interest.

The very breadth of GIS applications to policy problems makes GIS likely to be pulled into many different kinds of policy debates. Unlike the worlds of modeling for economic planning or welfare policy analysis, where idiosyncratic models served each policy need, GIS are likely to support a plethora of models for many policy needs. This too will be a challenge for GIS professionals because different policy debates take on widely different characteristics. Debates about land use or environmental pollution abatement typically pit economic interests of industrialists and land developers against environmental groups' interest in maintenance or restoration of areas and in limiting growth . . . Debates about traffic and transportation management often pit advocates for various transportation "solutions" (slow growth, roads, fixed-rail rapid transit) against one another, and increasingly, they pit governments short on resources for essential transportation infrastructure against developers who want to develop land but not pay for the full costs of infrastructure required to support such developments. GIS-based models can and will be used in each of these kinds of debates. Whether they are used constructively in the policy debate depends on the facility with which GIS professionals can adapt the systems to serve the arguments of different parties in the debates. If the models serve only particular interests, to the exclusion of others, the models will be challenged with the intent of destroying credibility in particular models or in modeling generally. (King & Kraemer, 1993, p. 358)

The power of GIS maps on the ways in which policy problems are framed is profound. The old maxim of "a picture is worth 1000 words" probably has two GIS-related corollaries: it is worth 2000 words if it is computer-generated and 5000 words if it is in color. That power can be used to either enhance or preempt meaningful citizen-to-citizen dialogue. But a mind set that GIS should conform to the demands of the deliberative process (and not vice versa) allows GIS to play a role in managing controversial situations that other methods arguably cannot.

Traditional scientific approaches are rarely effective in addressing the holistic problem of conflict resolution. Most are linear models, requiring a succession, or cascade, of individual parcel assignments. The final result is strongly biased by the ordering of parcel consideration. Even if a scientific solution is reached, it is viewed with suspicion by the layperson. Modern geographic information systems provide an alternative approach involving human rationalization and tradeoffs. This process involves statements like, "If you let me harvest this parcel, I will let you set aside that one for wildlife preservation." The statement is followed by a persuasive argument and group discussion. The dialogue is far from a mathematical optimization, but often closer to an effective solution. It uses the information system to focus discussions away from broad philosophical positions to a specific project area and its unique distribution of conditions and potential uses. (Berry & Ripple, 1996, pp. 121-122)

GIS certainly appears to be able to analyze and display data in ways that enhance learning, and because improved learning is an essential goal in Collaborative Learning processes, there should be no end to the potential use of GIS in Collaborative Learning projects. To date our use of GIS has been modest; we have distributed GIS-derived maps of the project area on several projects, and have used GIS-derived maps to display potential project alternatives. But we have never had the GIS readily accessible to the participants in a Collaborative Learning workshop so that they could construct their own management scenarios and get real-time answers to their "what if" questions. That sort of immediate link between the participants, their efforts to understand the situation and work through its complexity, and the technology would go far beyond any use of GIS in Collaborative Learning to date.

A BROADER RANGE OF APPLICATIONS

We hope that the Collaborative Learning approach will be adopted widely and used in situations in which it offers some real opportunity for improvement. That necessarily means that it will be used in a wider range of applications, since our range of uses—natural resource situations involving primarily public lands in the western United States—is clearly narrow. This wider range of applications will no doubt involve more variation in topics and in location.

A Broader Range of Topics

Our focus on natural resource-related decision situations is merely a function of our professional interests, and does not imply that Collaborative Learning is only applicable to those types of problems. Quite the contrary may be true: Collaborative Learning may have more applicability in policy arenas other than natural resources. Recall that Collaborative Learning is designed to work in situations characterized by complexity and controversy. While many natural resource decisions meet these criteria, so do decisions in other areas of endeavor. Most areas of public policy, from transportation planning, to education reform, to public health programs, have a set of decisions that are complex and controversial. Consequently, there is a role for participatory processes that enhance learning in virtually every aspect of public policy decision making, indicating a role for Collaborative Learning-style processes in more, rather than fewer, fields.

A Broader Range of Locations

Our history of conducting Collaborative Learning projects primarily in the western United States is merely a function of our location and does not imply that Collaborative Learning is applicable only in that locale. In fact, Collaborative Learning's relevance transcends any geographic region: Collaborative Learning should be applicable in areas outside of western U.S., including other countries. We have conducted our Collaborative Learning projects in the midst of our "day jobs" as resident faculty at a university. As a result, we have chosen projects in our region in order to manage other professional obligations and have had to decline opportunities for involvement in geographically distant projects.

Certainly, there is no reason that Collaborative Learning cannot be useful in a broad range of cultural and institutional settings. Recall the three foundations of Collaborative Learning: systems thinking, adult learning, and conflict management. All three of these foundations have been informed by work going on outside the United States. Systems thinking has been driven significantly by work in Europe and Australia, and American scholars are certainly playing catch-up in this arena. The soft systems-based work of Kathy Wilson (of Wilson & Morren, 1990) has been done throughout the world, most notably in Oceania and eastern Asia. Experiences in the international development arena have influenced adult learning theory; the 12 principles of effective adult learning presented in Chapter 5 come from Jane Vella's travels in Africa and elsewhere. Finally, the conflict management theories have been tested worldwide; many of them have been refined by cross-boundary disputes and international negotiations.

The European Extension Movement

During the past decade in Europe an area of inquiry has emerged with important similarities to our Collaborative Learning work. Researchers in agriculture, particularly extension educators, have focused considerable attention on participatory learning and knowledge systems among farmers. Probably the person most closely associated with this "European Extension Movement" (EEM) is Niels Röling (i.e., Röling & Jiggins, 1998). The program most closely identified with EEM is the Wageningen Extension Program of the Wageningen Agricultural University in The Netherlands. This extension program has been renamed "Communication and Innovation Studies" (CIS) to reflect its transformation away from a positivist model of science and technology transfer to one more grounded in the situation. The CIS Group's Web site notes that "keywords that best describe the main thrust of our research include knowledge transfer, (social) learning, informing, facilitating, negotiating, awareness-raising, and behavioural change" (http://www.sls.wau.nl/cis/). The efforts of Röling and his colleagues have been informed by some of the same writers who have influenced our Collaborative Learning work: Checkland, Habermas, Kolb, and so on. A doctoral dissertation, "Rapid Appraisal of Agricultural Knowledge Systems" (Engel, 1995), has specifically examined the role of knowledge among agriculturalists as a soft system a la Checkland (1981) and Wilson and Morren (1990).

There are at least five salient similarities between the European extensionists' efforts and our own. First, both attempt to synthesize existing theories to come up with new paradigms for involving stakeholders in processes of decision making and innovation. Second, both reject the traditional model of Western science, wherein the problem is given to discipline-based scientists who reduce the problem's complexity so that it can be understood in terms of their own particular intellectual discipline. Third, both the European Extension Movement and Collaborative Learning focus explicitly on adult experiential, participatory learning as a key to innovation and therefore build methods that strive to understand and augment those learning processes. Fourth, both feature a systems orientation that generates acceptance of emergent properties and systemic complexity. Lastly, EEM and CL are both action-oriented. Neither group is studying decision making and learning from afar; the European researchers and we are actively engaged with stakeholders, immersed in real situations, with real communities, on real issues. Practice is informing theory as much as theory is informing practice.

COLLABORATION AS CONTROVERSY

While participatory learning and collaborative decision making are taking place around the world, such practices are controversial. Consequently, we would like to acknowledge the "state of collaboration" in environmental policy at the dawn of the new century. As readers compare this book with other literature in the field, some may see it as simply about collaboration. In one sense it is: collaboration as a framework we call "Collaborative Learning." To the extent that this book is about collaboration or at least about one method for collaboration in environmental policy situations, the book's ideas may contribute to the current controversy over the value of community-level collaborations around environmental and natural resource management conflicts.

In 1987 Douglas Amy wrote a seminal book, *The Politics of Environmental Mediation*. In a chapter entitled "Mediation as Seduction," Amy voiced skepticism about the capacity and appropriateness of mediation to manage environmental and natural resource conflicts well. He noted that some aspects of the landscape had been compromised enough, that mediation required negotiation and compromise, and that some things in nature were simply non-negotiable.

Today, Amy's concerns resonate in discourse about community-level collaboration in natural resource and environmental policy. From the fields of conflict management, environmental dispute resolution, grassroots governance, and citizen activism, many community-based collaborations have emerged during the 1990s. Referred to by a variety of names, such as forums, councils, community or collaborative partnerships, collaborative coalitions, and resource management cooperatives, community-based collaborations (CBC) have increased in number throughout the 1990s.

Within the last decade, another phenomenon has appeared, informally linking the undercurrent philosophies of alternative dispute resolution (ADR), public participation and environmental problem solving. Known by varying names—such as community-based collaborative partnerships, watershed councils, consensus groups, coordinated resource management, and sustainable community initiatives, among others—these community-based initiatives bring together traditional disputants from all sides of controversial environmental issues (McClellan, 1996; Arrandale, 1997). Using processes that promote problem solving and focus on individual interests and shared concerns, collaborative partnerships are taking root across the United States, addressing issues as varied as watershed management, urban park protection, riparian restoration, forest management, endangered species recovery, and grazing management (Jones, 1996; McClellan, 1996). Although the processes use principles of alternative dispute resolution, the focus on building relationships for ongoing problem solving distinguishes collaborative partnerships from a one-time negotiated dispute resolution process (Wondolleck et al., 1996).

Community-based collaborations are typically place-based, tied to a landscape, a resource area, or a watershed. CBCs generally employ some manner of consensus decision making and seek the involvement of a broad and diverse array of stakeholders. CBC participants ideally include all parties desiring a voice in the given situation, parties that seek empowerment through the collaborative process. In many cases, CBCs bring together parties who may have been traditional adversaries (McClellan, 1996; Arrandale, 1997). CBCs draw upon elements of negotiation and mediation, but, as on-going enterprises, differ from single event environmental negotiations or mediations (Wondolleck et al., 1996). CBCs have typically emphasized problem solving in order to address both short- and long-term resource management issues, such as endangered species recovery, waste disposal procedures and siting, watershed management, forest and range stewardship, and habitat conservation planning (McClellan, 1996; Jones, 1996). Examples of CBCs include watershed councils (e.g., The Henry's Fork Watershed Council, Idaho; the Kenai Watershed Forum, Alaska); rangeland organizations (e.g., the Malpai Borderlands Group, Arizona and New Mexico; the Diablo Trust, Arizona), resource management partnerships (e.g., the Applegate Partnership, Oregon; the Minnesota Forest Resources Council; Canyon Country Partnership, Utah); and citizen coalitions (e.g., the Catron County Citizens Group, New Mexico; Friends of Marys Peak, Oregon).

The number of CBCs has increased in recent years for a variety of reasons. First, collaborative partnerships have received support on the national level. Both the Clinton administration and Republican Congressional leadership on a number of occasions stated a preference for local initiatives over "Potomocentric" control. The Environmental Protection Agency has fostered the development of watershed councils, while the Forest Service has advanced the idea of collaborative stewardship.

Second, CBCs are consistent with the recent and current resource management philosophies. Rangeland stewardship, ecosystem-based management, landscape-level planning, riparian restoration, watershed integrity, biodiversity, and sustainability are examples of management concepts that respect scientific, technical knowledge and local, traditional knowledge. Collaborative processes may best accommodate different forms of knowledge, ways of knowing, and learning styles (Walker & Daniels, 1998). Further, issues related to ecosystem-based management may be best conceived of as local (Sadler, 1994).

Third, many parties at the local level who have been enduring adversaries may be worn out fighting a "win-lose" battle. At some point parties may desire a more viable alternative that restores and sustains community rather than continually divides it. Wondolleck et al. (1996) assert that CBC activities can address complex and controversial natural resource management problems more innovatively and flexibly than traditional adversarial decision making. Doing so can lead to broad endorsement of, and participation in project implementation (Wondolleck et al., 1996). CBCs, by offering a fair procedure, may improve relationships between parties, including increasing trust and respect (Gieben, 1995; Weber, 1998).

While supporters assert that CBCs are compatible with basic principles and citizen involvement and democratic governance, such as inclusiveness and access (Barber, 2000), CBCs have not been universally embraced as a viable part of natural resource management. Critics of CBCs assert that locally-based stakeholder consensus processes generate "lowest common denominator" agreements (McCloskey, 1996). Some critics claim that CBCs ignore national interests and may co-opt the environmental advocacy movement in the United States (Mazza, 1997; Britell, 1997). Some national environmental groups have encouraged their members to not participate in partnerships; some environmental group leaders have expressed strong skepticism about CBCs (McCloskey, 1996). Concerns include doubts about the appropriateness of alternative dispute resolution techniques, coupled with a view that ADR methods may serve to de-legitimize conflict and co-opt environmental advocates (Britell, 1997; Modavi, 1996). Critics may question the legitimacy of local control of national resources and the scientific soundness of negotiated agreements. Congressional support for the proposals of at least two groups (located in Quincy and Tuolumne County, California) has fueled fears that local efforts will undermine national interests, compromise environmental standards, and preclude meaningful opportunities for non-CBC parties to review and comment on proposals (Duane, 1997; Blumburg & Knuffke, 1998).

CBC skeptics express a fundamental concern for the matter of precedent. Given the variability among local communities, CBCs may be vulnerable to criticisms that their actions do not correspond to clear and uniform standards for planning, implementation, and monitoring (Huber, 1997). As we noted in Chapter 3, there is an "entrenched conflict industry" consisting of parties—people and organizations—that have incentives different from those of CBCs. National organizations understandably prefer that conflicts and controversies be addressed at the national level where they hold standing as players. To the extent that CBCs are perceived to respond better to local interests than regional or national interests, particularly when dealing with resource areas "owned" by a state or national government, the controversy over them will continue.

CBCs as a part of environmental and natural resource policy decision making have both their supporters and detractors. CBC processes may give hope to members of local communities as they create anxiety for organizations that have long been active in normal policy development processes, such as organizing nationwide support and lobbying legislators at the state and federal level. These issues about CBCs have become more prominent with passage of the Quincy Library Group Forest Recovery and Economic Stability Act of 1997 (July) in the U.S. House of Representatives by a vote of 429-1 (Herger, 1997). This action granted national political legitimacy to a process that began as a CBC.

The controversy over community-based collaborations highlights both the promise and the risk of collaborative processes like Collaborative Learning. Collaborative Learning and other collaborative approaches offer parties in complex environmental and natural resource policy situations constructive methods for managing conflicts well and making the best decisions. But collaboration is neither easy nor appropriate for all situations. Collaboration provides a means for parties to engage one another meaningfully and productively but also opens up parties to manipulation and exploitation. As we noted in Chapter 4, parties need to assess the collaborative potential of a situation and apply Collaborative Learning thoughtfully and strategically.

Even the best decision making process, whether collaborative, adversarial, or unilateral, will be subject to criticism from those whose interests are not met. No single process or event will necessarily provide a voice for all parties at all levels. The challenge to find processes and methods to honor local, regional, and national interests is continual. Still, collaborative processes like Collaborative Learning have a role to play in incorporating the voices of all concerned parties in both the local and national environmental policy arenas.

NOTES

1. This issue of geography is one of the conundrums of public involvement concerning federal lands policy in the U.S. Presumably everyone in the United States is a stakeholder in the management of federal lands and ought to have access to the decision processes that affect those lands. Where then, should meetings be held? Should they be virtual, in cyberspace? A perennial critique of collaborative efforts is that they necessarily favor people in the local area where meetings occur, while not including the equally valid views of the mythical stakeholder in Chicago or Cleveland.

2. The most current information would likely be available on the Internet using searches beginning with "CSCL." For those people who are not CSCL specialists (like us), the discipline's reliance on electronic communication means that CSCL information is more web-accessible than many other fields.

References

Abe, H., & Wiseman, R. (1983). A cross-cultural confirmation of the dimensions. *International Journal of Intercultural Relations, 7*, 53–67.

Ackoff, R. L. (1974). *Redesigning the future.* New York: Wiley.

Ackoff, R. L. (1999). *Re-creating the corporation: A design of organizations for the 21st century.* New York: Oxford University Press.

Adler, R. B., & Towne, N. (1998). *Looking out, looking in: Interpersonal communication* (9th ed.). Fort Worth, TX: Harcourt College Publishers.

Amy, D. (1987). *The politics of environmental mediation.* New York: Columbia University Press.

Aronoff. S. (1989). *Geographic information systems: A management perspective.* Ottawa, Ontario, Canada: WDL.

Arrandale, T. (1997, July). Conservation by consensus. *Environment, 39*(2), 68.

Augsburger, D. (1992). *Conflict mediation across cultures—pathways and patterns.* Louisville, KY: Westminster/John Knox Press.

Axelrod, R. (1997). *The complexity of cooperation: Agent-based models of competition and collaboration.* Princeton, NJ: Princeton University Press.

Bacharach, S. B., & Lawler, E. J. (1976). The perception of power. *Social Forces, 55*, 123–134.

Bacharach, S. B., & Lawler, E. J. (1980). *Power and politics in organizations: The social psychology of conflict, coalitions, and bargaining.* San Francisco: Jossey-Bass.

Bacharach, S. B., & Lawler, E. J. (1981a). *Bargaining: Power, tactics, and outcomes.* San Francisco: Jossey-Bass.

Bacharach, S. B., & Lawler, E. J. (1981b). Power and tactics in bargaining. *Industrial and Labor Relations Review, 34*, 219–233.

Bacharach, S. B., & Lawler, E. J. (1986). Power dependence and power paradoxes in bargaining. *Negotiation Journal, 2*, 167–174.

Barber, B. (1984). *Strong democracy: Participatory politics for a new age.* Berkeley, CA: University of California Press.

Barber, B. (1999). *A place for us: How to make society civil and democracy strong.* New York: Hill & Wang.

Barnlund, D. C. (1991). Communication in a global village. In L. A. Samovar & R. E. Porter (Eds.), *Intercultural communication: A reader* (6th ed.), (pp. 22–32). Belmont, CA: Wadsworth.

Bazerman, M. H. (1998). *Judgment in managerial decision making* (4th ed.). New York: John Wiley.

Bazerman, M. H., & Neale, M. A. (1992). *Negotiating rationally*. New York: The Free Press.

Bennett, C. I. (1990). *Comprehensive multicultural education*. Boston: Allyn & Bacon.

Berry, J. K., & Ripple, W. J. (1996). Emergence of geographic information systems. In P. McDonald & J. Lassoie (Eds.), *The literature of forestry and agroforestry* (pp. 107–128). Ithaca, NY: Cornell University Press.

Bingham, G. (1986). *Resolving environmental disputes: A decade of experience*. Washington, DC: The Conservation Foundation.

Binnendijk, H. (Ed.). (1987). *National negotiating styles*. Washington, DC: U.S. Department of State Foreign Service Institute.

Blackburn, J. W., & Bruce, W. M. (Eds.). (1995). *Mediating environmental conflicts: Theory and practice*. Westport, CT: Quorum Books.

Blahna, D., & Yonts-Shepard, S. (1989). Public involvement in resource planning: Toward bridging the gap between policy and implementation. *Society and Natural Resources, 2,* 209–227.

Blatner, K. (1997). Evaluating the Collaborative Learning approach. Presentation as part of the panel: Putting out fires and working through conflicts: Wenatchee National Forest fire recovery planning. In K. Emerson, R. Yarde, & T. Heikkila (Eds.), *Environmental conflict resolution in the West: Conference proceedings* (p. 183). Tucson: Udall Center for Studies in Public Policy, University of Arizona.

Blatner, K. A., Carroll, M. S., Daniels, S. E., & Walker, G. B. (1999). Evaluation of the application of Collaborative Learning to the Wenatchee fire recovery effort. Unpublished manuscript, Department of Natural Resource Sciences, Washington State University, Pullman.

Blau, P. M. (1964). *Exchange and power in social life*. New York: Wiley.

Blumberg, L., & Knuffke, D. (1998). Count us out: Why the Wilderness Society opposed the Quincy Library Group legislation. *Chronicle of Community, 2*(2). 45–46.

Bochner, A. P., & Kelly, C. K. (1974). Interpersonal competence: A rationale, philosophy, and implementation of a conceptual framework. *Speech Teacher, 23,* 279–301.

Bohm, D., Factor, D., & Garrett, P. (1991/1998). Dialogue: A proposal. http://www.teleport.com/~mears/proposal.html.

Bohman, J. (1996). *Public deliberation: Pluralism, complexity, and democracy*. Cambridge: MIT Press.

Bohman, J., & Rehg, W. (1997). *Deliberative democracy: Essays on reason and politics*. Cambridge: MIT Press.

Bosworth, K., & Hamilton, S. J. (Eds.). (1994). *New directions for teaching and learning* (No. 59). San Francisco: Jossey-Bass.

Braiker, H. B., & Kelley, H. H. (1979). Conflict in the development of close relationships. In R. L. Burgess & T. L. Huston (Eds.), *Social exchange in developing relationships* (pp. 135–168). New York: Academic Press.

Brandenburg, A. M., & Carroll, M. S. (1995). Your place or mine?: The effect of place creation on environmental values and landscape meanings. *Society and Natural Resources, 8*(5), 381–398.

Brinkman, J. (1999a, 18 June) Some BPA plans to aid salmon take hit in review. *The Oregonian*, B1.

Brinkman, J. (1999b, 24 July). Crosscurrents to a consensus. *The Oregonian*, A1, A10.

Britell, J. (1997, 30 December). Partnerships, roundtables and Quincy-type groups are bad ideas that cannot resolve environmental conflicts. Unpublished essay, on the Word Wide Web at www.harborside.com/home/j/jbritell/welcome.

Brown, J. S., Collins, A., & Duguid, P. (1989). Situated cognition and the culture of learning. *Educational Researcher, 18*(1), 32–42.

Brown, M. (1996). A framework for assessing participation. In R. L. Flood & N.R.A. Romm (Eds.), *Critical systems thinking: Current research and practice* (pp. 195–214). New York: Plenum Press.

Bruner, J. (1966). *Toward a theory of instruction*. New York: W. W. Norton.

Bryson, J. M. (1988). *Strategic planning for public and nonprofit organizations*. San Francisco: Jossey-Bass.

Buckle, L. G., & Thomas-Buckle, S. (1986). Placing environmental mediation in context: Lessons from "failed" mediations. *Environmental Impact Assessment Review, 6*, 55–70.

Burgess, G., & Burgess, H. (1995). Beyond the limits: Dispute resolution of intractable environmental conflicts. In J. W. Blackburn & W. M. Bruce (Eds.), *Mediating environmental conflicts: Theory and practice* (pp. 101–119). Westport, CT: Quorum Books.

Burgess, H., & Burgess, G. (1996). Constructive confrontation: A transformative approach to intractable conflicts. *Mediation Quarterly, 13*, 305–322.

Burns, S. (1997, July). Critical steps in the development of community public lands partnership initiatives. Presentation at the Communities, Land Use, and Conflict Conference, Catron County, NM.

Burrell, N. A. (1990). To probe or not to probe: Evaluating mediators' question-asking behaviors. In M. A. Rahim (Ed.), *Theory and Research in Conflict Management* (pp. 54–72). New York: Praeger.

Bush, R.A.B., & Folger, J. P. (1994). *The promise of mediation: Responding to conflict through empowerment and recognition*. San Francisco: Jossey-Bass.

Buzan, T. (1983). *Use both sides of your brain*. New York: E. P. Dutton.

Cantrill, J. G. (1998). The environmental self and a sense of place: Communication foundations for regional ecosystem management. *Journal of Applied Communication Research, 26*, 301 - 318.

Carey, J. (1989). *Communication as culture: Essays on media and society*. New York: Unwin Hyman.

Carpenter, S., & Kennedy, W.J.D. (1988). *Managing public disputes: A practical guide to handling conflict and reaching agreements*. San Francisco: Jossey-Bass.

Carroll, M. S., Findley, A. J., Blatner, K. A., Rodriguez Mendez, S., Daniels, S. E., & Walker, G. B. (2000). *Social assessment for the Wenatchee National Forest wildfires of 1994: Targeted analysis for the Leavenworth, Entiat, and Chelan ranger districts*. Portland, OR: USDA-Forest Service Pacific Northwest Research Station.

Carroll, M. S., & Lee, R. G. (1990). Occupational community and identity among Pacific Northwest loggers: Implications for adapting to economic changes. In R. Lee, D. Field, & W. Burch (Eds.), *Community and forestry: Continuities in the sociology of natural resources* (pp. 141-155). Boulder, CO: Westview Press.

Checkland, P. (1981). *Systems thinking, systems practice*. New York: John Wiley & Sons.

Checkland, P., & Scholes, J. (1990). *Soft systems methodology in action*. New York: John Wiley & Sons.

Churchman, C. W. (1968). *The systems approach*. New York: Dell.

Churchman, C.W. (1971). *The design of inquiring systems: Basic concepts of systems and organisation.* New York: Basic Books.

Collaborative Learning Project (1998). http://www.greenville.org/uc/CLP/Default.

Collier, J. H. (Ed.). (1997). *Scientific and technical communication: Theory, practice, and policy.* Thousand Oaks, CA: Sage.

Collier, M. J. (1986). Culture and gender: Effects on assertive behavior and communication competence. In M. McLaughlin (Ed.), *Communication yearbook 9* (pp. 576–592). Beverly Hills, CA: Sage.

Collier, M. J. (1988). A comparison of conversations of among and between domestic culture groups: How intra- and intercultural competencies vary. *Communication Quarterly, 36,* 122–144.

Collier, M. J. (1989). Cultural and intercultural communication competence: Current approaches and directions for future research. *International Journal of Intercultural Relations, 13,* 287–302.

Collier, M. J. (1996) Communication competence problematics in ethnic friendships. *Communication Monographs, 63,* 314–336.

Collier, M. J., & Thomas, M. (1988). Identity in intercultural communication: An interpretive perspective. In Y. Kim & W. Gudykunst (Eds.), *Theories of intercultural communication* (pp. 99–120). Newbury Park, CA: Sage.

Cone, J. (1995). *A common fate: Endangered salmon and the people of the Pacific Northwest.* New York: Henry Holt.

Conrad, C. (1990). *Strategic organizational communication: An integrated perspective* (2nd ed.). Fort Worth, TX: Holt, Rinehart & Winston.

Cormick, G. (1982, Winter). Intervention and self-determination in environmental disputes: A mediator's perspective. *Resolve,* 1–7.

Cortner, H. J., & Moote, M. A. (1998). *The politics of ecosystem management.* Washington, DC: Island Press.

Cortner, H. J., & Shannon, M. A. (1993). Embedding public participation in its political context. *Journal of Forestry, 91*(7), 14–16.

Coser, L. (1956). *The functions of social conflict.* New York: The Free Press.

Cronon, W. (1998, November). *Impacts of different philosophies on natural resources.* Starker Lecture, Oregon State University, Corvallis.

Crowfoot, J., & Wondolleck, J. (1990). *Environmental disputes: Community involvement in conflict resolution.* Washington, DC: Island Press.

Cupach, W. R., & Canary, D. J. (1997). *Competence in interpersonal conflict.* New York: McGraw-Hill.

Dale, A. P., & Lane, M. P. (1994). Strategic perspectives analysis: A procedure for participatory and political social impact assessment. *Society and Natural Resources, 7*(2), 253–267.

Daniels, S. E., & Merrill, K. (1992). The committee of scientists: A forgotten link in national forest planning history. *Forest and Conservation History, 36*(3), 108–116.

Daniels, S. E., & Walker, G. B. (1993, June). *Managing natural resource disputes: The Collaborative Learning approach.* Paper presented at the National Conference on Peacemaking and Conflict Resolution, Portland, OR.

Daniels, S. E., & Walker, G. B. (1995a). Resolving local disputes amidst a national controversy: An exploratory analysis. *International Journal of Conflict Management, 6,* 290–311.

Daniels, S. E., & Walker, G. B. (1995b). Searching for effective natural resources policy: The special challenges of ecosystem management. *Natural Resources and Environmental Issues, 5,* 29–35.

Daniels, S. E., & Walker, G. B. (1996). Collaborative learning: Improving public deliberation in ecosystem-based management. *Environmental Impact Assessment Review 16*, 71–102.

Daniels, S. E., & Walker, G. B. (1999a). Rethinking public participation in natural resource management: Concepts from pluralism and five emerging approaches. In J. Anderson (Ed.), *Pluralism and sustainable forestry and rural development: Proceedings of an international workshop* (pp. 29-48). Rome, Italy: Food and Agriculture Organization of the United Nations.

Daniels, S. E., & Walker, G. B. (1999b, September). Payoffs, pitfalls, and blindsides: The implications of collaboration to foresters. Presentation at the Society of American Foresters annual meeting, Traverse City, MI.

Daniels, S. E., Walker, G. B., Boeder, J. R., & Means, J. E. (1993). Managing ecosystems and social conflict. In R. Everett & J. Tripp (Eds.), *Ecosystem management: Principles and applications* (Vol. 2, 347–359). Portland, OR: USDA Forest Service, Pacific Northwest Experiment Station.

Daniels, S. E., Walker, G. B., Carroll, M. S., & Blatner, K. A. (1996). Using Collaborative Learning in fire recovery planning. *Journal of Forestry, 94*(8), 4–9.

Davenport, J. (1993). Is there any way out of the andragogy morass? In M. Thorpe, R. Edwards, & A. Hanson (Eds.), *Culture and processes of adult learning: A reader* (pp. 109–117). London; New York: Routledge in association with the Open University.

DeLapp, J. (2000, February). The alternative development process. *Chugach National Forest Land and Resource Management Plan Revision Newsletter, 8*, 3.

Delli Priscoli, J. (1988). Alternative conflict management techniques in land-use decisions: Sanibel Island case study. In B. C. Dysart III & M. Clawson (Eds.), *Managing public lands in the public interest* (pp. 113–126). New York: Praeger.

Delli Priscoli, J. (1989). Public involvement, conflict management: means to EQ and social objectives. *Journal of Water Resource Planning and Management, 115*, 31–42.

Deutsch, M. (1973). *The resolution of conflict.* New Haven, CT: Yale University Press.

Dewey, J. (1938). *Experience and education.* New York: Macmillan.

Diemer, J. A., & Alvarez, R. C. (1995). Sustainable community, sustainable forestry: A participatory model. *Journal of Forestry, 93*(11), 10–14.

Dixon, K. M. (1993). *The relationship of benefits and fairness to political confidence in the U.S. Forest Service.* Unpublished master's thesis, School of Renewable Natural Resources, University of Arizona, Tucson.

Druckman, D. (1977). The person, role, and situation in international negotiation. In M. Hermann (Ed.), *The social psychology of political behavior* (pp. 409–456). Beverly Hills, CA: Sage.

Duane, T. P. (1997). Community participation in ecosystem management. *Ecology Law Quarterly, 24*(4), 300–320..

Dukes, E. F. (1996). *Resolving public conflict: Transforming community and governance.* Manchester, UK: Manchester University Press.

Dunn, T. (1994). Rapid rural appraisal: A description of the methodology and its application in teaching at Charles Stuart University. *Rural Society, 4*(3/4), 1-3. http://www.csu.edu.au/research/crsr/ruralsoc/v4n3p30.html.

Eisenberg, E. M., & Goodall, H. L. (1993). *Organizational communication: Balancing creativity and constraint.* New York: St. Martin's.

Emerson, R. M. (1962). Power-dependence relations. *American Sociological Review, 27*, 31–40.

Emerson, R. M. (1972a). Exchange theory, part I: A psychological basis for social exchange. In J. Berger, M. Zelditch, & B. Anderson (Eds.), *Sociological theories in progress* (Vol. 2), (pp. 38–57). Boston: Houghton Mifflin.

Emerson, R. M. (1972b). Exchange theory, part II: Exchange relations, exchange networks, and groups as exchange systems. In J. Berger, M. Zelditch, and B. Anderson (Eds.), *Sociological theories in progress* (Vol. 2), (pp. 58–87). Boston: Houghton Mifflin.

Emery, M. (1982). *Searching.* Canberra: Australian National University Centre for Continuing Education.

Emery, M. (1993). *Participative design for participative democracy.* Canberra: Australian National University Centre for Continuing Education.

Erlandson, D. A., Harris, E. L., Skipper, B. L., & Allen, S. D. (1993). *Doing naturalistic inquiry: A guide to methods.* Newbury Park, CA: Sage.

Faure, G-O., & Rubin, J. (1993). Organizing concepts and questions. In G. Sjostedt (Ed.), *International environmental negotiation* (pp. 17–26). Newbury Park, CA:Sage.

Federal institute for environmental conflict resolution opens under Udall Foundation (1999, February). Udall Center Update, 5.
http://udallcenter.arizona.edu/publications/update/update05.html.

Findley, A J. (1996). *Analyzing multiple worldviews of forestry: Local perceptions of the 1994 fires on the Wenatchee National Forest, Washington.* Unpublished master's thesis, Oregon State University, Corvallis.

Fisher R. (1972). *Basic negotiation strategy: International conflict for beginners.* New York: Bantam Books.

Fisher, R. J. (1997). *Interactive conflict resolution.* Syracuse, NY: Syracuse University Press.

Fisher, R., & Ury, W. (1981). *Getting to yes.* New York: Houghton Mifflin.

Fisher, R. Ury, W., & Patton, B. (1991). *Getting to yes* (2nd ed.). New York: Houghton Mifflin.

Fiske, S. T., & Taylor, S. T. (1991). *Social cognition* (2nd ed.). New York: McGraw-Hill.

Flood, R. L., & Jackson, M. C. (1991). *Creative problem solving: Total systems intervention.* Chichester, UK: John Wiley.

Folberg, J., & Taylor, A. (1984). *Mediation: A comprehensive guide to resolving conflicts without litigation.* San Francisco: Jossey-Bass.

Folger, J. P., Poole, M. S., & Stutman, R. K. (1997). *Working through conflict* (3rd ed.). New York: Longman.

Force, J. E., & Williams, K. L. (1989). A profile of National Forest planning participants. *Journal of Forestry, 87*(1), 33–38.

Forest plan revision timeline (1999, August). *Chugach National Forest Land and Resource Management Plan Revision Newsletter, 7,* 3.

Friedmann, J. (1973). *Retracking America: A theory of transactive planning.* Garden City, NY: Anchor Books.

Friedmann, J. (1987). *Planning in the public domain: From knowledge to action.* Princeton, NJ: Princeton University Press.

Friedmann, J. (1992). *Empowerment: The politics of alternative development.* Cambridge, MA: Blackwell.

Gale, R. P., & Cordray, S. M. (1994). Making sense of sustainability: Nine answers to "what should be sustained?" *Rural Sociology, 59(2),* 311–332.

Gieben, H. (1995, Summer). The misplaced search for objectivity in resource management. *Watershed Management Council Newsletter, 6*(3).
http://glinda.cnrs.humboldt.edu/wmc/news/sum_95/objectivity_rm.html.

Gleick, J. (1987). *Chaos: Making a new science.* New York: Penguin Books.

Glenn, E. (1966). Meaning and behavior; communication and culture. *Journal of Communication, 16,* 248–272.

Glenn, E., Witmeyer, D., & Stevenson, K. (1977). Cultural styles of persuasion. *International Journal of Intercultural Relations, 1,* 52-66.

Gorte, J. F. (1993). Spotted owls and sustainable communities. In G. H. Aplet, N. Johnson, J. T. Olson, & V. A. Sample, V. A. (Eds.), *Defining sustainable forestry* (pp. 294-302). Washington, DC: Island Press.

Gray, B. (1985). Conditions facilitating interorganizational collaboration. *Human Relations 38,* 911–936.

Gray, B. (1989). *Collaborating: Finding common ground for multiparty problems.* San Francisco: Jossey-Bass.

Griffin, E. (1997). *A first look at communication theory* (3rd ed.). New York: McGraw-Hill.

Grumbine, R. (1997). Reflections on "what is ecosystem management?" *Conservation Biology 11,* 41–47.

Gudykunst, W. B. (1994). *Bridging differences—effective intergroup communication* (2nd ed.). Thousand Oaks, CA: Sage.

Gudykunst, W. B., & Hammer, M. R. (1984). Dimensions of intercultural effectiveness: Culture specific or culture general? *International Journal of Intercultural Relations, 8,* 1–10.

Gudykunst, W., & Matsumoto, Y. (1996). Cross-cultural variability of communication in personal relationships. In W. Gudykunst, S. Ting-Toomey, & T. Nishida. (Eds.). *Communication in personal relationships across cultures* (pp. 20–38). Thousand Oaks, CA: Sage.

Hagestedt, A. (1999). Marys Peak. Oregon Offbeat(s) Network Web site. http://www.geocities.com/TheTropics/Resort/8991/marys.html).

Hall, E. T. (1959). *The silent language.* Greenwich, CT: Fawcett.

Hall, E. T. (1966). *The hidden dimension.* New York: Doubleday.

Hall, E. T. (1976). *Beyond culture.* Garden City, NY: Anchor Press.

Hall, E. T., & Hall, M. R. (1998). Key concepts underlying structures of culture. In J. N. Martin, T. K. Nakayama, & L. A. Flores (Eds.), *Readings in cultural contexts* (pp. 199–206). Mountain View, CA: Mayfield.

Hammer, M. R., Gudykunst, W. B., & Wiseman R. L. (1978). Dimensions of intercultural effectiveness: An exploratory study. *International Journal of Intercultural Relations, 2,* 382–393.

Harrison, J. E. (1997, November). Conflict management and culture. "Theories of Conflict and Conflict Management" course lecture, Department of Speech Communication, Oregon State University, Corvallis.

Harrison, J. E. (1999). *Community mediation and culture: A study of Oregon programs.* Unpublished master's thesis, Oregon State University, Corvallis.

Heifetz, R. A., & Sinder, R. M. (1988). Political leadership: Managing the public's problem solving. In R. B. Reich (Ed.), *The power of public ideas* (pp. 179–204). Cambridge: Harvard University Press.

Hendee, J. C., Lucas, R. C., Tracey, R. H., Clark, R. N., & Stankey, G. H. (1974). *Public involvement and the Forest Service: Experience, effectiveness, and suggested direction.* Washington, DC: USDA Forest Service, Land and Resource Management Planning.

Henning, D., & Mangun, W. (1989). *Managing the environmental crisis.* Durham, NC: Duke University Press.

Herger, W. (1997, 9 July). Victory for Quincy Library Bill. Congressional Press Release.

Heyerdahl, T. (1960). *Aku-Aku; The secret of Easter Island.* New York: Pocket

Books.

Heymann, F. V. (1998). From extension science to communication and innovation studies: New theoretical trends from Wageningen. *European Journal of Agricultural Education and Extension, 4*(4),:245–251.

Hocker, J. L., & Wilmot W. W. (1995). *Interpersonal conflict* (4th ed.). Dubuque, IA: Brown & Benchmark.

Hofstede, G. (1980). *Culture's consequences: International differences in work-related values.* Beverly Hills, CA: Sage.

Hofstede, G. (1991). *Cultures and organizations, software of the mind.* New York: McGraw-Hill.

Hofstede, G., & Bond, M. (1984). Hofstede's culture dimensions: An independent validation using Rokeach's value survey. *Journal of Cross-Cultural Psychology, 15,* 417–433.

Holling, C. S. (Ed.). (1978). *Adaptive environmental assessment and management.* New York: John Wiley & Sons.

Holmes, O. W. (no date). Communication quotations. Quotez Web site. http://www.geocities.com/Athens/Oracle/6517/communic.htm.

Huber, J. (1997, Fall). The citizens watershed movement in Washington state. *Watershed Management Council Networker, 7*(3), 14–17. http://glinda.cnrs.humboldt.edu/wmc/news/fall_97/7_citizens_watershed.html.

Hunter, D., Bailey, A., & Taylor, B. (1995). *The art of facilitation: How to create group synergy.* Tucson, AZ: Fisher Books.

Hunter, S. (1989). The roots of environmental conflict in the Tahoe Basin. In L. Kreisberg, T. Northrup, & S. Thorson (Eds.), *Intractable conflicts and their transformation* (pp. 25-40). Syracuse, NY: Syracuse University Press.

Hymes, D. (1962) The ethnography of speaking, In T. Gladwin, & W. C. Sturtevant (Eds.), *Anthropology and human behavior* (pp. 13–53). Washington, DC: Anthropological Society of Washington.

Hymes, D. (1972). Models of the interaction of language and social life. In J. J. Gumperz & D. Hymes (Eds.), *Directions in Sociolinguistics* (pp. 35–71). New York: Holt, Rinehart, & Winston.

Imahori, T. T., & Lanigan, M. L. (1989). Relational model of intercultural communication competence. *International Journal of Intercultural Relations, 13,* 269–286.

Jarvis, P. (1987). *Adult learning in the social context.* London, U.K.:Croom Helm.

Johnson, D. W. (1990). *Reaching out* (4th ed.). Englewood Cliffs, NJ: Prentice-Hall.

Jones, L. (1996, 13 May). Howdy neighbor!—as a last resort, westerners are starting talking to each other. *High Country News. 28* (9), 6–8.

Kaner, S., Lind, L., Toidi, C., Fisk, S., & Berger, D. (1996). *Facilitator's guide to participatory decision-making.* Philadelphia: New Society Publishers.

Katriel, T., & Philipsen, G. (1981). What we need is "communication": "Communication" as a cultural category in some American speech. *Communication Monographs, 48,* 301–317.

Keith, W. (1997). Science and communication: Beyond form and content. In J. H. Collier (Ed.), *Scientific and technical communication: Theory, practice, and policy* (pp. (pp. 299-326). Thousand Oaks, CA: Sage.

Keltner, J. W. (1987). *Mediation: Toward a civilized system of dispute resolution.* Annandale, VA: Speech Communication Association.

Keltner, J. W. (1994). *The management of struggle.* Cresskill, NJ: Hampton Press.

Kemmis, D. (1990). *Community and the politics of place*. Norman: University of Oklahoma Press.

Kim, Y. Y. (1991). Intercultural communication competence: A systems-theoretic view. In S. Ting-Toomey & F. Korzenny (Eds.), *Cross-Cultural Interpersonal Communication* (pp. 259–275). Newbury Park, CA: Sage.

Kimmins, J. P. (1997). *Forest ecology* (2nd ed.). New York: Macmillan.

King, J. L., & Kraemer, K. L. (1993). Models, facts, and the policy process: The political ecology of estimated truth. In M. F. Goodchild, B. O. Parks, & L. T. Steyaert (Eds.), *Environmental modeling with GIS* (pp. 353–360). New York: Oxford University Press.

Kiser, A. G. (1998). *Masterful facilitation: Becoming a catalyst for meaningful change*. New York: AMACOM Business Books.

Knight, R. L., & Landres, P. B. (Eds.). (1998). *Stewardship across boundaries*. Washington, DC: Island Press.

Knowles, M. S. (Ed.). (1980). *The modern practice of adult learning: From pedagogy to andragogy* (2nd ed.). Chicago: Follett.

Knowles, M. S. et al. (1984). *Andragogy in action: Applying modern principles of adult learning*. San Francisco: Jossey-Bass.

Kolb, D. A. (1984). *Experiential learning: Experience as the source of learning and development*. Englewood Cliffs, NJ: Prentice-Hall.

Kolb, D. A. (1993). The process of experiential learning. In M. Thorpe, R. Edwards, & A. Hanson (Eds.), *Culture and processes of adult learning: A reader* (pp. 138–156). London & New York: Routledge in association with the Open University.

Krannich, R. S., Carroll, M. S., Daniels, S. E., & Walker, G. B. (1994). *Incorporating social assessment and public involvement processes into ecosystem-based resource management: Applications to the East Side Ecosystem Management Project*. Boise, ID: USDA Forest Service Interior Columbia River Basin Ecosystem Management Project.

Kreps, G. L. (1990). *Organizational communication* (2nd ed.). New York: Longman.

Kriesberg, L. (1989). Conclusion: Research and policy implications. In L. Kriesberg, T. Northrup, & S. Thorson (Eds.), *Intractable conflicts and their transformation* (pp. 210–220). Syracuse, NY: Syracuse University Press.

Krishnamurti, J. (1972). *You are the world: An authentic report of talks and discussions in American universities*. New York: Harper & Row.

Krueger, W. (1992). Building consensus for rangeland uses. *Rangelands, 14*(1), 38–41.

Kumar, V. S. (1998). Computer-Supported Collaborative Learning: Issues for Research. www.cs.usask.ca/grads/vsk719/academic/890/project2/project2.html.

Lane Council of Governments (1993, June). *Collaborative problem solving and consensus building in resource planning and management*. Salem: Oregon Department of Land Conservation and Development.

Lang, W. L. (1996). River of change: Salmon, time, and crisis on the Columbia River. In J. Cone & S. Ridlington (Eds.), *The Northwest salmon crisis: A documentary history* (pp. 348-363). Corvallis: Oregon State University Press.

Lang, W. (1991). Negotiations on the environment. In V. Kremenyuk (Ed.), *International negotiation: Analysis, approaches, issues* (pp. 343-356). San Francisco: Jossey-Bass.

Lange, J. I. (1993). The logic of competing information campaigns: Conflict over old growth and the spotted owl. *Communication Monographs, 60,* 239–257.

Lave, J. (1988). *Cognition in practice: Mind, mathematics, and culture in everyday life*. Cambridge, U.K.: Cambridge University Press.

Lawler, E. J., & Bacharach, S. B. (1976). Outcome alternatives and value as criteria for multistrategy evaluations. *Journal of Personality and Social Psychology, 34,* 885–894.

Lawler, E. J., & Bacharach, S. B. (1979). Power dependence in individual bargaining: The expected utility of influence. *Industrial and Labor Relations Review, 32,* 196–204.

Lee, K. (1993). *Compass and gyroscope: Integrating science and politics for the environment.* Washington, DC: Island Press.

Lee, R. G. (1994). *Broken trust, broken land: Freeing ourselves from the war over the environment.* Wilsonville, OR: Bookpartners

Levine, S. (1998). *Getting to resolution: Turning conflict into collaboration.* San Francisco: Berrett-Koehler.

Lewicki, R. J., & Litterer, J. A. (1985). *Negotiation.* Burr Ridge, IL: Irwin.

Lewicki, R. J., Litterer, J. A., Minton, J. W., & Saunders, D. M. (1994). *Negotiation* (2nd ed.). Burr Ridge, IL: Irwin.

Lewicki, R. J., Saunders, D, M., & Minton, J. W. (1999). *Negotiation* (3rd ed.). Boston: Irwin McGraw-Hill.

Lewicki, R. J., Saunders, D. M., & Minton, J. W. (2001). *Essentials of negotiation* (2nd ed.). Boston: McGraw-Hill Irwin.

Lewin, K. (1951). *Field theory in social science.* New York: HarperCollins.

Little, R.L., & Krannich, R. S. (1989). A model for assessing the social impacts of natural resource utilization on resource-dependent communities. *Impact Assessment Bulletin, 6*(2), 21–35.

Lofland, J. & Lofland, L. H. (1995). *Analyzing social settings* (3rd ed.). Belmont, CA: Wadsworth.

Lovins, A. (1979). *The energy controversy: Soft path questions and answers.* San Francisco: Friends of the Earth Books.

Low, A. (1976) *Zen and creative management.* Garden City, NY: Anchor Press.

Lustig, M., & Koester, J. (1993). *Intercultural competence: Interpersonal communication across cultures.* New York: HarperCollins.

Lyden, F. J., Twight, B. W., & Tuchmann, T. E. (1990). Citizen participation in long-range planning. *Natural Resources Journal, 30,* 123–138.

Majone, G. (1988). Policy analysis and public deliberation. In R. B. Reich (Ed.), *The power of public ideas* (pp. 157–178). Cambridge: Harvard University Press.

Martin, J. N., & Hammer, M. R. (1989). Behavioral categories of intercultural communication competence: Everyday communicators' perceptions. *International Journal of Intercultural Relations, 13,* 303–332.

Maser, C. (1996). *Resolving environmental conflict: Towards sustainable community development.* Delray Beach, FL: St. Lucie Press.

Mathews, D. (1994). *Politics for people: Finding a responsible public voice.* Urbana: University of Illinois Press.

Mazza, P. (1997, 20 August). Cooptation or constructive engagement? Quincy library group's effort to bring together loggers and environmentalists under fire. *Cascadia Planet.* http://www.tnews.com/text/quincy_library.html.

McCain, J. (1998, 22 October). Remarks of Senator John McCain inaugurating the U.S. Institute for Environmental Conflict Resolution. Press Release. http://www.senate.gov/~mccain/udallenv.htm.

McClellan, M. (1996, 13 May). A sampling of the WLA's collaboration efforts. *High Country News, 28* (9), 15.

McCloskey, M. (1995, November). *Report of the Chairman of the Sierra Club to the Board of Directors.* San Francisco.

McCloskey, M. (1996, 13 May). The skeptic: Collaboration has its limits. *High*

Country News, 28(9), 7.

McCorkle, S., & Mills, J. L. (1992). Rowboat in a hurricane: Metaphors of interpersonal conflict management. *Communication Reports, 5*, 57–66.

McManman, D. (1997, 9 November). Much already has been spent with little being accomplished. *Tri-City Herald*, C1.

Merriam, S. B. (1993a). Adult learning: Where have we come from? Where are we headed? In S. B. Merriam (Ed.), *New Directions for Adult and Continuing Education: No. 57. An update on adult learning theory* (pp. 5–14). San Francisco: Jossey-Bass.

Merriam, S. B. (1993b). Editor's notes. In S. B. Merriam (Ed.), *New Directions for Adult and Continuing Education: No. 57. An update on adult learning theory* (pp. 1–4). San Francisco: Jossey-Bass

Mitroff, I. (1998). *Smart thinking for crazy times*. San Francisco: Barrett-Koehler.

Modavi, N. (1996). Mediation of environmental conflicts in hawaii: Win-win or co-optation? *Sociological Perspectives, 39*(2): 301–316.

Moore, C. W. (1986). *The mediation process*. San Francisco: Jossey-Bass.

Moore, C. W. (1996). *The mediation process*, 2nd ed. San Francisco: Jossey-Bass.

Moore, C. (1988). Techniques to break impasse. In J. Folberg, & A. Milne, (Eds.), *Divorce mediation: Theory and practice* (pp. 251-276). New York: Guilford.

Moore, C. (1996). *The mediation process* (2nd ed.). San Francisco: Jossey-Bass.

Moore, M. P. (1993). Constructing irreconcilable conflict: The function of synecdoche in the spotted owl controversy. *Communication Monographs, 60*, 258–274.

Nadler, L. B., Nadler, M. K., & Broome, B. J. (1985). Culture and the management of conflict situations. In W. Gudykunst, L. Stewart, & S. Ting-Toomey (Eds.), *Communication, culture, and organizational processes* (pp. 87–113).. Beverly Hills, CA: Sage.

Neale, M. A., & Bazerman, M. H. (1985). The effects of framing and negotiator overconfidence on bargainer behavior. *Academy of Management Journal 28*(1), 34–49.

Nega, T. (1998). *Annotated bibliography on adaptive environmental assessment and management 1973–1996* (ISEES Sustainability Series). St. Paul: University of Minnesota Institute for Social, Economic, and Ecological Sustainability.

O'Leary, R. (1995). Environmental mediation and public managers: What do we know and how do we know it? In J. W. Blackburn & W. M. Bruce (Eds.). *Mediating environmental conflicts: Theory and practice* (17-35). Westport, CT: Quorum Books.

O'Leary, R. (1997). Environmental mediation and public managers: What do we know and how do we know it? Indiana Conflict Resolution Institute Research Paper: Environmental Mediation. Indiana University School of Public and Environmental Affairs. http://www.spea.indiana.edu/icri.

Orenstein, S. (1997). Managing salmon recovery in the northwest. Presentation as part of the panel: Collaborative processes in natural resource management. In K. Emerson, R. Yarde, & T. Heikkila (Eds.), *Environmental conflict resolution in the West: Conference proceedings* (p. 144). Tucson: Udall Center for Studies in Public Policy, University of Arizona.

Osborne, D., & Gaebler, T. (1992). *Reinventing government: How the entrepreneurial spirit is transforming the public sector.* Reading, MA: Addison-Wesley.

OSU Extension Service (1993). *Oregon directory of forest interest groups.* Corvallis: Oregon State University Extension Service.

Ozawa, C (1991). *Recasting science: Consensual processes in public policy making.* Boulder, CO: Westview.

Pacheco, R. (1997). Mediation as a dominant institution. Presentation as part of the panel: Cross-cultural challenges in western environmental conflicts. In K. Emerson, R. Yarde, & T. Heikkila (Eds.), *Environmental conflict resolution in the West: Conference proceedings* (pp. 20–22). Tucson: Udall Center for Studies in Public Policy, University of Arizona.

Parks, B. O. (1993). The need for integration. In M. F. Goodchild, B. O. Parks, and L. T. Steyaert (Eds.), *Environmental modeling with GIS* (pp. 353–360). New York: Oxford University Press.

Partridge, M. (1995, January 15). Environmentalists, loggers talk fire-recovery. *Wenatchee World*, 10.

Paulson, Michael (1999, 15 March). Time to protect our rich salmon heritage. *Seattle Post-Intelligencer*, B1.

Pearce, W. B. (1994). *Interpersonal communication: Making social worlds.* New York: HarperCollins.

Pearce, W. B., & Cronen, V. (1981). *Communication, action, and meaning: The creation of social realities.* New York: Praeger.

Perry, C. R. (1993). The environment of words: A communications primer. In J. K. Berry & J. C. Gordon (Eds.), *Environmental leadership* (pp. 46–66). Washington DC: Island Press.

Peterson, R., & Tracy, L. (1979). Systematic management of human resources. Reading, MA: Addison-Wesley.

Peterson, T. R. (1997). *Sharing the earth: The rhetoric of sustainable development.* Columbia: University of South Carolina Press.

Pfeiffer, J. W., & Jones, J. E. (1973–1983) *A Handbook of structured experiences for human relations training,* annual, Volumes 1-10. San Diego, CA: University Associates.

Pierce, J., Steger, M., Steel, B., & Lovrich, N. (1992). *Citizens, political communication, and interest groups: Environmental organizations in Canada and the United States.* Westport, CT: Praeger.

President's Council on Sustainable Development (1997, April). *Lessons learned from collaborative approaches.* PCSD Web site: http://docs.whitehouse.gov/PCSD/Publications/Lessons_Learned.html.

Pribram, K. (1949). *Conflicting patterns of thought.* Washington, DC: Public Affairs Press.

Pruitt, D. G. (1981). *Negotiation behavior.* New York: Academic.

Pruitt, D. G. (1983). Achieving integrative agreements. In M. H. Bazerman & R. J. Lewicki (Eds.), *Negotiating in Organizations* (pp. 35-50). Beverly Hills, CA: Sage.

Pruitt, D. G., & Kressel, K. (1989). Introduction: An overview of mediation research. In K. Kressel & D. G. Pruitt (Eds.), *Mediation research* (pp. 1–8). San Francisco: Jossey-Bass.

Pruitt, D. G., & Rubin, J. Z. (1986). *Social conflict.* New York: Random House.

Putnam, L. L., & Holmer, M. (1992). Framing, reframing, and issue development. In L. L. Putnam & M. E. Roloff (Eds.), *Communication and negotiation* (pp. 128–155). Thousand Oaks, CA: Sage.

Putnam, L. L., & Poole, M. S. (1987). Conflict and negotiation. In F. M. Jablin, L. L. Putnam, K. H. Roberts, & L. W. Porter (Eds.), *Handbook of organizational communication* (pp. 549–599). Newbury Park, CA: Sage.

Raiffa, H. (1982). *The art & science of negotiation.* Cambridge: Harvard University Press

Ramirez, R. (1983). Action learning: A strategic approach for organizations facing turbulent conditions. *Human Relations, 36*(8), 725–742.

Reich, R. (1985). Public administration and public deliberation: An interpretive essay. *Yale Law Journal, 94*, 1617–1641.

Reich, R. B. (1988). Policy making in a democracy. In R. B. Reich (Ed.), *The power of public ideas* (pp. 123–156). Cambridge: Harvard University Press.

Revision Update (2000). Current events, Chugach National Forest Web site. http://www.fs.fed.us/r10/chugach/revision.

Rescher, N. (1993). *Pluralism: Against the demand for consensus*. Oxford, U.K.: Claredon/Oxford University Press.

Reychler, L. (1979). *Patterns of diplomatic thinking*. New York: Praeger.

Rivlin, A. M. (1993). Values, institutions, and sustainable forestry. In G. H. Aplet, N. Johnson, J. T. Olson, & V. A. Sample. (Eds.), *Defining sustainable forestry* (pp. 255–259). Washington, DC: Island Press.

Robbins, W. G. (1996). The world of Columbia River salmon: Nature, culture, and the great river of the West. In J. Cone & S. Ridlington (Eds.), *The Northwest salmon crisis: A documentary history* (pp. 2–24) Corvallis: Oregon State University Press.

Roberts, C. (1999). Five kinds of systems thinking. In P. Senge, A. Kleiner, C. Roberts, R. Ross, G. Roth, & B. Smith, *The dance of change: The challenges to sustaining momentum in learning organizations* (pp. 137–149). New York: Currency Doubleday.

Rokeach, M. (1979). *Understanding human values: Individual and societal*. New York: Free Press.

Rogoff, B.L.J. (1984). *Everyday cognition: Its development in social context*. Cambridge: Harvard University Press.

Röling, N. G., & J. Jiggins. (1998). The ecological knowledge system. In N. G. Röling & M.A.E. Wagemakers (Eds.), *Facilitating Sustainable Agriculture. Participatory learning and adaptive management in times of environmental uncertainty*. Cambridge, U.K.: Cambridge University Press.

Roloff, M. E., & Berger, C. R. (1982). Social cognition and communication: An introduction. In M. E. Roloff & C. R. Berger (Eds.), *Social cognition and communication* (pp. 9–32). Beverly Hills, CA, USA: Sage.

Rolston, H. III. (1988). *Environmental ethics: Duties to and values in the natural world*. Philadelphia: Temple University Press.

Romm, J. (1993). Sustainable forestry, an adaptive social process. . In G. H. Aplet, N. Johnson, J. T. Olson, & V. A. Sample (Eds.), *Defining sustainable forestry* (pp. 280–293). Washington, DC: Island Press.

Ross, R., & Roberts, C. (1998). Balancing inquiry and advocacy. Society for Organizational Learning, http: //www.sol-ne.org/pra/tool/inquiry.html.

Ruben, B. (1976). Assessing communication competency for intercultural adaptation. *Group and Organization Studies, 1*, 334–354.

Ruben, B. D. (1989). The study of cross-cultural competence: Traditions and contemporary issues. *International Journal of Intercultural Relations, 13*, 229–240.

Ruben, B., & Kealey, D. (1979). Behavioral assessment of communication competency and the perception of cross-cultural adaptation. *International Journal of Intercultural Relations, 3*, 15–47.

Rubin, J. Z., Pruitt, D. G., & Kim, S. H. (1994). *Social conflict: Escalation, stalemate, and settlement* (2nd ed.). New York: Random House.

Sadler, R. (1994, November). Why can't we get to "yes" anymore? Watershed Management Council Newsletter, *6*(3). http://glinda.cnrs.humboldt.edu/wmc/news/sum 95/why_yes.html.

Salwasser, H. (1994). Ecosystem management: Can it sustain diversity and productivity? *Journal of Forestry, 92*(8), 6–7, 9–10.

Schelling T. C. (1960). *The strategy of conflict.* Cambridge: Harvard University Press.

Schön, D. A. (1983). *The reflective practitioner: How professionals think in action.* New York: Basic Books.

Schön, D. A. (1987). *Educating the reflective practitioner: Toward a new design for teaching and learning in the professions.* San Francisco: Jossey-Bass.

Scott, W. R. (1998). *Organizations: Rational, natural, and open systems* (4th ed.). New York: Pretinve Hall.

Selin, S., & Chavez, D. (1995). Developing a collaborative model for environmental planning and management. *Environmental Management, 19,* 189–195.

Selin, S. W., Schuett, M. A., & Carr, D. S. (1997). Has collaborative planning taken root in the National Forests? *Journal of Forestry, 95*(5), 25–28.

Senge, P. (1990). *The fifth discipline: The art & practice of the learning organization.* New York: Currency Doubleday.

Senge, P. M., Roberts, C., Ross, R. B., Smith, B. J., & Kleiner, A. (1994). *The fifth discipline fieldbook: Strategies and tools for building a learning organization.* New York: Currency Doubleday.

Senge, P., Kleiner, A., Roberts, C., Ross, R., Roth, G., & Smith, B. (1999). *The dance of change: The challenges to sustaining momentum in learning organizations.* New York: Currency Doubleday.

Shackleton, V., & Ali, A. (1990). Work-related values of managers: A test of the Hofstede model. *Journal of Cross-Cultural Psychology, 21,* 109–118.

Sherman, J. D. (2000). *Business dynamics systems: Thinking and modeling for a complex world.* Boston: McGraw-Hill.

Sirmon, J. (1993). National leadership. In J. K. Berry & J. C. Gordon (Eds.), *Environmental leadership* (pp. 165–184). Washington DC: Island Press.

Sirmon, J., Shands, W. E., & Liggett, C. (1995). Communities of interests and open decisionmaking. *Journal of Forestry, 91*(7), 17–21.

Siuslaw National Forest (1993). *Draft environmental impact statement for the Oregon Dunes National Recreation Area management plan.* USDA-Forest Service, Pacific Northwest Region.

Siuslaw National Forest (1994). *Record of decision: Dunes management plan.* USDA-Forest Service, Pacific Northwest Region.

Spitzberg, B. H. (1983). Communication competence as knowledge, skill, and impression. *Communication Education, 32,* 323–329.

Sptizberg. B. H. (1989). Issues in the development of a theory of interpersonal competence in the intercultural context. *International Journal of Intercultural Relations, 13,* 241–268.

Spitzberg, B. H. (1991). Intercultural communication competence. In L. A. Samovar & R. E. Porter (Eds.), *Intercultural communication: A reader* (6th ed.) (pp. 353–365). Belmont, CA: Wadsworth.

Spitzberg, B. H., & Cupach, W. R. (1984). *Interpersonal communication competence.* Beverly Hills, CA: Sage.

Stanfield, R. L. (1988). Policy implications in managing public lands. In B. C. Dysart III & M. Clawson (Eds.), *Managing public lands in the public interest* (pp. 127–132). New York: Praeger.

Summary of the general procedures for forest planning (2000). The revision process, Chugach National Forest Web site. http://www.fs.fed.us/r10/chugach/revision.

Susskind L., & Cruikshank, J. (1987). *Breaking the impasse: Consensual approaches to resolving public disputes.* New York: Basic Books.

Susskind, L., & Field, P. (1996). *Dealing with an angry public: The mutual gains approach to resolving disputes.* New York: The Free Press.

Susskind, L. E., & Landry, E. M. (1991). Implementing a mutual gains approach to collective bargaining. *Negotiation Journal, 7*(1): 5–10.

Susskind, L., Levy, P. F., & Thomas-Larmer, J. (1999). *Negotiating environmental agreements: How to avoid escalating confrontation, needless costs, and unnecessary litigation.* Washington, DC: Island Press.

Sypher, B. D. (1984). The importance of social cognitive abilities in organizations. In R. N. Bostrom (Ed.), *Competence in communication* (pp. 103–127). Beverly Hills, CA: Sage.

Tannen, D. (1998). *The argument culture: Moving from debate to dialogue.* New York: Simon & Schuster.

Tarnow, K., Watt, P., & Silverberg, D. (1996). *Collaborative approaches to decision making and conflict resolution.* Salem: Oregon Department of Land Conservation and Development.

Taylor, A. (1988). A general theory of divorce mediation. In J. Folberg & A. Milne (Eds.), *Divorce mediation: Theory and practice* (pp. 61–82). New York: Guilford

Tennant, M., & Pogson, P. (1995). *Learning and change in the adult years: A developmental perspective.* San Francisco: Jossey-Bass.

Thompson, L. (1990). Negotiation behavior and outcomes: Empirical evidence and theoretical issues. *Psychological Bulletin, 108*, 515–532.

Thompson, L. (1991). Information exchange in negotiation. *Journal of Experimental Social Psychology, 27*, 161–179.

Thompson L., & Hastie. R (1990). Judgment tasks and biases in negotiation. In *Research on negotiation in organizations, Vol. 2* (pp. 31–54). JAI Press.

Ting-Toomey, S. (1985). Toward a theory of conflict and culture. In W. Gudykunst, L. Stewart, & S. Ting-Toomey (Eds.), *Communication, culture, and organizational processes* (pp. 71–86). Beverly Hills, CA: Sage.

Ting-Toomey, S. (1988). Intercultural conflict styles: A face-negotiation theory. In Y. Kim & W. Gudykunst (Eds.), *Theories in intercultural communication* (pp. 213–235). Newbury Park, CA: Sage.

Ting-Toomey, S. (1999). *Communicating across cultures.* New York: Guilford.

Ting-Toomey, S., & Chung, L. (1996). Cross-cultural interpersonal communication: theoretical trends and research directions. In W. Gudykunst, S. Ting-Toomey, & T. Nishida (Eds.), *Communication in personal relationships across cultures* (pp. 252–270). Thousand Oaks, CA: Sage.

Tjosvold, D. (1990). The goal interdependence approach to communication in conflict: An organizational study. In M. A. Rahim (Ed.), *Theory and research in conflict management* (pp. 15–27). New York: Praeger.

Tjosvold, D. (1991). *The conflict-positive organization: Stimulate diversity and create unity.* Reading, MA: Addison-Wesley.

Tjosvold, D. (1993). *Learning to manage conflict: Getting people to work together productively.* New York: Lexington.

Tjosvold, D., & van de Vliert, E. (1994). Applying cooperative and competitive conflict theory to mediation. *Mediation Quarterly, 11*, 303–311.

Tracy. L., & Peterson, R. (1986). A behavioral theory of labor negotiations—How well has it aged? *Negotiation Journal, 2*(1), 93–108.

Triandis, H. C. (1982). [Review of *Culture's Consequences: International Differences in Work-related Values*]. *Human Organization, 41*, 86–90.

Twight, B. W. (1977). Confidence or more controversy: Whither public involvement? *Journal of Forestry, 75*(1), 93–95.

Twight, B. W., & Paterson, J. J. (1979). Conflict and public involvement: Measuring consensus. *Journal of Forestry, 77*(12), 771–774.

Ury, W. (1991). *Getting past no: Negotiating with difficult people.* New York: Bantam Books.

Ury, W., Goldberg, S., & Brett, J. (1993). *Getting disputes resolved: Designing systems to cut the cost of conflict.* Cambridge: Harvard University Program on Negotiation.

USDA-Forest Service (1990). *Critique of land management planning, volume 2: National Forest planning: Searching for a common vision.* Document FS-453. Washington, DC: U.S. Government Printing Office.

U.S. Institute for Environmental Conflict Resolution (2000). Web site. http://www.ecr.gov/index.htm.

Vella, J. (1994). *Learning to listen: Learning to teach.* San Francisco: Jossey-Bass.

Vietor, D. M., & Cralle, H. T. (1990) Comparison: Stage 5 of the soft systems approach. In K. Wilson & G.E.B. Morren, *Systems approaches for improvements in agriculture and resource management* (pp. 212–236). New York: MacMillan.

Vira, B., Dubois, O., Daniels, S. E., & Walker, G. B. (1998). Institutional pluralism in forestry: Considerations of analytical and operational tools. *Unasylva, 49*(3), 35–42.

Walker, G. B. (1987). Communicating across cultures: Argument and international negotiation. In F. van Eemeren, R. Grootendorst, J. Blair, & C. Willard (Eds.), *Argumentation: Analysis and practices* (pp. 238–250). Dordrecht, The Netherlands: Foris.

Walker, G. B. (1990). Cultural orientations of argument in international disputes: Negotiating the Law of the Sea. In F. Korzenny & S. Ting-Toomey (Eds.), *Communicating for peace: Diplomacy and negotiation* (pp. 96–117). Newbury Park, CA: Sage.

Walker, G. B. (1991, June). *Argumentation, collaborative argument skills, and mediation.* Paper presented at the biannual National Conference on Peacemaking and Conflict Resolution, Charlotte, NC.

Walker, G. B. (1992, June). *Toward a theory of conflict communication competence.* Paper presented at the meeting of the International Association for Conflict Management, Minneapolis, MN.

Walker, G. B. (1996, May). *An analytic framework to improve conflict diagnostic skills.* Paper presented at the Sixth International Symposium on Society and Resource Management, State College, PA.

Walker, G. B., & Daniels, S. E. (1994, August). *Collaborative Learning and the management of natural resource disputes.* Paper presented at the meeting of the Rural Sociological Society, Portland, OR.

Walker, G. B., & Daniels, S. E. (1995, February). *Managing conflict in fire recovery planning: Public participation as Collaborative Learning.* Paper presented at the meeting of the Western States Communication Association, Portland, OR.

Walker, G. B., & Daniels, S. E. (1996). The Clinton administration, the Northwest Forest Conference, and managing conflict: When talk and structure collide. *Society and Natural Resources, 9*, 77–91.

Walker, G. B., & Daniels, S. E. (1997). Foundations of natural resource conflict: Conflict theory and public policy. In B. Solberg & S. Miina (Eds.), *Proceedings: Conflict management public participation in land management* (pp. 13-36). Joensuu, Finland: European Forest Institute.

Walker, G. B., & Daniels, S. E. (1998, June). Natural resource policy and the paradox of public involvement: Bring scientists and citizens together. Paper presented at the American Forests Workshop on Rural Communities and Sustainable Forestry, Bend, OR.

Wall, J. A. (1985). *Negotiation: Theory and practice.* Glenview, IL: Scott, Foresman.

Walters, C .J. (1986). *Adaptive management of renewable resources.* New York: McGraw-Hill.

Walters, C. J., & Holling, C.S. (1990). Large-scale management experiments and learning by doing. *Ecology, 71*(6), 2060–2068.

Walton, R. E., & McKersie, R. B. (1965). *A behavioral theory of labor negotiations: An analysis of a social interaction system.* New York: McGraw-Hill.

Weaver, R. G., & Farrell, J. D. (1997). *Managers as facilitators: A practical guide to getting work done in a changing workplace.* San Francisco: Barrett-Koehler.

Webber, M. M., & Rittel, H. W. J. (1973). Dilemmas in a general theory of planning. *Policy Sciences, 2*(4), 155–169.

Weber, E. P. (1998). *Pluralism by the rules: Conflict and cooperation in environmental regulation.* Washington, DC: Georgetown University Press.

Webne-Behrman, H. (1998). *The practice of facilitation: Managing group process and solving problems.* Westport, CT: Quorum Books.

Wehr. P. (1979). *Conflict regulation.* Boulder, CO: Westview.

Weick, K. (1976). Educational organizations as loosely coupled systems. *Administrative Science Quarterly, 21, 1–19.*

Weisbord, M. R., & Janoff, S. (1995). *Future Search.* San Francisco: Berrett-Koehler.

Wenatchee National Forest (1994, 12 September). Fire information sheet.

Wenzel, J. W. (1990). Three perspectives on argument: Rhetoric, dialectic, and logic. In R. Trapp & J. Schuetz (Eds.), *Perspectives on argument: Essays in honor of Wayne Brockriede* (pp. 9–26). Prospect Heights, IL: Waveland Press.

Wheatley, M. J. (1992). *Leadership and the new science: Learning about organization from an orderly world.* San Francisco: Berrett-Koehler Publishers.

Wiemann, J. M. (1977). Explication and test of a model of communicative competence. *Human Communication Research, 3,* 195–213.

Wilkinson, C. (1992). *Crossing the next meridian: Land, water, and the future of the west.* Washington, DC: Island Press.

Wilmot, W. W., & Hocker, J. L. (1998). *Interpersonal conflict* (5th ed.). Boston: McGraw-Hill.

Wilmot, W. W., & Hocker, J. L. (2001). *Interpersonal conflict* (6th ed.). Boston: McGraw-Hill.

Wilson, A. K. (1993). The promise of situated cognition. In S. B. Merriam (Ed.), *New directions for adult and continuing education: No. 57. An update on adult learning theory* (pp. 71–80). San Francisco: Jossey-Bass.

Wilson, K., & Morren, G.E.B. (1990). *Systems approaches for improvements in agriculture and resource management.* New York: MacMillan.

Wiseman, R. L., Hammer, M. R., & Nishida, H. (1989). Predictors of intercultural communication competence. *International Journal of Intercultural Relations, 13,* 349–370.

Wolcott, H. F. (1995). *The art of fieldwork.* Walnut Creek, CA: Altamira Press.

Wondolleck, J. (1988). *Public lands conflict and resolution: Managing national forest disputes.* New York: Plenum Press.

Wondolleck, J. M., Manring, N. J., & Crowfoot, J. E. (1996). Teetering at the top of the ladder: The experience of citizen group participants in alternative dispute resolution processes. *Sociological Perspectives, 39*(2), 249–262.

Yankelovich, D. (1991). *Coming to public judgment: Making democracy work in a complex world.* Syracuse, NY: Syracuse University Press.

Yankelovich, D. (1999*). The magic of dialogue.* New York: Simon & Schuster.

Index

About the Authors

STEVEN E. DANIELS is Director of the Western Rural Development Center at Utah State University in Logan. The WRDC is one of four regional centers for applied social science and community development; its mission is to strengthen rural families, communities, and businesses by facilitating collaborative socioeconomic research and extension through higher education institutions in the western region. Dr. Daniels is a professor in the Department of Sociology, Social Work and Anthropology and the Department of Forest Resources at Utah State University. Earlier, he was a faculty member in the Department of Forest Resources at Oregon State University.

GREGG B. WALKER is Professor and Chair of the Department of Speech Communication, Adjunct Professor of Forest Resources, and Director of the Peace Studies program at Oregon State University in Corvallis. In addition, Professor Walker conducts training programs on collaborative decision making, designs collaborative public participation processes, facilitates collaborative learning community workshops, and researchs community-level collaborative efforts. He is on the roster at the U.S. Institute for Environmental Conflict Resolution as a facilitator, designer, and trainer.